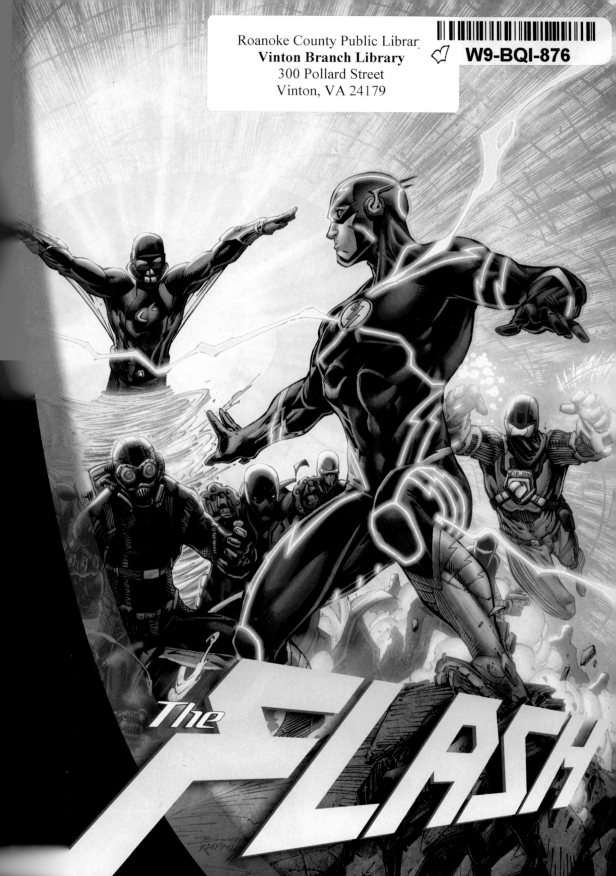

Roanoke County Public Library
Vinton Branch Library
300 Pollard Street
Vinton, VA 24179

W9-BQI-876

The FLASH

VOLUME 6 **OUT OF TIME**

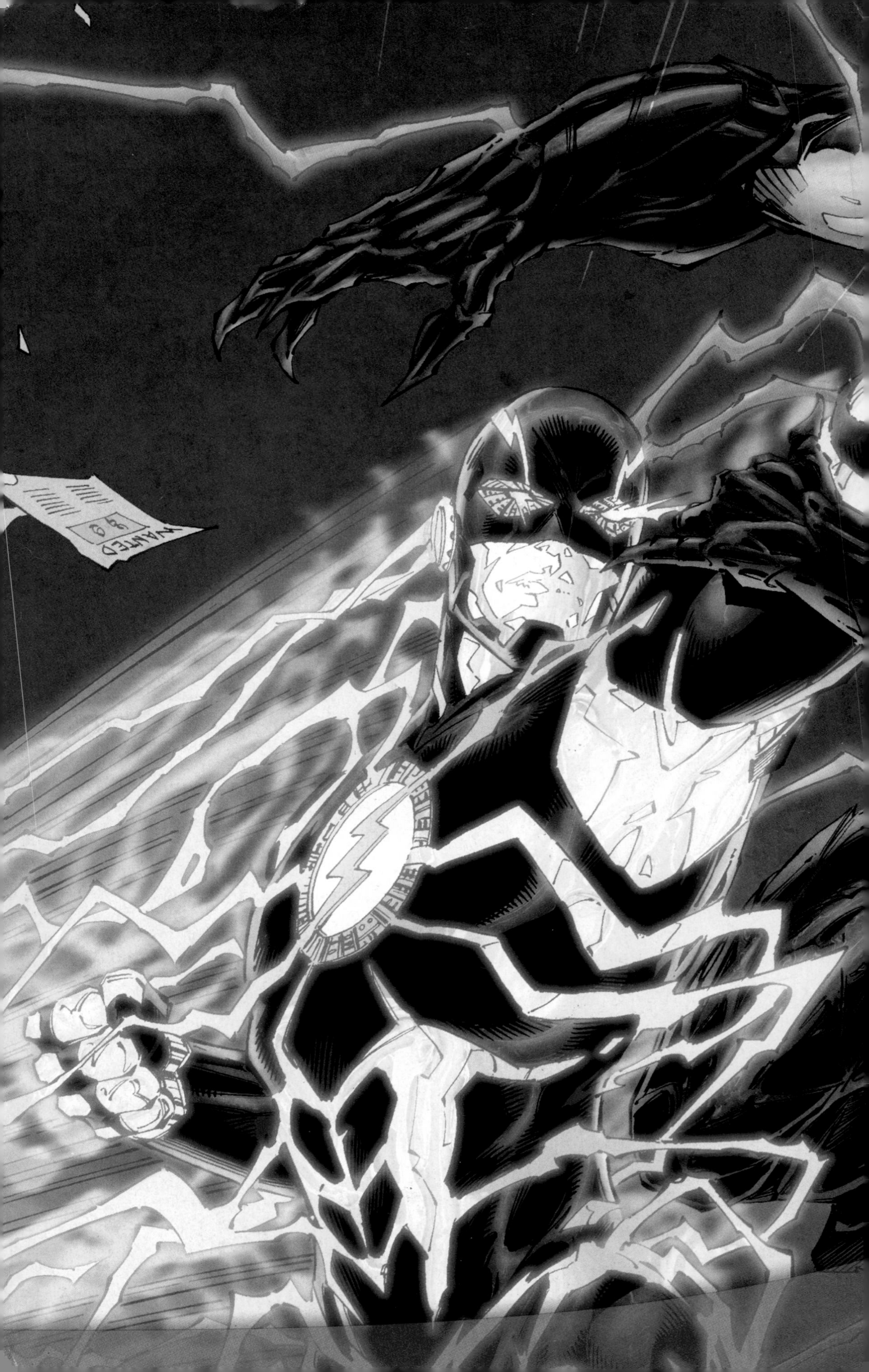
WANTED

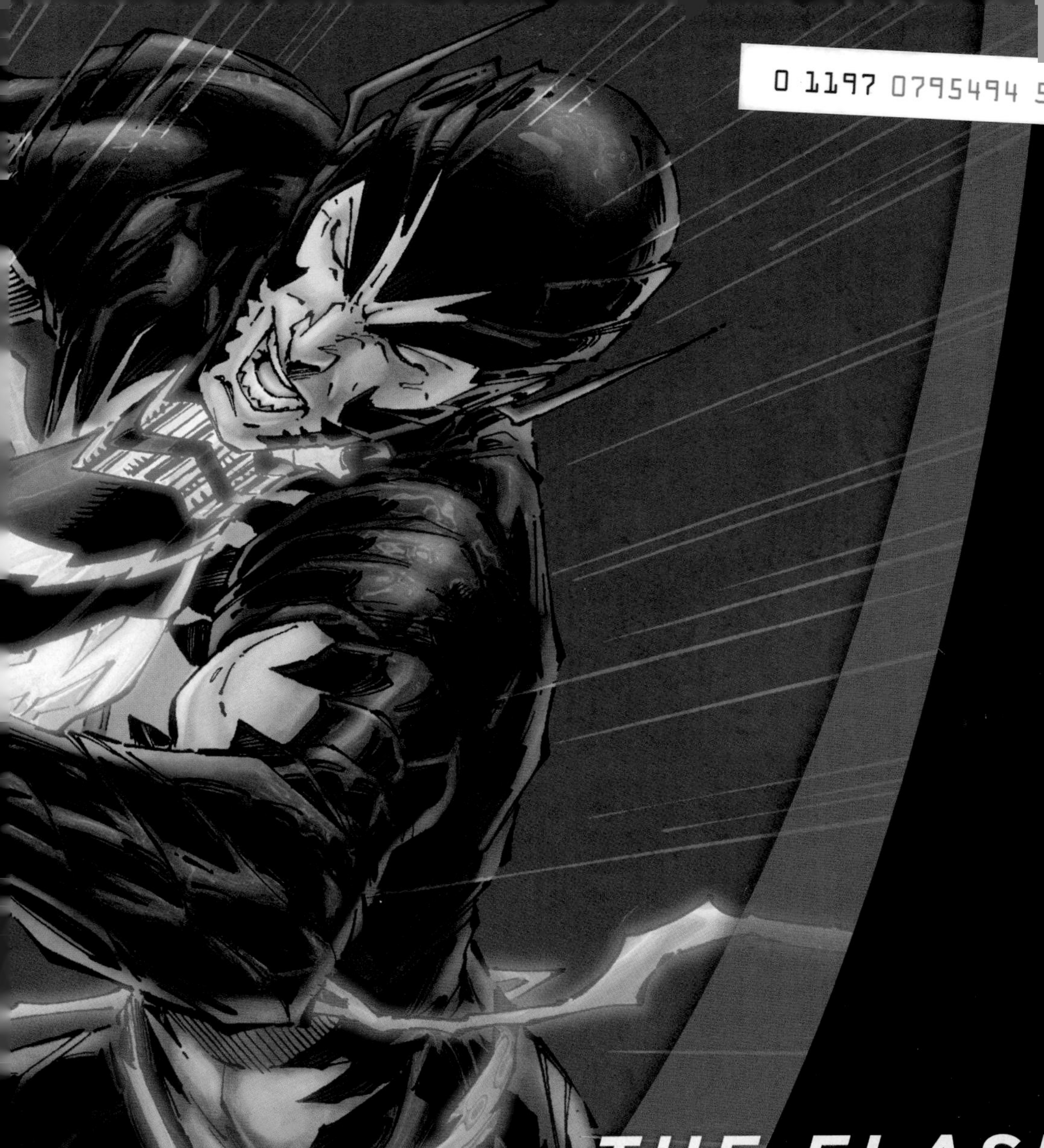

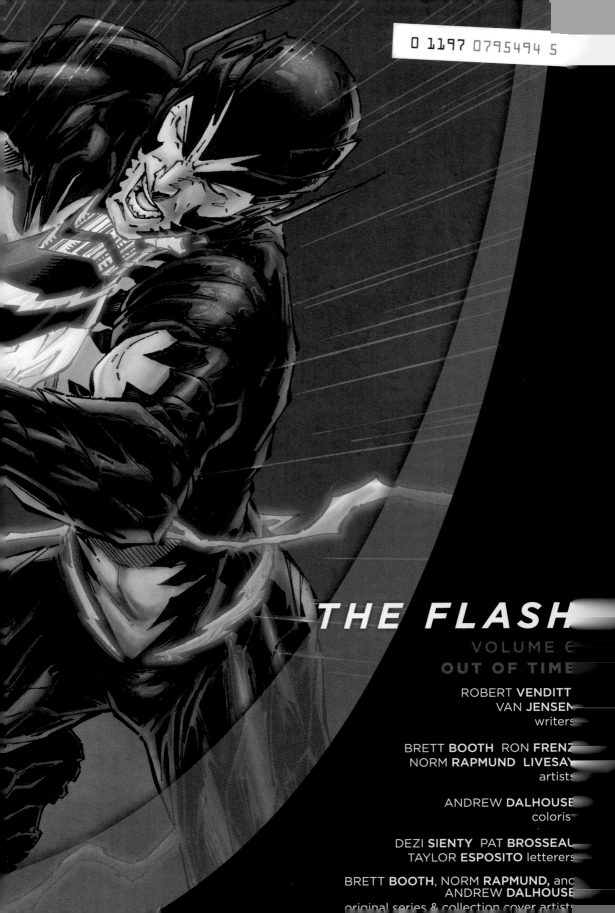

THE FLASH

VOLUME 6
OUT OF TIME

ROBERT **VENDITTI**
VAN **JENSEN**
writers

BRETT **BOOTH** RON **FRENZ**
NORM **RAPMUND** **LIVESAY**
artists

ANDREW **DALHOUSE**
colorist

DEZI **SIENTY** PAT **BROSSEAU**
TAYLOR **ESPOSITO** letterers

BRETT **BOOTH**, NORM **RAPMUND,** and
ANDREW **DALHOUSE**
original series & collection cover artists

BRIAN CUNNINGHAM Editor – Original Series KATE DURRÉ, AMEDEO TURTURRO Assistant Editors – Original Series
JEB WOODARD Group Editor – Collected Editions PAUL SANTOS Editor – Collected Edition
STEVE COOK Design Director – Books ROBBIE BIEDERMAN Publication Design

BOB HARRAS Senior VP – Editor-in-Chief, DC Comics

DIANE NELSON President DAN DIDIO and JIM LEE Co-Publishers GEOFF JOHNS Chief Creative Officer
AMIT DESAI Senior VP – Marketing & Global Franchise Management NAIRI GARDINER Senior VP – Finance
SAM ADES VP – Digital Marketing BOBBIE CHASE VP – Talent Development MARK CHIARELLO Senior VP – Art, Design & Collected Editions
JOHN CUNNINGHAM VP – Content Strategy ANNE DEPIES VP – Strategy Planning & Reporting
DON FALLETTI VP – Manufacturing Operations LAWRENCE GANEM VP – Editorial Administration & Talent Relations
ALISON GILL Senior VP – Manufacturing & Operations HANK KANALZ Senior VP – Editorial Strategy & Administration
JAY KOGAN VP – Legal Affairs DEREK MADDALENA Senior VP – Sales & Business Development
JACK MAHAN VP – Business Affairs DAN MIRON VP – Sales Planning & Trade Development
NICK NAPOLITANO VP – Manufacturing Administration CAROL ROEDER VP – Marketing
EDDIE SCANNELL VP – Mass Account & Digital Sales COURTNEY SIMMONS Senior VP – Publicity & Communications
JIM (SKI) SOKOLOWSKI VP – Comic Book Specialty & Newsstand Sales SANDY YI Senior VP – Global Franchise Management

THE FLASH VOLUME 6: OUT OF TIME

Published by DC Comics. Compilation Copyright © 2015 DC Comics. All Rights Reserved.

Originally published in single magazine form as THE FLASH 30-35, THE FLASH ANNUAL 3, THE FLASH: FUTURES END 1 © 2014 DC Comics.
All Rights Reserved. All characters, their distinctive likenesses and related elements featured in this publication are trademarks of DC Comics.
MAD and Alfred E. Neuman © and TM E.C. Publications, Inc. The stories, characters and incidents featured in this publication are entirely
fictional. DC Comics does not read or accept unsolicited ideas, stories or artwork.

DC Comics, 2900 West Alameda Ave., Burbank, CA 91505
Printed by RR Donnelley, Owensville, MO, USA. 12/11/15. First Printing.
ISBN: 978-1-4012-5874-0

PEFC Certified

Printed on paper from
sustainably managed
forests and controlled
sources

PEFC/29-31-75 www.pefc.org

Library of Congress Cataloging-in-Publication Data

Venditti, Robert.
The Flash. Volume 6, Out of Time / Van Jensen, Brett Booth.
pages cm. — (The New 52!)
ISBN 978-1-4012-5874-0
1. Graphic novels. I. Booth, Brett, illustrator. II. Title. III. Title: Out of Time.

PN6728.F53B84 2015
741.5'973—dc23

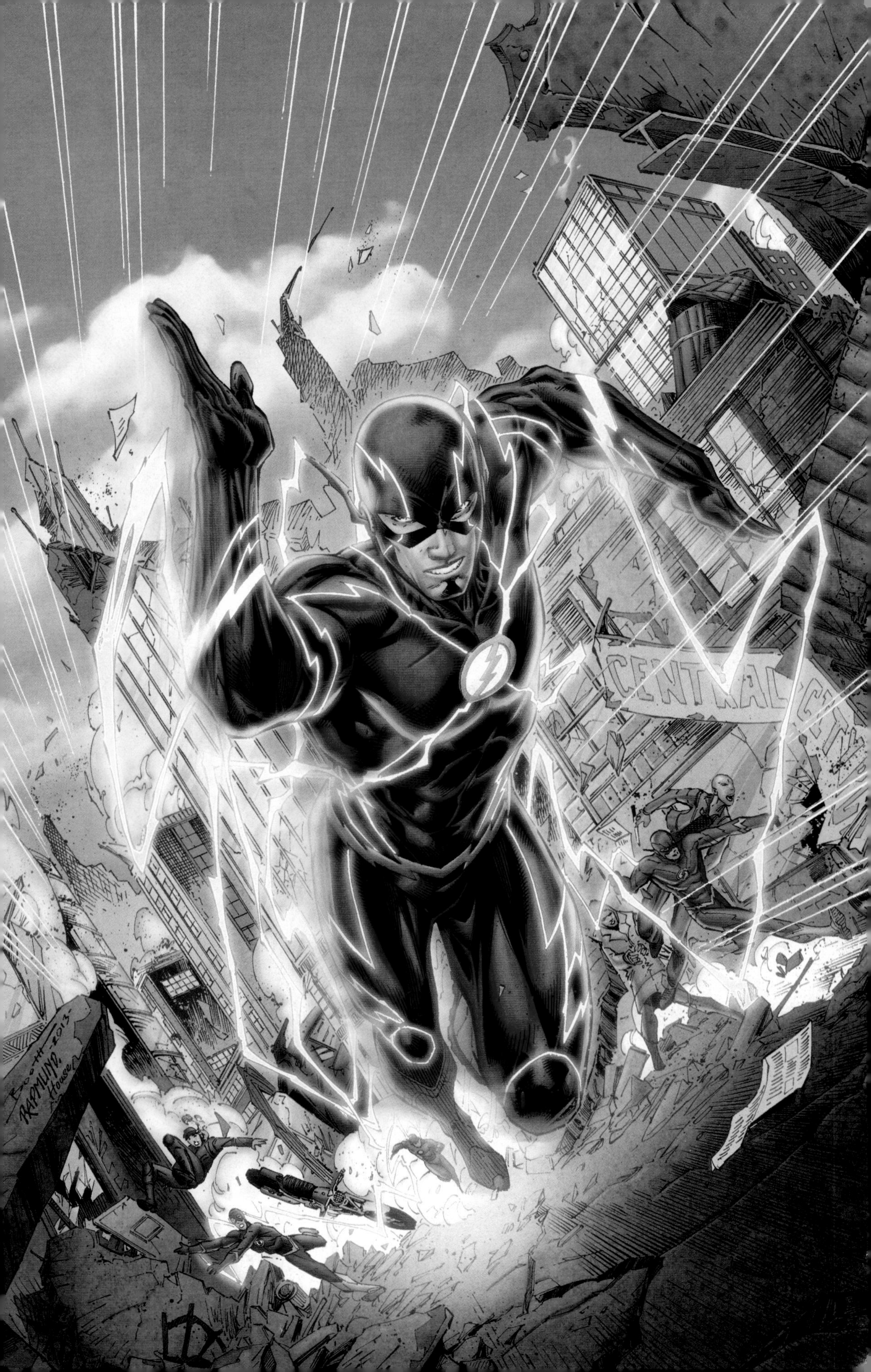
CENTRAL

LOST TIME

ROBERT VENDITTI & VAN JENSEN writers **BRETT BOOTH** penciller **NORM RAPMUND** inker

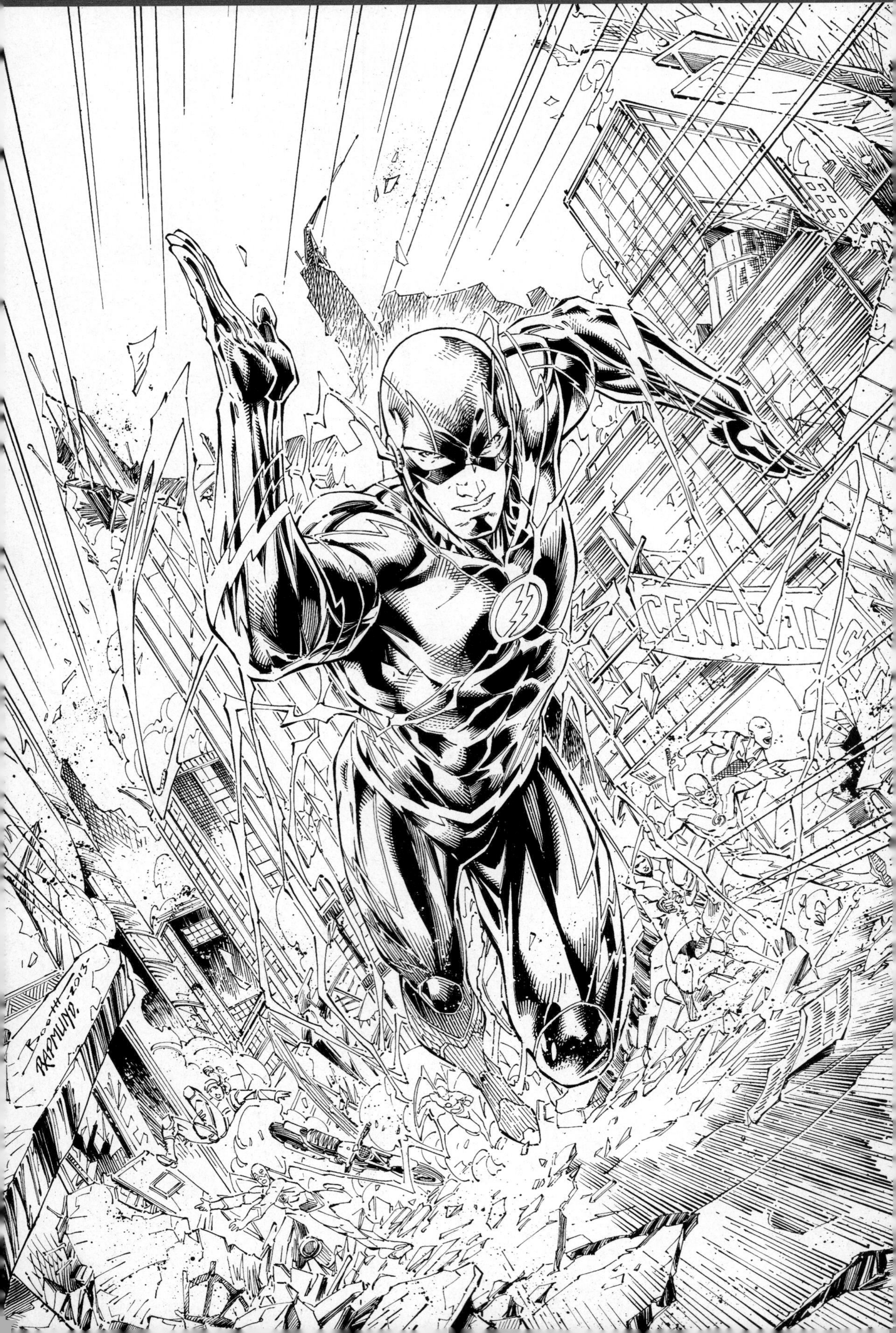
CENTRAL C

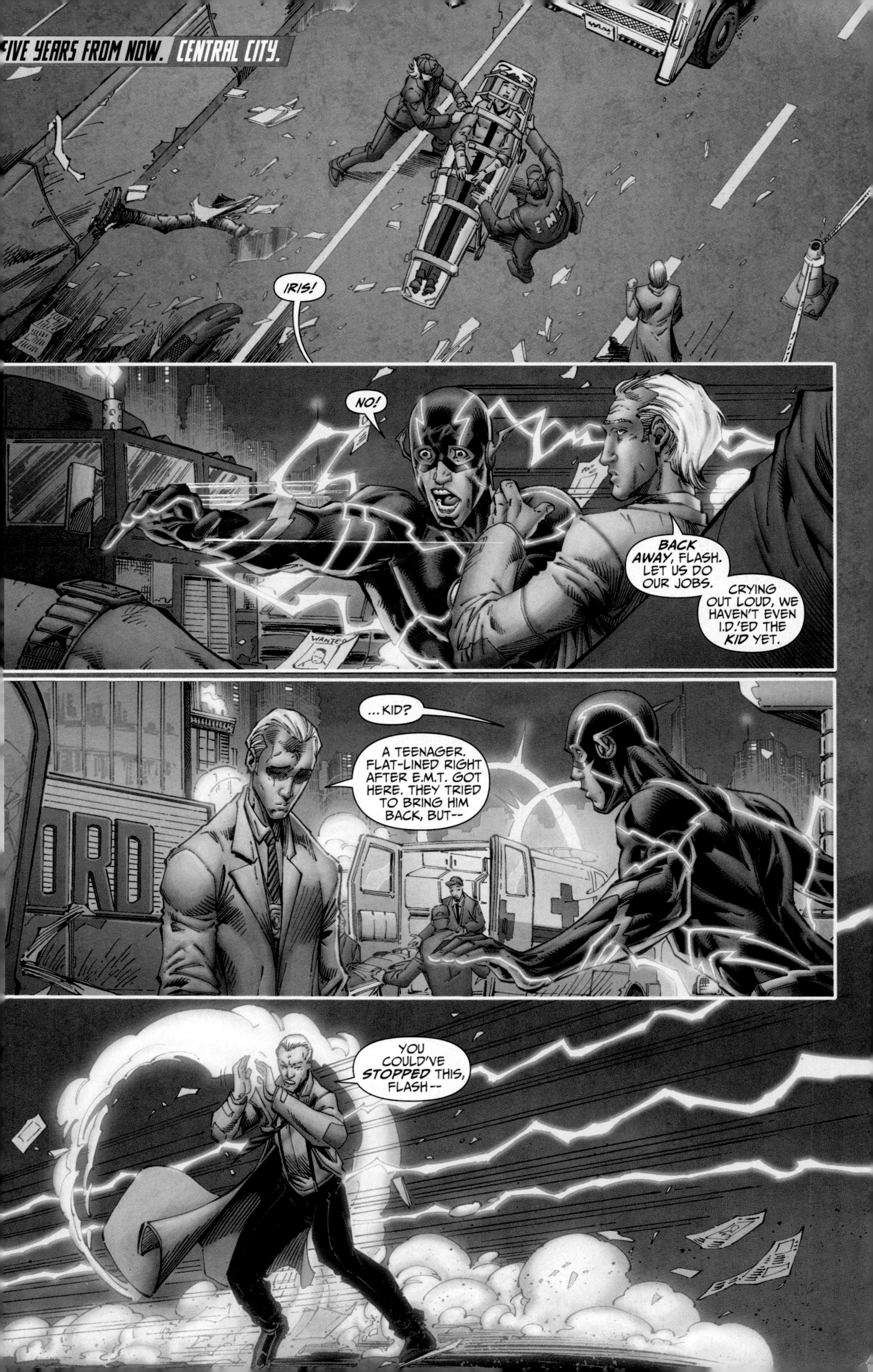
FIVE YEARS FROM NOW. CENTRAL CITY.
IRIS!
NO!
BACK AWAY, FLASH. LET US DO OUR JOBS.
CRYING OUT LOUD, WE HAVEN'T EVEN I.D.'ED THE KID YET.
...KID?
A TEENAGER. FLAT-LINED RIGHT AFTER E.M.T. GOT HERE. THEY TRIED TO BRING HIM BACK, BUT--
YOU COULD'VE STOPPED THIS, FLASH--

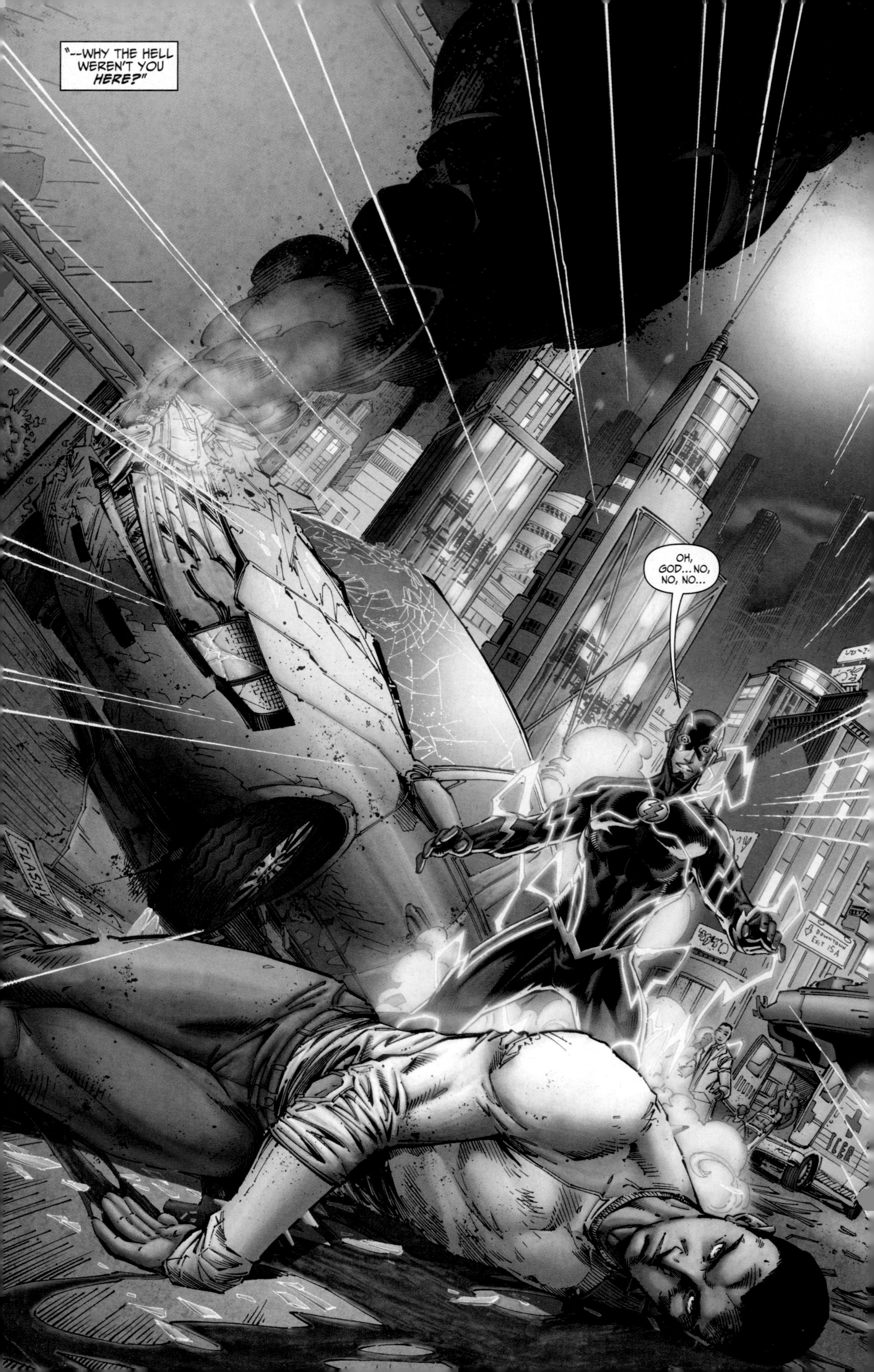
"--WHY THE HELL WEREN'T YOU *HERE?*"
OH, GOD... NO, NO, NO...

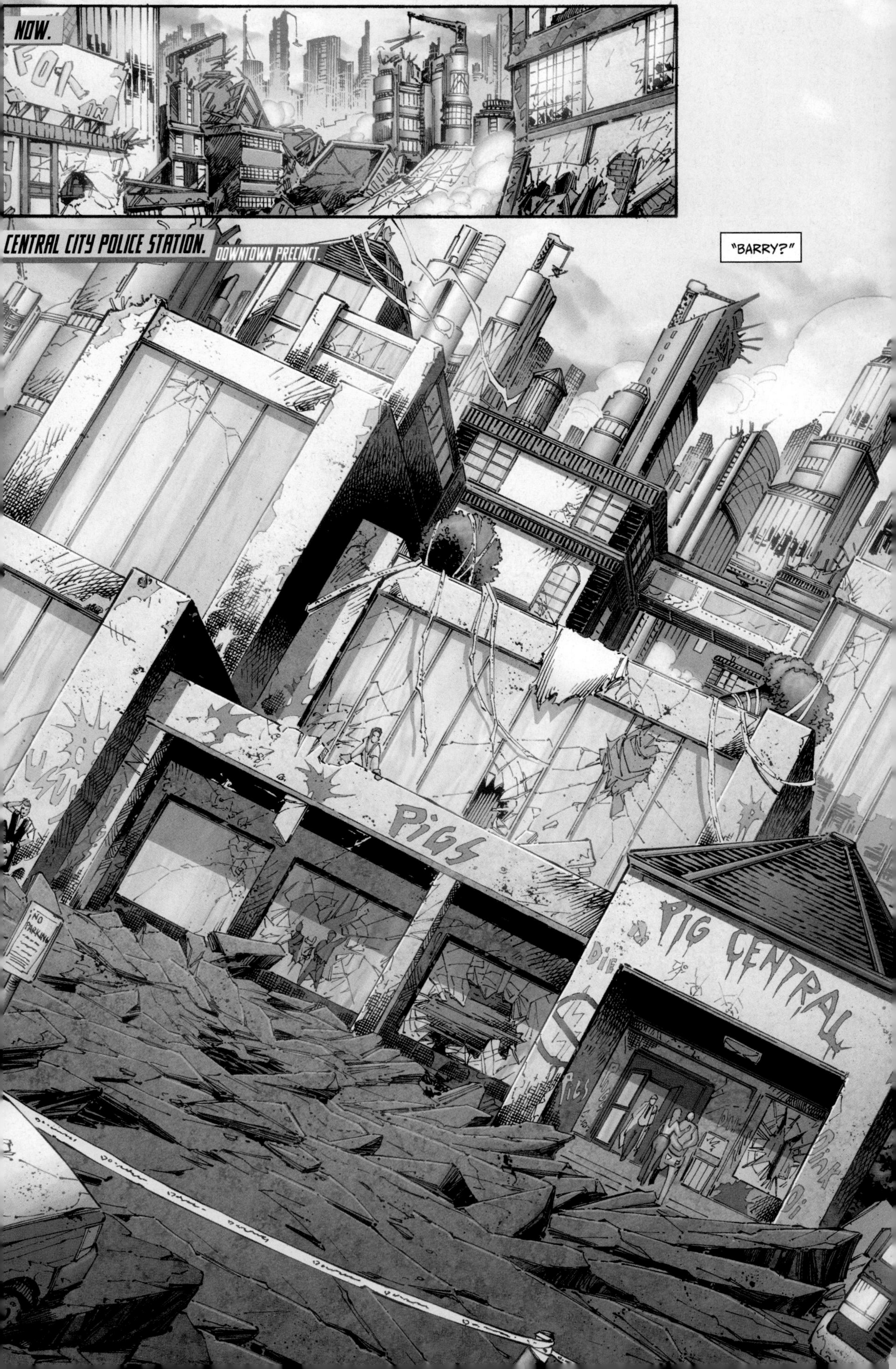
NOW.
CENTRAL CITY POLICE STATION.
DOWNTOWN PRECINCT.
"BARRY?"
PIGS
PIG CENTRAL
DIE
NO PARKING

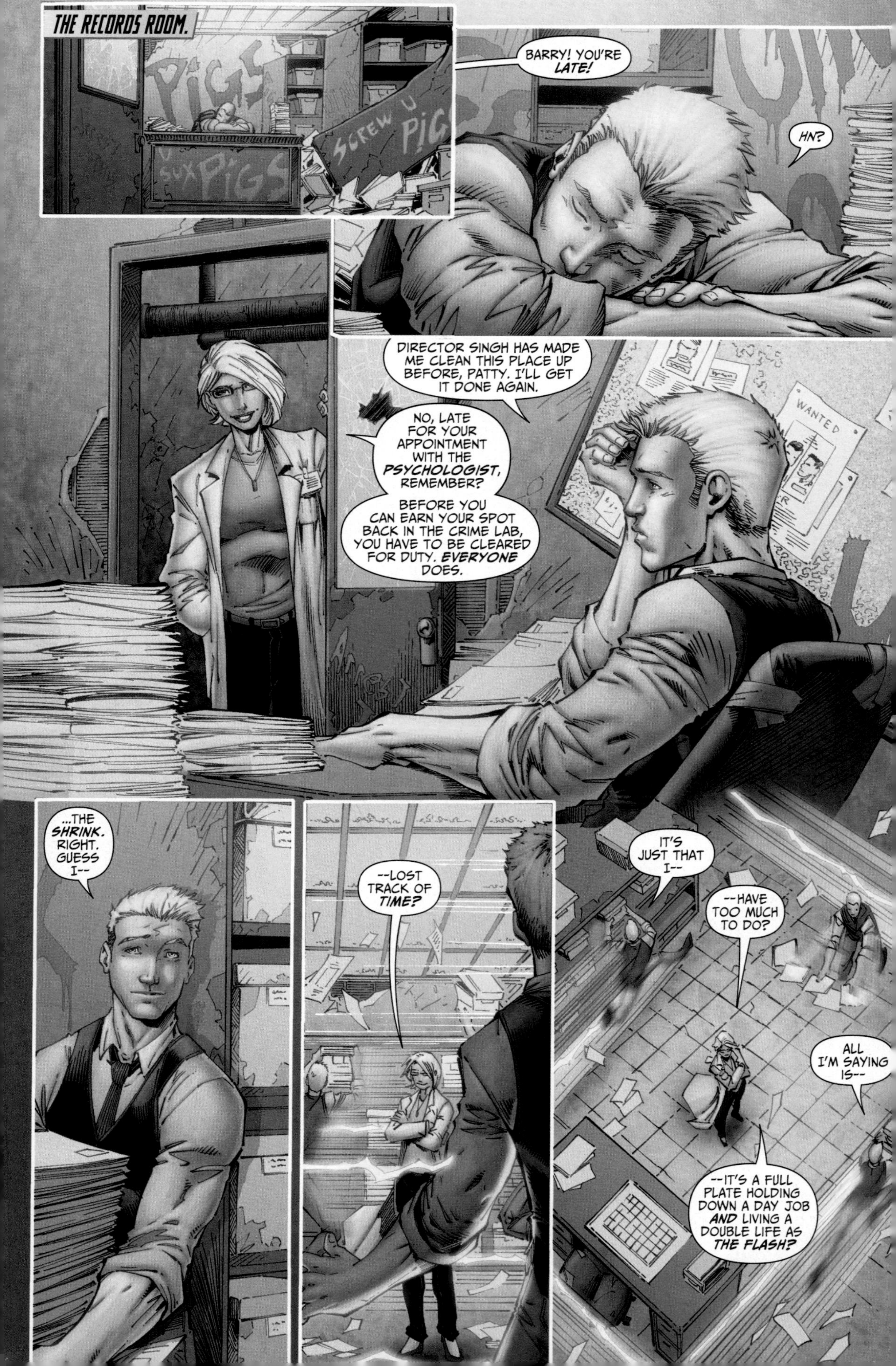
THE RECORDS ROOM.
PIGS
SCREW U PIGS
U SUX PIGS
BARRY! YOU'RE LATE!
HN?
DIRECTOR SINGH HAS MADE ME CLEAN THIS PLACE UP BEFORE, PATTY. I'LL GET IT DONE AGAIN.
NO, LATE FOR YOUR APPOINTMENT WITH THE PSYCHOLOGIST, REMEMBER?
BEFORE YOU CAN EARN YOUR SPOT BACK IN THE CRIME LAB, YOU HAVE TO BE CLEARED FOR DUTY. EVERYONE DOES.
WANTED
...THE SHRINK. RIGHT. GUESS I--
--LOST TRACK OF TIME?
IT'S JUST THAT I--
--HAVE TOO MUCH TO DO?
ALL I'M SAYING IS--
--IT'S A FULL PLATE HOLDING DOWN A DAY JOB AND LIVING A DOUBLE LIFE AS THE FLASH?

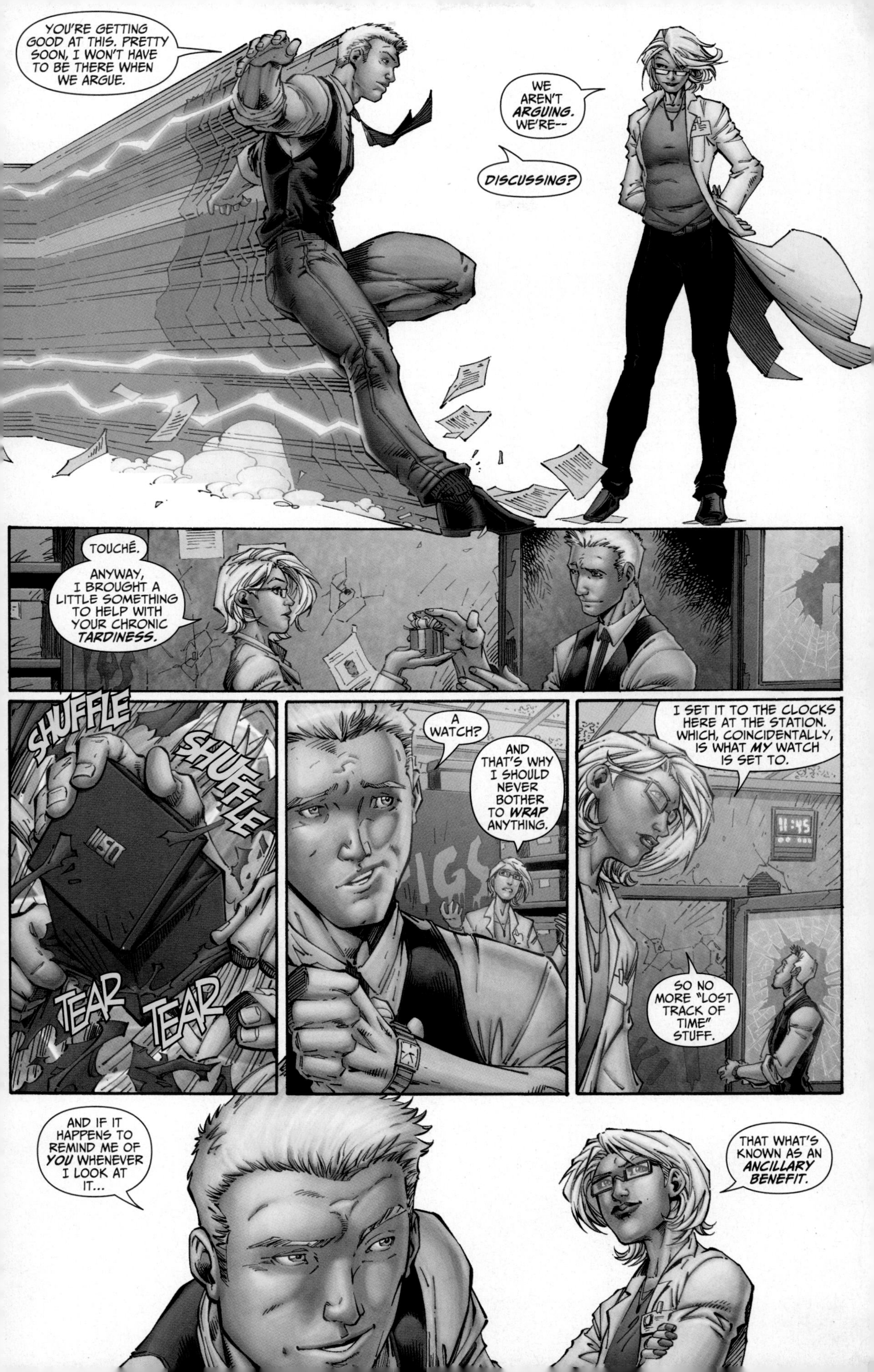

YOU'RE GETTING GOOD AT THIS. PRETTY SOON, I WON'T HAVE TO BE THERE WHEN WE ARGUE.
WE AREN'T ARGUING. WE'RE--
DISCUSSING?
TOUCHÉ.
ANYWAY, I BROUGHT A LITTLE SOMETHING TO HELP WITH YOUR CHRONIC TARDINESS.
SHUFFLE
SHUFFLE
TEAR
TEAR
A WATCH?
AND THAT'S WHY I SHOULD NEVER BOTHER TO WRAP ANYTHING.
I SET IT TO THE CLOCKS HERE AT THE STATION. WHICH, COINCIDENTALLY, IS WHAT MY WATCH IS SET TO.
SO NO MORE "LOST TRACK OF TIME" STUFF.
AND IF IT HAPPENS TO REMIND ME OF YOU WHENEVER I LOOK AT IT...
THAT WHAT'S KNOWN AS AN ANCILLARY BENEFIT.

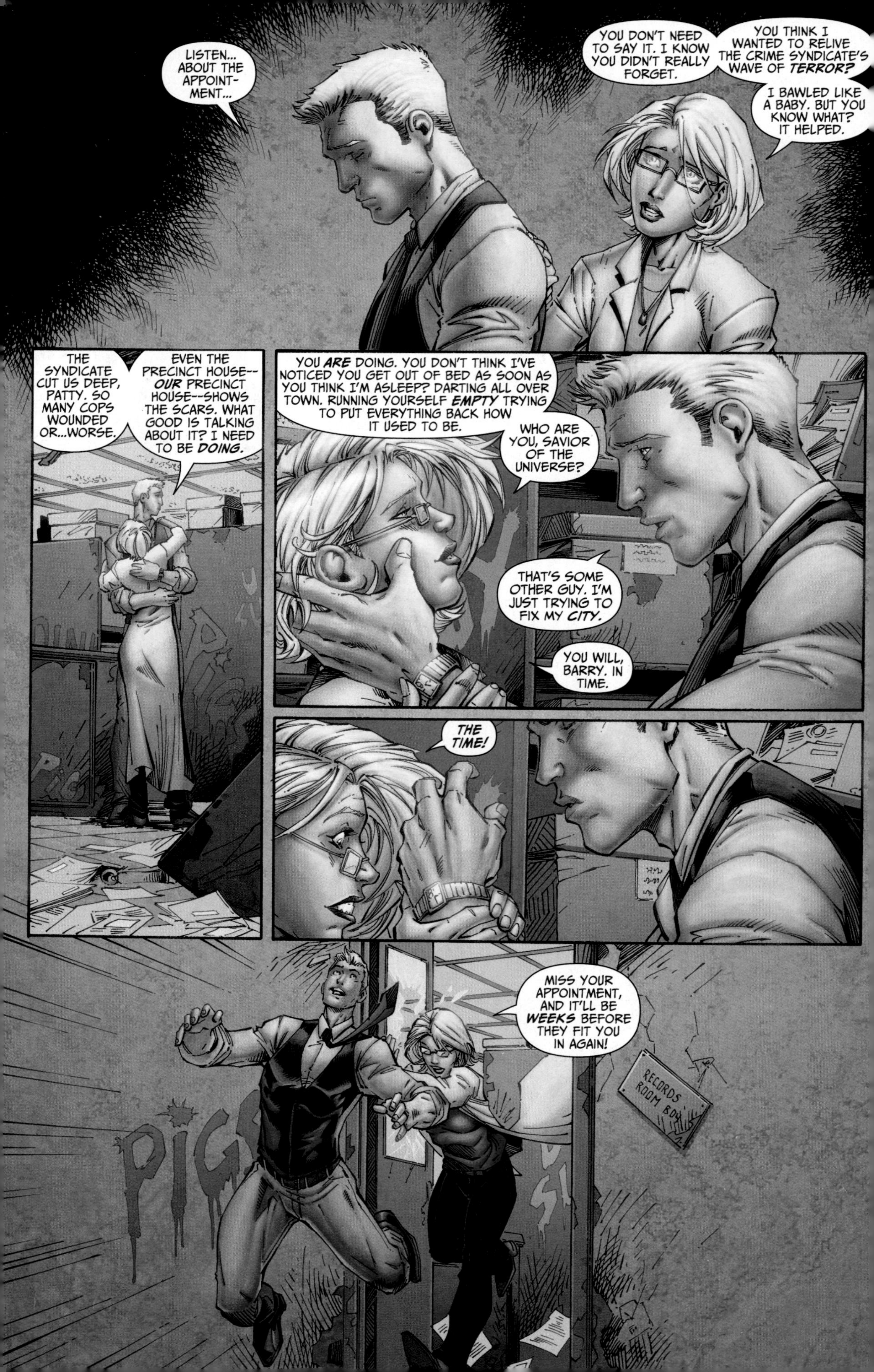

LISTEN... ABOUT THE APPOINTMENT...
YOU DON'T NEED TO SAY IT. I KNOW YOU DIDN'T REALLY FORGET.
YOU THINK I WANTED TO RELIVE THE CRIME SYNDICATE'S WAVE OF TERROR?
I BAWLED LIKE A BABY. BUT YOU KNOW WHAT? IT HELPED.
THE SYNDICATE CUT US DEEP, PATTY. SO MANY COPS WOUNDED OR...WORSE.
EVEN THE PRECINCT HOUSE-- OUR PRECINCT HOUSE--SHOWS THE SCARS. WHAT GOOD IS TALKING ABOUT IT? I NEED TO BE DOING.
PIGS
YOU ARE DOING. YOU DON'T THINK I'VE NOTICED YOU GET OUT OF BED AS SOON AS YOU THINK I'M ASLEEP? DARTING ALL OVER TOWN. RUNNING YOURSELF EMPTY TRYING TO PUT EVERYTHING BACK HOW IT USED TO BE.
WHO ARE YOU, SAVIOR OF THE UNIVERSE?
THAT'S SOME OTHER GUY. I'M JUST TRYING TO FIX MY CITY.
YOU WILL, BARRY. IN TIME.
THE TIME!
MISS YOUR APPOINTMENT, AND IT'LL BE WEEKS BEFORE THEY FIT YOU IN AGAIN!
RECORDS ROOM B
PIGS

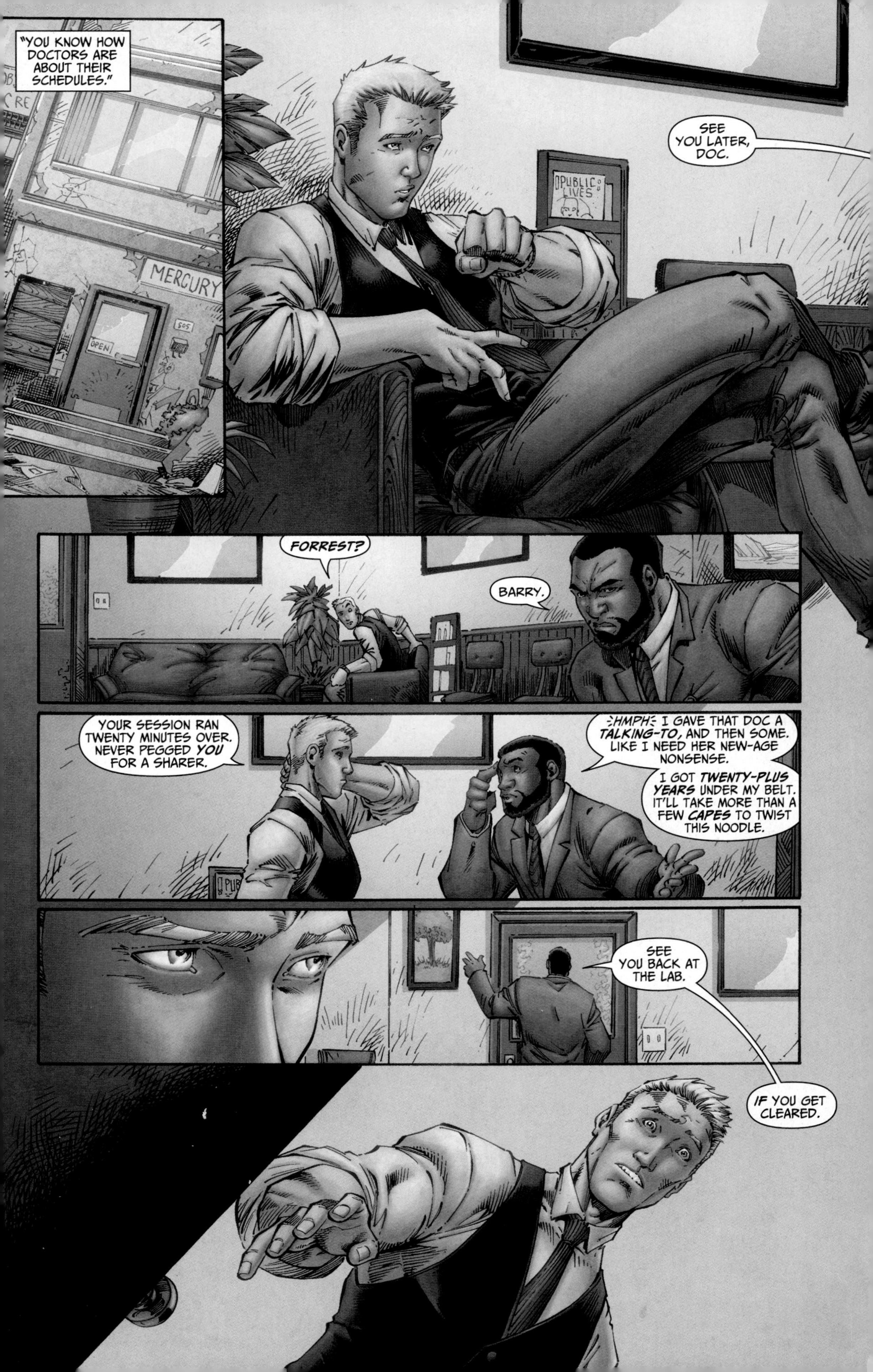
"YOU KNOW HOW DOCTORS ARE ABOUT THEIR SCHEDULES."
MERCURY
OPEN
PUBLIC LIVES
SEE YOU LATER, DOC.
FORREST?
BARRY.
YOUR SESSION RAN TWENTY MINUTES OVER. NEVER PEGGED *YOU* FOR A SHARER.
HMPH I GAVE THAT DOC A *TALKING-TO,* AND THEN SOME. LIKE I NEED HER NEW-AGE NONSENSE.
I GOT *TWENTY-PLUS YEARS* UNDER MY BELT. IT'LL TAKE MORE THAN A FEW *CAPES* TO TWIST THIS NOODLE.
SEE YOU BACK AT THE LAB.
IF YOU GET CLEARED.

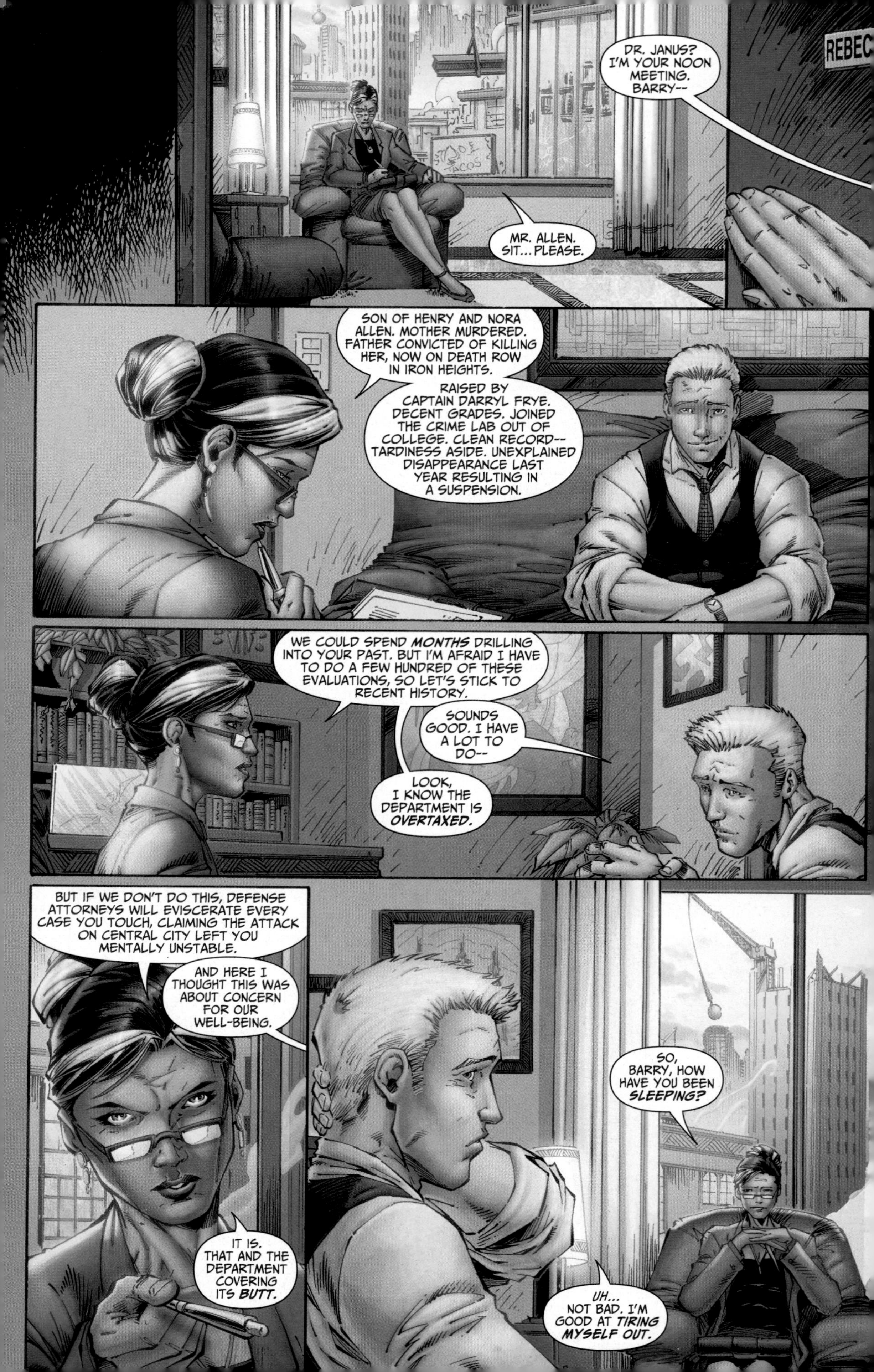
REBEC
DR. JANUS? I'M YOUR NOON MEETING. BARRY--
MR. ALLEN. SIT... PLEASE.
SON OF HENRY AND NORA ALLEN. MOTHER MURDERED. FATHER CONVICTED OF KILLING HER, NOW ON DEATH ROW IN IRON HEIGHTS.
RAISED BY CAPTAIN DARRYL FRYE. DECENT GRADES. JOINED THE CRIME LAB OUT OF COLLEGE. CLEAN RECORD-- TARDINESS ASIDE. UNEXPLAINED DISAPPEARANCE LAST YEAR RESULTING IN A SUSPENSION.
WE COULD SPEND MONTHS DRILLING INTO YOUR PAST. BUT I'M AFRAID I HAVE TO DO A FEW HUNDRED OF THESE EVALUATIONS, SO LET'S STICK TO RECENT HISTORY.
SOUNDS GOOD. I HAVE A LOT TO DO--
LOOK, I KNOW THE DEPARTMENT IS OVERTAXED.
BUT IF WE DON'T DO THIS, DEFENSE ATTORNEYS WILL EVISCERATE EVERY CASE YOU TOUCH, CLAIMING THE ATTACK ON CENTRAL CITY LEFT YOU MENTALLY UNSTABLE.
AND HERE I THOUGHT THIS WAS ABOUT CONCERN FOR OUR WELL-BEING.
IT IS. THAT AND THE DEPARTMENT COVERING ITS BUTT.
SO, BARRY, HOW HAVE YOU BEEN SLEEPING?
UH... NOT BAD. I'M GOOD AT TIRING MYSELF OUT.

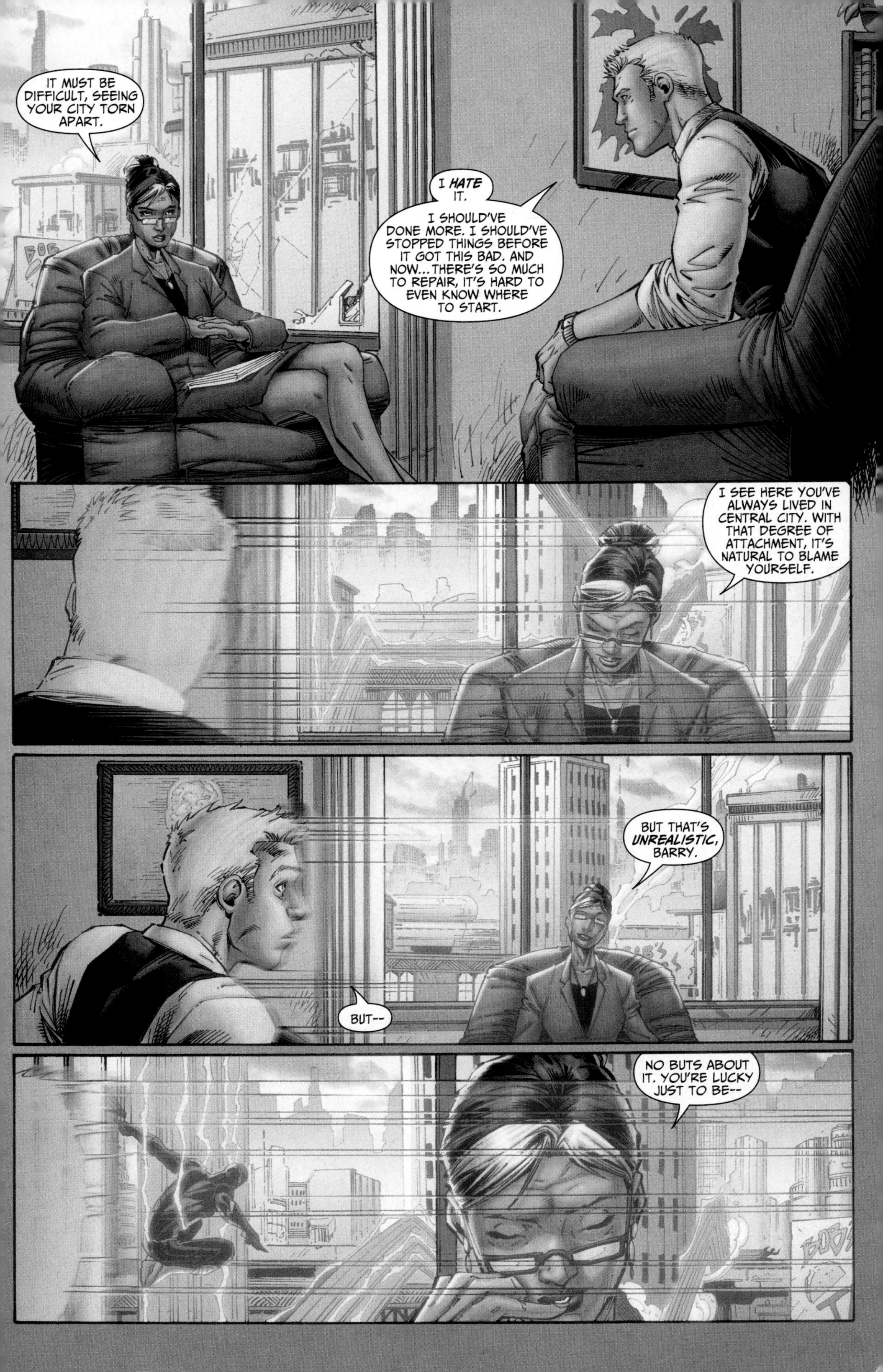
IT MUST BE DIFFICULT, SEEING YOUR CITY TORN APART.
I HATE IT.
I SHOULD'VE DONE MORE. I SHOULD'VE STOPPED THINGS BEFORE IT GOT THIS BAD. AND NOW...THERE'S SO MUCH TO REPAIR, IT'S HARD TO EVEN KNOW WHERE TO START.
I SEE HERE YOU'VE ALWAYS LIVED IN CENTRAL CITY. WITH THAT DEGREE OF ATTACHMENT, IT'S NATURAL TO BLAME YOURSELF.
BUT THAT'S UNREALISTIC, BARRY.
BUT--
NO BUTS ABOUT IT. YOU'RE LUCKY JUST TO BE--

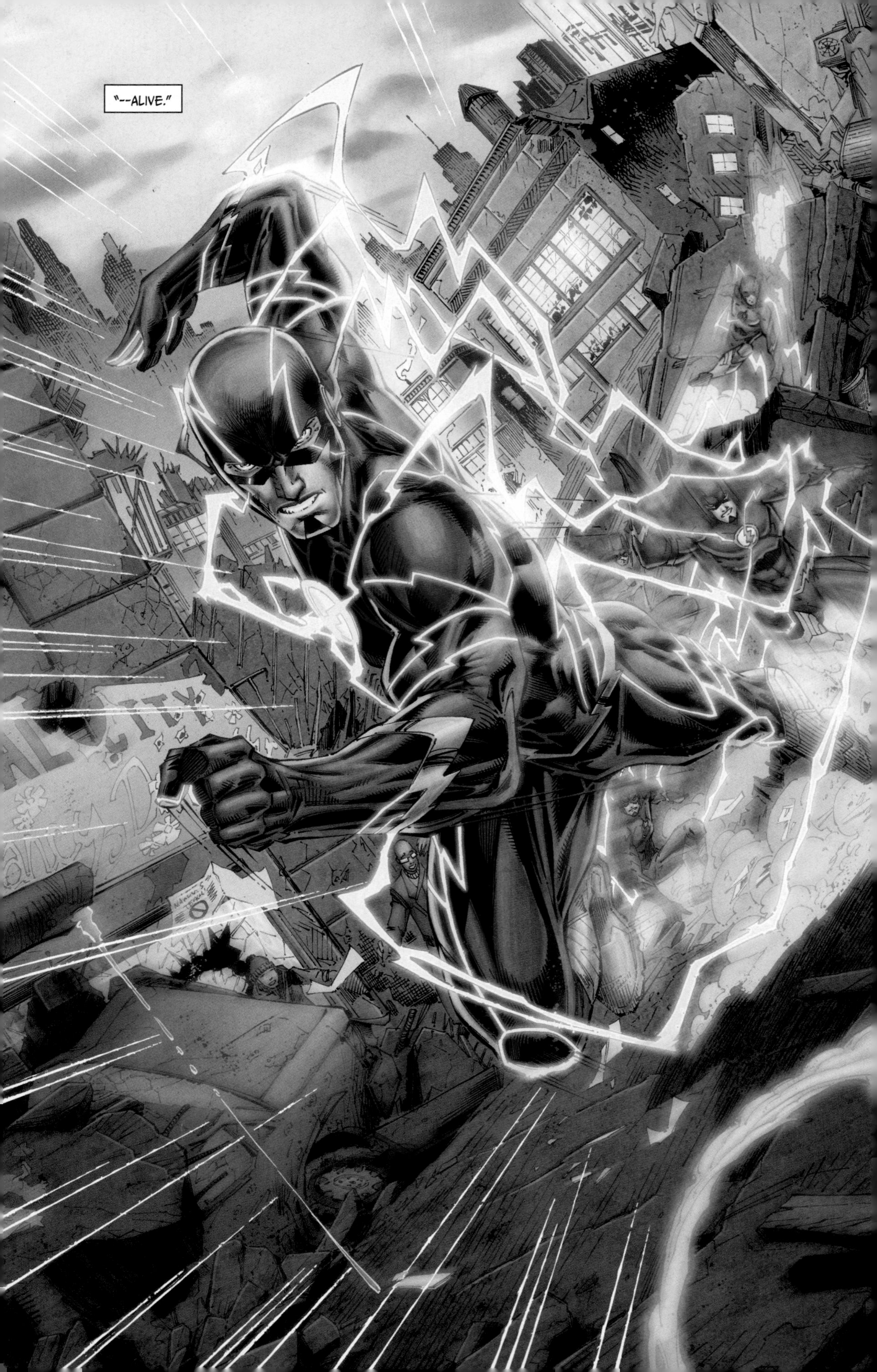
"--ALIVE."

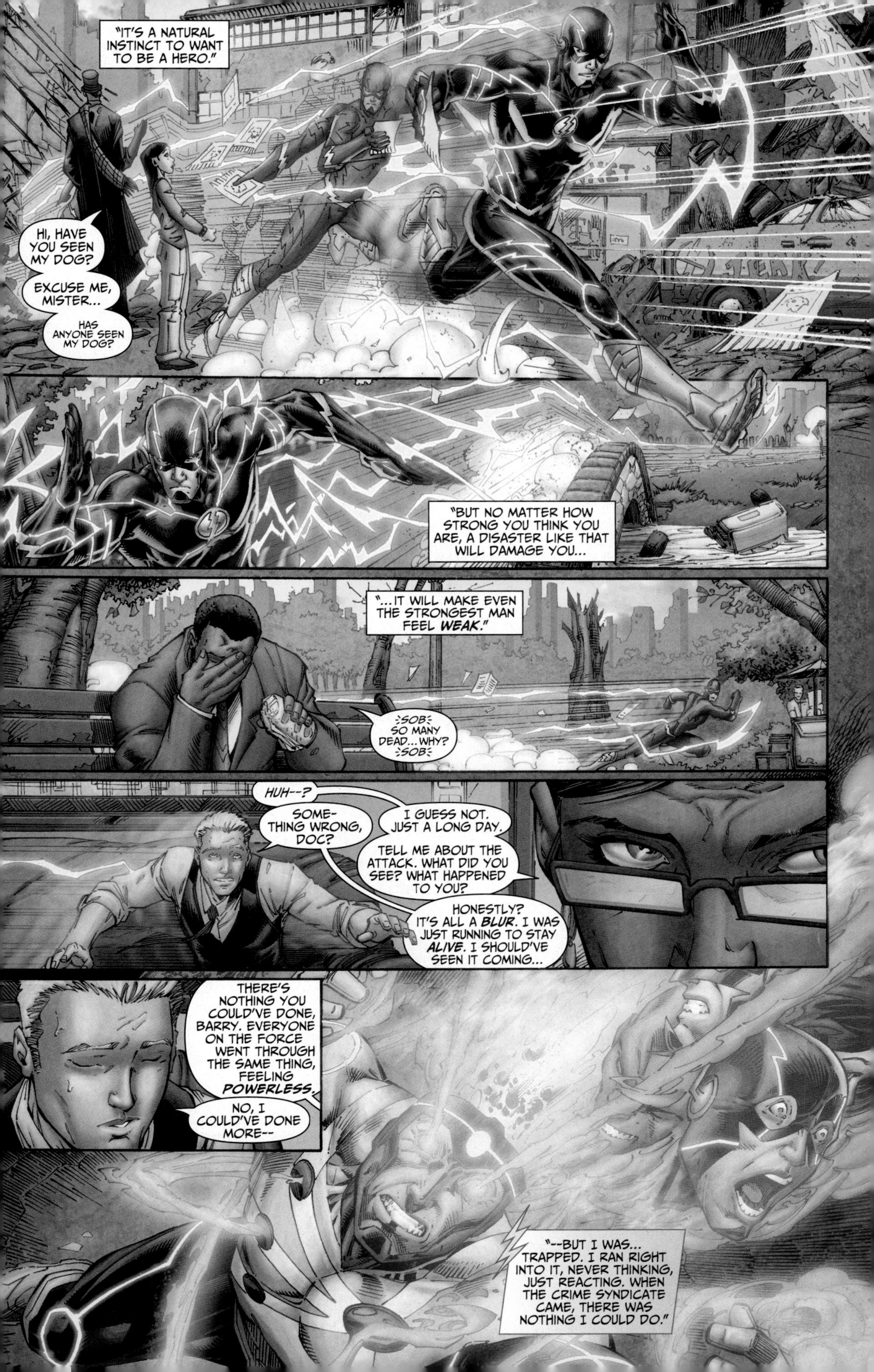

"IT'S A NATURAL INSTINCT TO WANT TO BE A HERO."
HI, HAVE YOU SEEN MY DOG?
EXCUSE ME, MISTER...
HAS ANYONE SEEN MY DOG?
"BUT NO MATTER HOW STRONG YOU THINK YOU ARE, A DISASTER LIKE THAT WILL DAMAGE YOU...
"...IT WILL MAKE EVEN THE STRONGEST MAN FEEL WEAK."
SOB SO MANY DEAD...WHY? SOB
HUH--?
SOME-THING WRONG, DOC?
I GUESS NOT. JUST A LONG DAY.
TELL ME ABOUT THE ATTACK. WHAT DID YOU SEE? WHAT HAPPENED TO YOU?
HONESTLY? IT'S ALL A BLUR. I WAS JUST RUNNING TO STAY ALIVE. I SHOULD'VE SEEN IT COMING...
THERE'S NOTHING YOU COULD'VE DONE, BARRY. EVERYONE ON THE FORCE WENT THROUGH THE SAME THING, FEELING POWERLESS.
NO, I COULD'VE DONE MORE--
"--BUT I WAS... TRAPPED. I RAN RIGHT INTO IT, NEVER THINKING, JUST REACTING. WHEN THE CRIME SYNDICATE CAME, THERE WAS NOTHING I COULD DO."

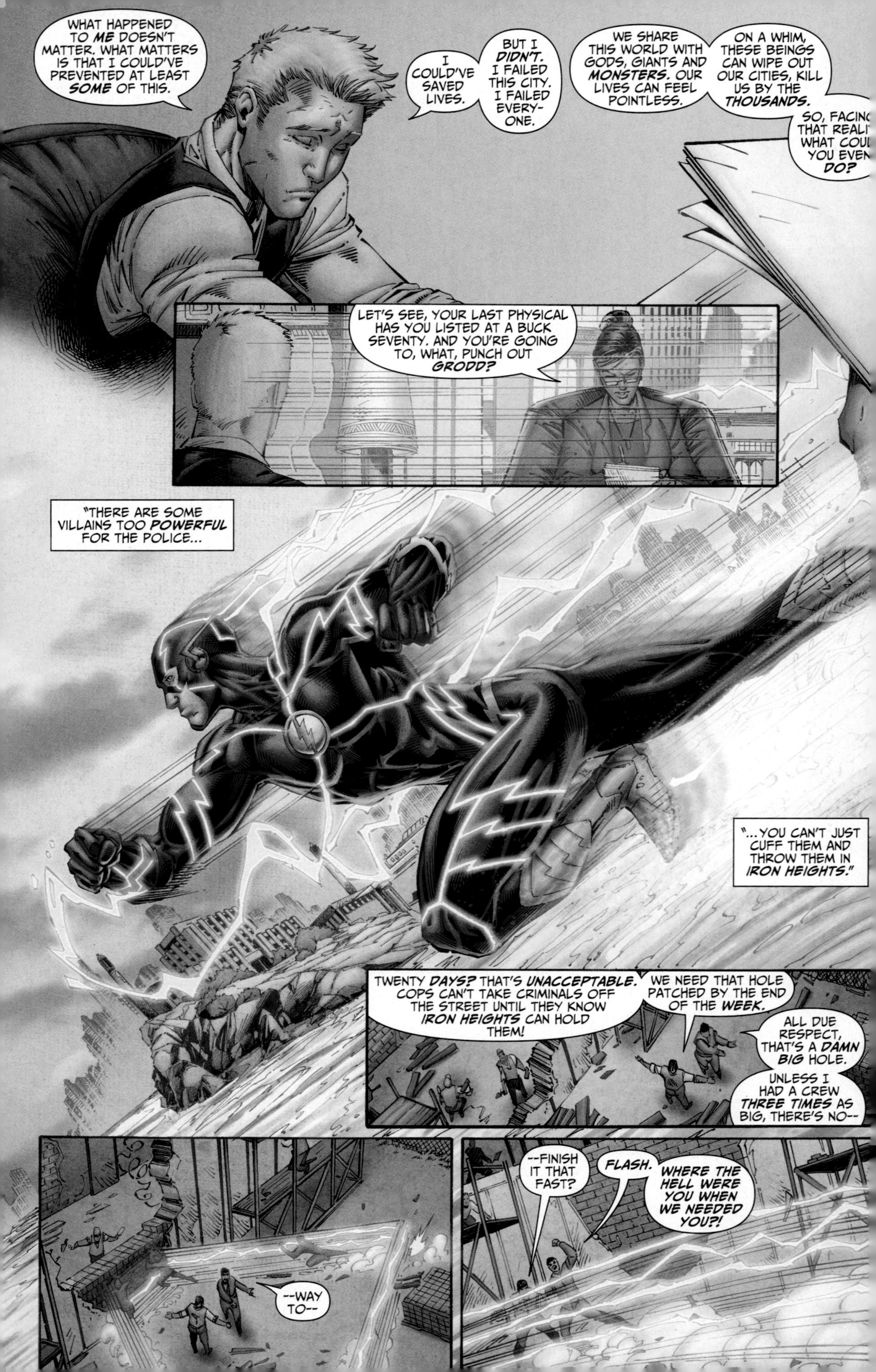
WHAT HAPPENED TO ME DOESN'T MATTER. WHAT MATTERS IS THAT I COULD'VE PREVENTED AT LEAST SOME OF THIS.
I COULD'VE SAVED LIVES.
BUT I DIDN'T. I FAILED THIS CITY. I FAILED EVERY-ONE.
WE SHARE THIS WORLD WITH GODS, GIANTS AND MONSTERS. OUR LIVES CAN FEEL POINTLESS.
ON A WHIM, THESE BEINGS CAN WIPE OUT OUR CITIES, KILL US BY THE THOUSANDS.
LET'S SEE, YOUR LAST PHYSICAL HAS YOU LISTED AT A BUCK SEVENTY. AND YOU'RE GOING TO, WHAT, PUNCH OUT GRODD?
"THERE ARE SOME VILLAINS TOO POWERFUL FOR THE POLICE...
"...YOU CAN'T JUST CUFF THEM AND THROW THEM IN IRON HEIGHTS."
TWENTY DAYS? THAT'S UNACCEPTABLE. COPS CAN'T TAKE CRIMINALS OFF THE STREET UNTIL THEY KNOW IRON HEIGHTS CAN HOLD THEM!
WE NEED THAT HOLE PATCHED BY THE END OF THE WEEK.
ALL DUE RESPECT, THAT'S A DAMN BIG HOLE.
UNLESS I HAD A CREW THREE TIMES AS BIG, THERE'S NO--
--WAY TO--
--FINISH IT THAT FAST?
FLASH.
WHERE THE HELL WERE YOU WHEN WE NEEDED YOU?!

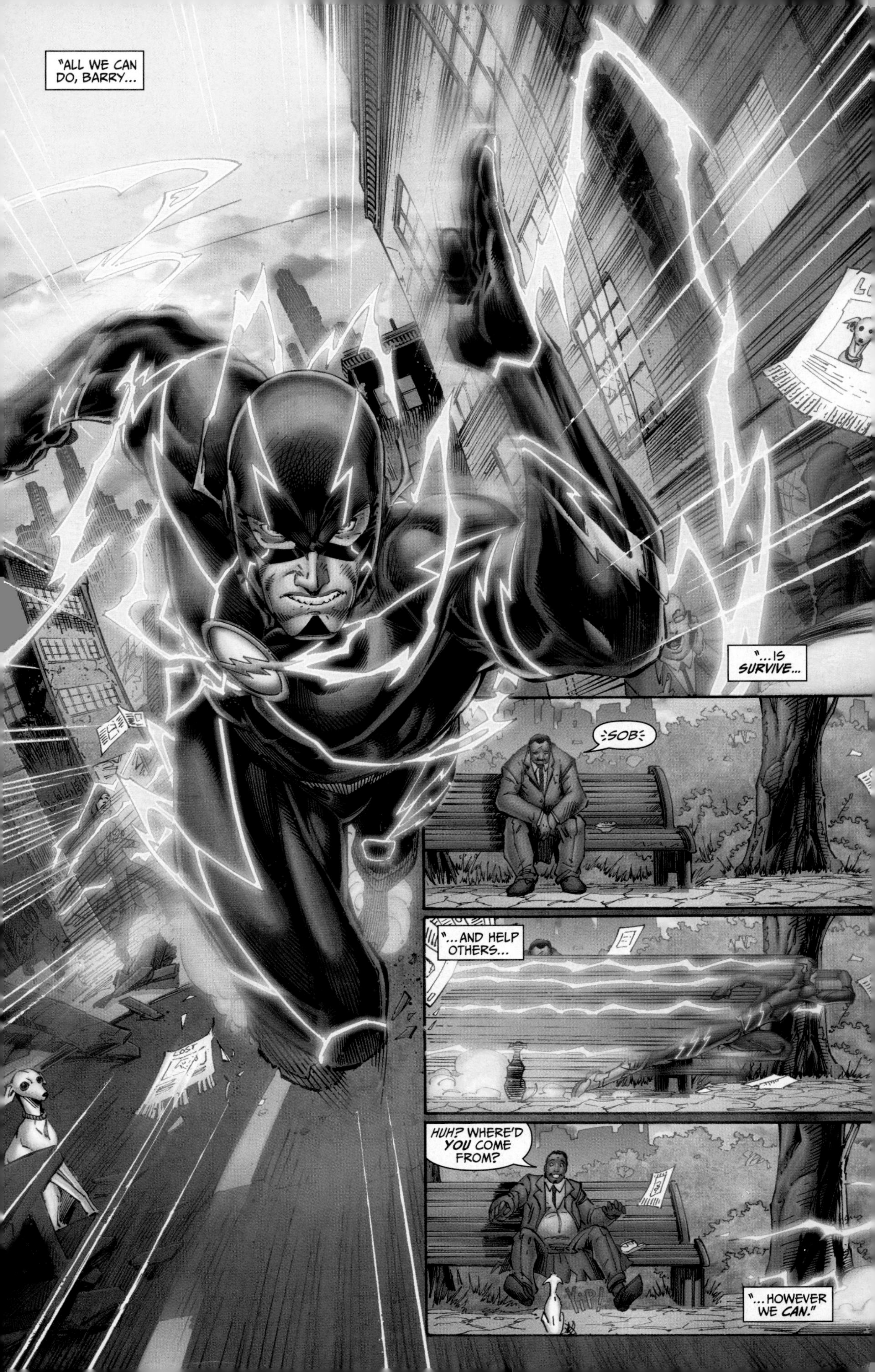
"ALL WE CAN DO, BARRY...
"...IS SURVIVE...
SOB
"...AND HELP OTHERS...
HUH? WHERE'D YOU COME FROM?
YIP!
"...HOWEVER WE CAN."

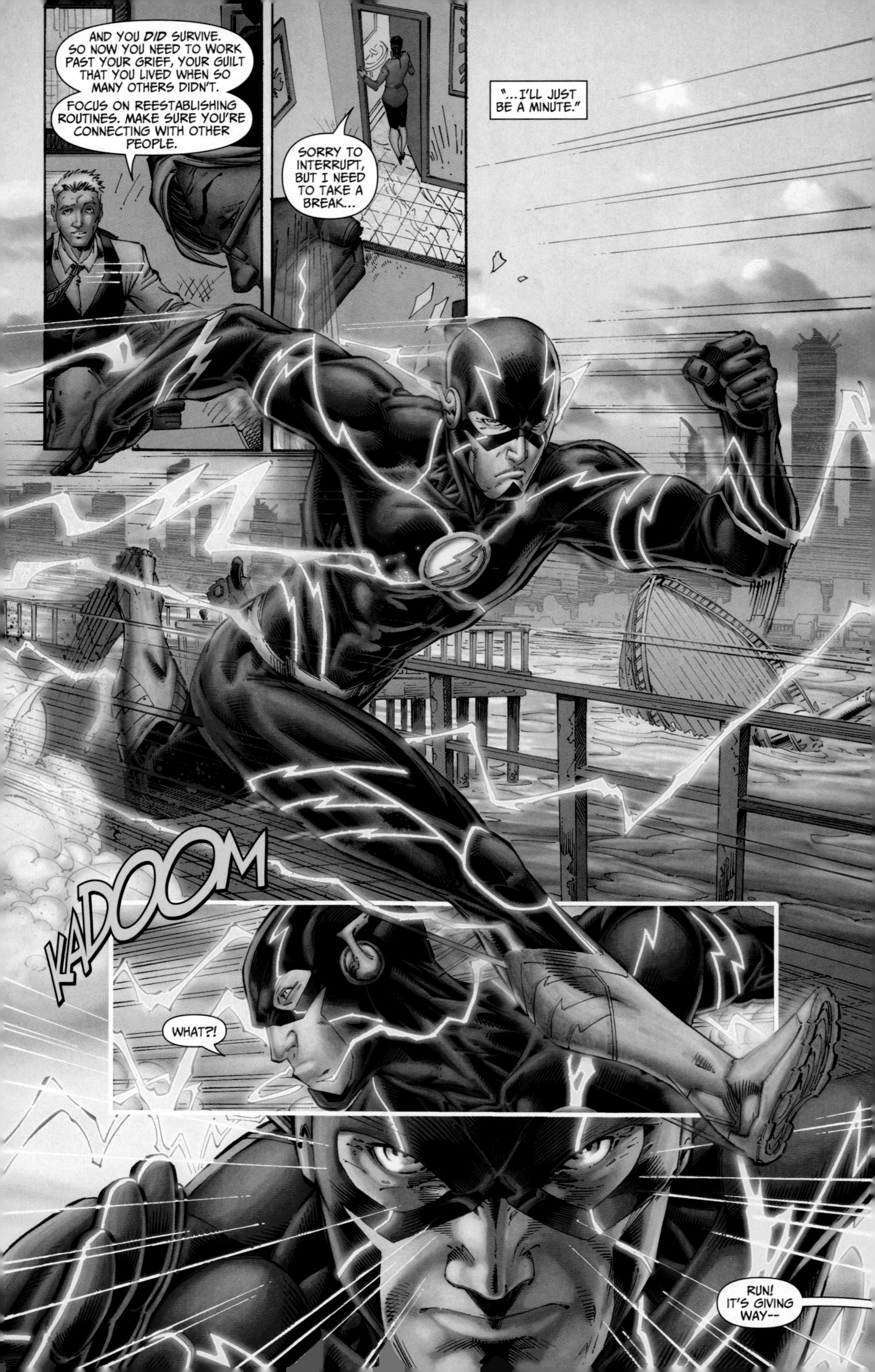
AND YOU *DID* SURVIVE. SO NOW YOU NEED TO WORK PAST YOUR GRIEF, YOUR GUILT THAT YOU LIVED WHEN SO MANY OTHERS DIDN'T.
FOCUS ON REESTABLISHING ROUTINES. MAKE SURE YOU'RE CONNECTING WITH OTHER PEOPLE.
SORRY TO INTERRUPT, BUT I NEED TO TAKE A BREAK...
"...I'LL JUST BE A MINUTE."
KADOOM
WHAT?!
RUN! IT'S GIVING WAY--

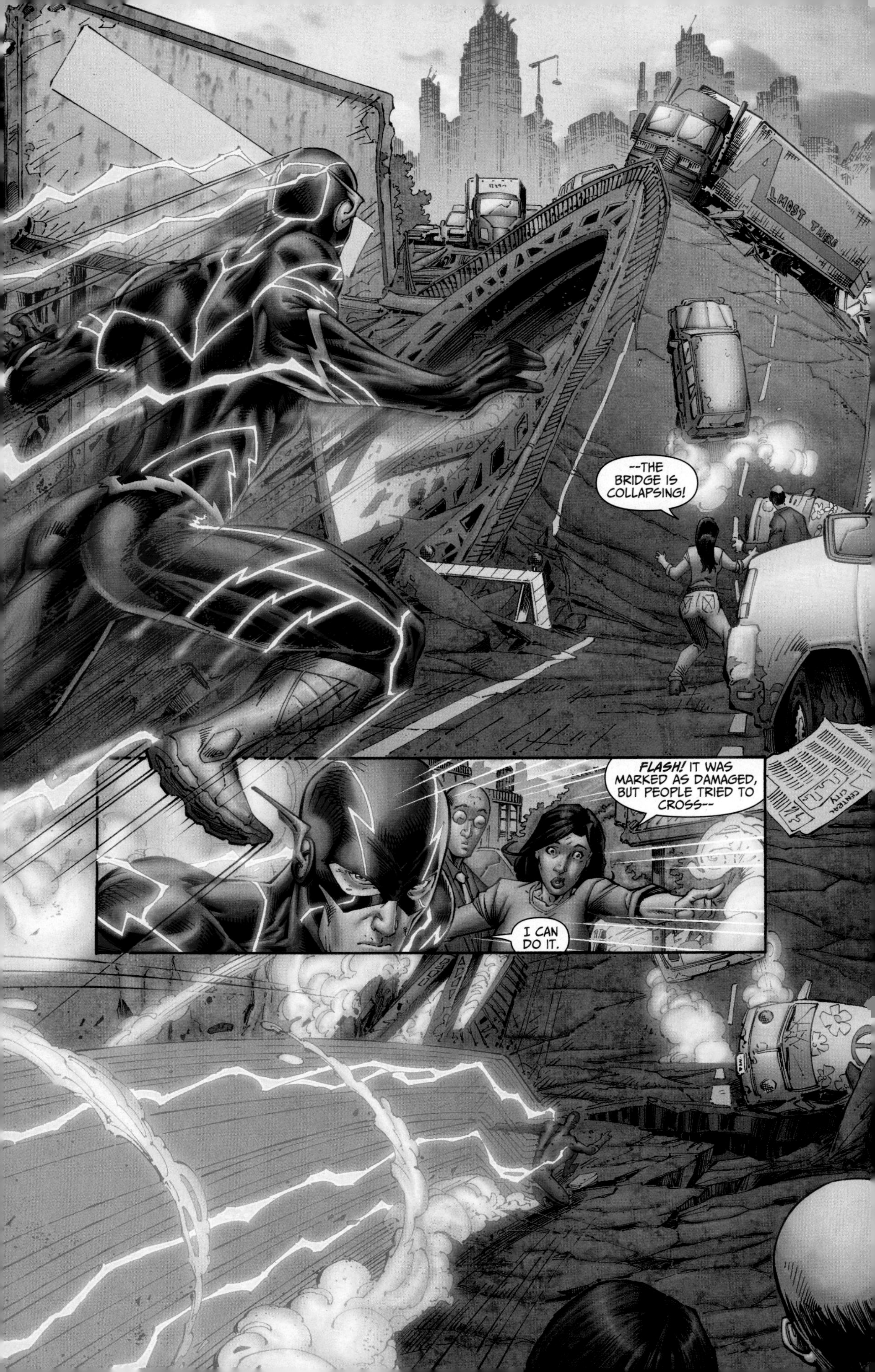
ALMOST THERE
--THE BRIDGE IS COLLAPSING!
FLASH! IT WAS MARKED AS DAMAGED, BUT PEOPLE TRIED TO CROSS--
I CAN DO IT.

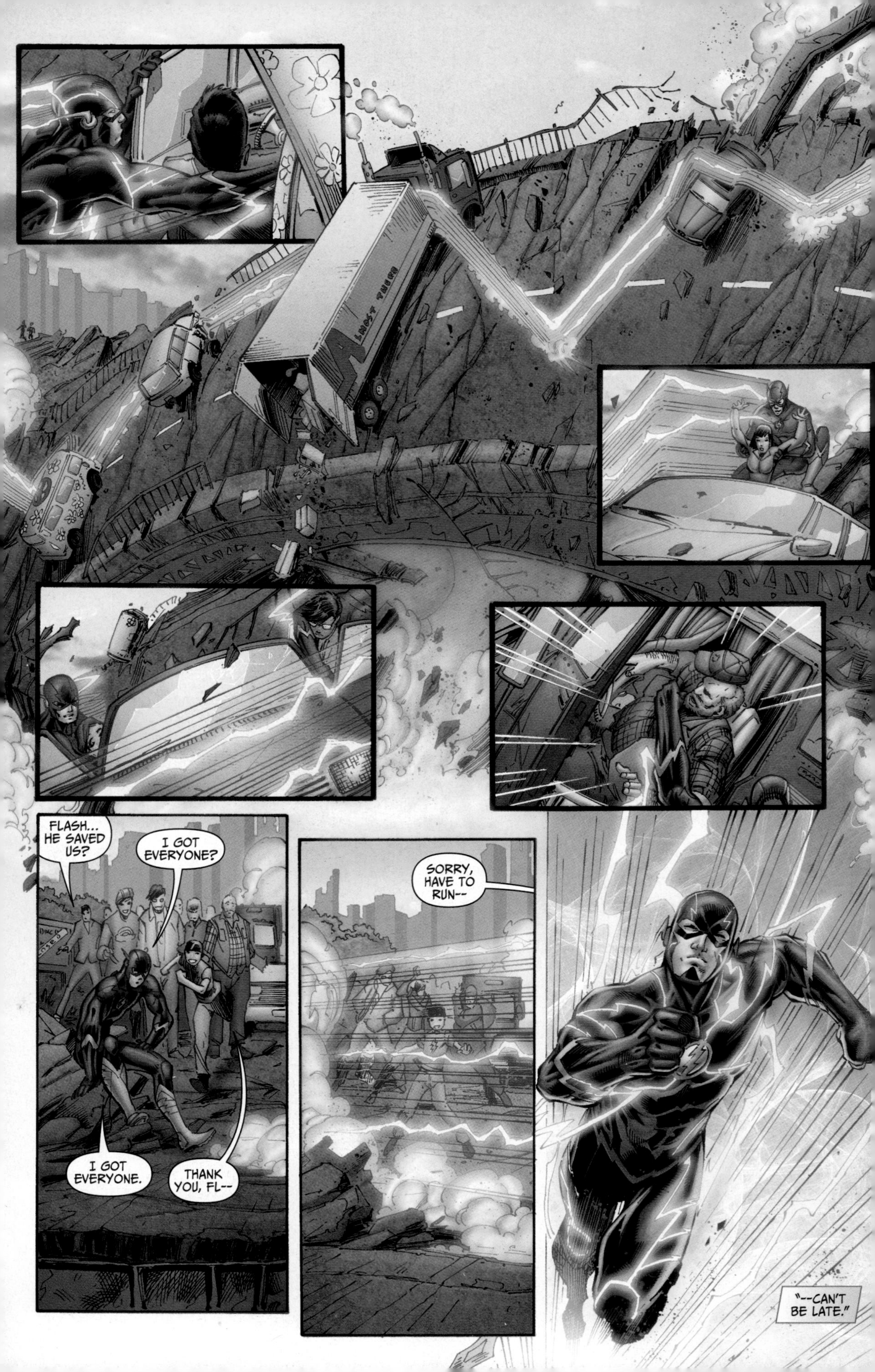
FLASH... HE SAVED US?
I GOT EVERYONE?
I GOT EVERYONE.
THANK YOU, FL--
SORRY, HAVE TO RUN--
"--CAN'T BE LATE."

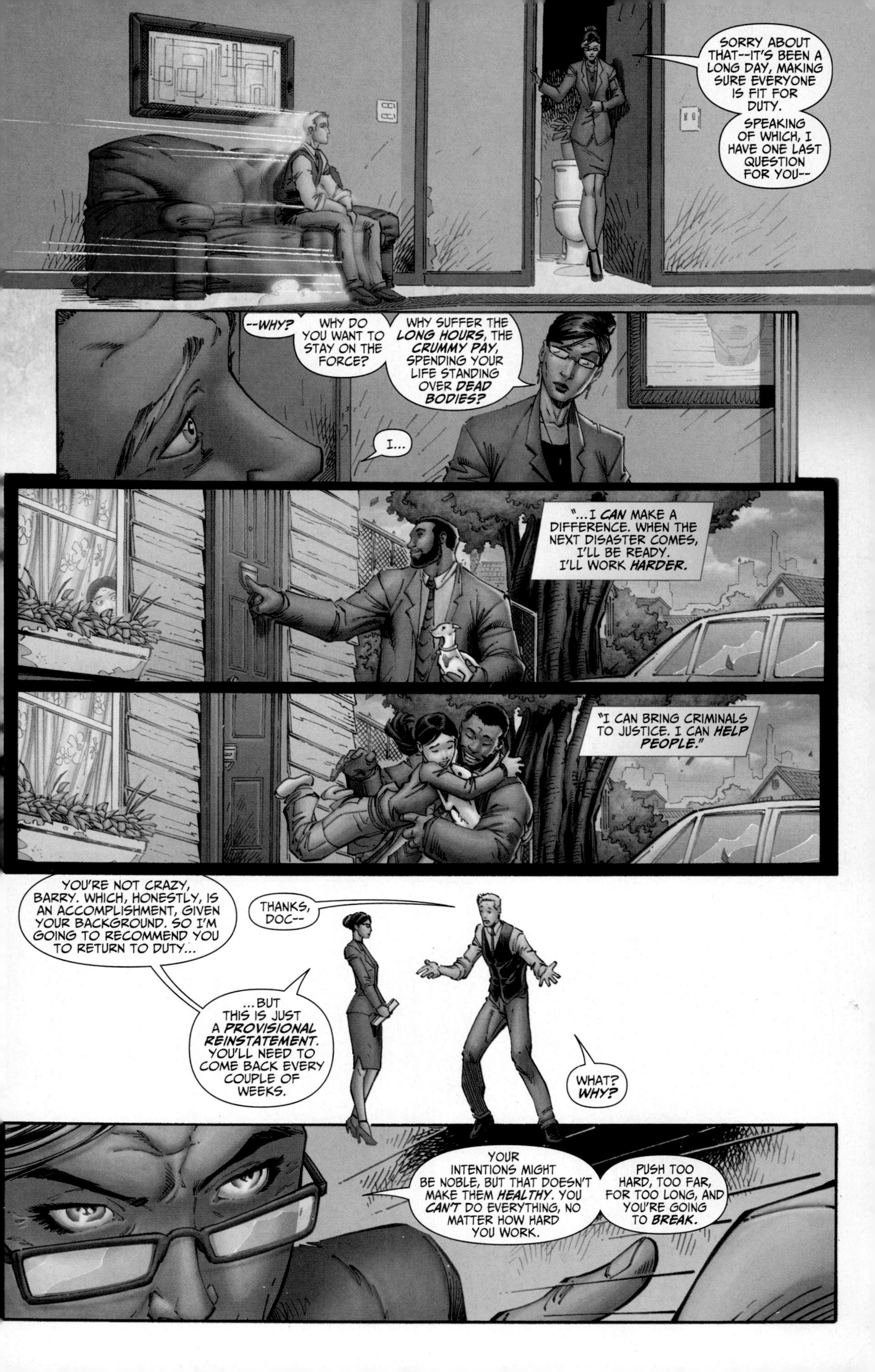
SORRY ABOUT THAT--IT'S BEEN A LONG DAY, MAKING SURE EVERYONE IS FIT FOR DUTY.
SPEAKING OF WHICH, I HAVE ONE LAST QUESTION FOR YOU--
--WHY?
WHY DO YOU WANT TO STAY ON THE FORCE?
WHY SUFFER THE LONG HOURS, THE CRUMMY PAY, SPENDING YOUR LIFE STANDING OVER DEAD BODIES?
I...
"...I CAN MAKE A DIFFERENCE. WHEN THE NEXT DISASTER COMES, I'LL BE READY. I'LL WORK HARDER.
"I CAN BRING CRIMINALS TO JUSTICE. I CAN HELP PEOPLE."
YOU'RE NOT CRAZY, BARRY. WHICH, HONESTLY, IS AN ACCOMPLISHMENT, GIVEN YOUR BACKGROUND. SO I'M GOING TO RECOMMEND YOU TO RETURN TO DUTY...
THANKS, DOC--
...BUT THIS IS JUST A PROVISIONAL REINSTATEMENT. YOU'LL NEED TO COME BACK EVERY COUPLE OF WEEKS.
WHAT? WHY?
YOUR INTENTIONS MIGHT BE NOBLE, BUT THAT DOESN'T MAKE THEM HEALTHY. YOU CAN'T DO EVERYTHING, NO MATTER HOW HARD YOU WORK.
PUSH TOO HARD, TOO FAR, FOR TOO LONG, AND YOU'RE GOING TO BREAK.

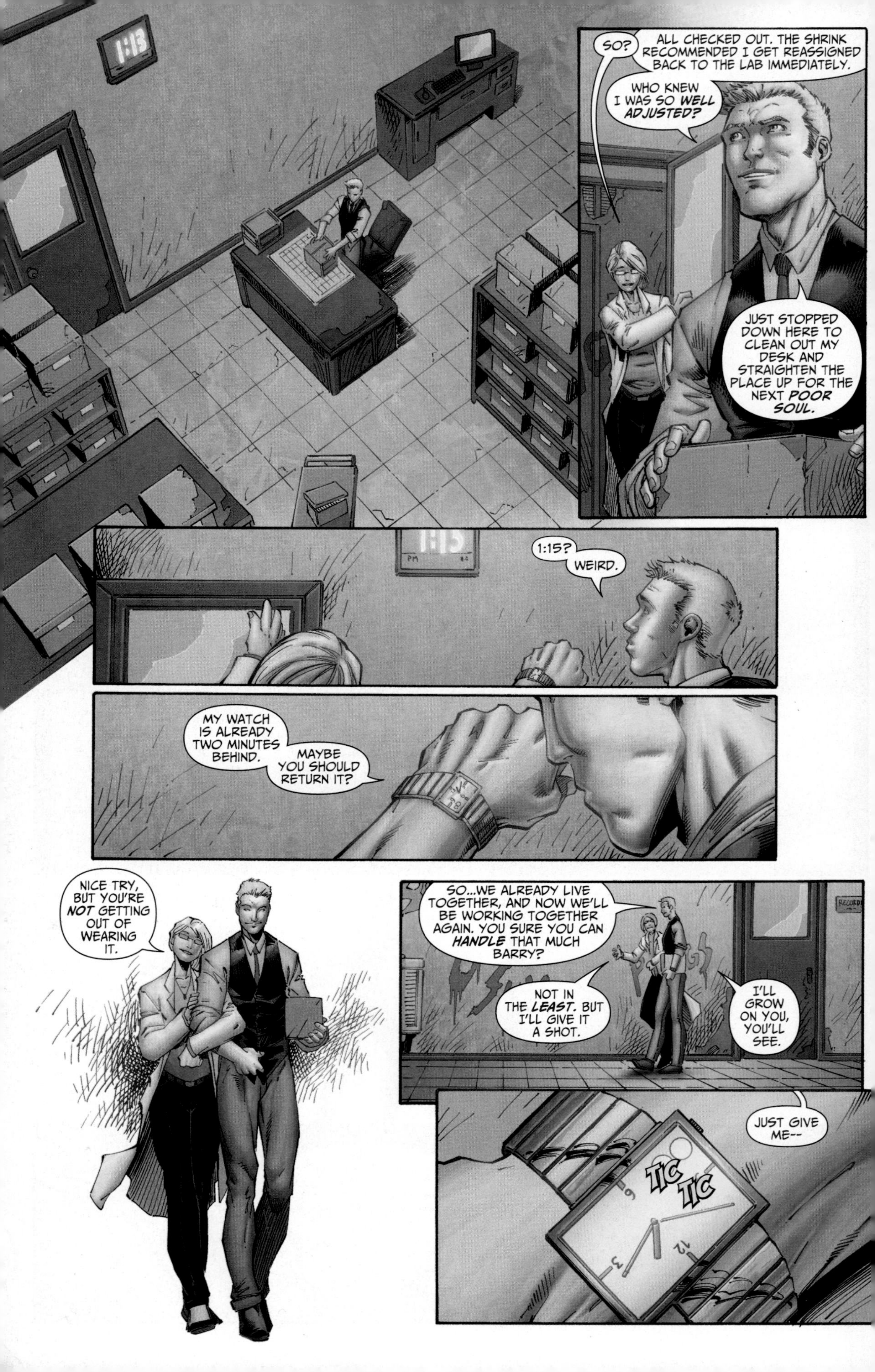
1:13
SO?
ALL CHECKED OUT. THE SHRINK RECOMMENDED I GET REASSIGNED BACK TO THE LAB IMMEDIATELY.
WHO KNEW I WAS SO WELL ADJUSTED?
JUST STOPPED DOWN HERE TO CLEAN OUT MY DESK AND STRAIGHTEN THE PLACE UP FOR THE NEXT POOR SOUL.
1:15
PM
1:15? WEIRD.
MY WATCH IS ALREADY TWO MINUTES BEHIND.
MAYBE YOU SHOULD RETURN IT?
NICE TRY, BUT YOU'RE NOT GETTING OUT OF WEARING IT.
SO...WE ALREADY LIVE TOGETHER, AND NOW WE'LL BE WORKING TOGETHER AGAIN. YOU SURE YOU CAN HANDLE THAT MUCH BARRY?
NOT IN THE LEAST. BUT I'LL GIVE IT A SHOT.
I'LL GROW ON YOU, YOU'LL SEE.
JUST GIVE ME--
TIC
TIC

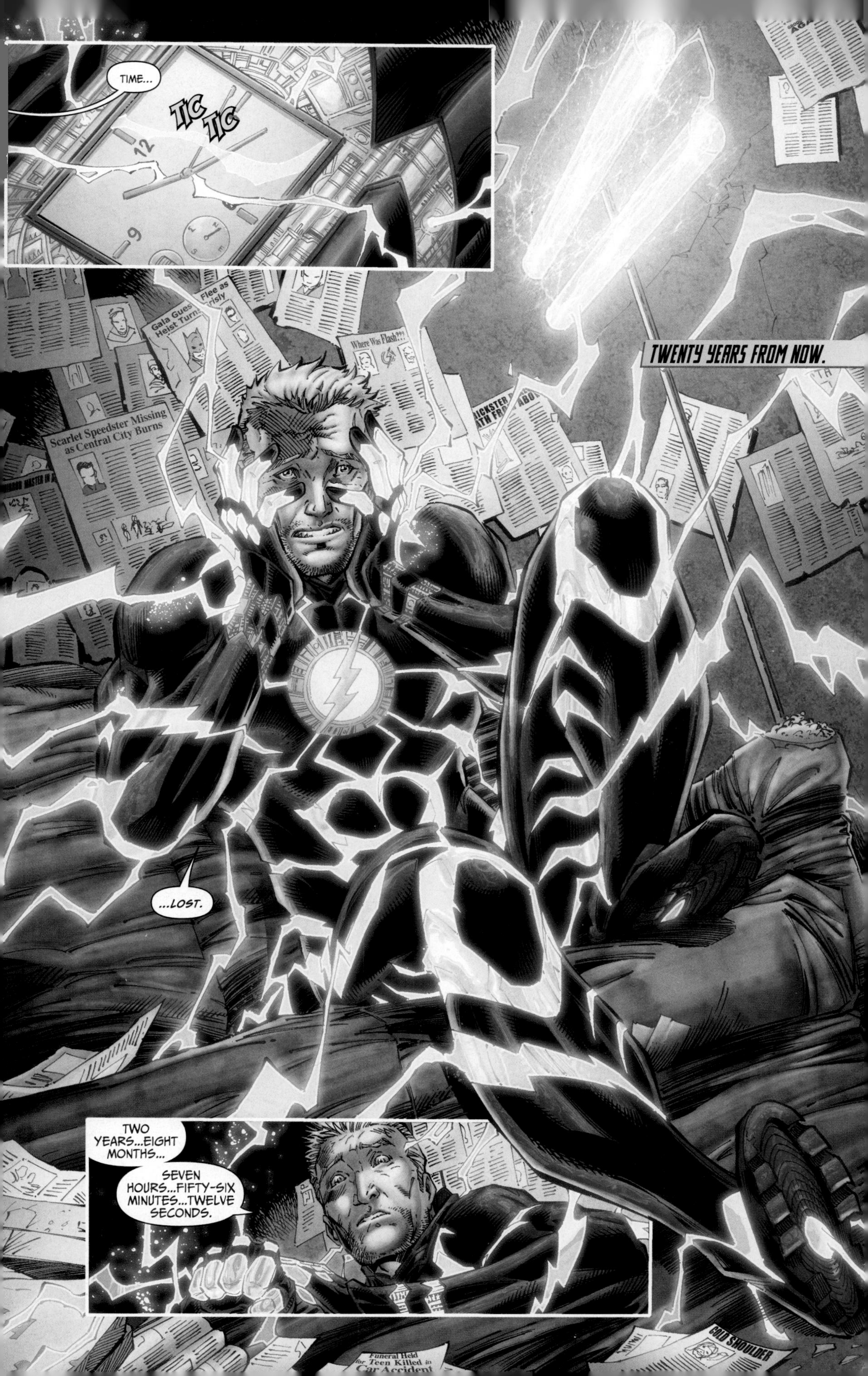
TIME...
TIC TIC
TWENTY YEARS FROM NOW.
Where Was Flash???
Scarlet Speedster Missing as Central City Burns
...LOST.
TWO YEARS...EIGHT MONTHS...
SEVEN HOURS...FIFTY-SIX MINUTES...TWELVE SECONDS.
Funeral Held for Teen Killed in Car Accident

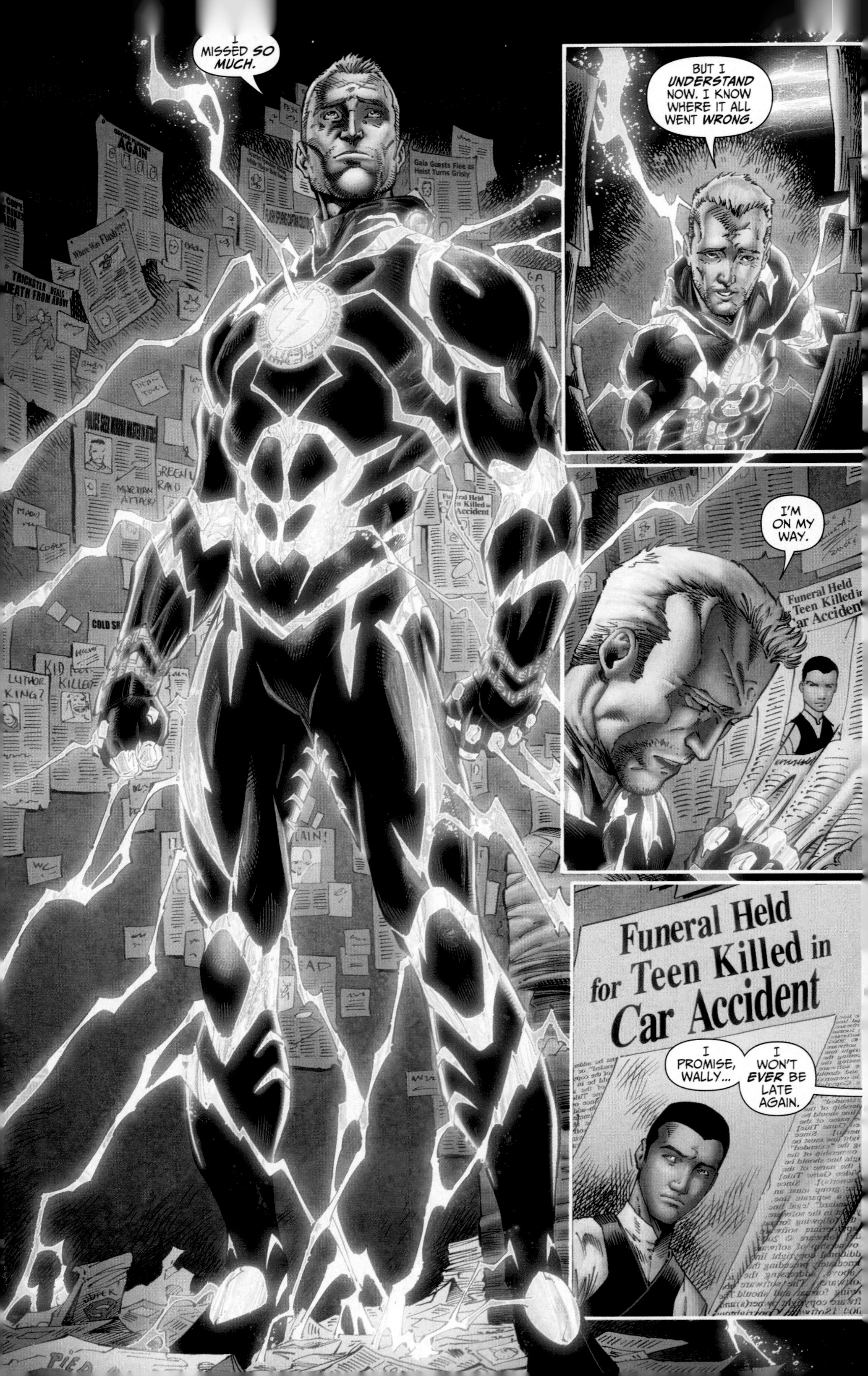

I MISSED SO MUCH.
Gala Guests Flee as Heist Turns Grisly
Where Was Flash???
TRICKSTER DEALS DEATH FROM ABOVE
LUTHOR KING?
BUT I UNDERSTAND NOW. I KNOW WHERE IT ALL WENT WRONG.
I'M ON MY WAY.
Funeral Held for Teen Killed in Car Accident
Funeral Held for Teen Killed in Car Accident
I PROMISE, WALLY...
I WON'T EVER BE LATE AGAIN.

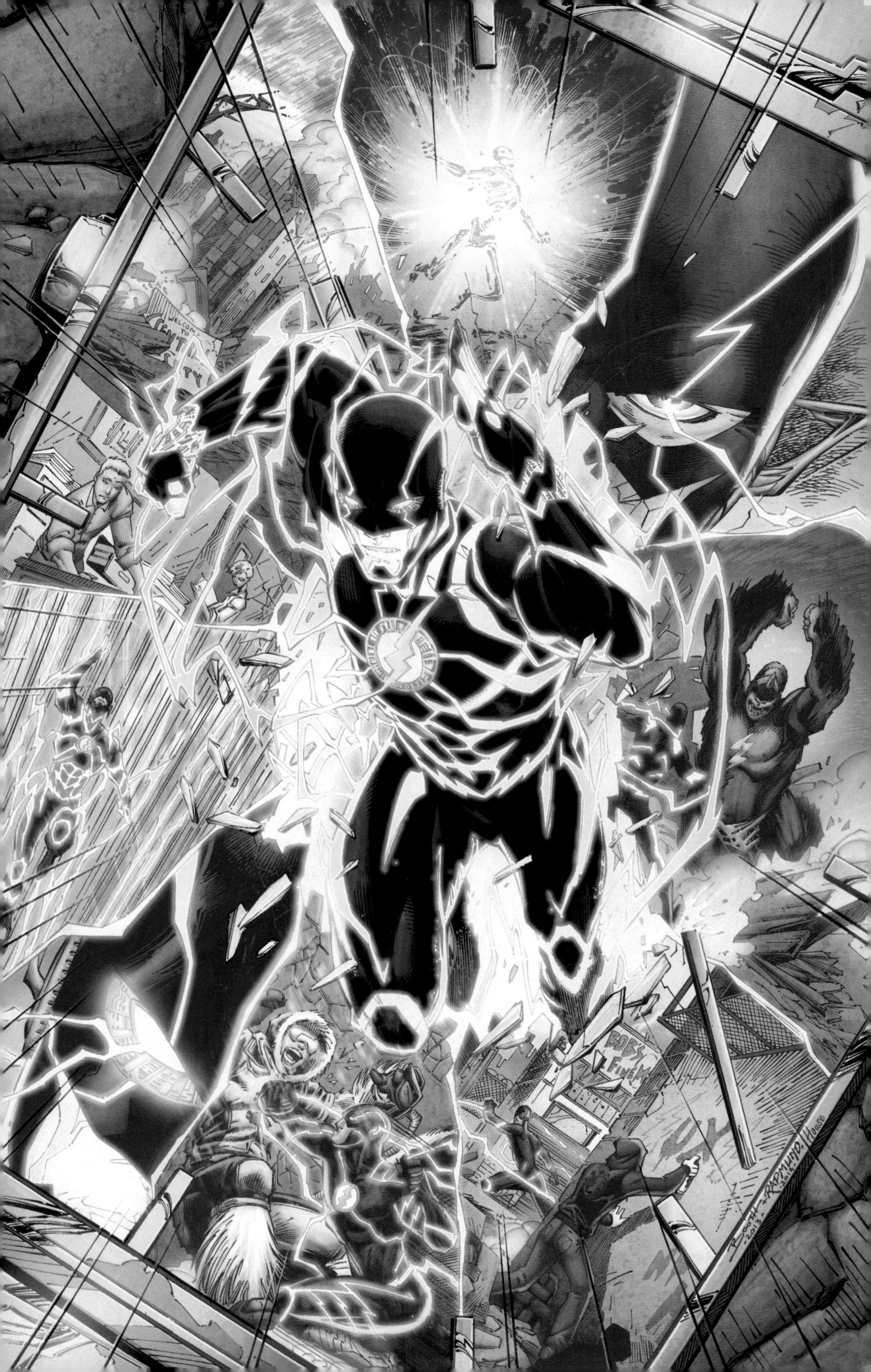
WELCOME TO
BOB'S

SLIP

ROBERT VENDITTI & VAN JENSEN writers BRETT BOOTH penciller NORM RAPMUND inker (Future Flash)
RON FRENZ penciller LIVESAY inker (Present Flash)

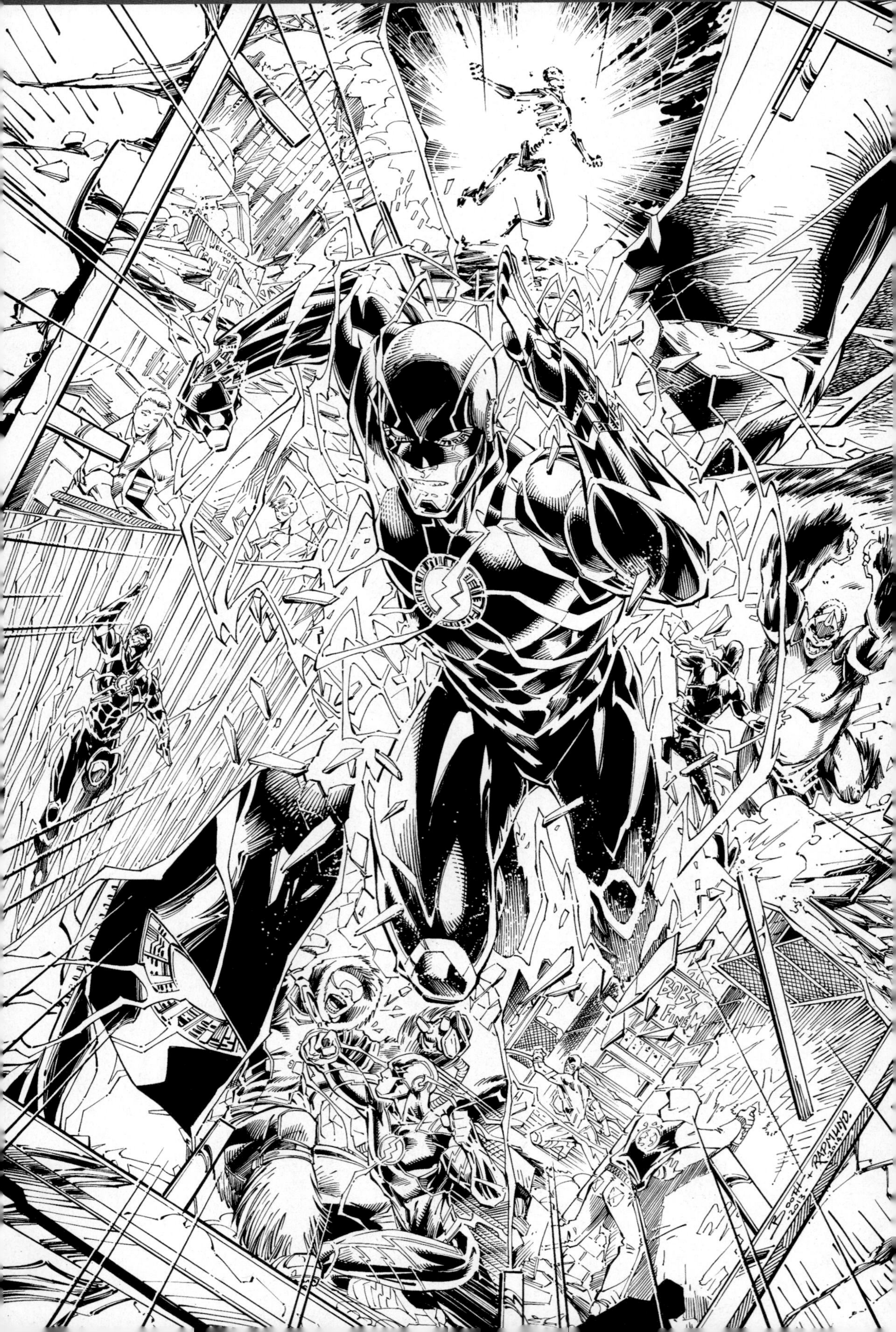

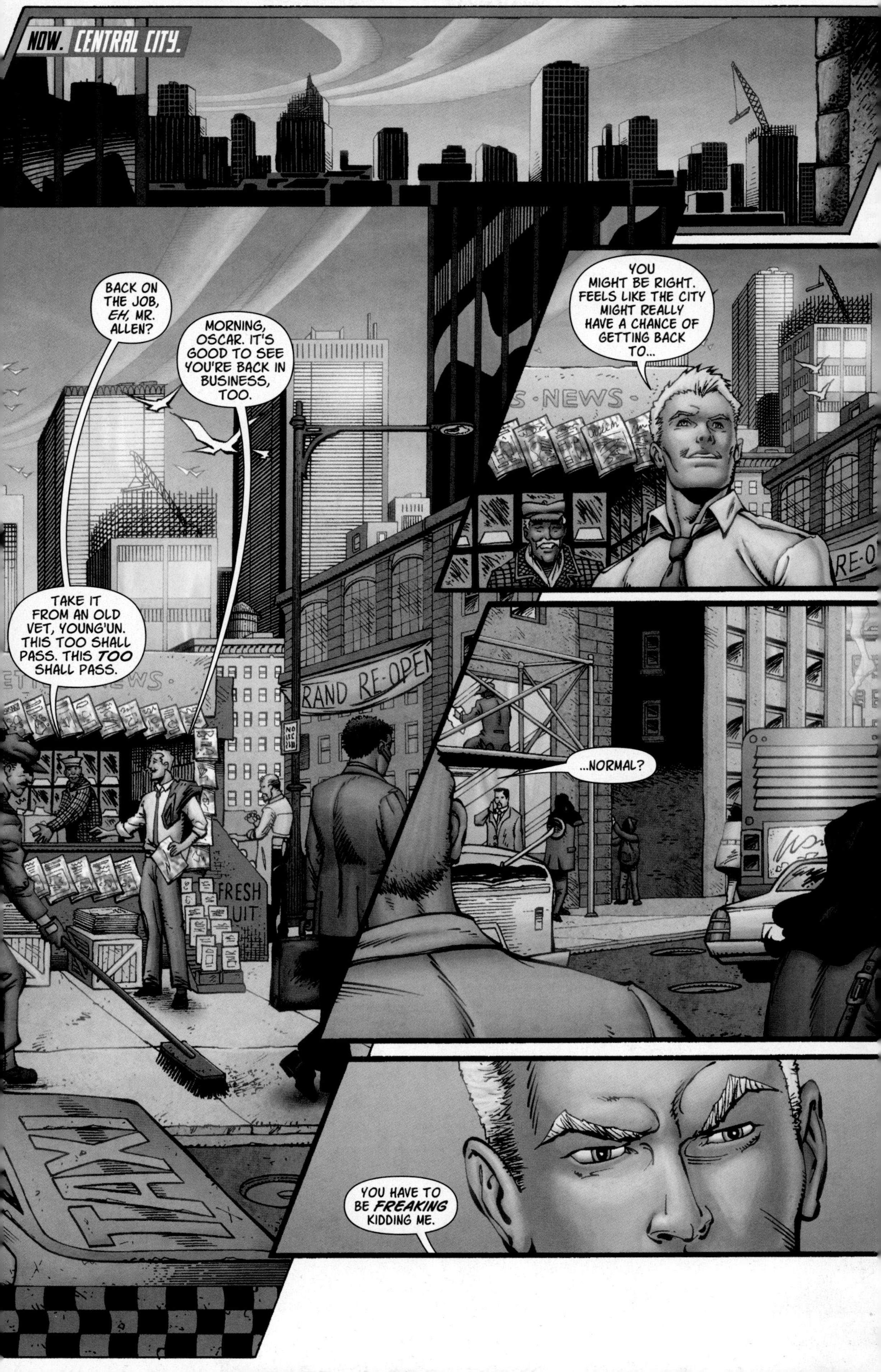
NOW. CENTRAL CITY.
BACK ON THE JOB, *EH,* MR. ALLEN?
MORNING, OSCAR. IT'S GOOD TO SEE YOU'RE BACK IN BUSINESS, TOO.
TAKE IT FROM AN OLD VET, YOUNG'UN. THIS TOO SHALL PASS. THIS ***TOO*** SHALL PASS.
NEWS
RAND RE-OPEN
FRESH UIT
YOU MIGHT BE RIGHT. FEELS LIKE THE CITY MIGHT REALLY HAVE A CHANCE OF GETTING BACK TO...
S·NEWS
...NORMAL?
YOU HAVE TO BE ***FREAKING*** KIDDING ME.

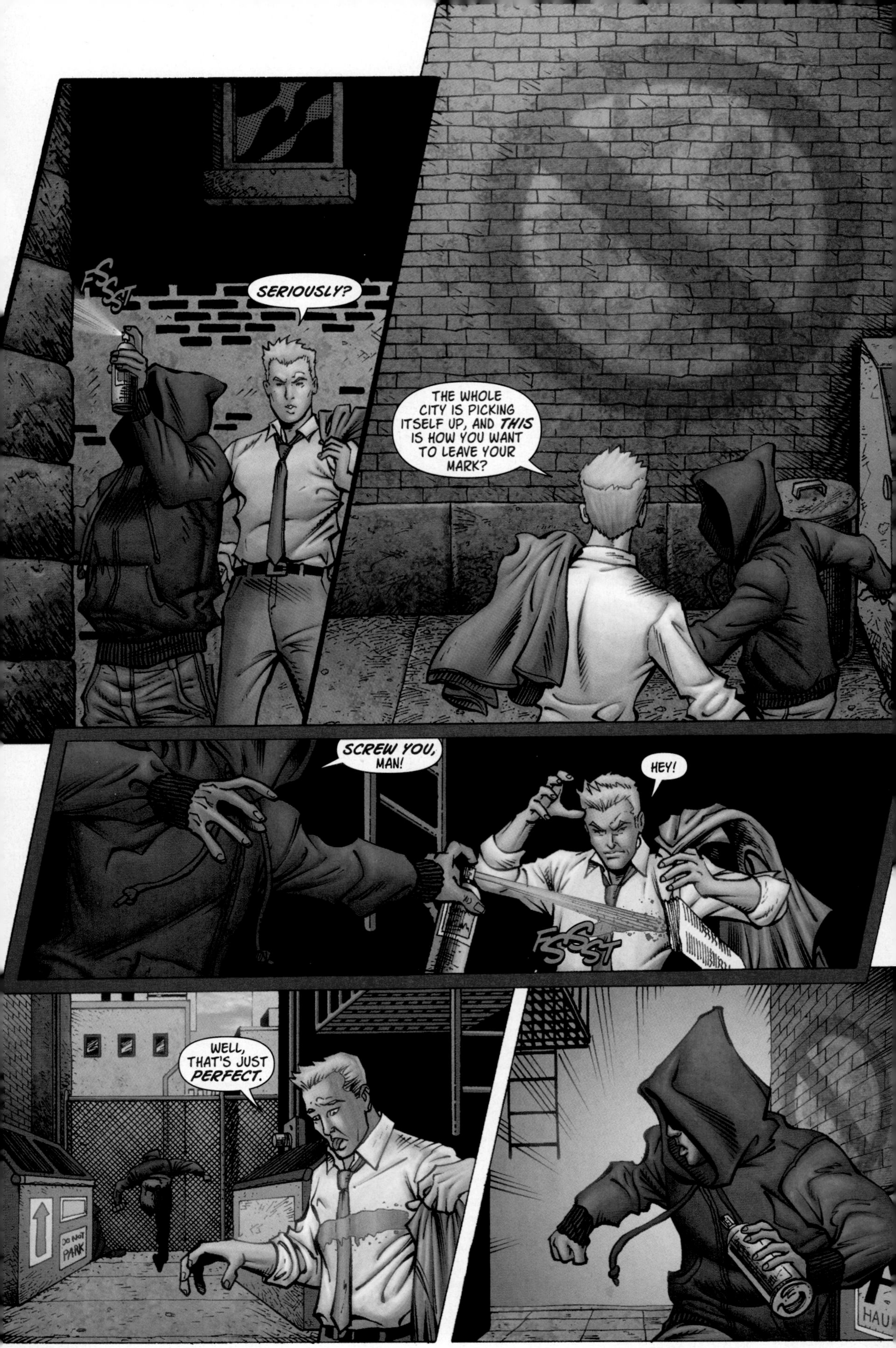
FSSST
SERIOUSLY?
THE WHOLE CITY IS PICKING ITSELF UP, AND THIS IS HOW YOU WANT TO LEAVE YOUR MARK?
SCREW YOU, MAN!
HEY!
FSSST
WELL, THAT'S JUST PERFECT.
DO NOT PARK

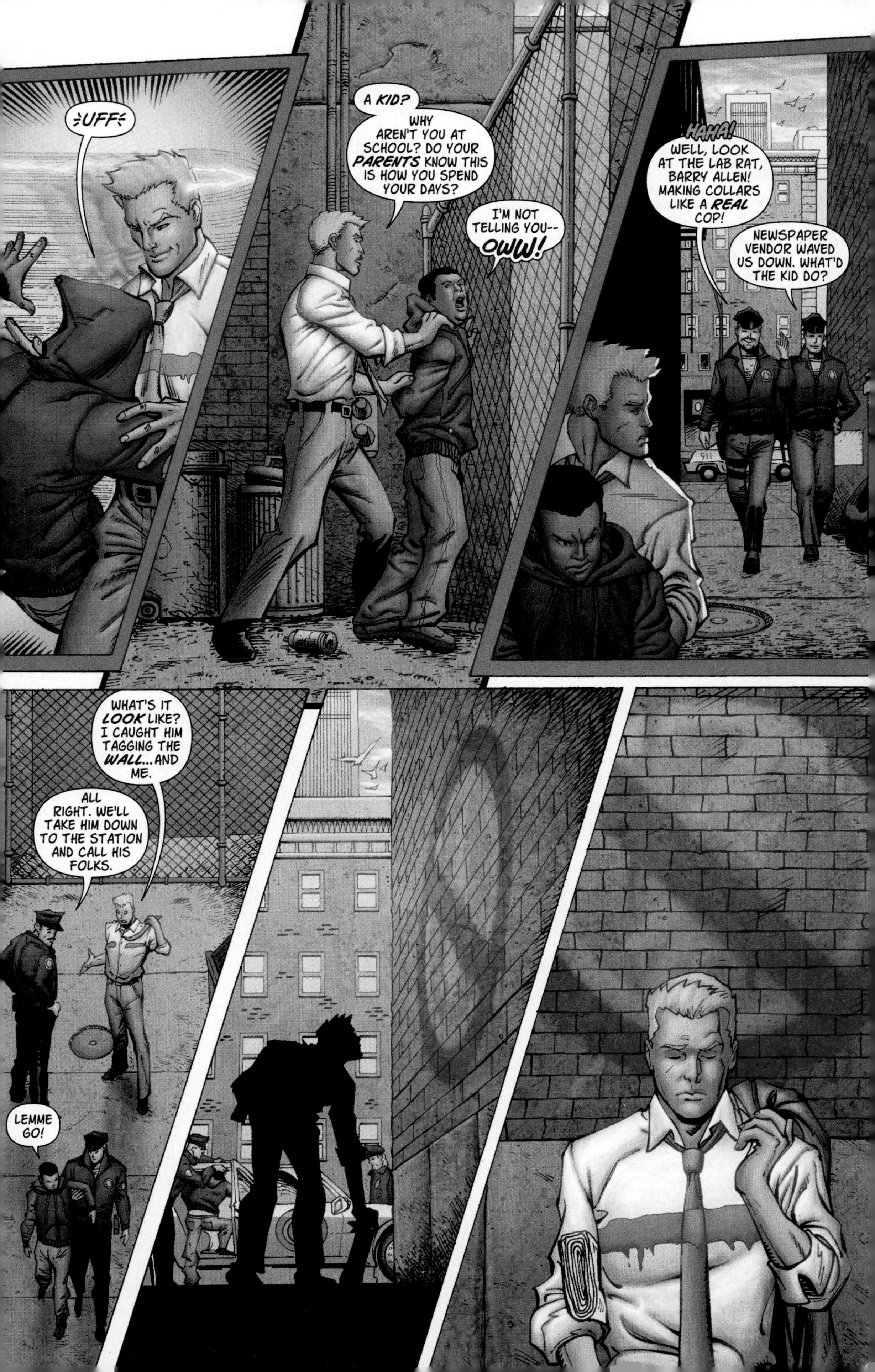
UFF
A KID?
WHY AREN'T YOU AT SCHOOL? DO YOUR PARENTS KNOW THIS IS HOW YOU SPEND YOUR DAYS?
I'M NOT TELLING YOU-- OWW!
HAHA!
WELL, LOOK AT THE LAB RAT, BARRY ALLEN! MAKING COLLARS LIKE A REAL COP!
NEWSPAPER VENDOR WAVED US DOWN. WHAT'D THE KID DO?
WHAT'S IT LOOK LIKE? I CAUGHT HIM TAGGING THE WALL...AND ME.
ALL RIGHT. WE'LL TAKE HIM DOWN TO THE STATION AND CALL HIS FOLKS.
LEMME GO!

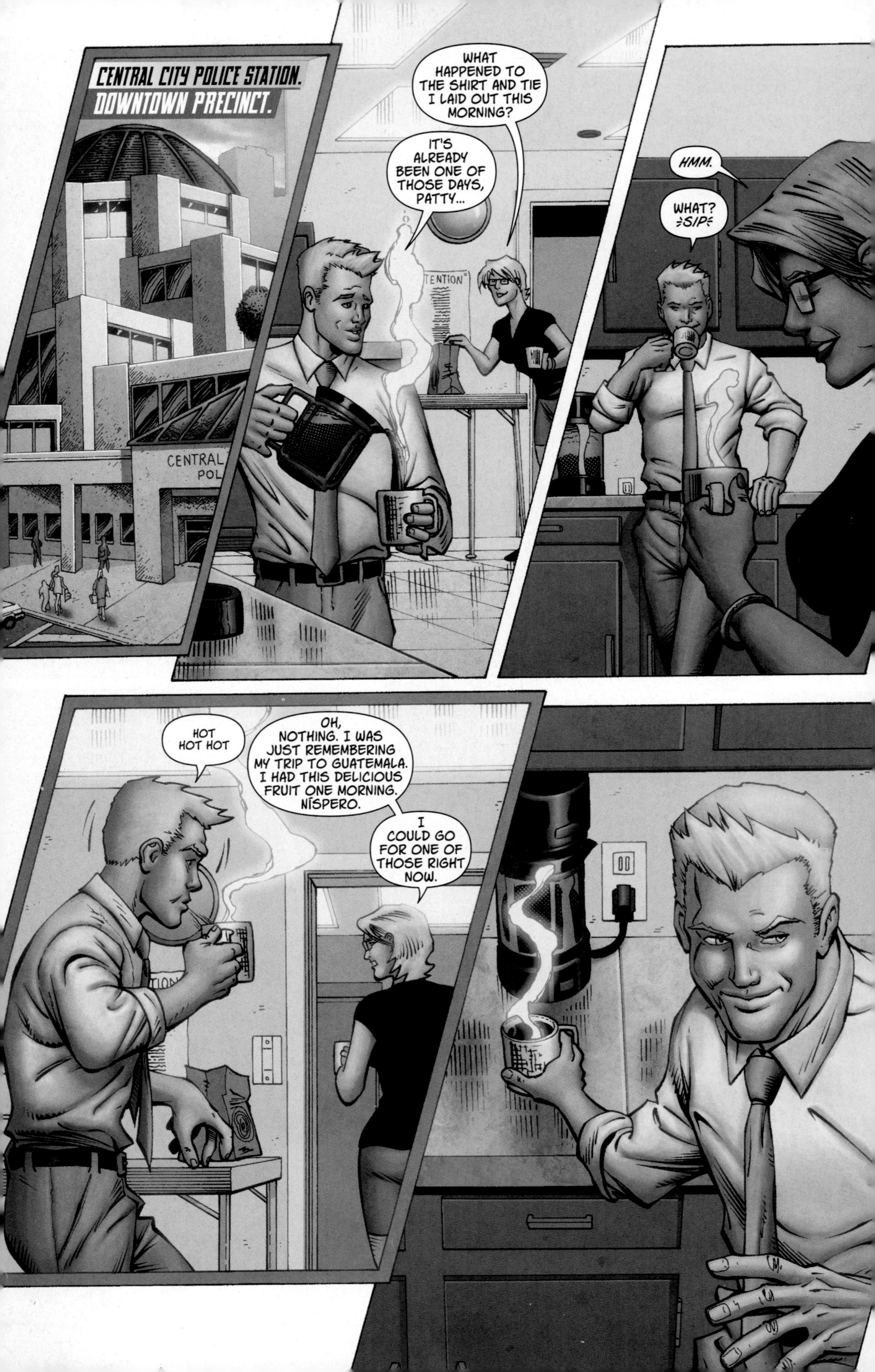
CENTRAL CITY POLICE STATION.
DOWNTOWN PRECINCT.
CENTRAL
POL
WHAT HAPPENED TO THE SHIRT AND TIE I LAID OUT THIS MORNING?
IT'S ALREADY BEEN ONE OF THOSE DAYS, PATTY...
TENTION
HMM.
WHAT? SIP
HOT HOT HOT
OH, NOTHING. I WAS JUST REMEMBERING MY TRIP TO GUATEMALA. I HAD THIS DELICIOUS FRUIT ONE MORNING. NÍSPERO.
I COULD GO FOR ONE OF THOSE RIGHT NOW.
TION

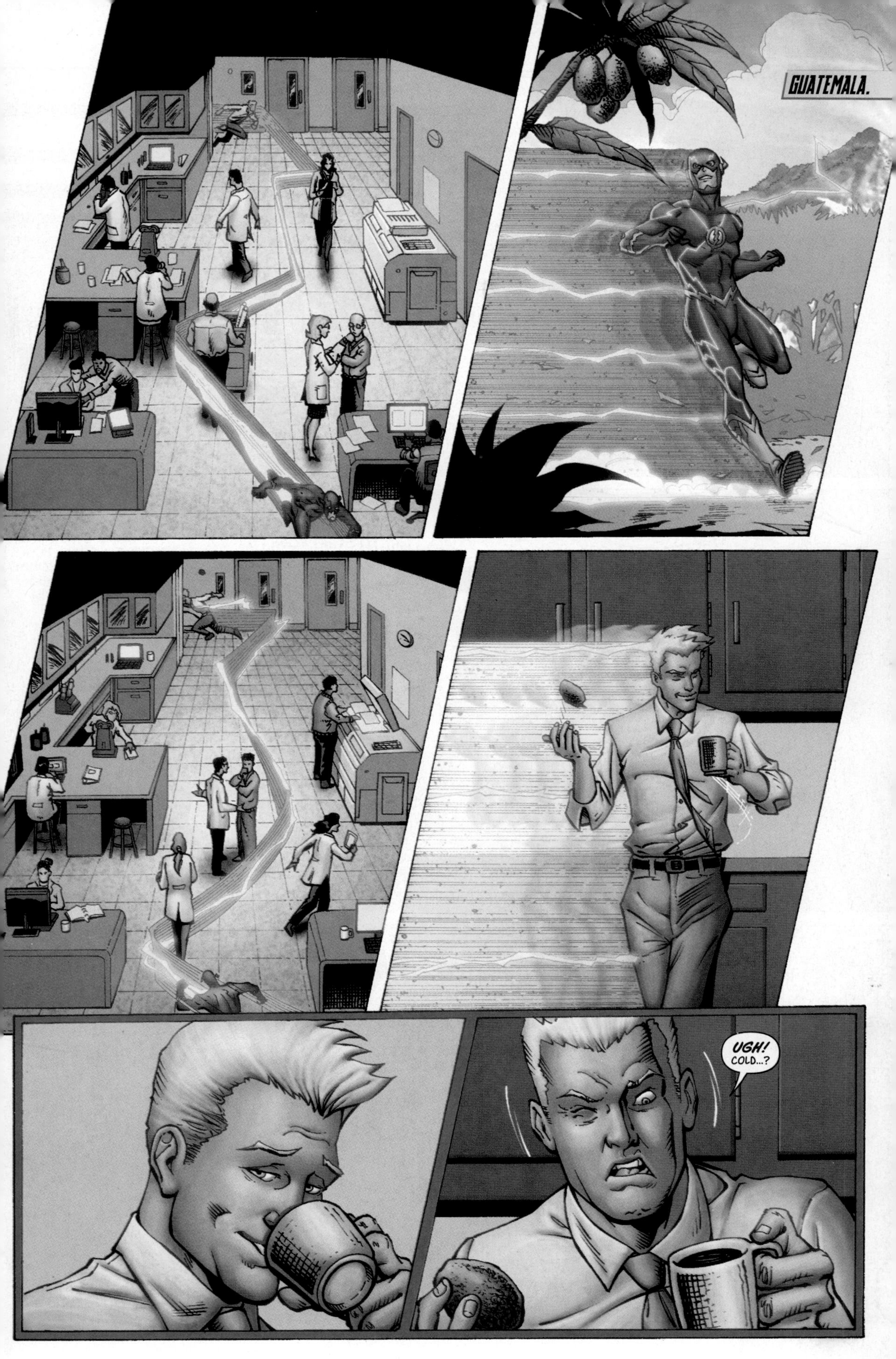
GUATEMALA.
UGH!
COLD...?

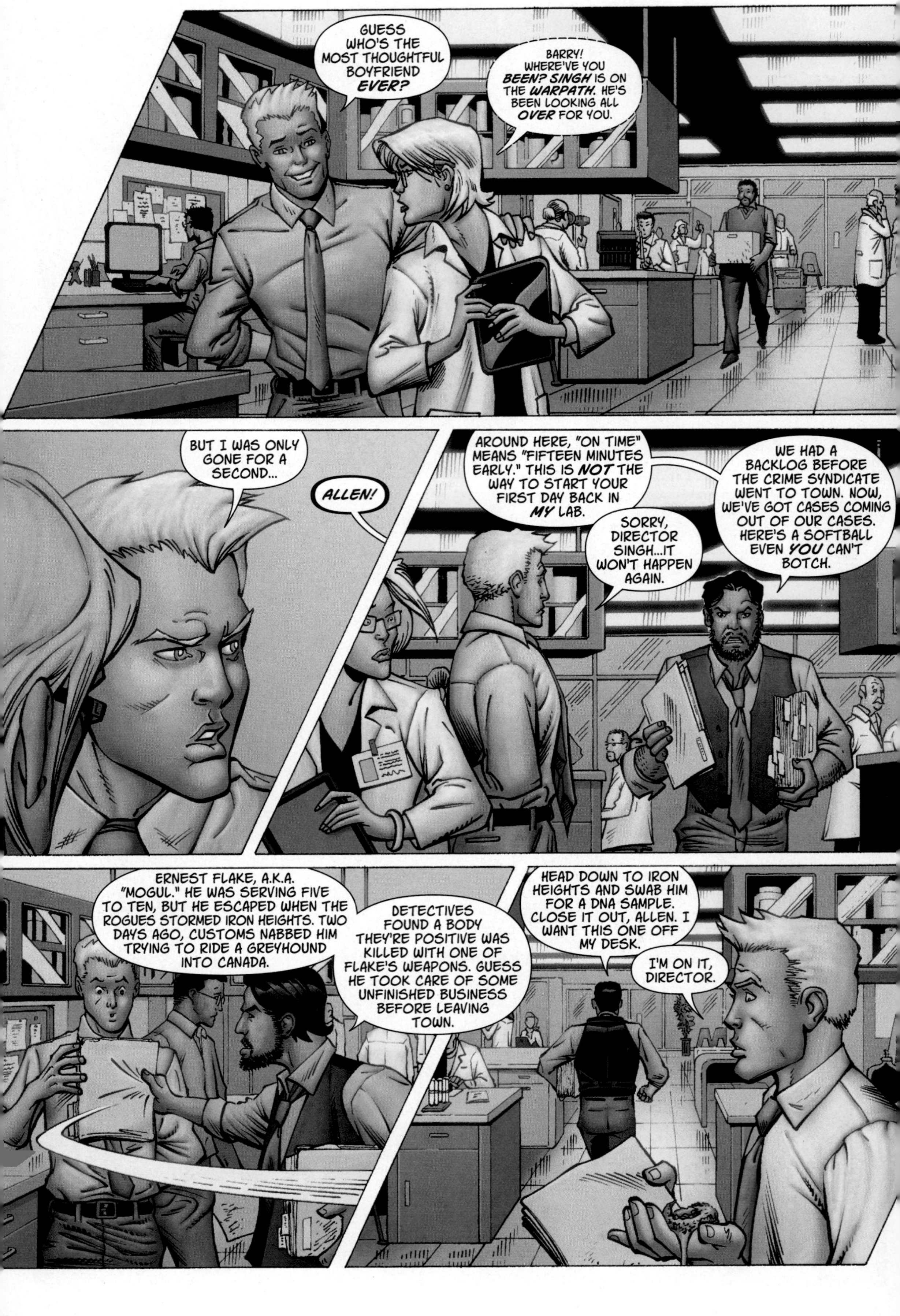
GUESS WHO'S THE MOST THOUGHTFUL BOYFRIEND EVER?
BARRY! WHERE'VE YOU BEEN? SINGH IS ON THE WARPATH. HE'S BEEN LOOKING ALL OVER FOR YOU.
BUT I WAS ONLY GONE FOR A SECOND...
ALLEN!
AROUND HERE, "ON TIME" MEANS "FIFTEEN MINUTES EARLY." THIS IS NOT THE WAY TO START YOUR FIRST DAY BACK IN MY LAB.
SORRY, DIRECTOR SINGH...IT WON'T HAPPEN AGAIN.
WE HAD A BACKLOG BEFORE THE CRIME SYNDICATE WENT TO TOWN. NOW, WE'VE GOT CASES COMING OUT OF OUR CASES. HERE'S A SOFTBALL EVEN YOU CAN'T BOTCH.
ERNEST FLAKE, A.K.A. "MOGUL." HE WAS SERVING FIVE TO TEN, BUT HE ESCAPED WHEN THE ROGUES STORMED IRON HEIGHTS. TWO DAYS AGO, CUSTOMS NABBED HIM TRYING TO RIDE A GREYHOUND INTO CANADA.
DETECTIVES FOUND A BODY THEY'RE POSITIVE WAS KILLED WITH ONE OF FLAKE'S WEAPONS. GUESS HE TOOK CARE OF SOME UNFINISHED BUSINESS BEFORE LEAVING TOWN.
HEAD DOWN TO IRON HEIGHTS AND SWAB HIM FOR A DNA SAMPLE. CLOSE IT OUT, ALLEN. I WANT THIS ONE OFF MY DESK.
I'M ON IT, DIRECTOR.

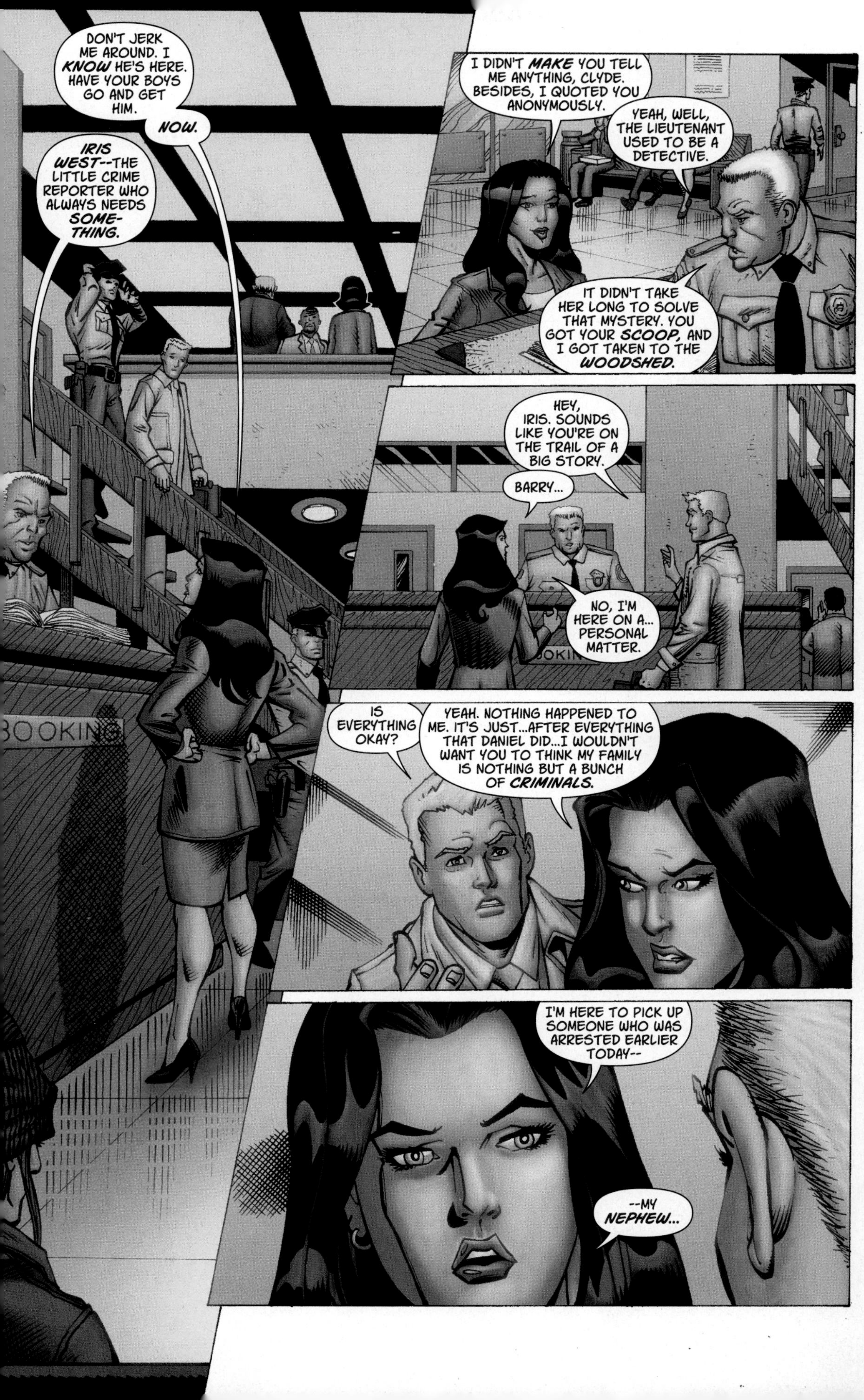
DON'T JERK ME AROUND. I *KNOW* HE'S HERE. HAVE YOUR BOYS GO AND GET HIM.
NOW.
IRIS WEST--THE LITTLE CRIME REPORTER WHO ALWAYS NEEDS *SOME-THING.*
BOOKING
I DIDN'T *MAKE* YOU TELL ME ANYTHING, CLYDE. BESIDES, I QUOTED YOU ANONYMOUSLY.
YEAH, WELL, THE LIEUTENANT USED TO BE A DETECTIVE.
IT DIDN'T TAKE HER LONG TO SOLVE THAT MYSTERY. YOU GOT YOUR *SCOOP,* AND I GOT TAKEN TO THE *WOODSHED.*
HEY, IRIS. SOUNDS LIKE YOU'RE ON THE TRAIL OF A BIG STORY.
BARRY...
NO, I'M HERE ON A... PERSONAL MATTER.
IS EVERYTHING OKAY?
YEAH. NOTHING HAPPENED TO ME. IT'S JUST...AFTER EVERYTHING THAT DANIEL DID...I WOULDN'T WANT YOU TO THINK MY FAMILY IS NOTHING BUT A BUNCH OF *CRIMINALS.*
I'M HERE TO PICK UP SOMEONE WHO WAS ARRESTED EARLIER TODAY--
--MY *NEPHEW...*

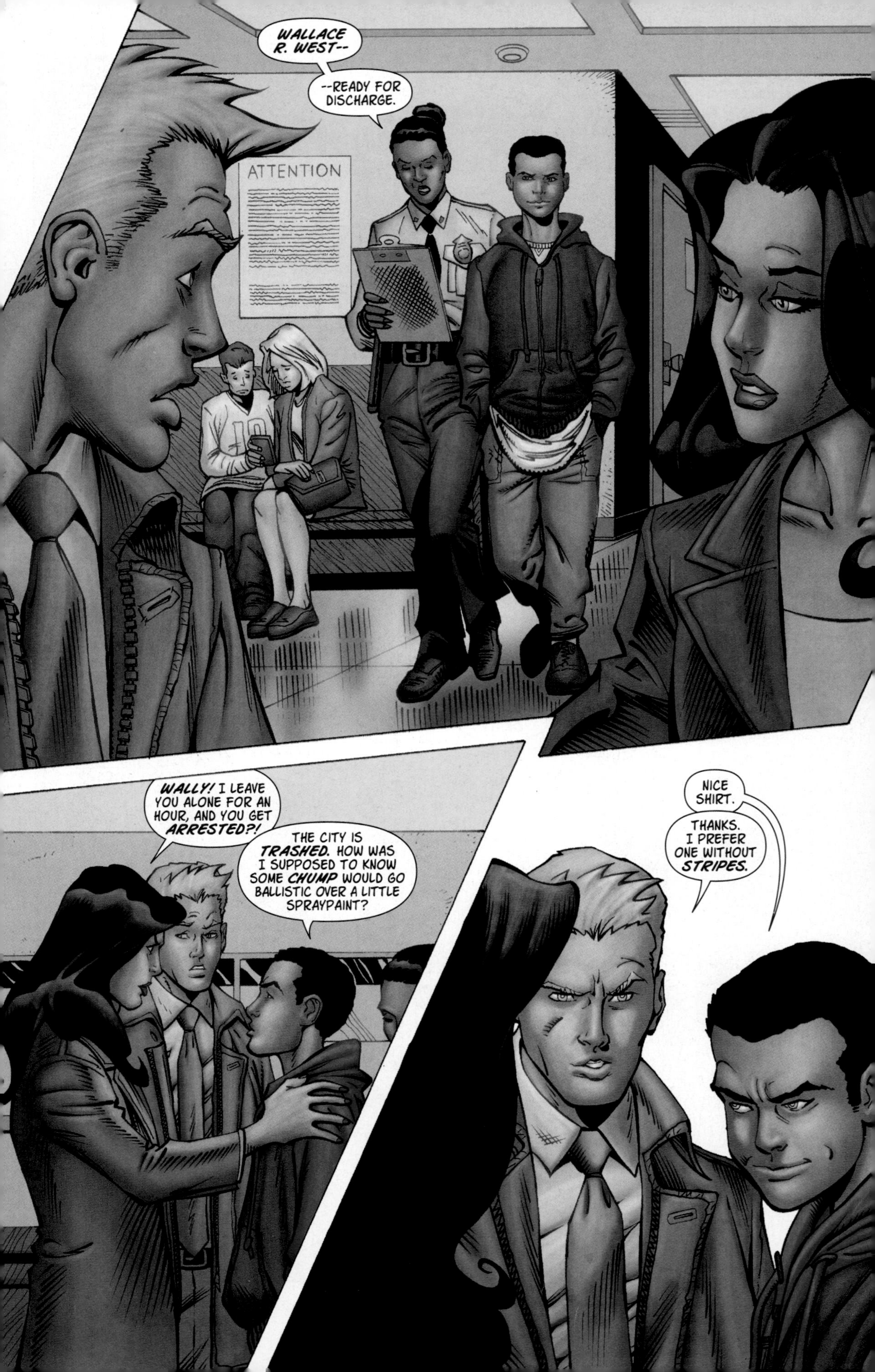

WALLACE R. WEST--
--READY FOR DISCHARGE.
ATTENTION
WALLY! I LEAVE YOU ALONE FOR AN HOUR, AND YOU GET ARRESTED?!
THE CITY IS TRASHED. HOW WAS I SUPPOSED TO KNOW SOME CHUMP WOULD GO BALLISTIC OVER A LITTLE SPRAYPAINT?
NICE SHIRT.
THANKS. I PREFER ONE WITHOUT STRIPES.

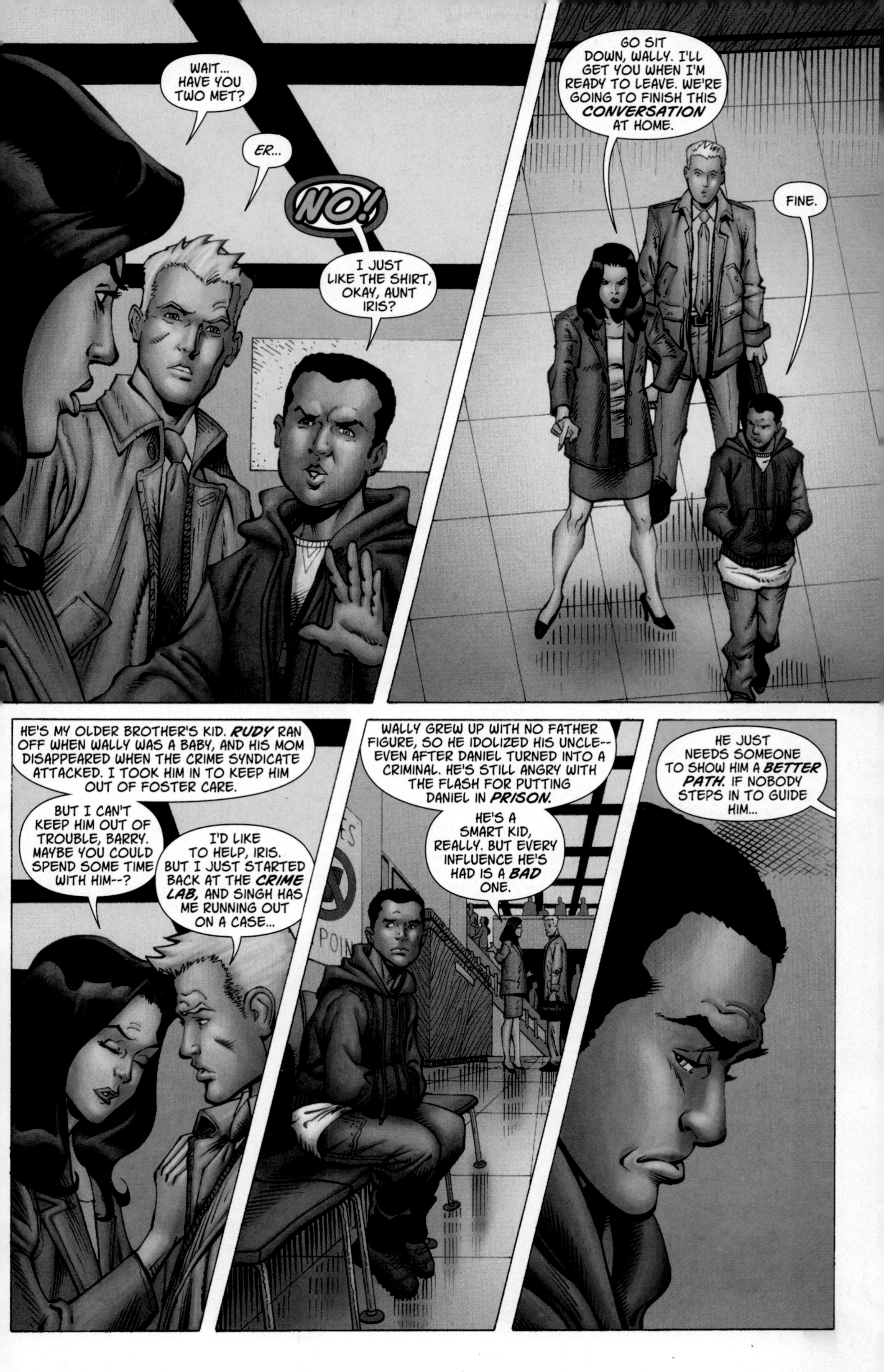
WAIT... HAVE YOU TWO MET?
ER...
NO!
I JUST LIKE THE SHIRT, OKAY, AUNT IRIS?
GO SIT DOWN, WALLY. I'LL GET YOU WHEN I'M READY TO LEAVE. WE'RE GOING TO FINISH THIS CONVERSATION AT HOME.
FINE.
HE'S MY OLDER BROTHER'S KID. RUDY RAN OFF WHEN WALLY WAS A BABY, AND HIS MOM DISAPPEARED WHEN THE CRIME SYNDICATE ATTACKED. I TOOK HIM IN TO KEEP HIM OUT OF FOSTER CARE.
BUT I CAN'T KEEP HIM OUT OF TROUBLE, BARRY. MAYBE YOU COULD SPEND SOME TIME WITH HIM--?
I'D LIKE TO HELP, IRIS. BUT I JUST STARTED BACK AT THE CRIME LAB, AND SINGH HAS ME RUNNING OUT ON A CASE...
WALLY GREW UP WITH NO FATHER FIGURE, SO HE IDOLIZED HIS UNCLE-- EVEN AFTER DANIEL TURNED INTO A CRIMINAL. HE'S STILL ANGRY WITH THE FLASH FOR PUTTING DANIEL IN PRISON.
HE'S A SMART KID, REALLY. BUT EVERY INFLUENCE HE'S HAD IS A BAD ONE.
HE JUST NEEDS SOMEONE TO SHOW HIM A BETTER PATH. IF NOBODY STEPS IN TO GUIDE HIM...

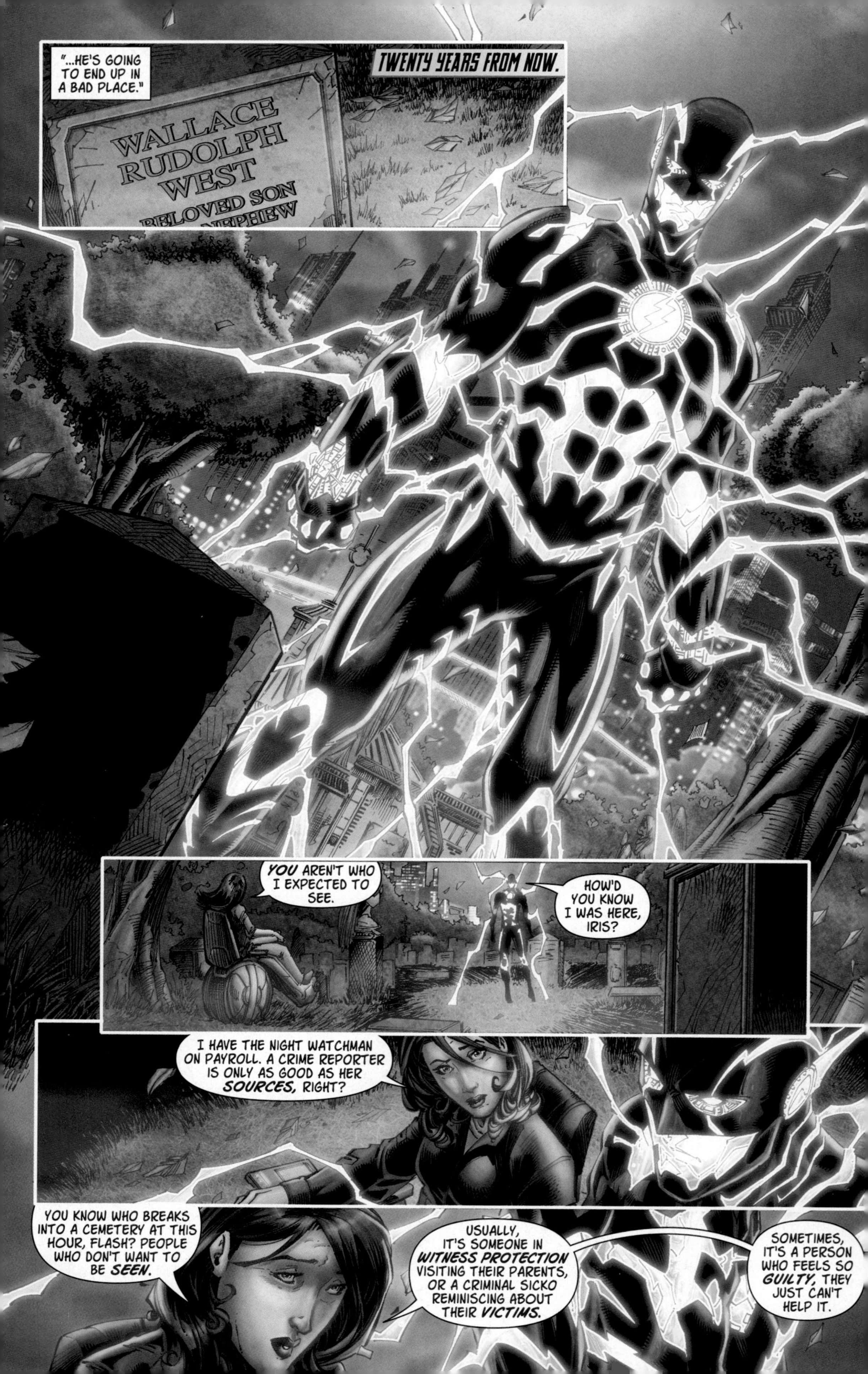

"...HE'S GOING TO END UP IN A BAD PLACE."
TWENTY YEARS FROM NOW.
WALLACE RUDOLPH WEST BELOVED SON
YOU AREN'T WHO I EXPECTED TO SEE.
HOW'D YOU KNOW I WAS HERE, IRIS?
I HAVE THE NIGHT WATCHMAN ON PAYROLL. A CRIME REPORTER IS ONLY AS GOOD AS HER SOURCES, RIGHT?
YOU KNOW WHO BREAKS INTO A CEMETERY AT THIS HOUR, FLASH? PEOPLE WHO DON'T WANT TO BE SEEN.
USUALLY, IT'S SOMEONE IN WITNESS PROTECTION VISITING THEIR PARENTS, OR A CRIMINAL SICKO REMINISCING ABOUT THEIR VICTIMS.
SOMETIMES, IT'S A PERSON WHO FEELS SO GUILTY, THEY JUST CAN'T HELP IT.

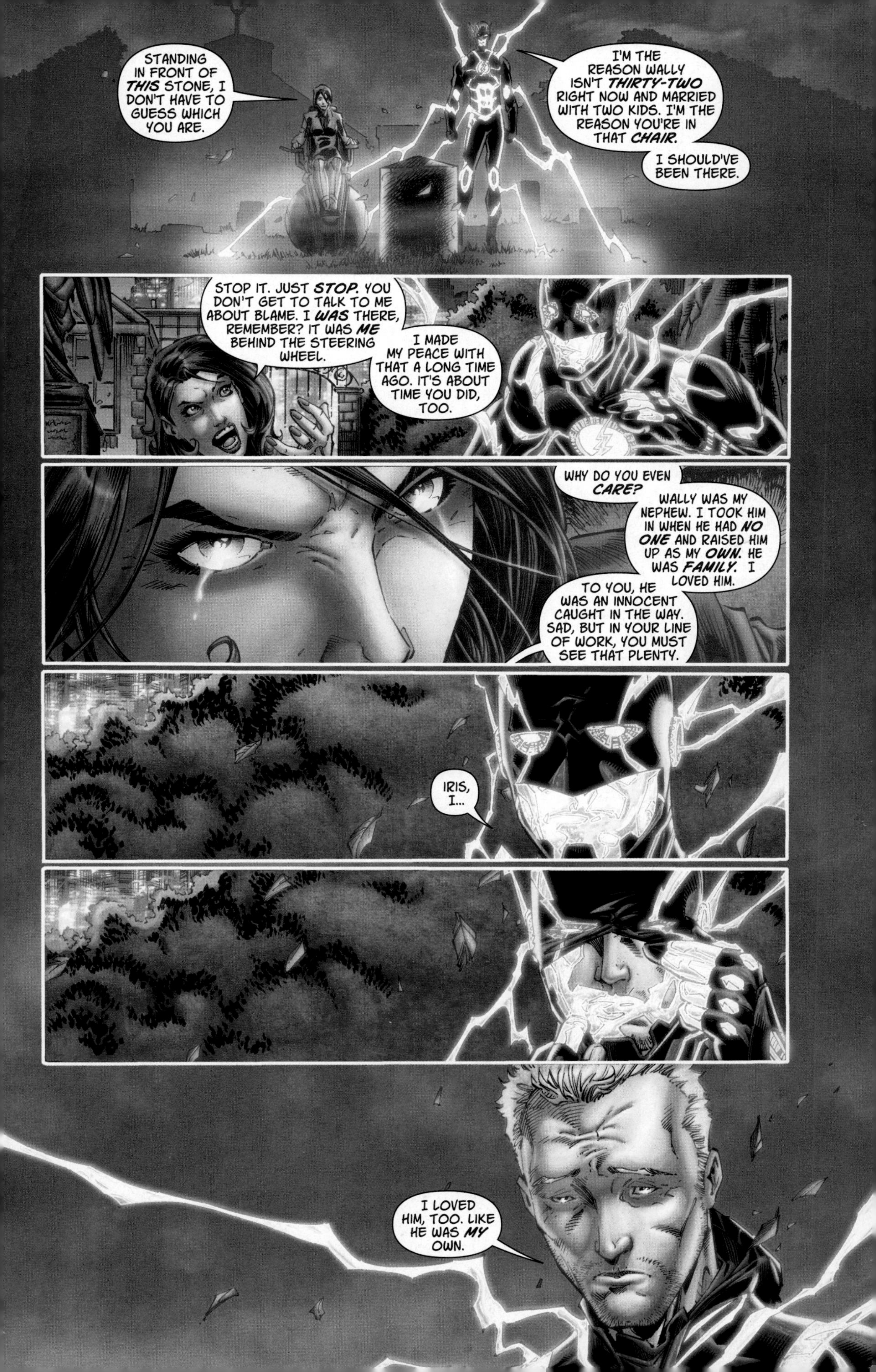
STANDING IN FRONT OF THIS STONE, I DON'T HAVE TO GUESS WHICH YOU ARE.
I'M THE REASON WALLY ISN'T THIRTY-TWO RIGHT NOW AND MARRIED WITH TWO KIDS. I'M THE REASON YOU'RE IN THAT CHAIR.
I SHOULD'VE BEEN THERE.
STOP IT. JUST STOP. YOU DON'T GET TO TALK TO ME ABOUT BLAME. I WAS THERE, REMEMBER? IT WAS ME BEHIND THE STEERING WHEEL.
I MADE MY PEACE WITH THAT A LONG TIME AGO. IT'S ABOUT TIME YOU DID, TOO.
WHY DO YOU EVEN CARE?
WALLY WAS MY NEPHEW. I TOOK HIM IN WHEN HE HAD NO ONE AND RAISED HIM UP AS MY OWN. HE WAS FAMILY. I LOVED HIM.
TO YOU, HE WAS AN INNOCENT CAUGHT IN THE WAY. SAD, BUT IN YOUR LINE OF WORK, YOU MUST SEE THAT PLENTY.
IRIS, I...
I LOVED HIM, TOO. LIKE HE WAS MY OWN.

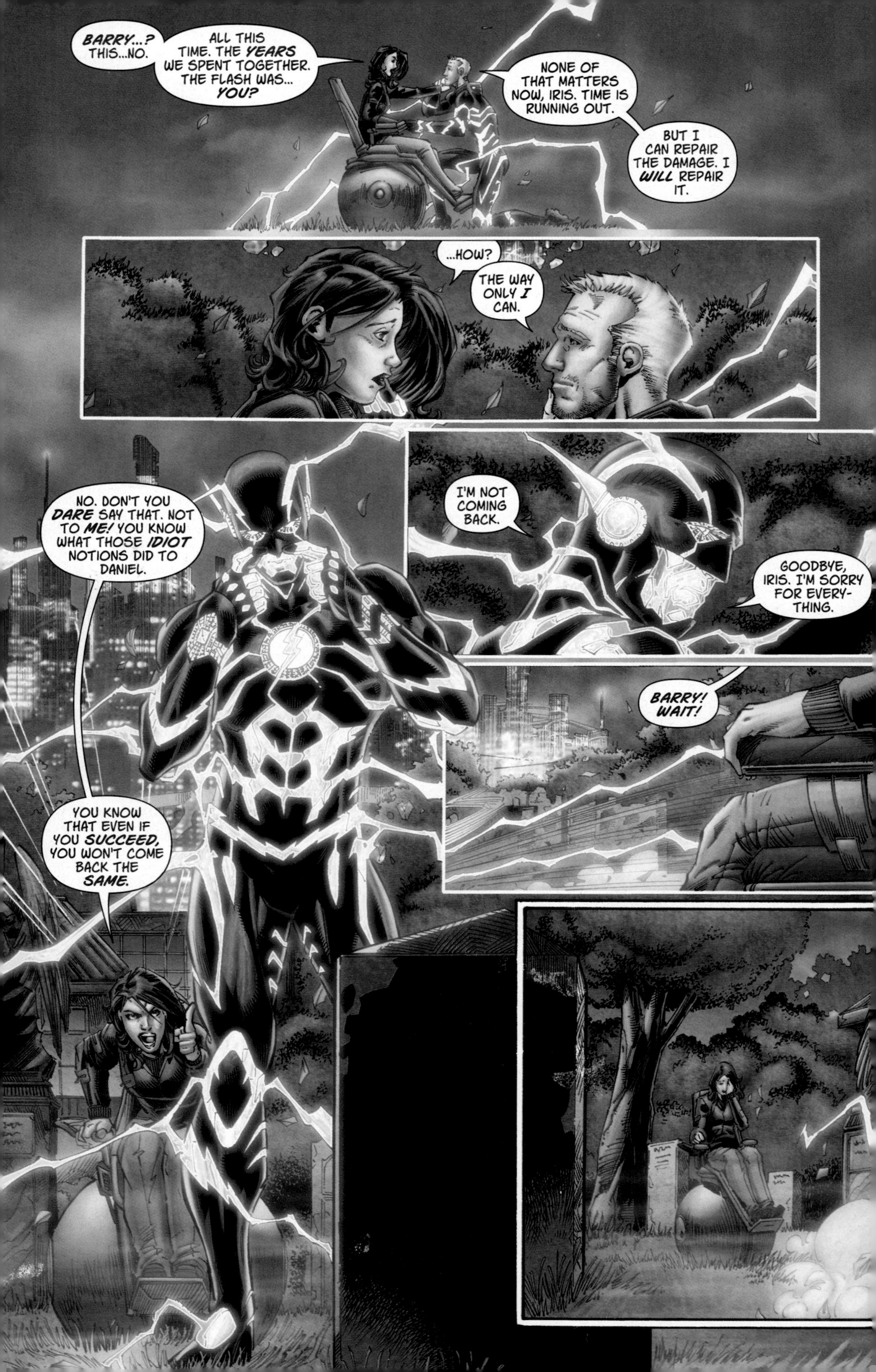
BARRY...? THIS...NO.
ALL THIS TIME. THE YEARS WE SPENT TOGETHER. THE FLASH WAS... YOU?
NONE OF THAT MATTERS NOW, IRIS. TIME IS RUNNING OUT.
BUT I CAN REPAIR THE DAMAGE. I WILL REPAIR IT.
...HOW?
THE WAY ONLY I CAN.
I'M NOT COMING BACK.
NO. DON'T YOU DARE SAY THAT. NOT TO ME! YOU KNOW WHAT THOSE IDIOT NOTIONS DID TO DANIEL.
YOU KNOW THAT EVEN IF YOU SUCCEED, YOU WON'T COME BACK THE SAME.
GOODBYE, IRIS. I'M SORRY FOR EVERY-THING.
BARRY! WAIT!

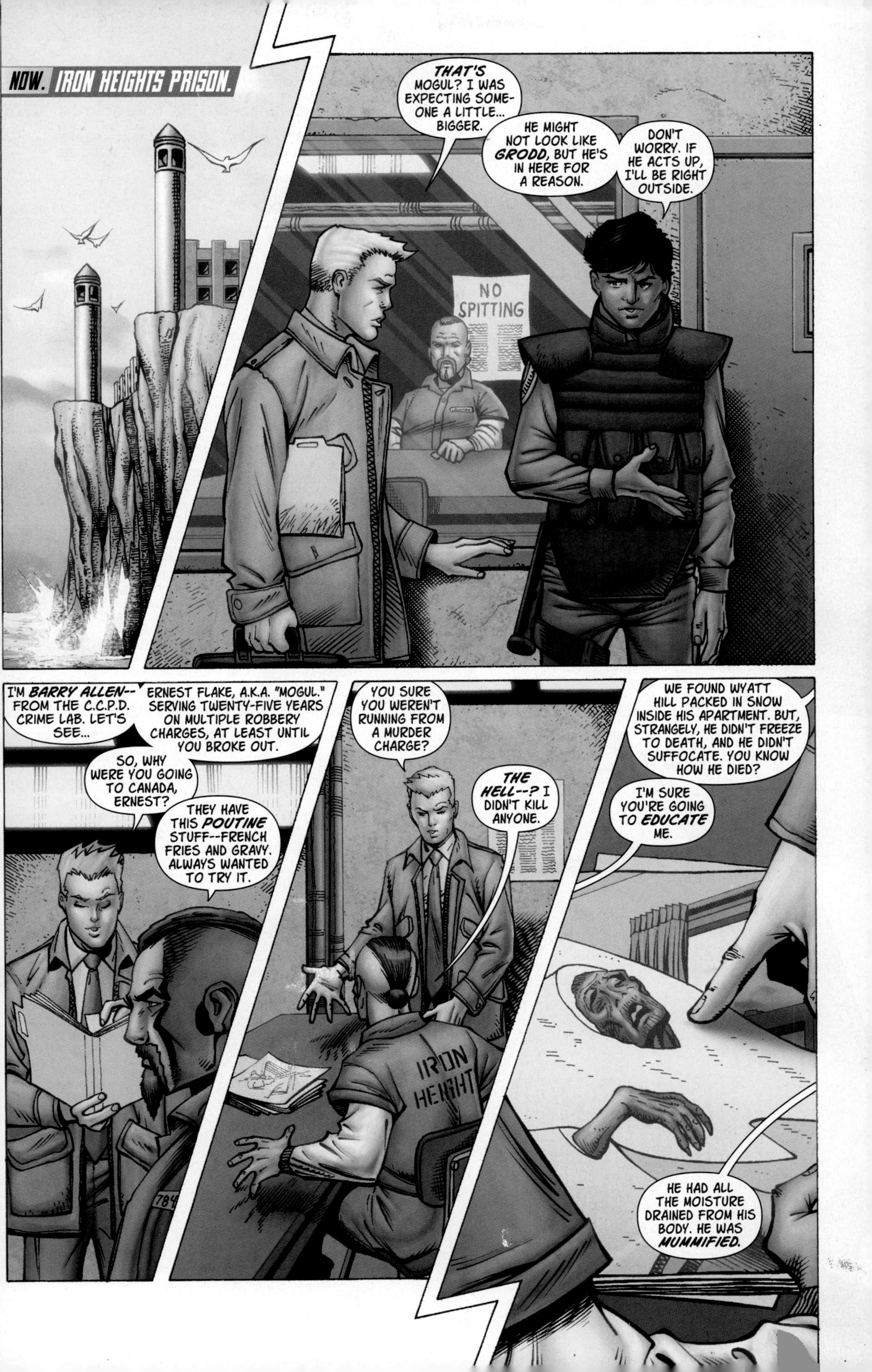
NOW. IRON HEIGHTS PRISON.
THAT'S MOGUL? I WAS EXPECTING SOME-ONE A LITTLE... BIGGER.
HE MIGHT NOT LOOK LIKE GRODD, BUT HE'S IN HERE FOR A REASON.
DON'T WORRY. IF HE ACTS UP, I'LL BE RIGHT OUTSIDE.
NO SPITTING
I'M BARRY ALLEN-- FROM THE C.C.P.D. CRIME LAB. LET'S SEE...
ERNEST FLAKE, A.K.A. "MOGUL." SERVING TWENTY-FIVE YEARS ON MULTIPLE ROBBERY CHARGES, AT LEAST UNTIL YOU BROKE OUT.
SO, WHY WERE YOU GOING TO CANADA, ERNEST?
THEY HAVE THIS POUTINE STUFF--FRENCH FRIES AND GRAVY. ALWAYS WANTED TO TRY IT.
YOU SURE YOU WEREN'T RUNNING FROM A MURDER CHARGE?
THE HELL--? I DIDN'T KILL ANYONE.
IRON HEIGHT
WE FOUND WYATT HILL PACKED IN SNOW INSIDE HIS APARTMENT. BUT, STRANGELY, HE DIDN'T FREEZE TO DEATH, AND HE DIDN'T SUFFOCATE. YOU KNOW HOW HE DIED?
I'M SURE YOU'RE GOING TO EDUCATE ME.
HE HAD ALL THE MOISTURE DRAINED FROM HIS BODY. HE WAS MUMMIFIED.

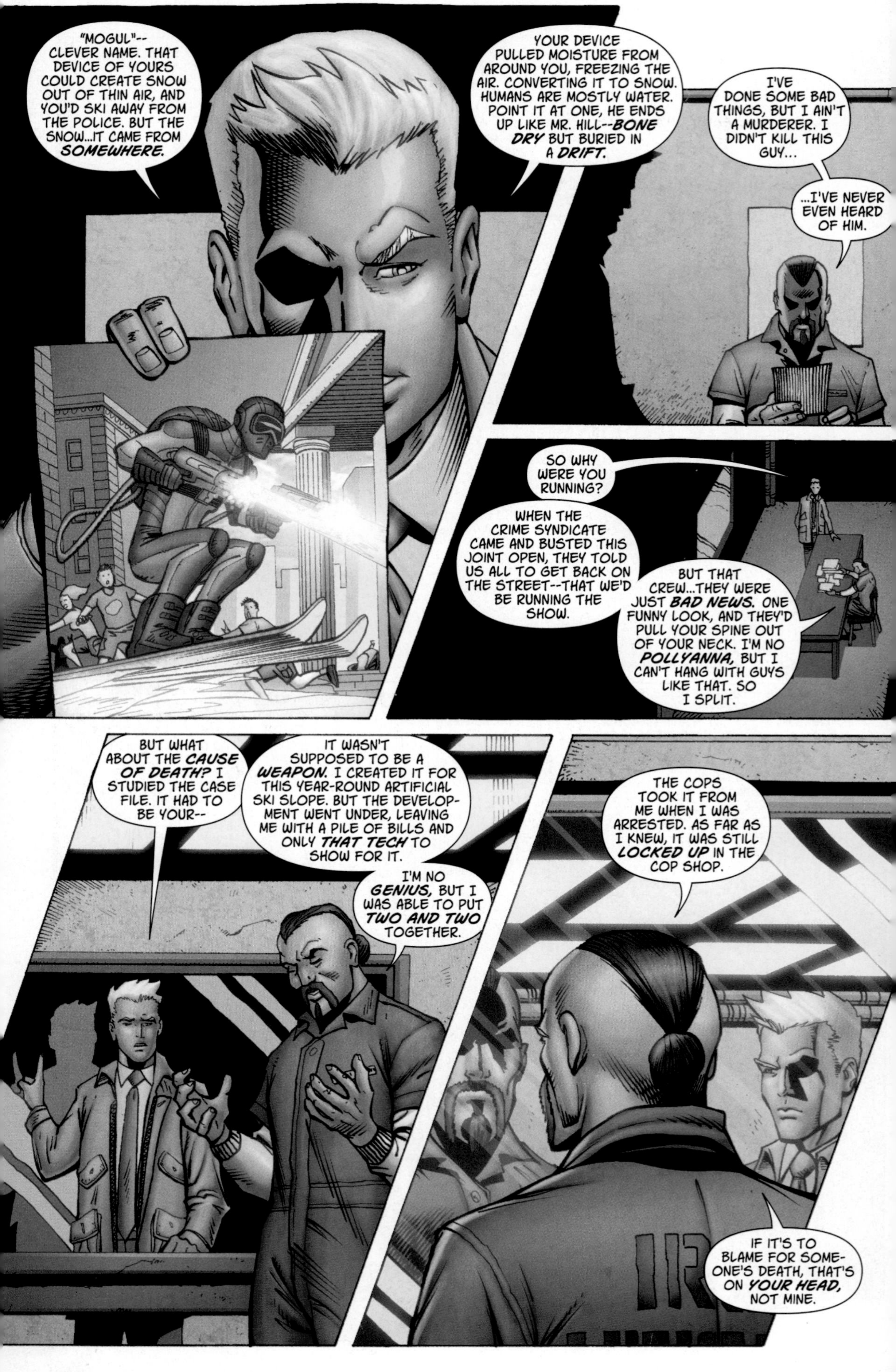
"MOGUL"--CLEVER NAME. THAT DEVICE OF YOURS COULD CREATE SNOW OUT OF THIN AIR, AND YOU'D SKI AWAY FROM THE POLICE. BUT THE SNOW...IT CAME FROM SOMEWHERE.
YOUR DEVICE PULLED MOISTURE FROM AROUND YOU, FREEZING THE AIR. CONVERTING IT TO SNOW. HUMANS ARE MOSTLY WATER. POINT IT AT ONE, HE ENDS UP LIKE MR. HILL--BONE DRY BUT BURIED IN A DRIFT.
I'VE DONE SOME BAD THINGS, BUT I AIN'T A MURDERER. I DIDN'T KILL THIS GUY...
...I'VE NEVER EVEN HEARD OF HIM.
SO WHY WERE YOU RUNNING?
WHEN THE CRIME SYNDICATE CAME AND BUSTED THIS JOINT OPEN, THEY TOLD US ALL TO GET BACK ON THE STREET--THAT WE'D BE RUNNING THE SHOW.
BUT THAT CREW...THEY WERE JUST BAD NEWS. ONE FUNNY LOOK, AND THEY'D PULL YOUR SPINE OUT OF YOUR NECK. I'M NO POLLYANNA, BUT I CAN'T HANG WITH GUYS LIKE THAT. SO I SPLIT.
BUT WHAT ABOUT THE CAUSE OF DEATH? I STUDIED THE CASE FILE. IT HAD TO BE YOUR--
IT WASN'T SUPPOSED TO BE A WEAPON. I CREATED IT FOR THIS YEAR-ROUND ARTIFICIAL SKI SLOPE. BUT THE DEVELOPMENT WENT UNDER, LEAVING ME WITH A PILE OF BILLS AND ONLY THAT TECH TO SHOW FOR IT.
I'M NO GENIUS, BUT I WAS ABLE TO PUT TWO AND TWO TOGETHER.
THE COPS TOOK IT FROM ME WHEN I WAS ARRESTED. AS FAR AS I KNEW, IT WAS STILL LOCKED UP IN THE COP SHOP.
IF IT'S TO BLAME FOR SOMEONE'S DEATH, THAT'S ON YOUR HEAD, NOT MINE.

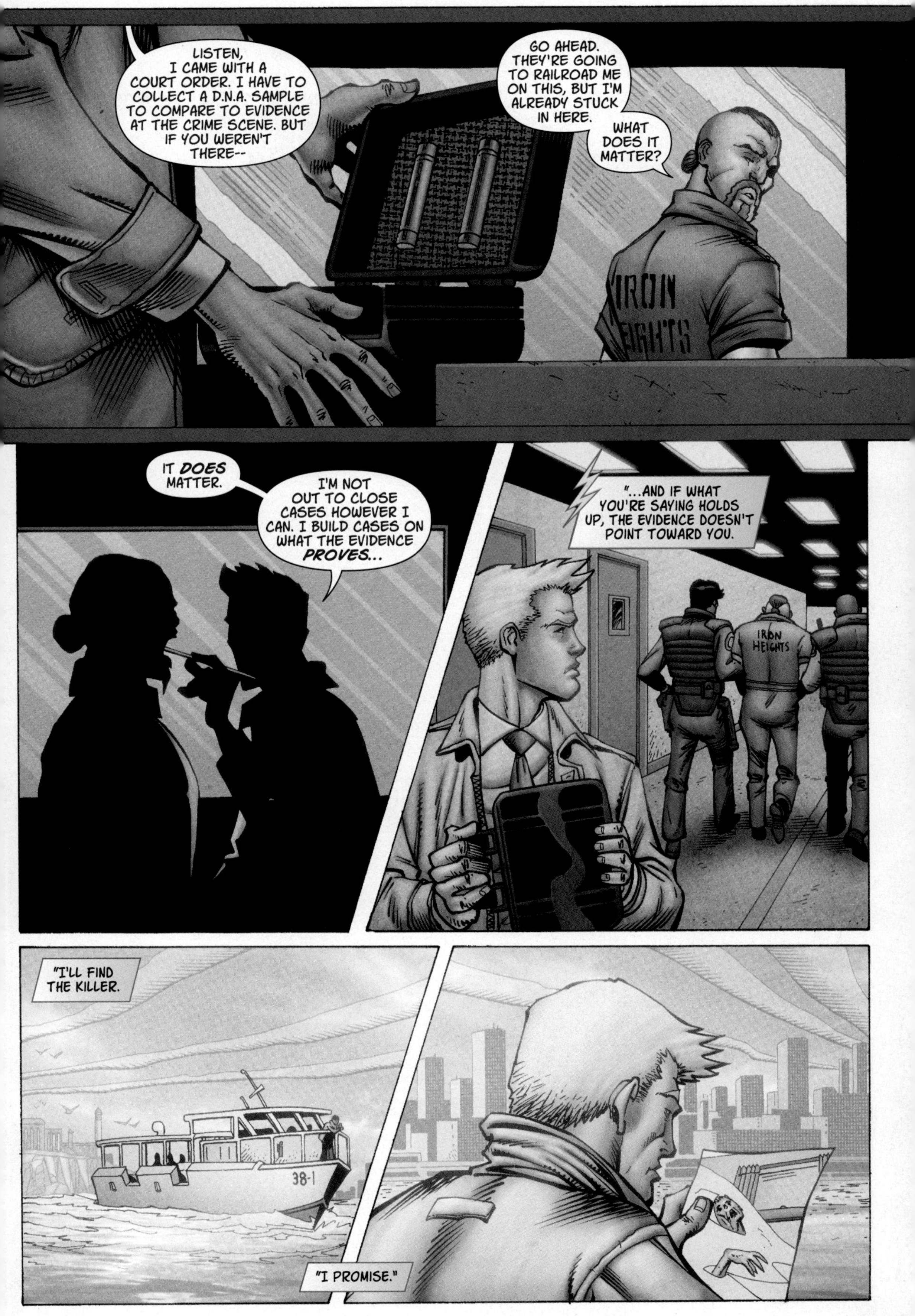
LISTEN, I CAME WITH A COURT ORDER. I HAVE TO COLLECT A D.N.A. SAMPLE TO COMPARE TO EVIDENCE AT THE CRIME SCENE. BUT IF YOU WEREN'T THERE--
GO AHEAD. THEY'RE GOING TO RAILROAD ME ON THIS, BUT I'M ALREADY STUCK IN HERE.
WHAT DOES IT MATTER?
IRON HEIGHTS
IT *DOES* MATTER.
I'M NOT OUT TO CLOSE CASES HOWEVER I CAN. I BUILD CASES ON WHAT THE EVIDENCE *PROVES*...
"...AND IF WHAT YOU'RE SAYING HOLDS UP, THE EVIDENCE DOESN'T POINT TOWARD YOU.
IRON HEIGHTS
"I'LL FIND THE KILLER.
38-1
"I PROMISE."

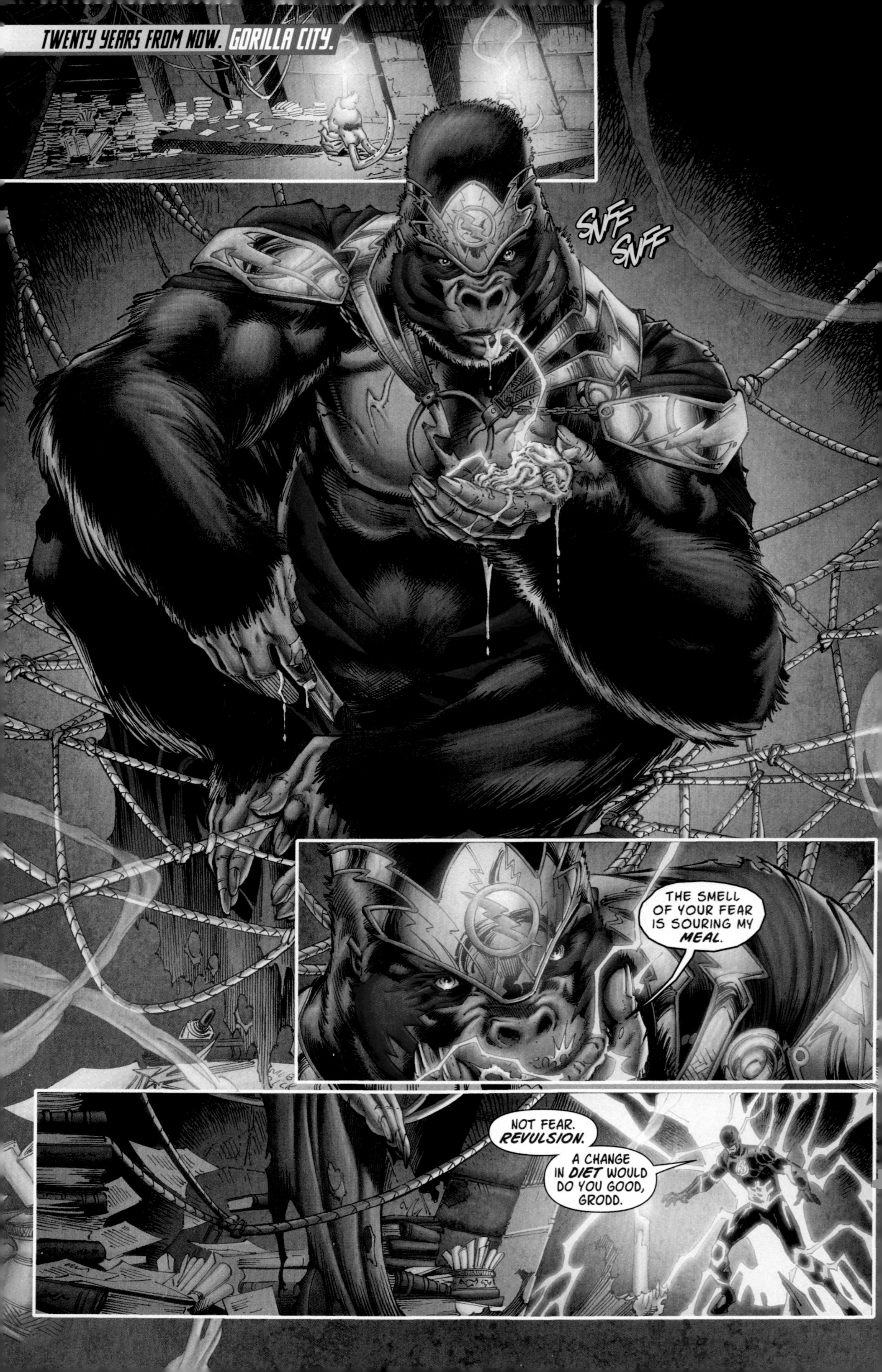
TWENTY YEARS FROM NOW. GORILLA CITY.
SNFF SNFF
THE SMELL OF YOUR FEAR IS SOURING MY MEAL.
NOT FEAR. REVULSION.
A CHANGE IN DIET WOULD DO YOU GOOD, GRODD.

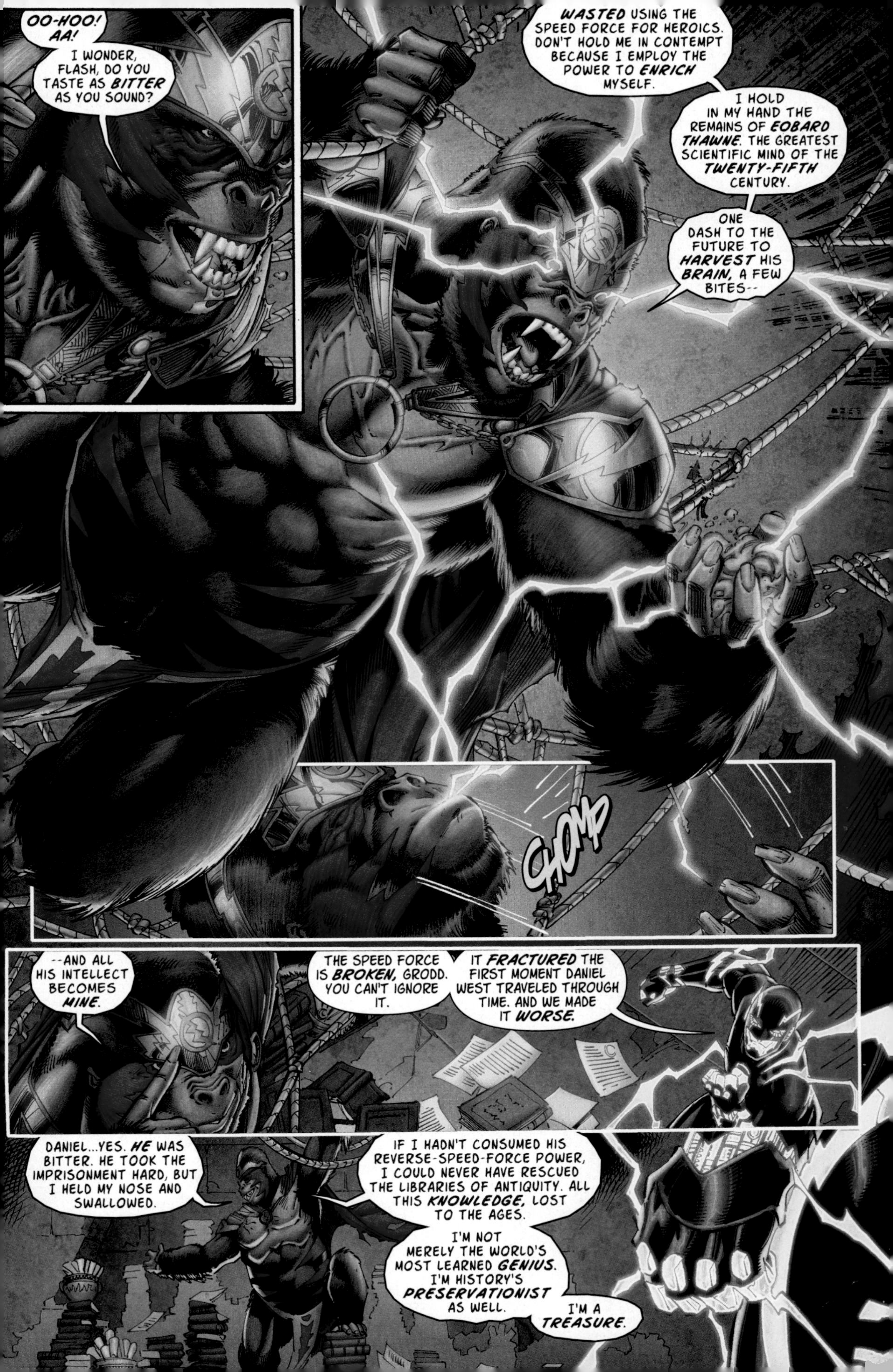
OO-HOO! AA!
I WONDER, FLASH, DO YOU TASTE AS BITTER AS YOU SOUND?
WASTED USING THE SPEED FORCE FOR HEROICS. DON'T HOLD ME IN CONTEMPT BECAUSE I EMPLOY THE POWER TO ENRICH MYSELF.
I HOLD IN MY HAND THE REMAINS OF EOBARD THAWNE. THE GREATEST SCIENTIFIC MIND OF THE TWENTY-FIFTH CENTURY.
ONE DASH TO THE FUTURE TO HARVEST HIS BRAIN, A FEW BITES--
CHOMP
--AND ALL HIS INTELLECT BECOMES MINE.
THE SPEED FORCE IS BROKEN, GRODD. YOU CAN'T IGNORE IT.
IT FRACTURED THE FIRST MOMENT DANIEL WEST TRAVELED THROUGH TIME. AND WE MADE IT WORSE.
DANIEL...YES. HE WAS BITTER. HE TOOK THE IMPRISONMENT HARD, BUT I HELD MY NOSE AND SWALLOWED.
IF I HADN'T CONSUMED HIS REVERSE-SPEED-FORCE POWER, I COULD NEVER HAVE RESCUED THE LIBRARIES OF ANTIQUITY. ALL THIS KNOWLEDGE, LOST TO THE AGES.
I'M NOT MERELY THE WORLD'S MOST LEARNED GENIUS. I'M HISTORY'S PRESERVATIONIST AS WELL.
I'M A TREASURE.

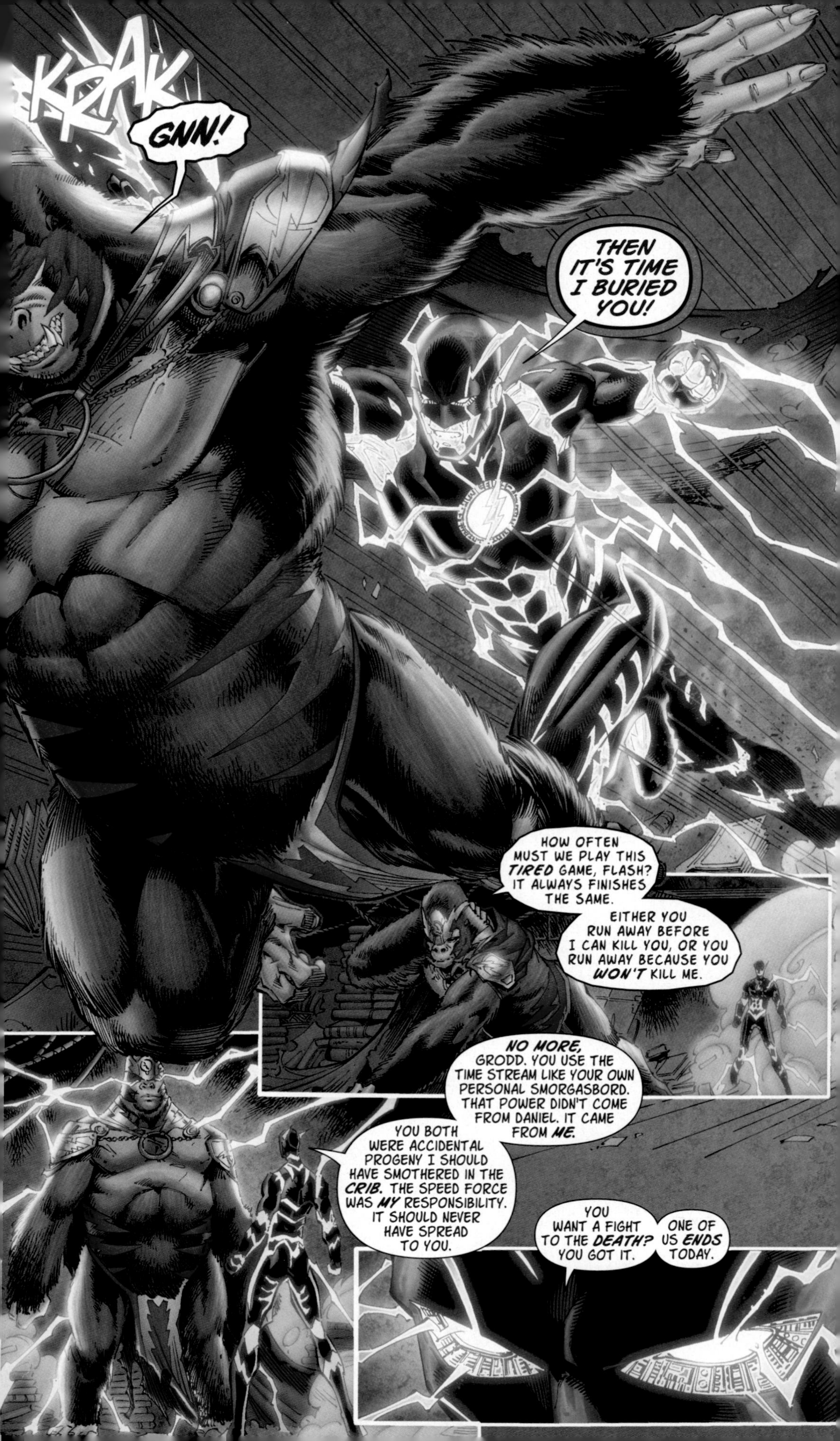

KRAK
GNN!
THEN IT'S TIME I BURIED YOU!
HOW OFTEN MUST WE PLAY THIS TIRED GAME, FLASH? IT ALWAYS FINISHES THE SAME.
EITHER YOU RUN AWAY BEFORE I CAN KILL YOU, OR YOU RUN AWAY BECAUSE YOU WON'T KILL ME.
NO MORE, GRODD. YOU USE THE TIME STREAM LIKE YOUR OWN PERSONAL SMORGASBORD. THAT POWER DIDN'T COME FROM DANIEL. IT CAME FROM ME.
YOU BOTH WERE ACCIDENTAL PROGENY I SHOULD HAVE SMOTHERED IN THE CRIB. THE SPEED FORCE WAS MY RESPONSIBILITY. IT SHOULD NEVER HAVE SPREAD TO YOU.
YOU WANT A FIGHT TO THE DEATH? YOU GOT IT.
ONE OF US ENDS TODAY.

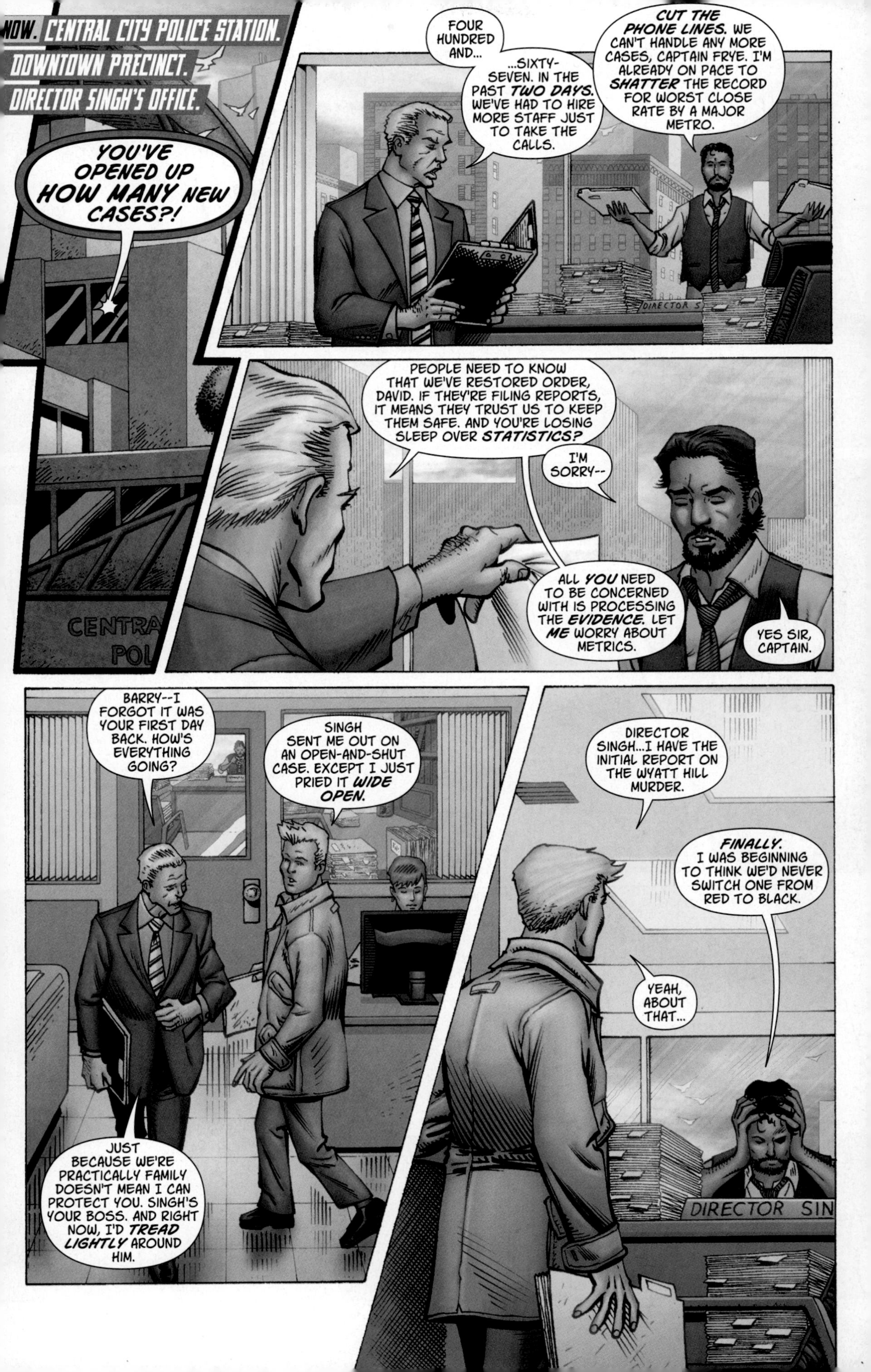
NOW. CENTRAL CITY POLICE STATION.
DOWNTOWN PRECINCT.
DIRECTOR SINGH'S OFFICE.
YOU'VE OPENED UP HOW MANY NEW CASES?!
CENTRA
POL
FOUR HUNDRED AND...
...SIXTY-SEVEN. IN THE PAST TWO DAYS. WE'VE HAD TO HIRE MORE STAFF JUST TO TAKE THE CALLS.
CUT THE PHONE LINES. WE CAN'T HANDLE ANY MORE CASES, CAPTAIN FRYE. I'M ALREADY ON PACE TO SHATTER THE RECORD FOR WORST CLOSE RATE BY A MAJOR METRO.
DIRECTOR S
PEOPLE NEED TO KNOW THAT WE'VE RESTORED ORDER, DAVID. IF THEY'RE FILING REPORTS, IT MEANS THEY TRUST US TO KEEP THEM SAFE. AND YOU'RE LOSING SLEEP OVER STATISTICS?
I'M SORRY--
ALL YOU NEED TO BE CONCERNED WITH IS PROCESSING THE EVIDENCE. LET ME WORRY ABOUT METRICS.
YES SIR, CAPTAIN.
BARRY--I FORGOT IT WAS YOUR FIRST DAY BACK. HOW'S EVERYTHING GOING?
SINGH SENT ME OUT ON AN OPEN-AND-SHUT CASE. EXCEPT I JUST PRIED IT WIDE OPEN.
JUST BECAUSE WE'RE PRACTICALLY FAMILY DOESN'T MEAN I CAN PROTECT YOU. SINGH'S YOUR BOSS. AND RIGHT NOW, I'D TREAD LIGHTLY AROUND HIM.
DIRECTOR SINGH...I HAVE THE INITIAL REPORT ON THE WYATT HILL MURDER.
FINALLY. I WAS BEGINNING TO THINK WE'D NEVER SWITCH ONE FROM RED TO BLACK.
YEAH, ABOUT THAT...
DIRECTOR SIN

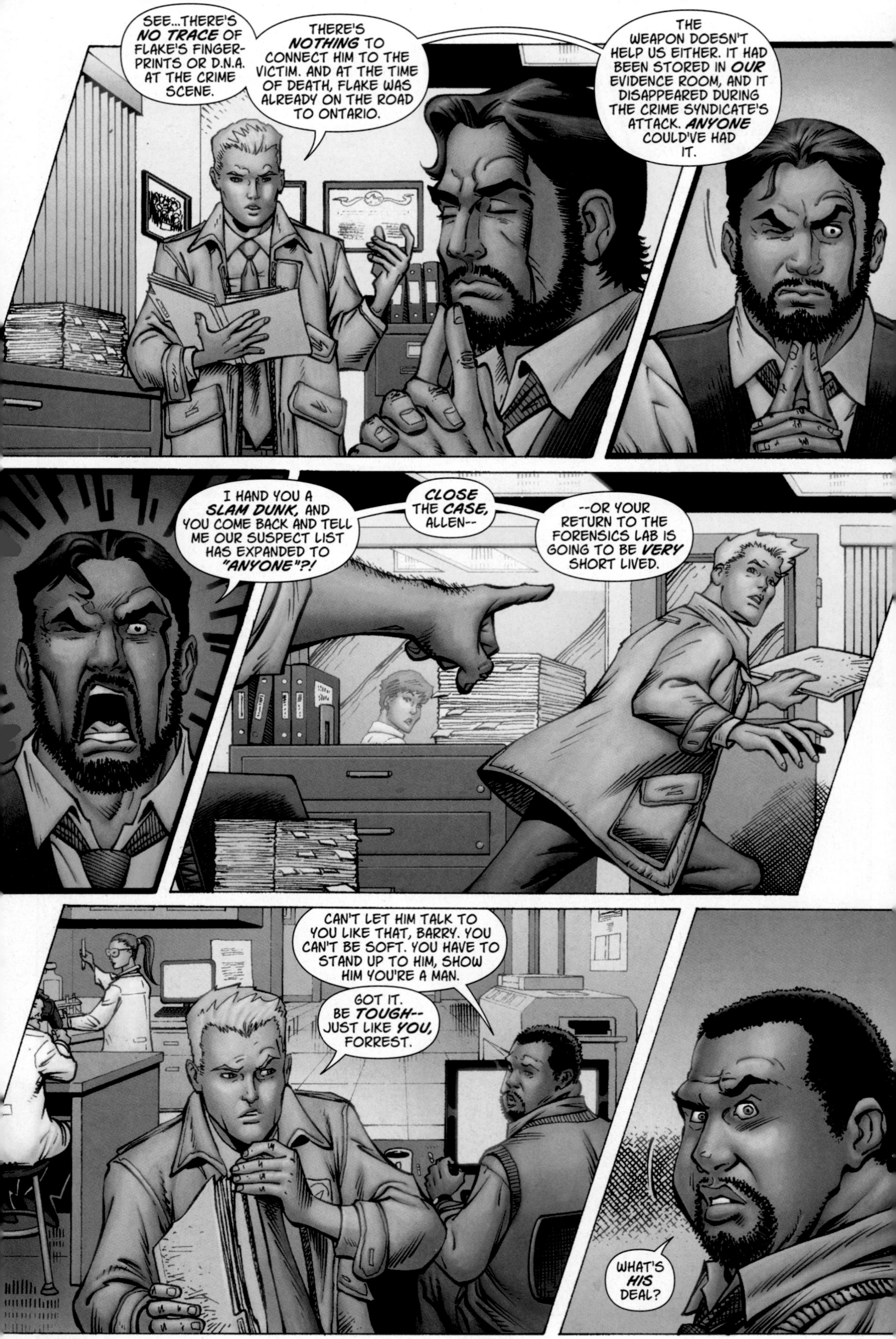
SEE...THERE'S NO TRACE OF FLAKE'S FINGER-PRINTS OR D.N.A. AT THE CRIME SCENE.
THERE'S NOTHING TO CONNECT HIM TO THE VICTIM. AND AT THE TIME OF DEATH, FLAKE WAS ALREADY ON THE ROAD TO ONTARIO.
THE WEAPON DOESN'T HELP US EITHER. IT HAD BEEN STORED IN OUR EVIDENCE ROOM, AND IT DISAPPEARED DURING THE CRIME SYNDICATE'S ATTACK. ANYONE COULD'VE HAD IT.
I HAND YOU A SLAM DUNK, AND YOU COME BACK AND TELL ME OUR SUSPECT LIST HAS EXPANDED TO "ANYONE"?!
CLOSE THE CASE, ALLEN--
--OR YOUR RETURN TO THE FORENSICS LAB IS GOING TO BE VERY SHORT LIVED.
CAN'T LET HIM TALK TO YOU LIKE THAT, BARRY. YOU CAN'T BE SOFT. YOU HAVE TO STAND UP TO HIM, SHOW HIM YOU'RE A MAN.
GOT IT. BE TOUGH-- JUST LIKE YOU, FORREST.
WHAT'S HIS DEAL?

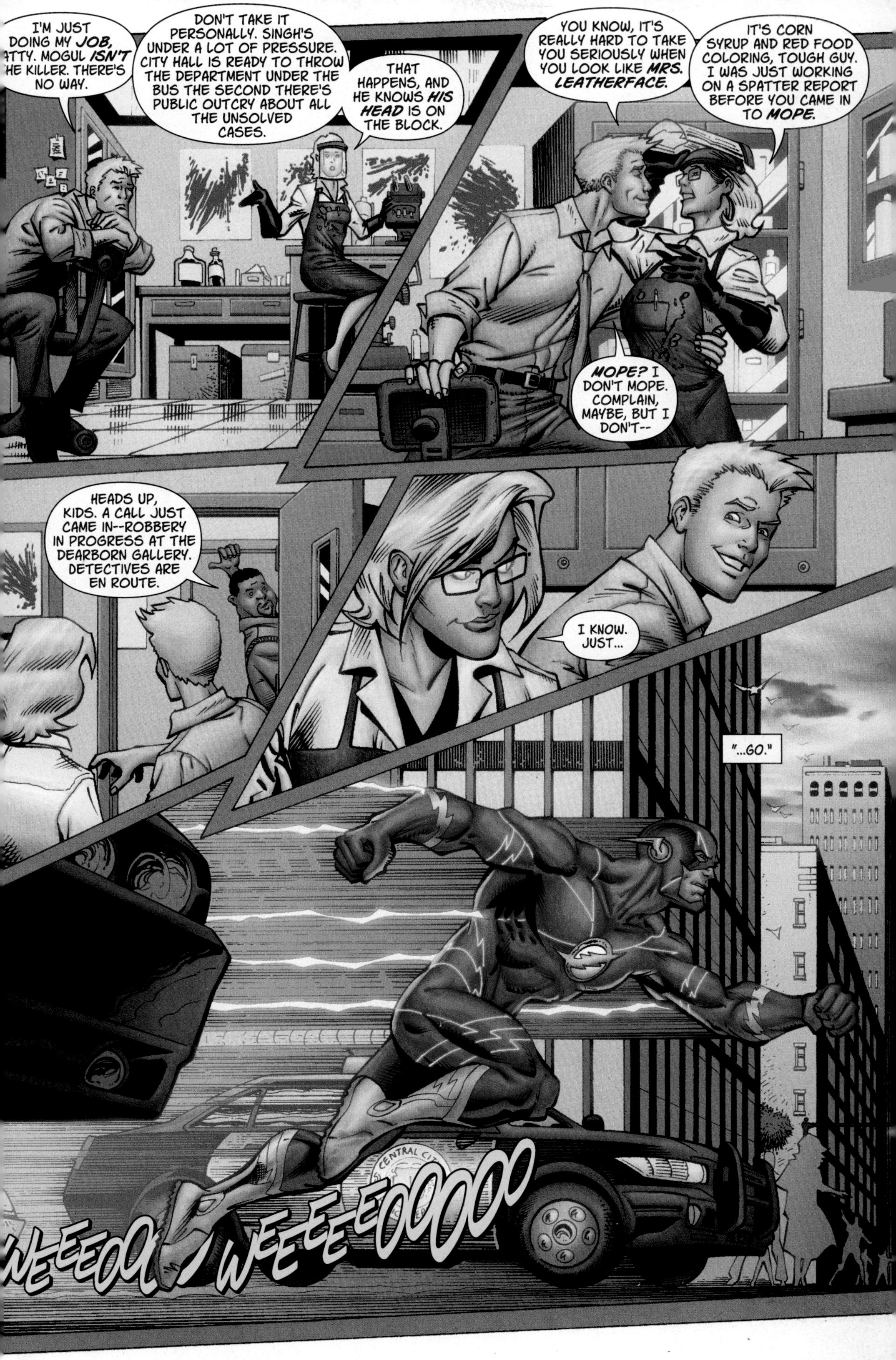
I'M JUST DOING MY JOB, PATTY. MOGUL ISN'T THE KILLER. THERE'S NO WAY.
DON'T TAKE IT PERSONALLY. SINGH'S UNDER A LOT OF PRESSURE. CITY HALL IS READY TO THROW THE DEPARTMENT UNDER THE BUS THE SECOND THERE'S PUBLIC OUTCRY ABOUT ALL THE UNSOLVED CASES.
THAT HAPPENS, AND HE KNOWS HIS HEAD IS ON THE BLOCK.
YOU KNOW, IT'S REALLY HARD TO TAKE YOU SERIOUSLY WHEN YOU LOOK LIKE MRS. LEATHERFACE.
IT'S CORN SYRUP AND RED FOOD COLORING, TOUGH GUY. I WAS JUST WORKING ON A SPATTER REPORT BEFORE YOU CAME IN TO MOPE.
MOPE? I DON'T MOPE. COMPLAIN, MAYBE, BUT I DON'T--
HEADS UP, KIDS. A CALL JUST CAME IN--ROBBERY IN PROGRESS AT THE DEARBORN GALLERY. DETECTIVES ARE EN ROUTE.
I KNOW. JUST...
"...GO."
WEEEOO WEEEEOOOOO

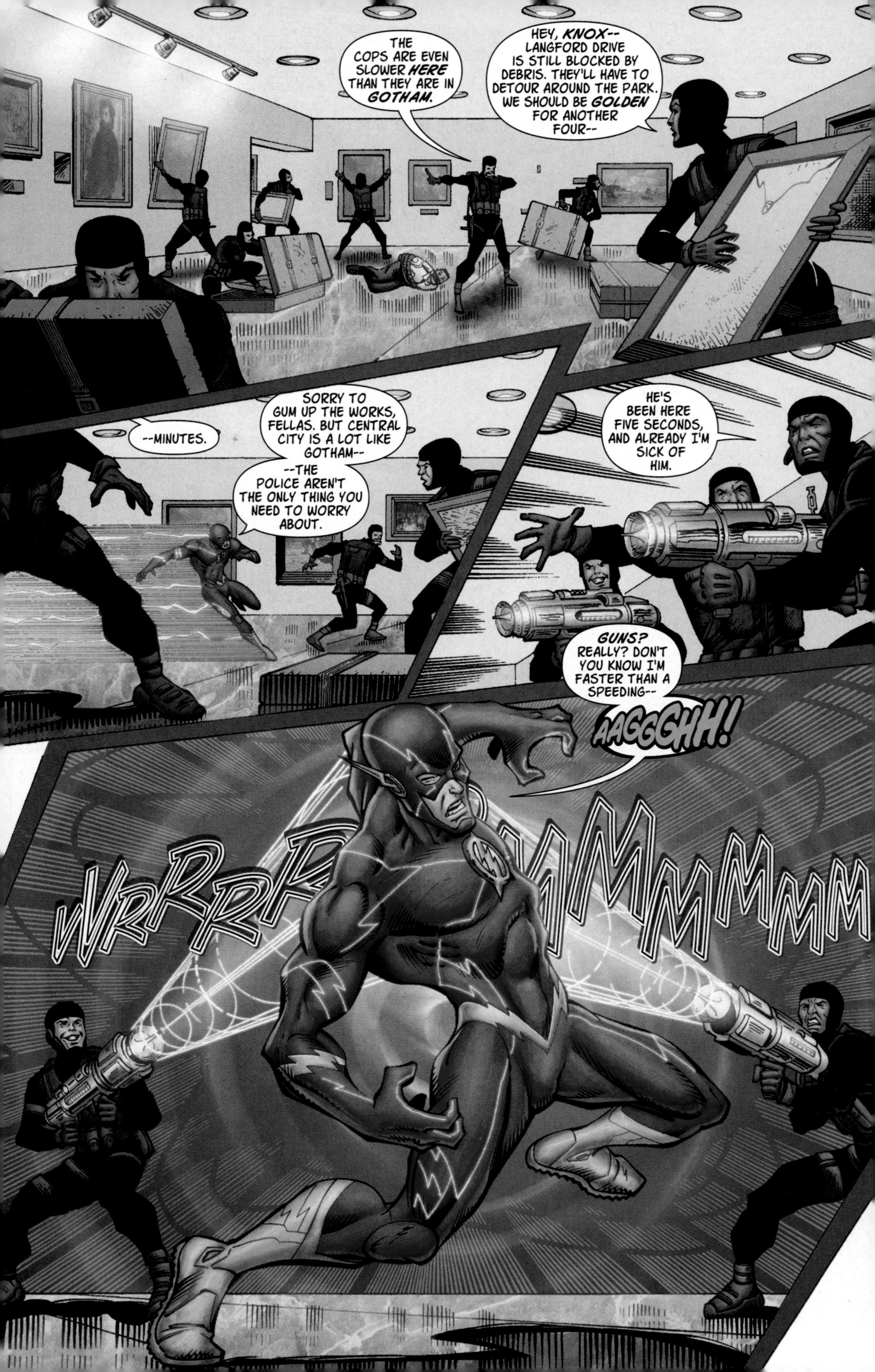
THE COPS ARE EVEN SLOWER HERE THAN THEY ARE IN GOTHAM.
HEY, KNOX-- LANGFORD DRIVE IS STILL BLOCKED BY DEBRIS. THEY'LL HAVE TO DETOUR AROUND THE PARK. WE SHOULD BE GOLDEN FOR ANOTHER FOUR--
--MINUTES.
SORRY TO GUM UP THE WORKS, FELLAS. BUT CENTRAL CITY IS A LOT LIKE GOTHAM--
--THE POLICE AREN'T THE ONLY THING YOU NEED TO WORRY ABOUT.
HE'S BEEN HERE FIVE SECONDS, AND ALREADY I'M SICK OF HIM.
GUNS? REALLY? DON'T YOU KNOW I'M FASTER THAN A SPEEDING--
AAGGGHH!
WRRRRRMMMMMMMM

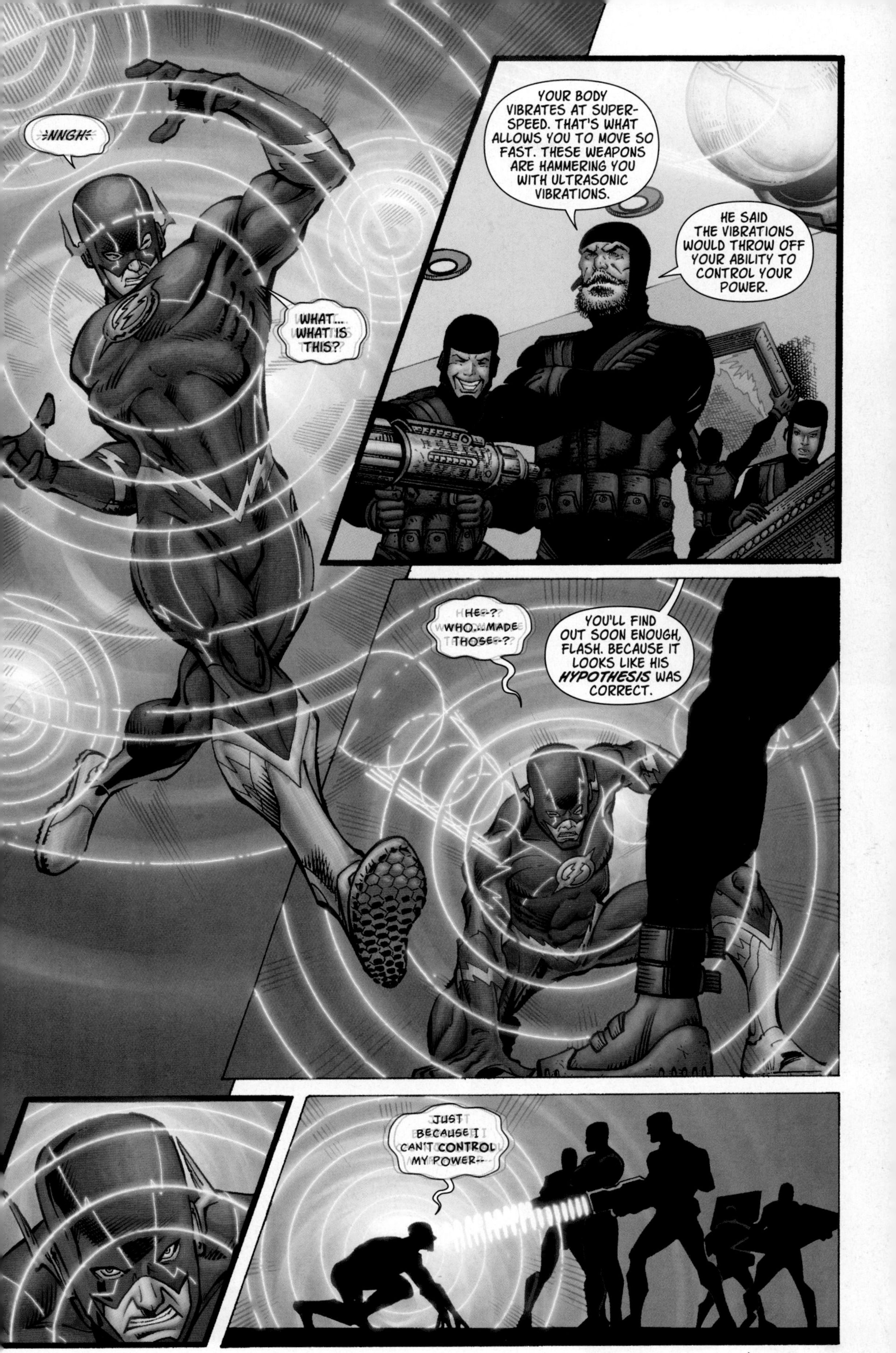
NNGH
YOUR BODY VIBRATES AT SUPER-SPEED. THAT'S WHAT ALLOWS YOU TO MOVE SO FAST. THESE WEAPONS ARE HAMMERING YOU WITH ULTRASONIC VIBRATIONS.
HE SAID THE VIBRATIONS WOULD THROW OFF YOUR ABILITY TO CONTROL YOUR POWER.
WHAT... WHAT IS THIS?
HE--? WHO...MADE THOSE--?
YOU'LL FIND OUT SOON ENOUGH, FLASH. BECAUSE IT LOOKS LIKE HIS HYPOTHESIS WAS CORRECT.
JUST BECAUSE I CAN'T CONTROL MY POWER--

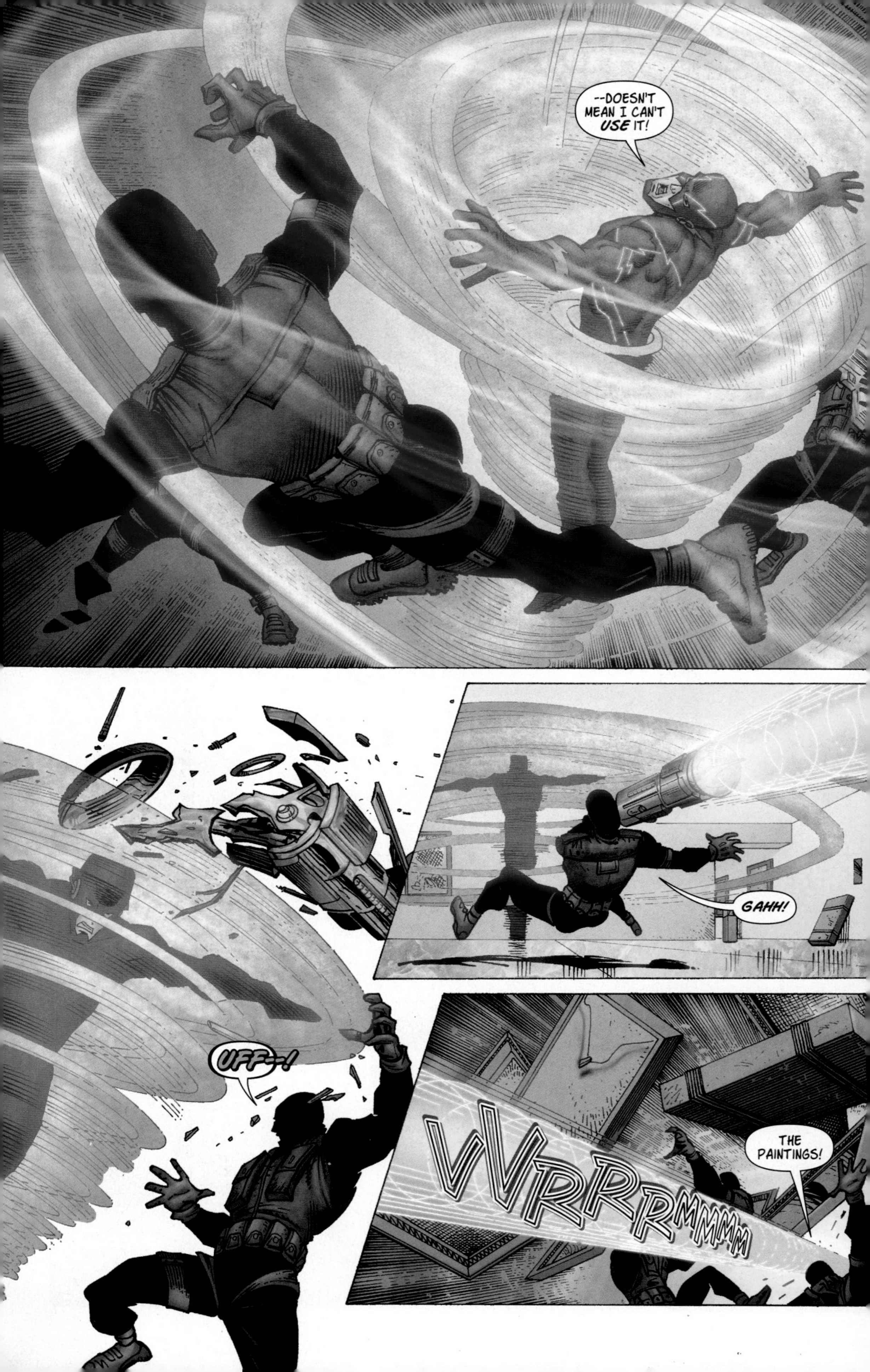
--DOESN'T MEAN I CAN'T USE IT!
GAHH!
UFF--!
WWRRRMMMMM
THE PAINTINGS!

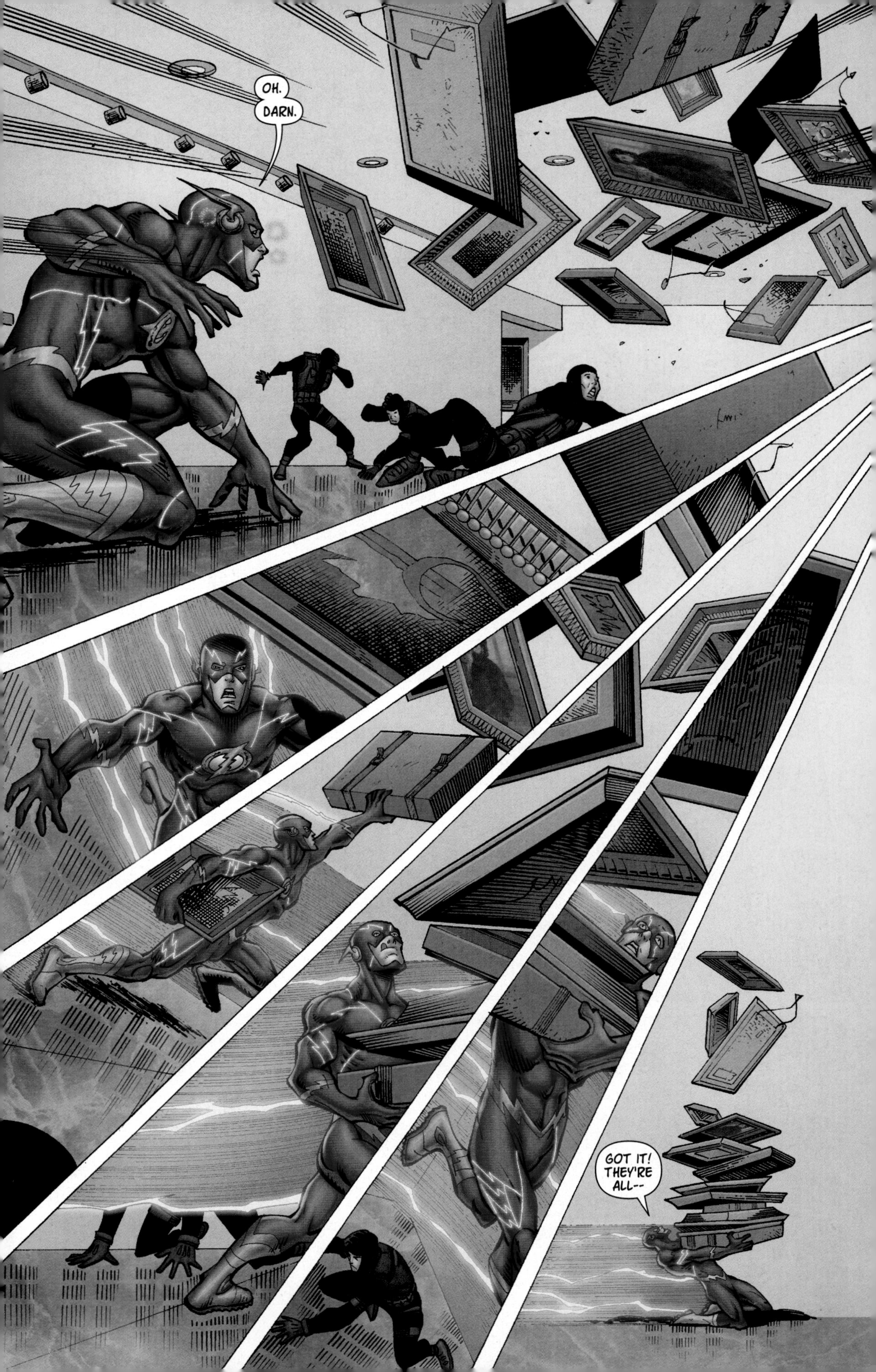
OH.
DARN.
GOT IT! THEY'RE ALL--

--SAFE? IMPRESSIVE, FLASH. BUT IT LOOKS LIKE IT WAS ALL FOR NOTHING.

YOU CAN'T HIT ME WITHOUT *DESTROYING* THE PAINTINGS. YOU DESTROY THEM, AND THERE GOES YOUR *BIG SCORE*.

SO LET'S POINT THOSE WEAPONS AWAY FROM THE *PICASSO*.

TRUTH BE TOLD, I ALWAYS PREFERRED THE *RENAISSANCE*. BESIDES, THE PAINTINGS WERE NEVER OUR *ONLY* TARGET.

VREEEE

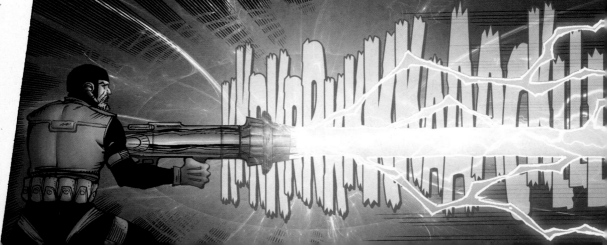

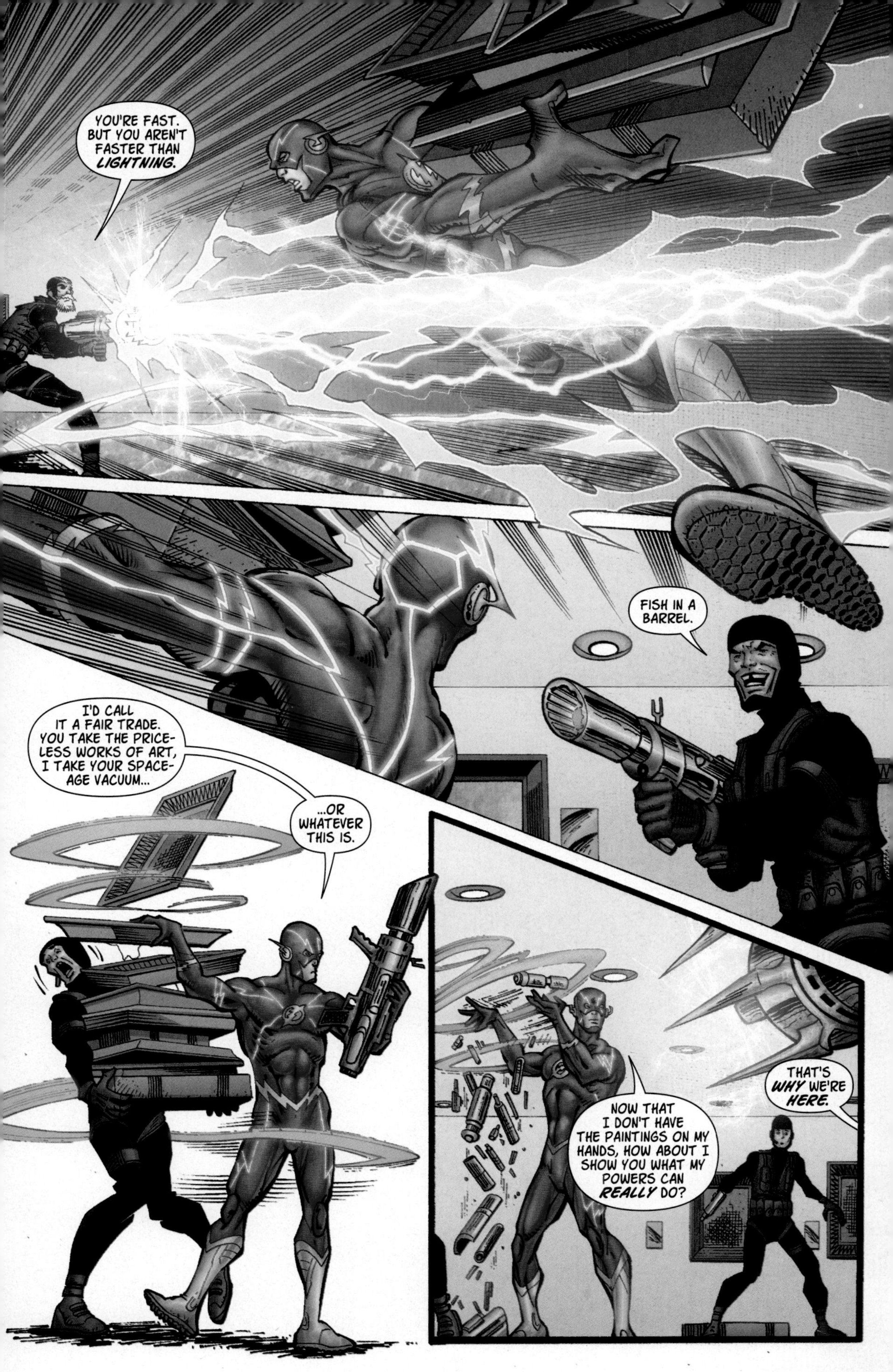
YOU'RE FAST. BUT YOU AREN'T FASTER THAN *LIGHTNING*.
FISH IN A BARREL.
I'D CALL IT A FAIR TRADE. YOU TAKE THE PRICELESS WORKS OF ART, I TAKE YOUR SPACE-AGE VACUUM...
...OR WHATEVER THIS IS.
NOW THAT I DON'T HAVE THE PAINTINGS ON MY HANDS, HOW ABOUT I SHOW YOU WHAT MY POWERS CAN *REALLY* DO?
THAT'S *WHY* WE'RE *HERE*.

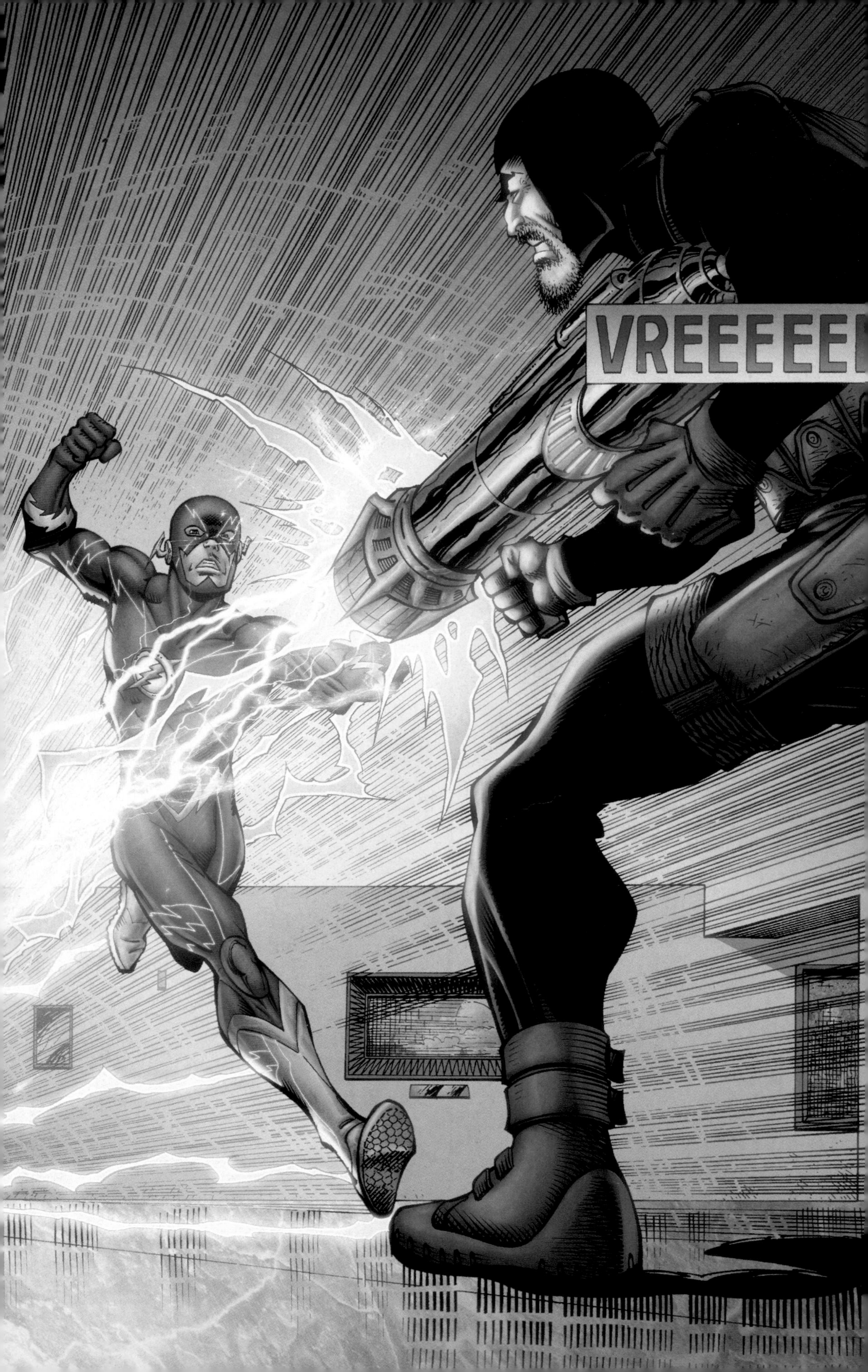
VREEEEEE

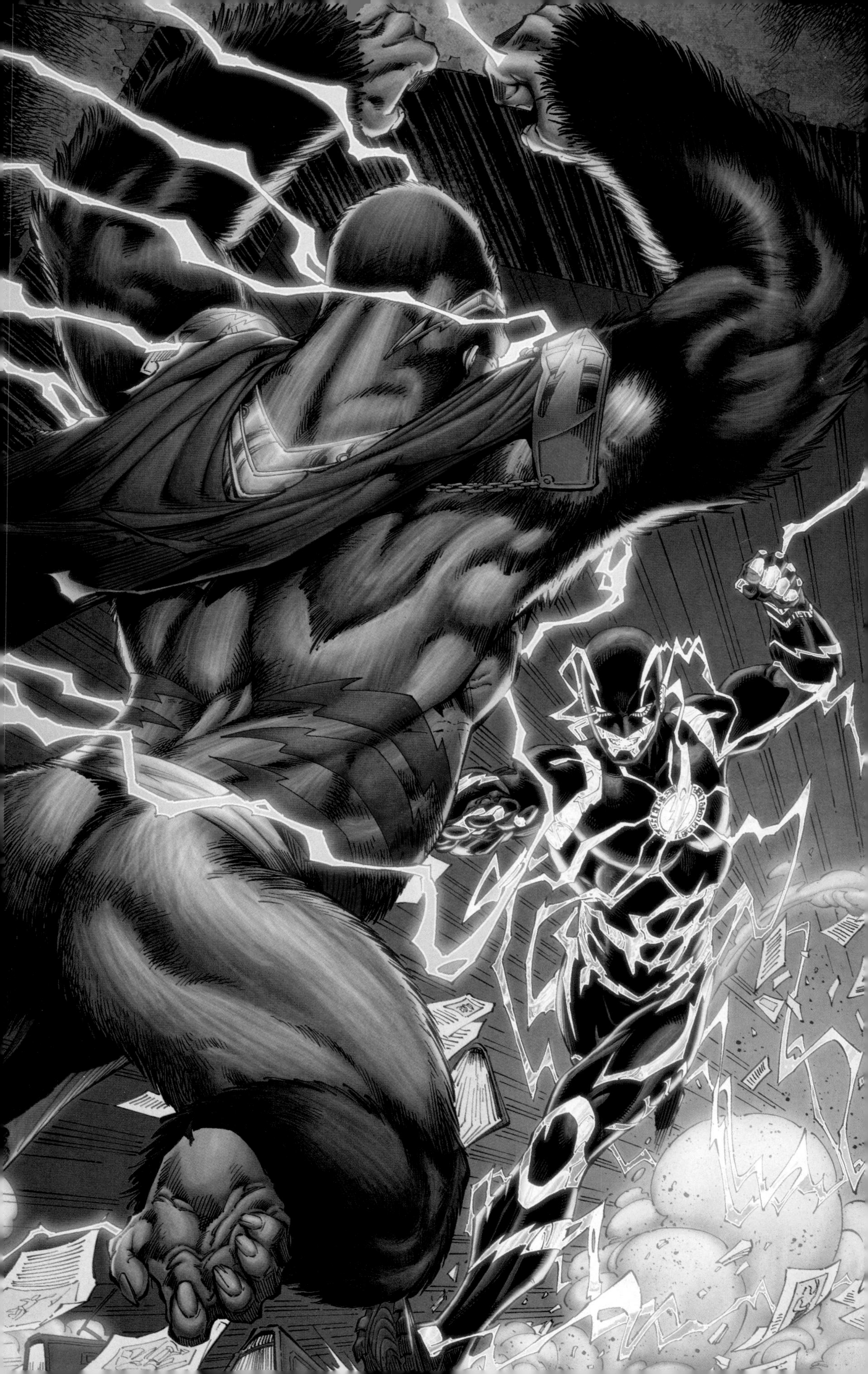

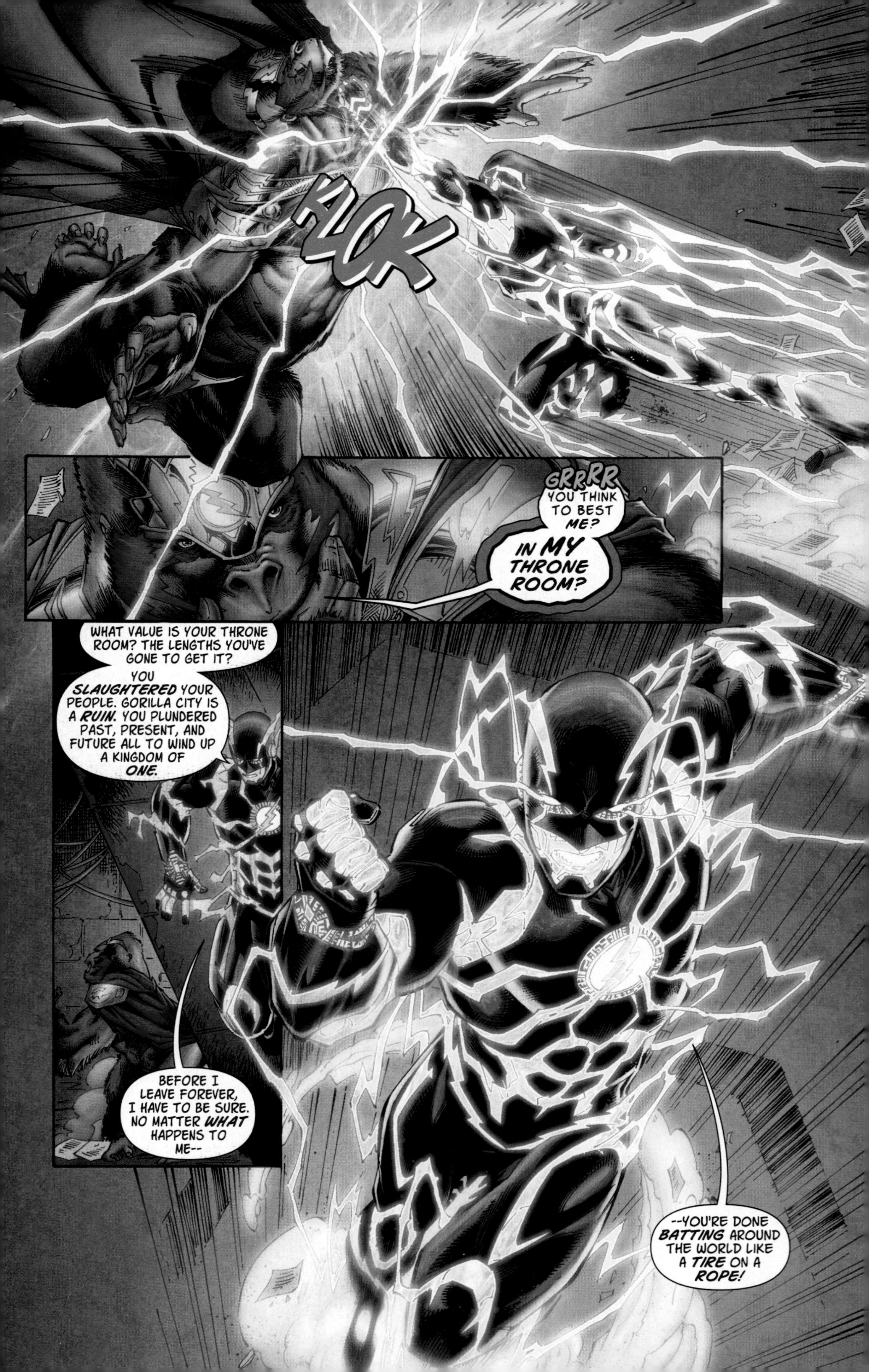
KLOK
GRRRR
YOU THINK TO BEST ME?
IN MY THRONE ROOM?
WHAT VALUE IS YOUR THRONE ROOM? THE LENGTHS YOU'VE GONE TO GET IT?
YOU SLAUGHTERED YOUR PEOPLE. GORILLA CITY IS A RUIN. YOU PLUNDERED PAST, PRESENT, AND FUTURE ALL TO WIND UP A KINGDOM OF ONE.
BEFORE I LEAVE FOREVER, I HAVE TO BE SURE. NO MATTER WHAT HAPPENS TO ME--
--YOU'RE DONE BATTING AROUND THE WORLD LIKE A TIRE ON A ROPE!

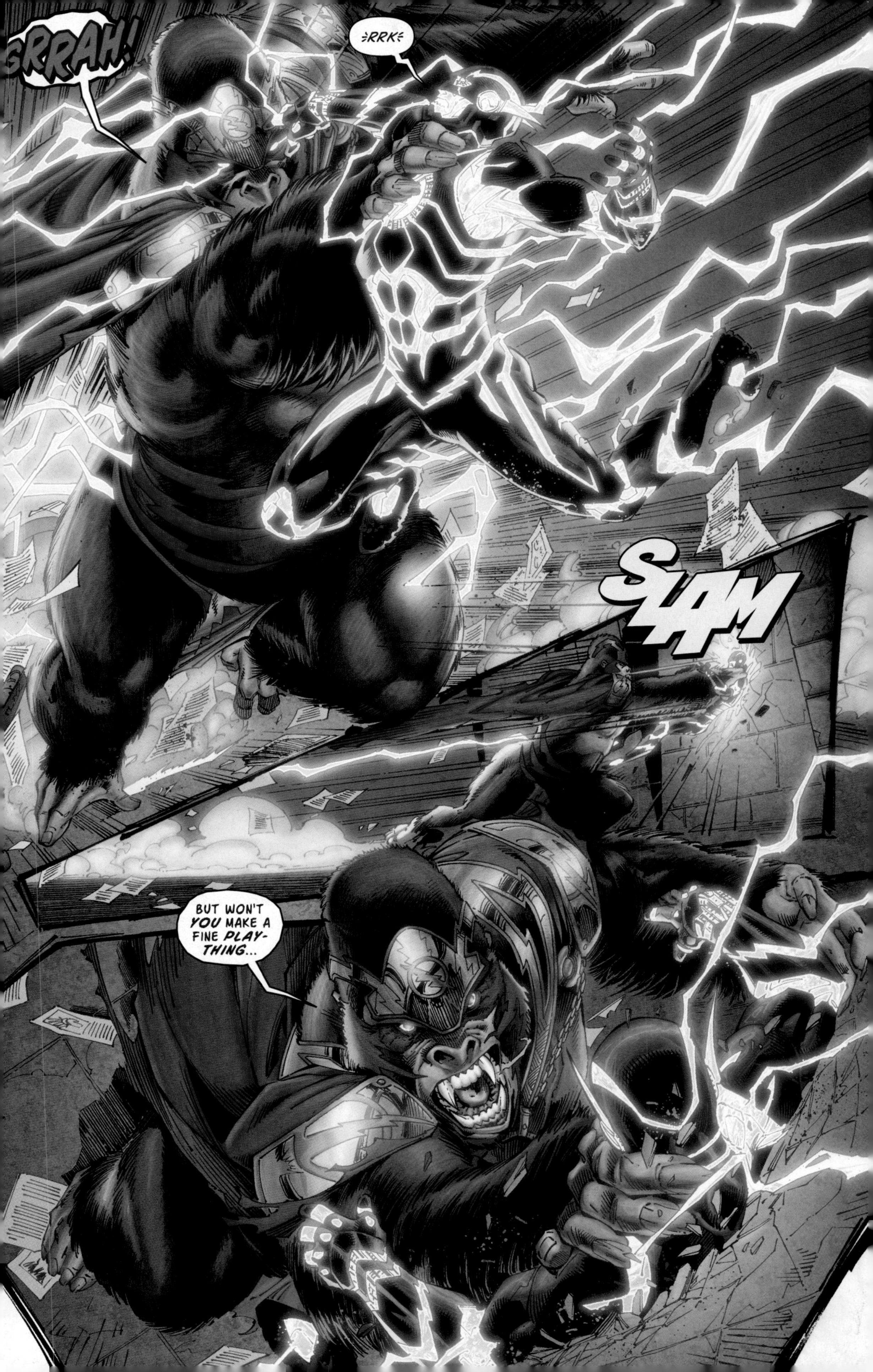
GRRAH!
RRK
SLAM
BUT WON'T YOU MAKE A FINE PLAY-THING...

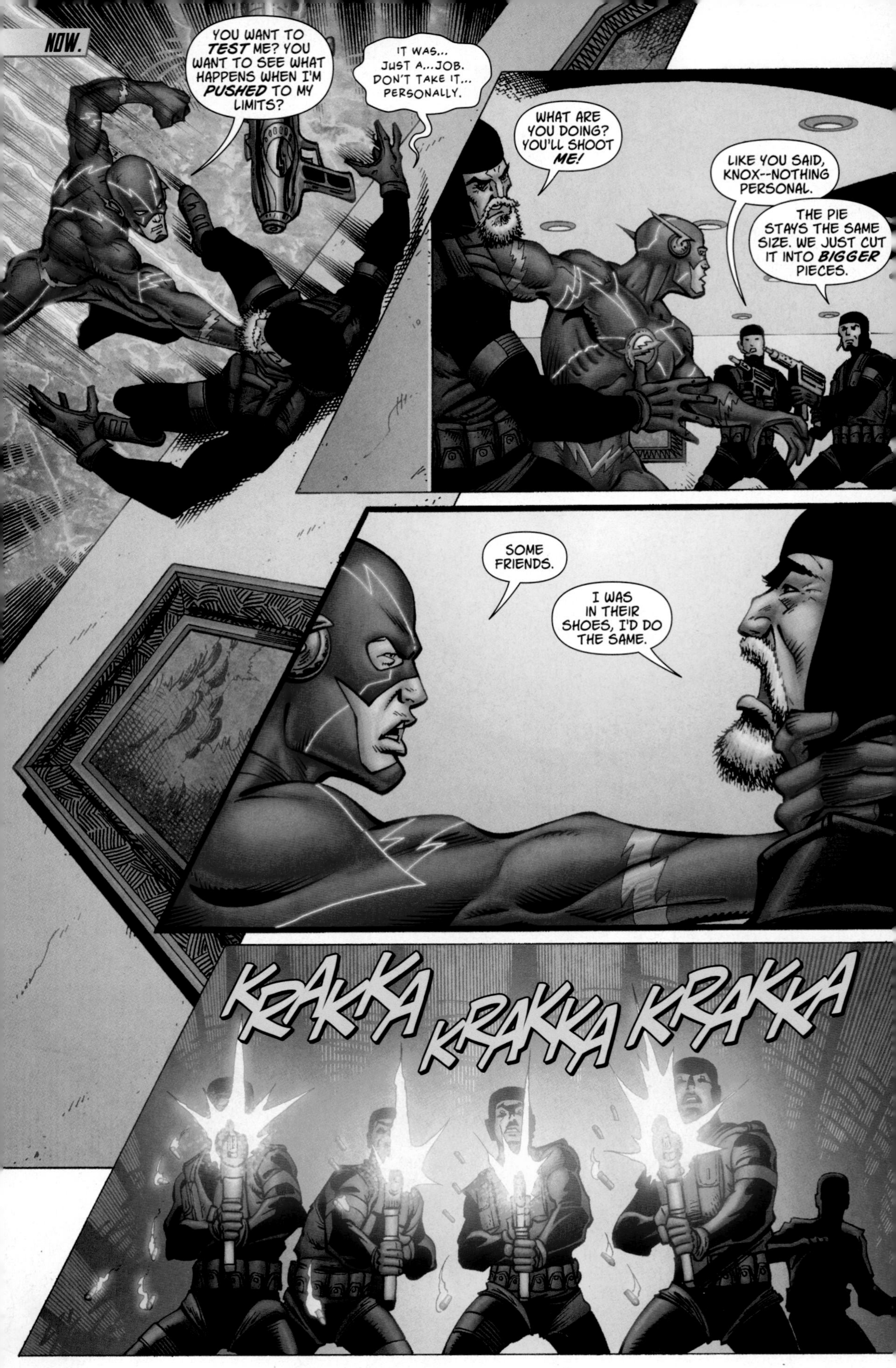
NOW.
YOU WANT TO TEST ME? YOU WANT TO SEE WHAT HAPPENS WHEN I'M PUSHED TO MY LIMITS?
IT WAS... JUST A...JOB. DON'T TAKE IT... PERSONALLY.
WHAT ARE YOU DOING? YOU'LL SHOOT ME!
LIKE YOU SAID, KNOX--NOTHING PERSONAL.
THE PIE STAYS THE SAME SIZE. WE JUST CUT IT INTO BIGGER PIECES.
SOME FRIENDS.
I WAS IN THEIR SHOES, I'D DO THE SAME.
KRAKKA KRAKKA KRAKKA

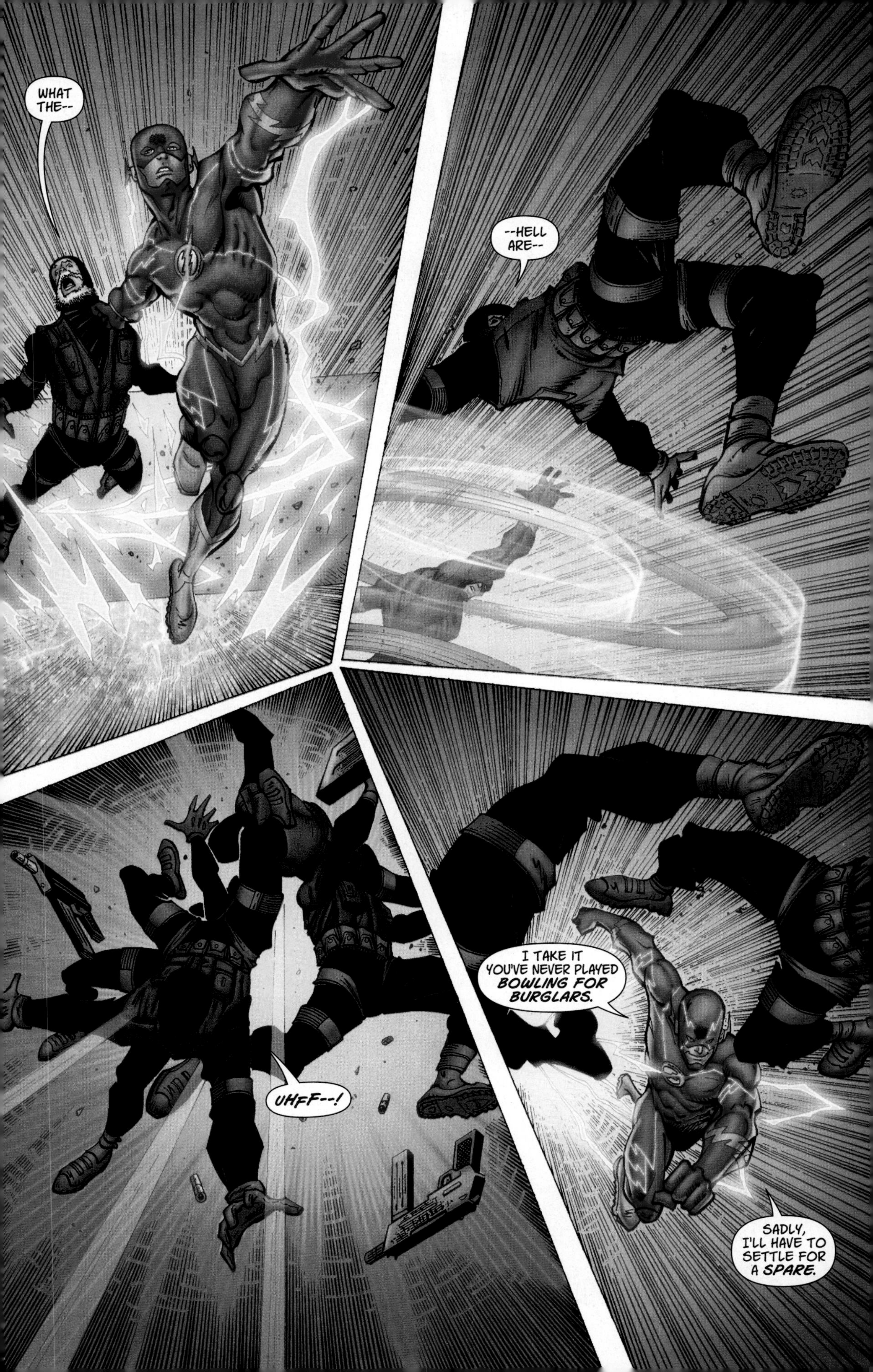
WHAT THE--
--HELL ARE--
UHFF--!
I TAKE IT YOU'VE NEVER PLAYED BOWLING FOR BURGLARS.
SADLY, I'LL HAVE TO SETTLE FOR A SPARE.

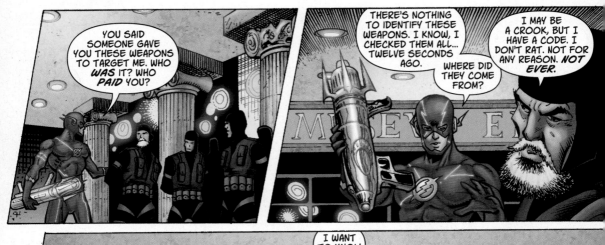

YOU SAID SOMEONE GAVE YOU THESE WEAPONS TO TARGET ME. WHO *WAS* IT? WHO *PAID* YOU?

THERE'S NOTHING TO IDENTIFY THESE WEAPONS. I KNOW, I CHECKED THEM ALL... TWELVE SECONDS AGO.

WHERE DID THEY COME FROM?

I MAY BE A CROOK, BUT I HAVE A CODE. I DON'T RAT. NOT FOR ANY REASON. *NOT EVER.*

I WANT TO KNOW *WHY.*

WHY WHAT?

IF I'D BEEN KILLED, IT WOULD'VE BEEN ON THEIR HEADS, NOT YOURS.

I HAD A CHANCE TO SAVE YOU, SO I HAD TO TRY. TO LET YOU DIE... IT'D BE NO DIFFERENT FROM KILLING YOU MYSELF.

I WON'T TAKE A LIFE.

NOT FOR ANY REASON.

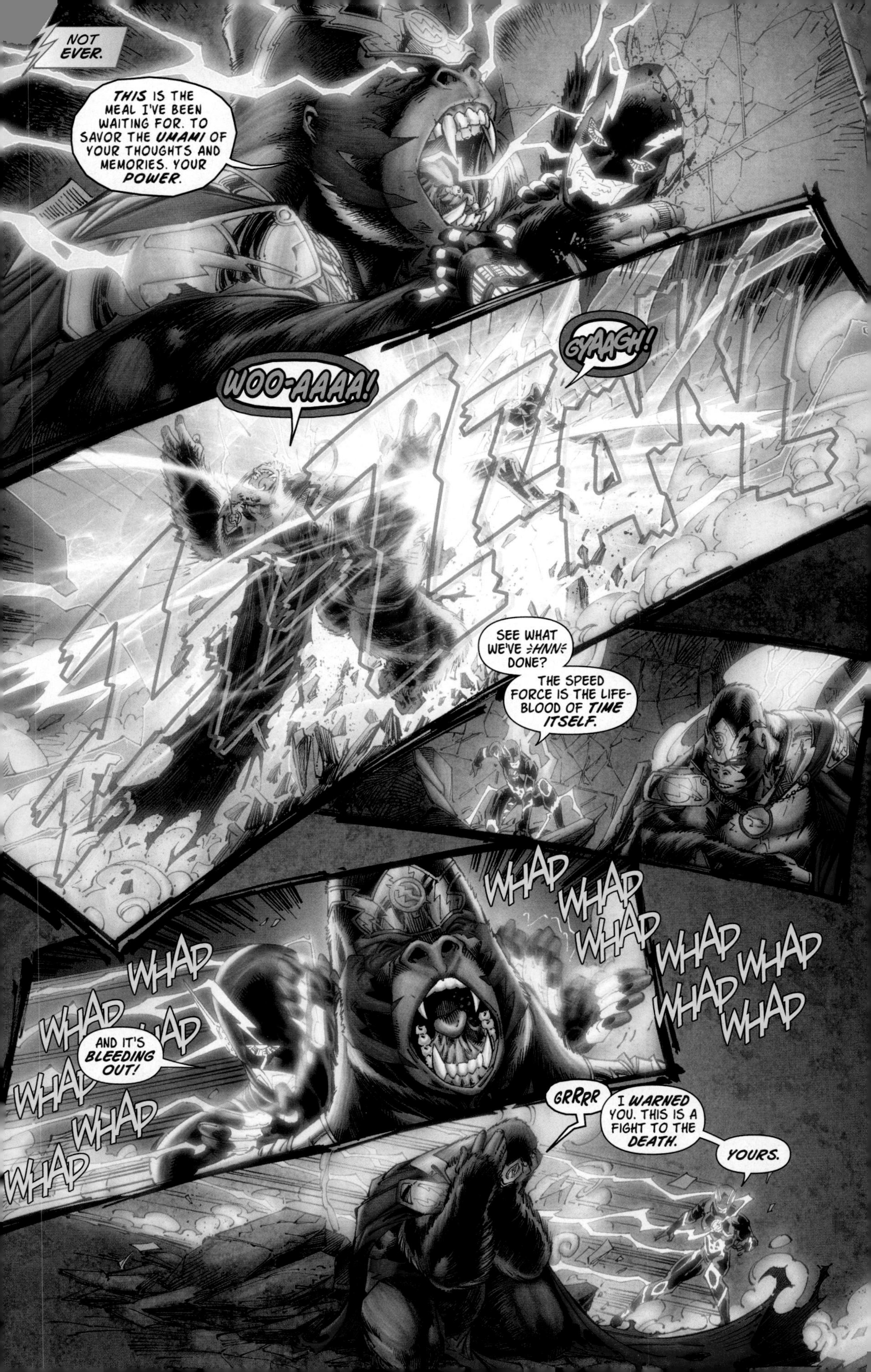
NOT EVER.
THIS IS THE MEAL I'VE BEEN WAITING FOR. TO SAVOR THE UMAMI OF YOUR THOUGHTS AND MEMORIES. YOUR POWER.
WOO-AAAA!
GYAAGH!
SEE WHAT WE'VE ≠HNN≠ DONE?
THE SPEED FORCE IS THE LIFE-BLOOD OF TIME ITSELF.
WHAP WHAP WHAP WHAP WHAP WHAP WHAP WHAP
WHAP WHAP WHAP WHAP WHAP WHAP WHAP
AND IT'S BLEEDING OUT!
GRRRR
I WARNED YOU. THIS IS A FIGHT TO THE DEATH.
YOURS.

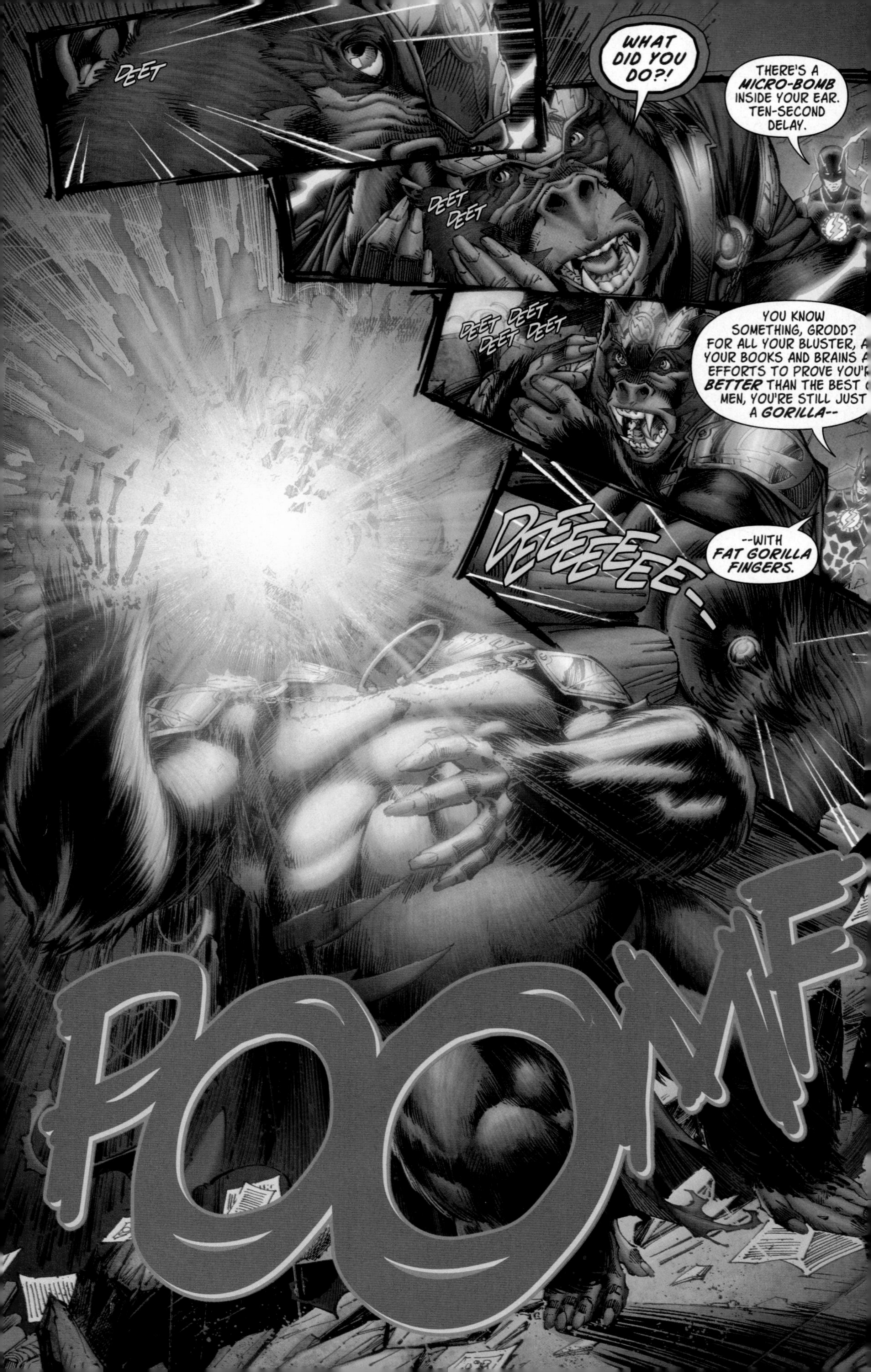
DEET
WHAT DID YOU DO?!
THERE'S A MICRO-BOMB INSIDE YOUR EAR. TEN-SECOND DELAY.
DEET DEET
DEET DEET DEET DEET
YOU KNOW SOMETHING, GRODD? FOR ALL YOUR BLUSTER, A YOUR BOOKS AND BRAINS A EFFORTS TO PROVE YOU'R BETTER THAN THE BEST MEN, YOU'RE STILL JUST A GORILLA--
DEEEEEEEE--
--WITH FAT GORILLA FINGERS.
POOOMF

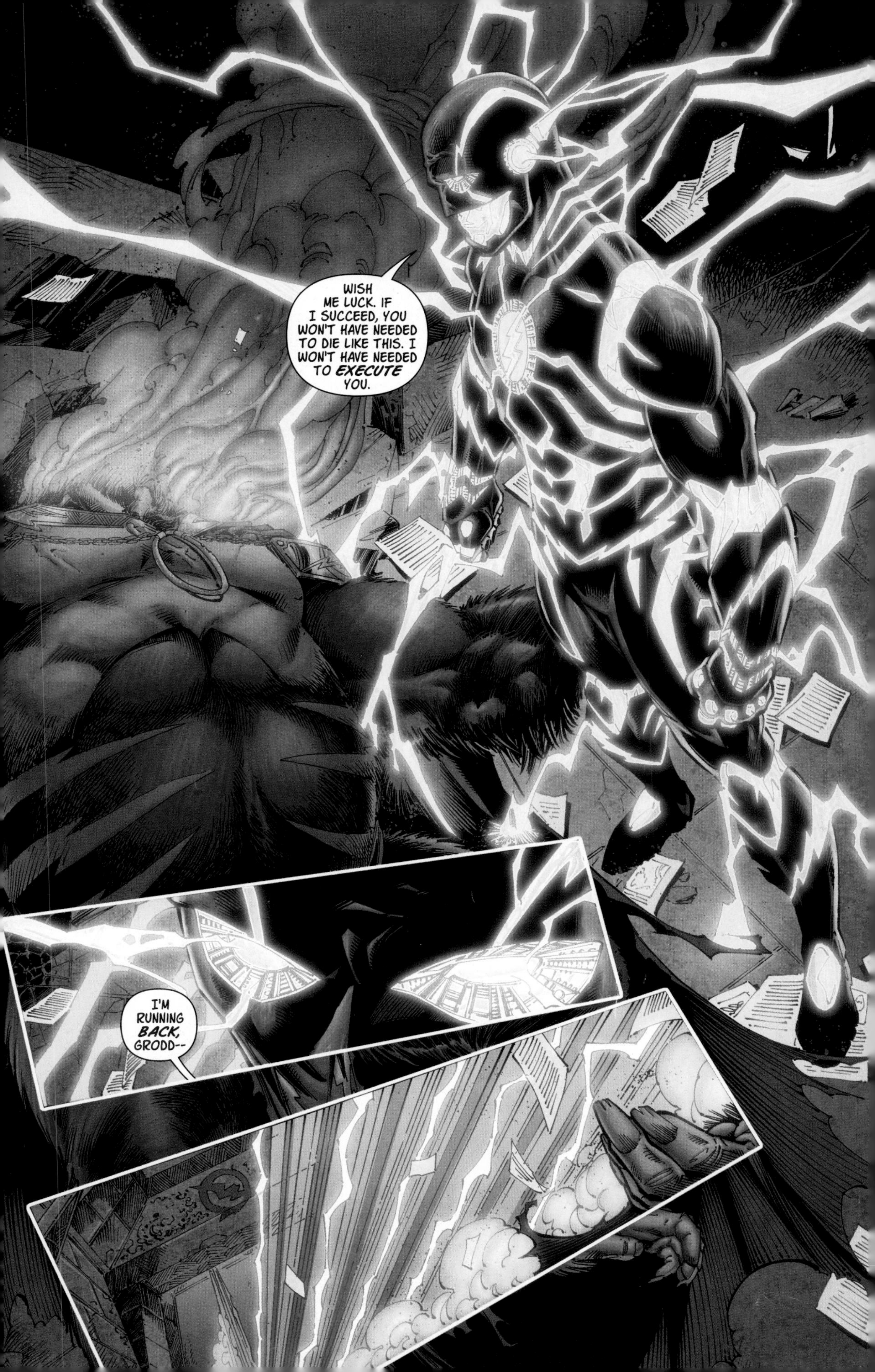
WISH ME LUCK. IF I SUCCEED, YOU WON'T HAVE NEEDED TO DIE LIKE THIS. I WON'T HAVE NEEDED TO **EXECUTE** YOU.
I'M RUNNING **BACK,** GRODD--

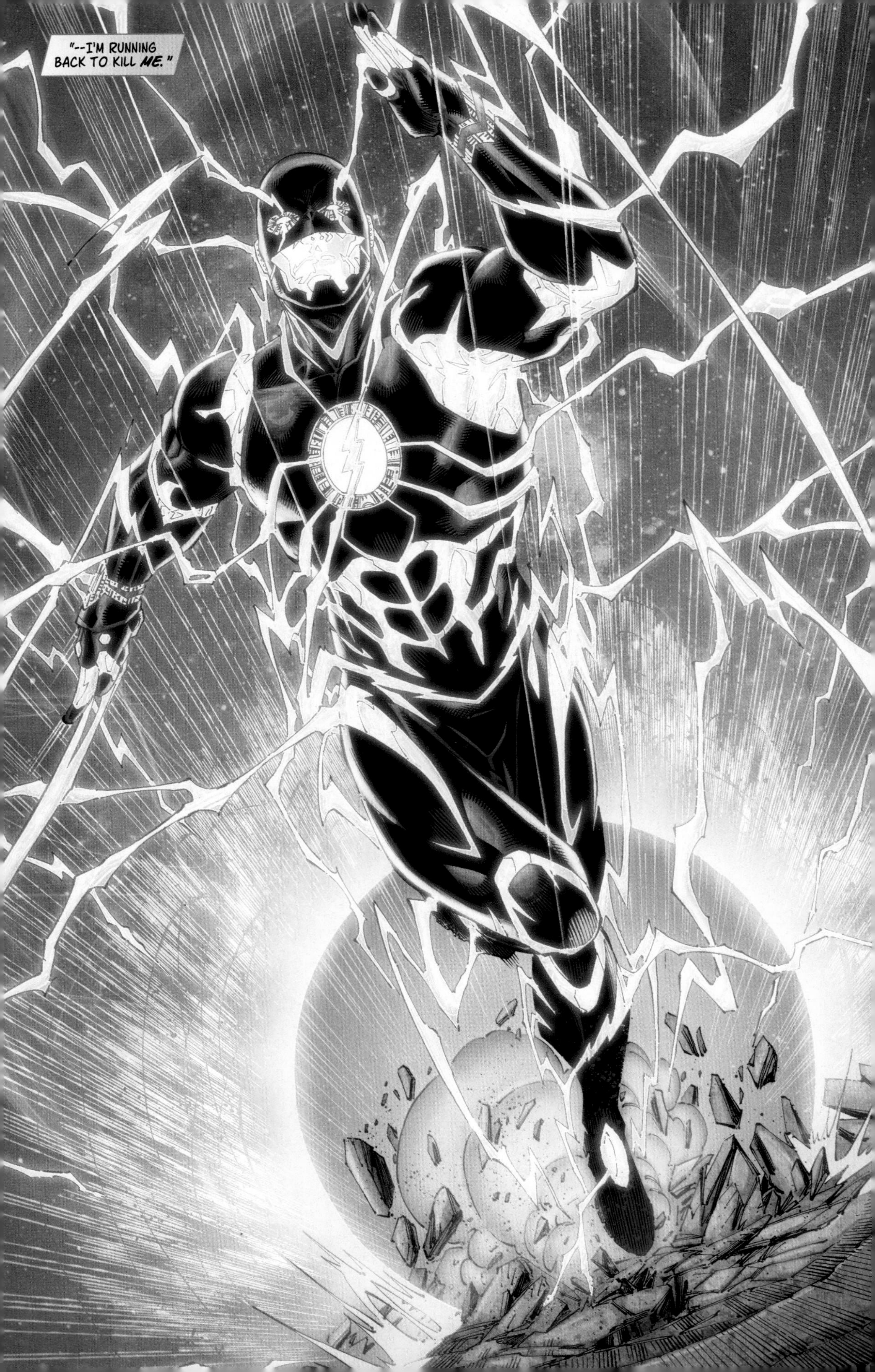
"--I'M RUNNING BACK TO KILL ME."

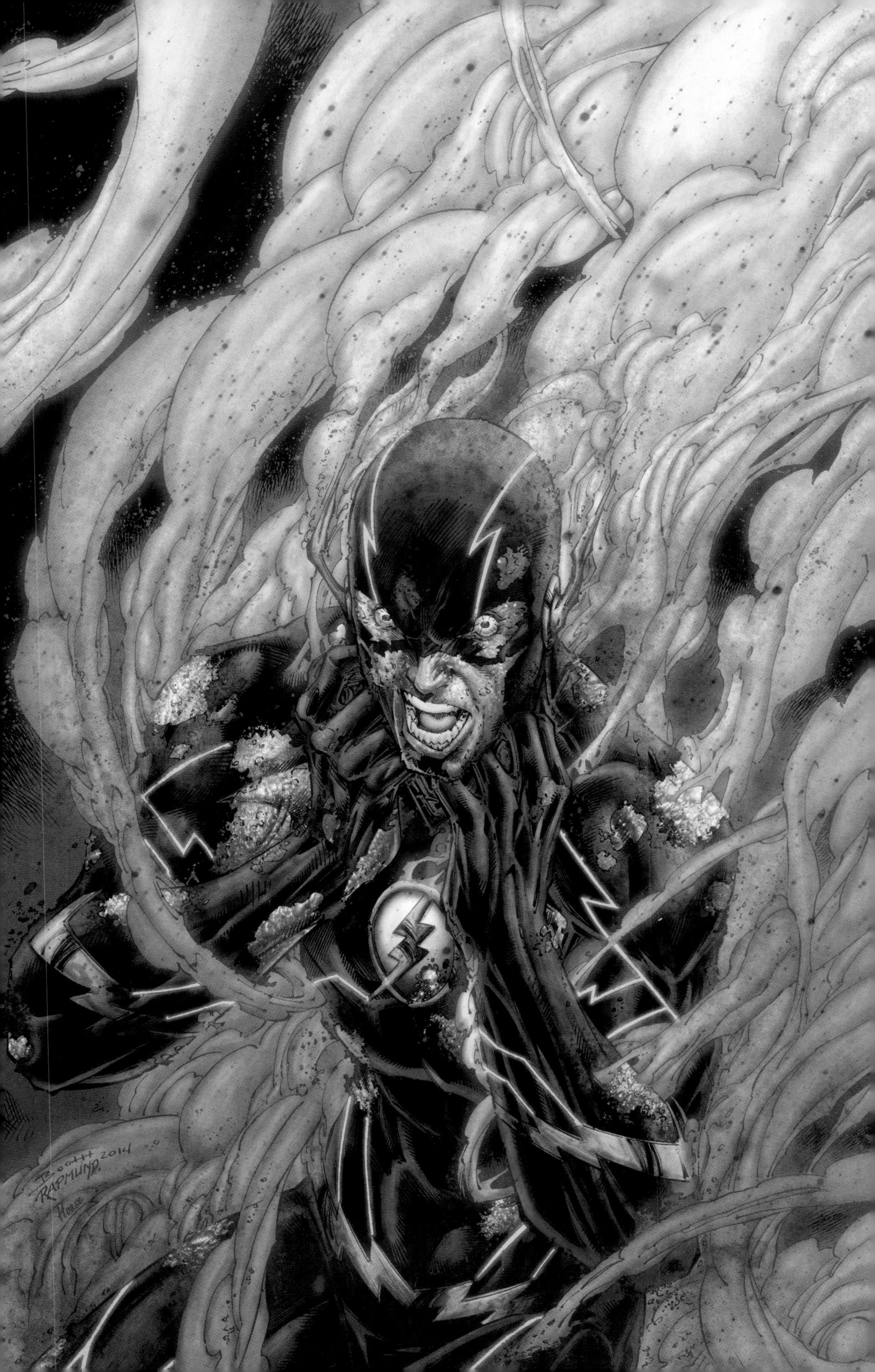
BOOTH
RAPMUND 2014

THROUGH A LOOKING GLASS DARKLY

ROBERT VENDITTI & VAN JENSEN writers BRETT BOOTH penciller NORM RAPMUND inker

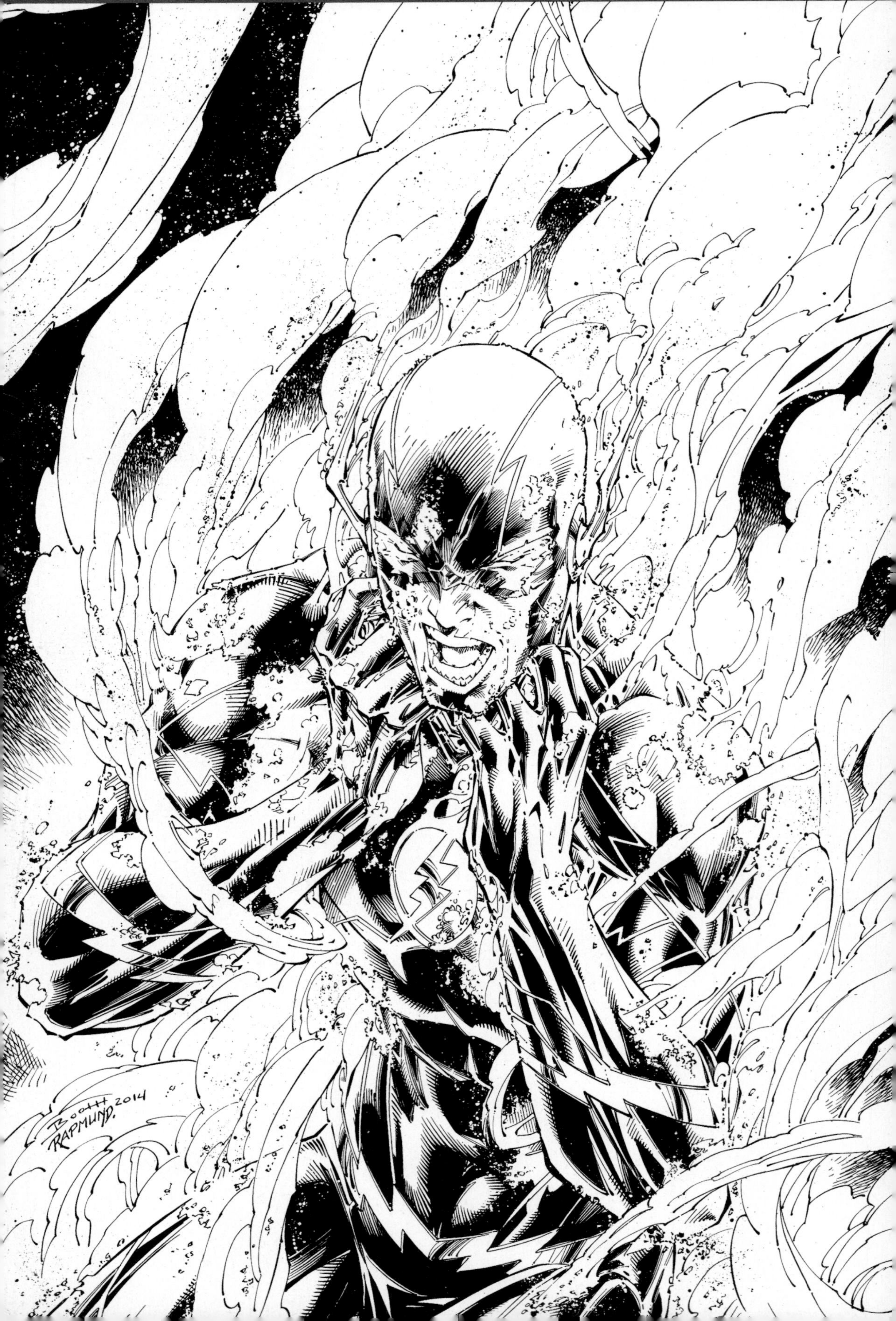
BOOTH 2014
RAPMUND

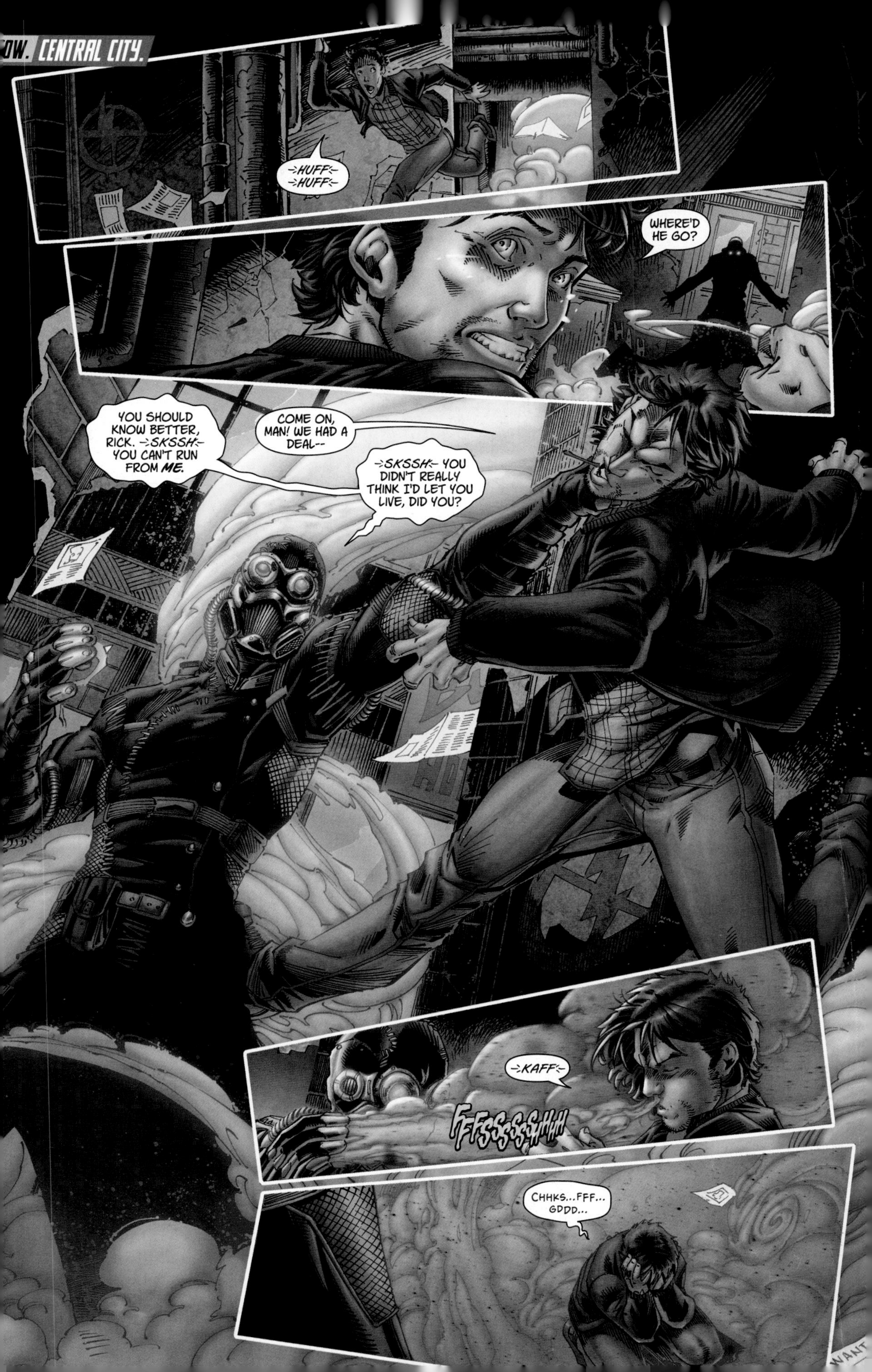

...OW. CENTRAL CITY.
-HUFF- -HUFF-
WHERE'D HE GO?
YOU SHOULD KNOW BETTER, RICK. -SKSSH- YOU CAN'T RUN FROM ME.
COME ON, MAN! WE HAD A DEAL--
-SKSSH- YOU DIDN'T REALLY THINK I'D LET YOU LIVE, DID YOU?
-KAFF-
FFFSSSSSSHHH
CHHKS...FFF... GDDD...

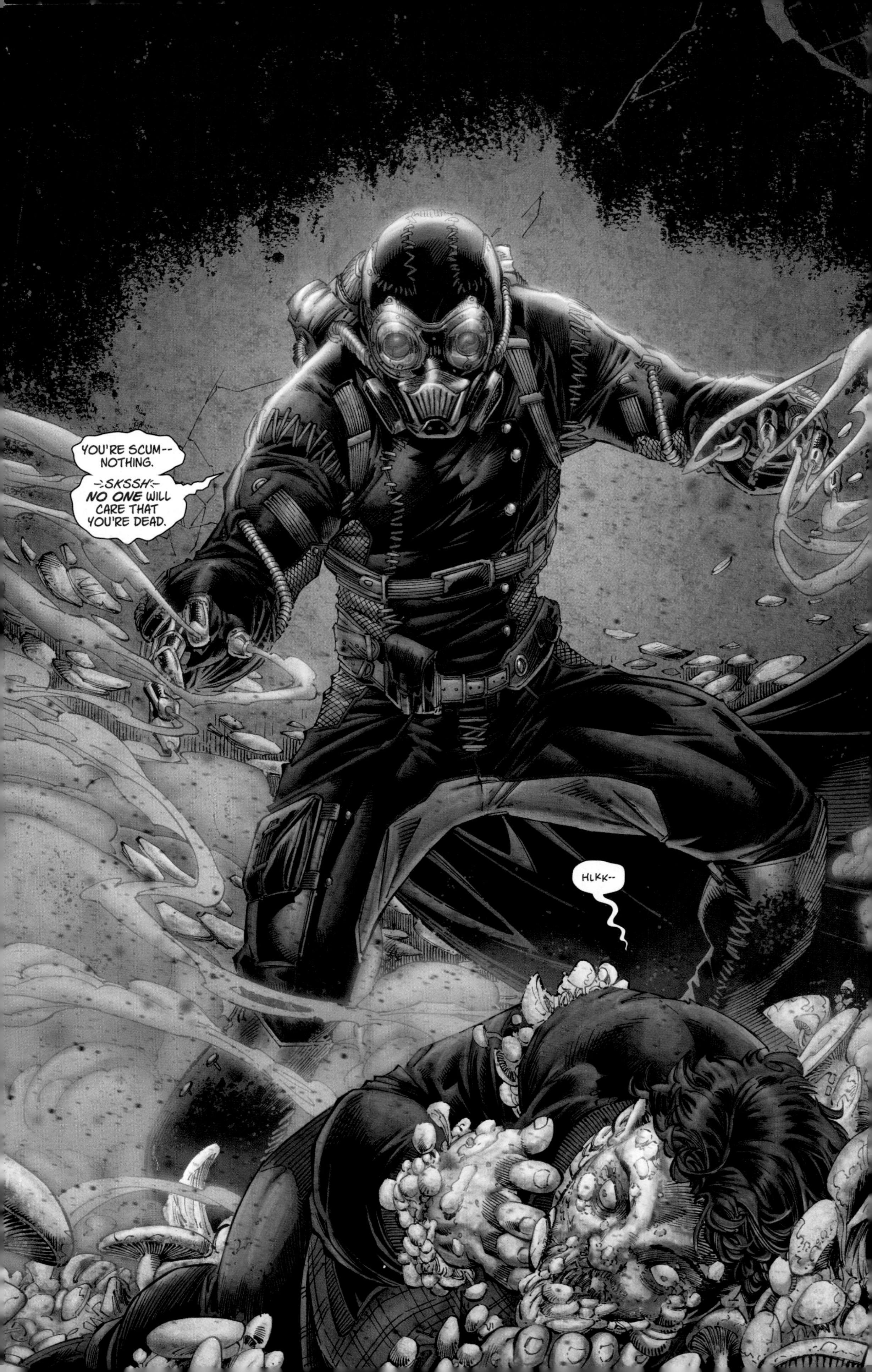
YOU'RE SCUM-- NOTHING.
-SKSSH- NO ONE WILL CARE THAT YOU'RE DEAD.
HLKK--

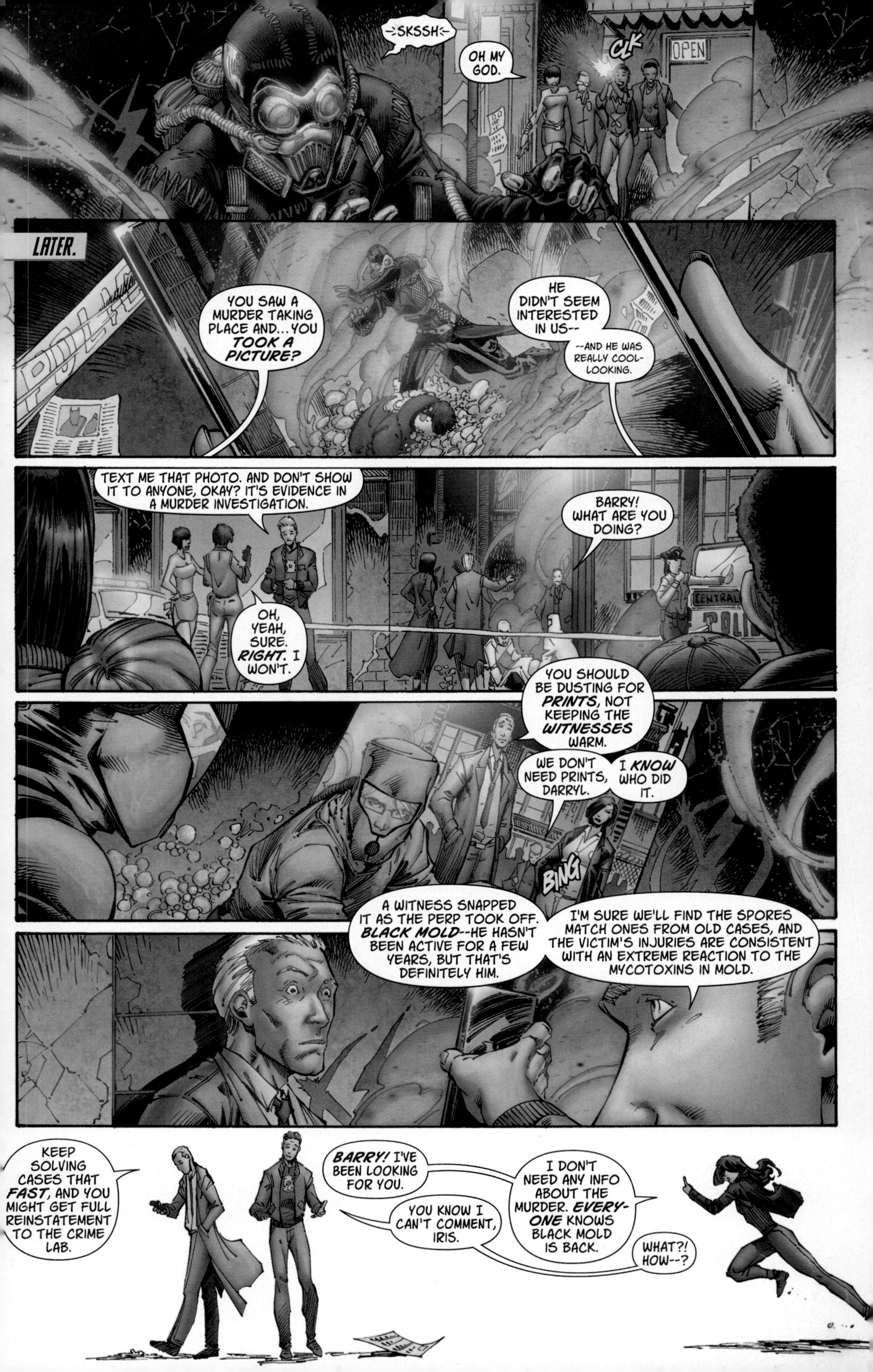
-SKSSH-
OH MY GOD.
CLK
OPEN
LATER.
YOU SAW A MURDER TAKING PLACE AND... YOU TOOK A PICTURE?
HE DIDN'T SEEM INTERESTED IN US--
--AND HE WAS REALLY COOL-LOOKING.
TEXT ME THAT PHOTO. AND DON'T SHOW IT TO ANYONE, OKAY? IT'S EVIDENCE IN A MURDER INVESTIGATION.
OH, YEAH, SURE. RIGHT. I WON'T.
BARRY! WHAT ARE YOU DOING?
YOU SHOULD BE DUSTING FOR PRINTS, NOT KEEPING THE WITNESSES WARM.
WE DON'T NEED PRINTS, DARRYL.
I KNOW WHO DID IT.
BING
A WITNESS SNAPPED IT AS THE PERP TOOK OFF. BLACK MOLD--HE HASN'T BEEN ACTIVE FOR A FEW YEARS, BUT THAT'S DEFINITELY HIM.
I'M SURE WE'LL FIND THE SPORES MATCH ONES FROM OLD CASES, AND THE VICTIM'S INJURIES ARE CONSISTENT WITH AN EXTREME REACTION TO THE MYCOTOXINS IN MOLD.
KEEP SOLVING CASES THAT FAST, AND YOU MIGHT GET FULL REINSTATEMENT TO THE CRIME LAB.
BARRY! I'VE BEEN LOOKING FOR YOU.
YOU KNOW I CAN'T COMMENT, IRIS.
I DON'T NEED ANY INFO ABOUT THE MURDER. EVERYONE KNOWS BLACK MOLD IS BACK.
WHAT?! HOW--?

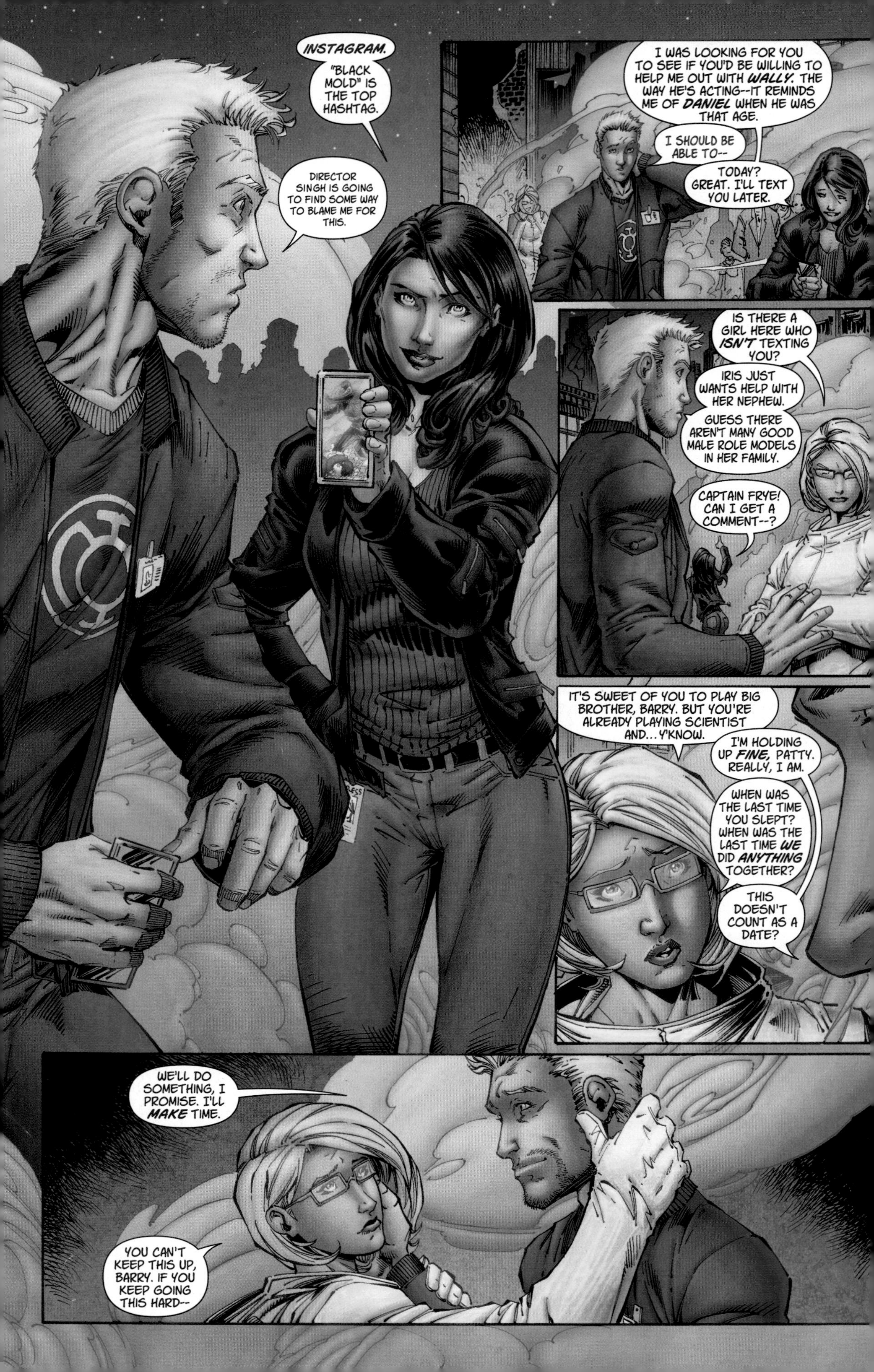
INSTAGRAM. "BLACK MOLD" IS THE TOP HASHTAG.
DIRECTOR SINGH IS GOING TO FIND SOME WAY TO BLAME ME FOR THIS.
I WAS LOOKING FOR YOU TO SEE IF YOU'D BE WILLING TO HELP ME OUT WITH WALLY. THE WAY HE'S ACTING--IT REMINDS ME OF DANIEL WHEN HE WAS THAT AGE.
I SHOULD BE ABLE TO--
TODAY? GREAT. I'LL TEXT YOU LATER.
IS THERE A GIRL HERE WHO ISN'T TEXTING YOU?
IRIS JUST WANTS HELP WITH HER NEPHEW.
GUESS THERE AREN'T MANY GOOD MALE ROLE MODELS IN HER FAMILY.
CAPTAIN FRYE! CAN I GET A COMMENT--?
IT'S SWEET OF YOU TO PLAY BIG BROTHER, BARRY. BUT YOU'RE ALREADY PLAYING SCIENTIST AND... Y'KNOW.
I'M HOLDING UP FINE, PATTY. REALLY, I AM.
WHEN WAS THE LAST TIME YOU SLEPT? WHEN WAS THE LAST TIME WE DID ANYTHING TOGETHER?
THIS DOESN'T COUNT AS A DATE?
WE'LL DO SOMETHING, I PROMISE. I'LL MAKE TIME.
YOU CAN'T KEEP THIS UP, BARRY. IF YOU KEEP GOING THIS HARD--

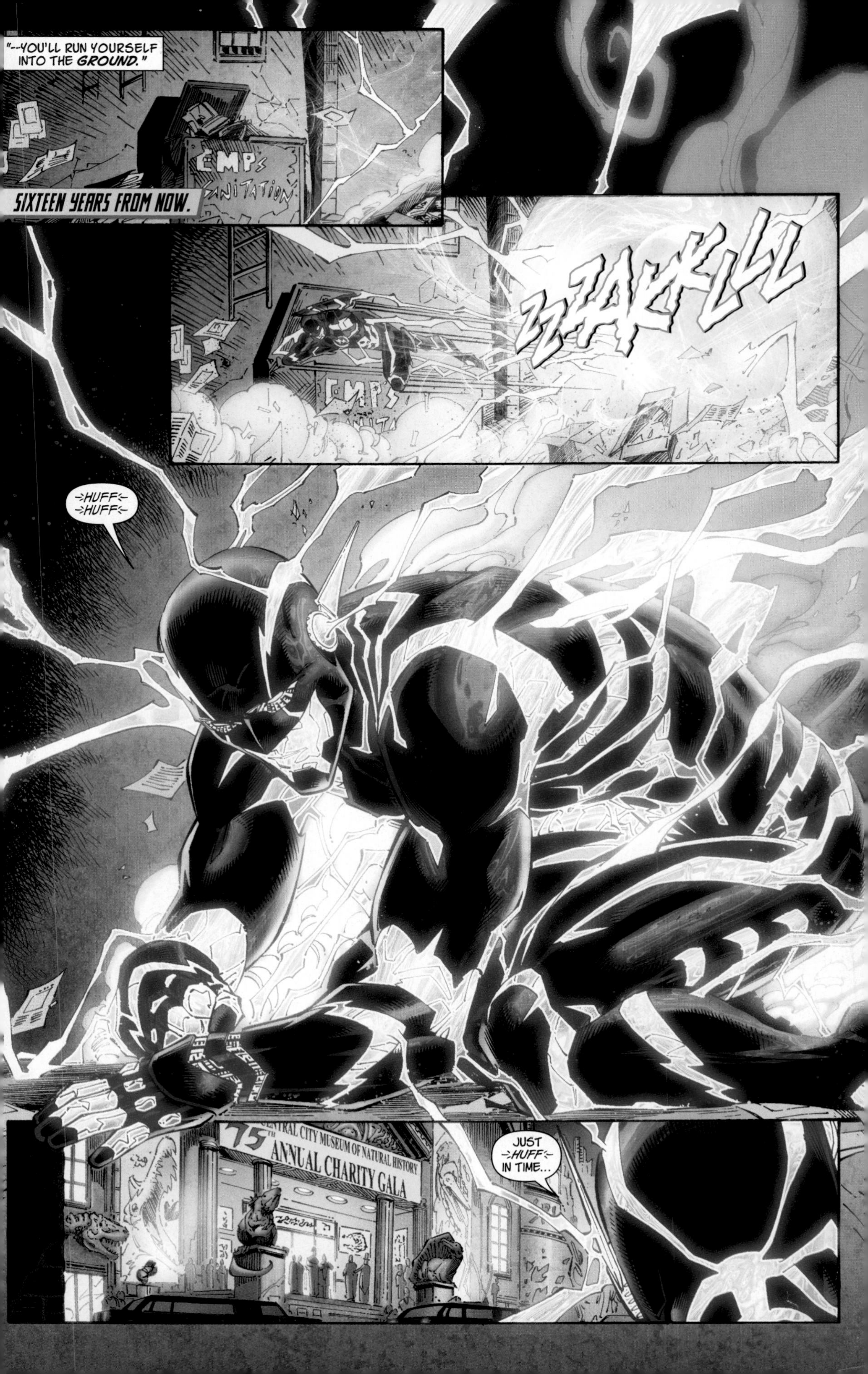

"--YOU'LL RUN YOURSELF INTO THE GROUND."
SIXTEEN YEARS FROM NOW.
ZZZAKKLLL
-HUFF- -HUFF-
CENTRAL CITY MUSEUM OF NATURAL HISTORY 75TH ANNUAL CHARITY GALA
JUST -HUFF- IN TIME...

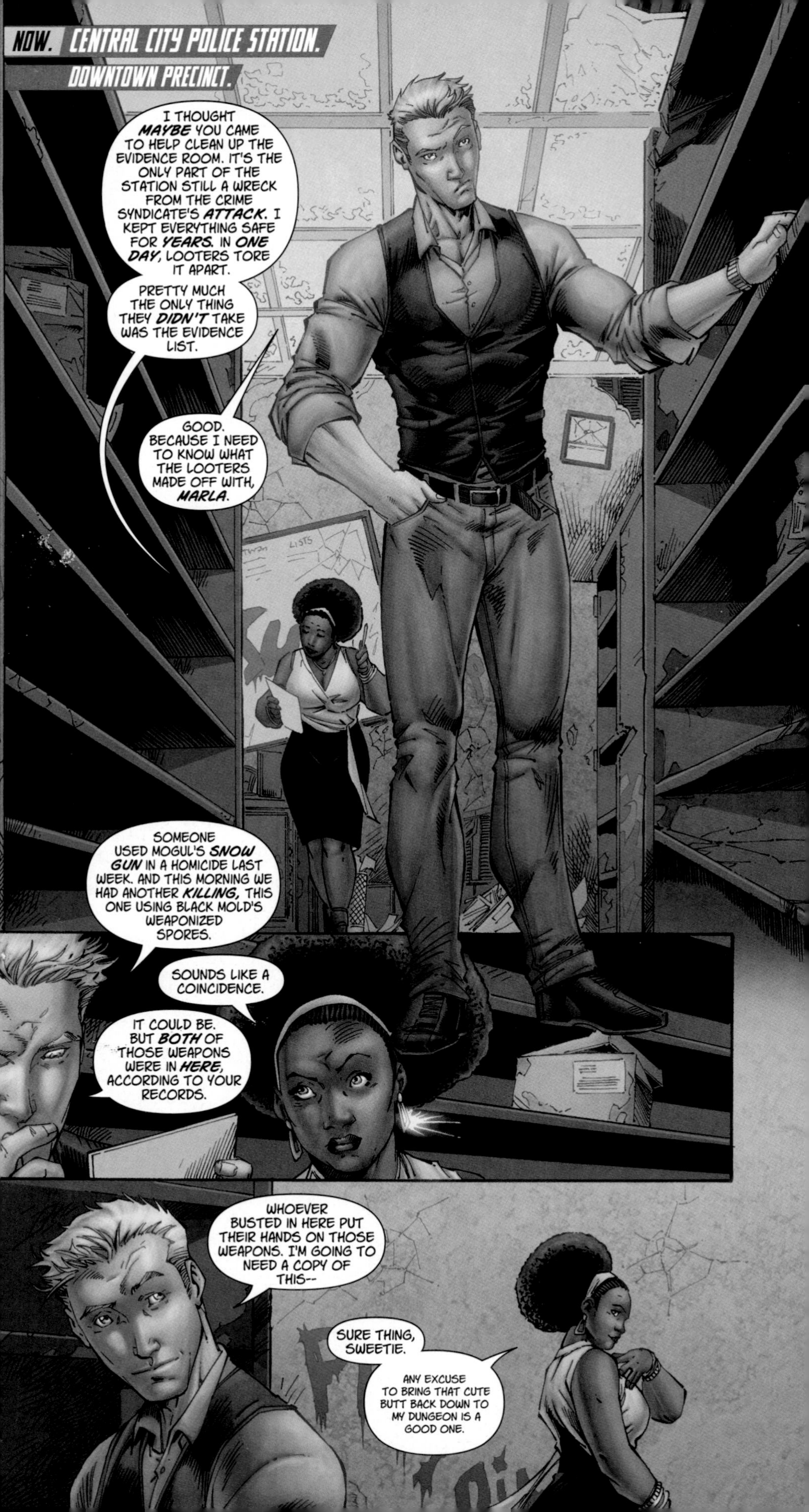
NOW. CENTRAL CITY POLICE STATION.
DOWNTOWN PRECINCT.
I THOUGHT MAYBE YOU CAME TO HELP CLEAN UP THE EVIDENCE ROOM. IT'S THE ONLY PART OF THE STATION STILL A WRECK FROM THE CRIME SYNDICATE'S ATTACK. I KEPT EVERYTHING SAFE FOR YEARS. IN ONE DAY, LOOTERS TORE IT APART.
PRETTY MUCH THE ONLY THING THEY DIDN'T TAKE WAS THE EVIDENCE LIST.
GOOD. BECAUSE I NEED TO KNOW WHAT THE LOOTERS MADE OFF WITH, MARLA.
LISTS
SOMEONE USED MOGUL'S SNOW GUN IN A HOMICIDE LAST WEEK. AND THIS MORNING WE HAD ANOTHER KILLING, THIS ONE USING BLACK MOLD'S WEAPONIZED SPORES.
SOUNDS LIKE A COINCIDENCE.
IT COULD BE. BUT BOTH OF THOSE WEAPONS WERE IN HERE, ACCORDING TO YOUR RECORDS.
WHOEVER BUSTED IN HERE PUT THEIR HANDS ON THOSE WEAPONS. I'M GOING TO NEED A COPY OF THIS--
SURE THING, SWEETIE.
ANY EXCUSE TO BRING THAT CUTE BUTT BACK DOWN TO MY DUNGEON IS A GOOD ONE.

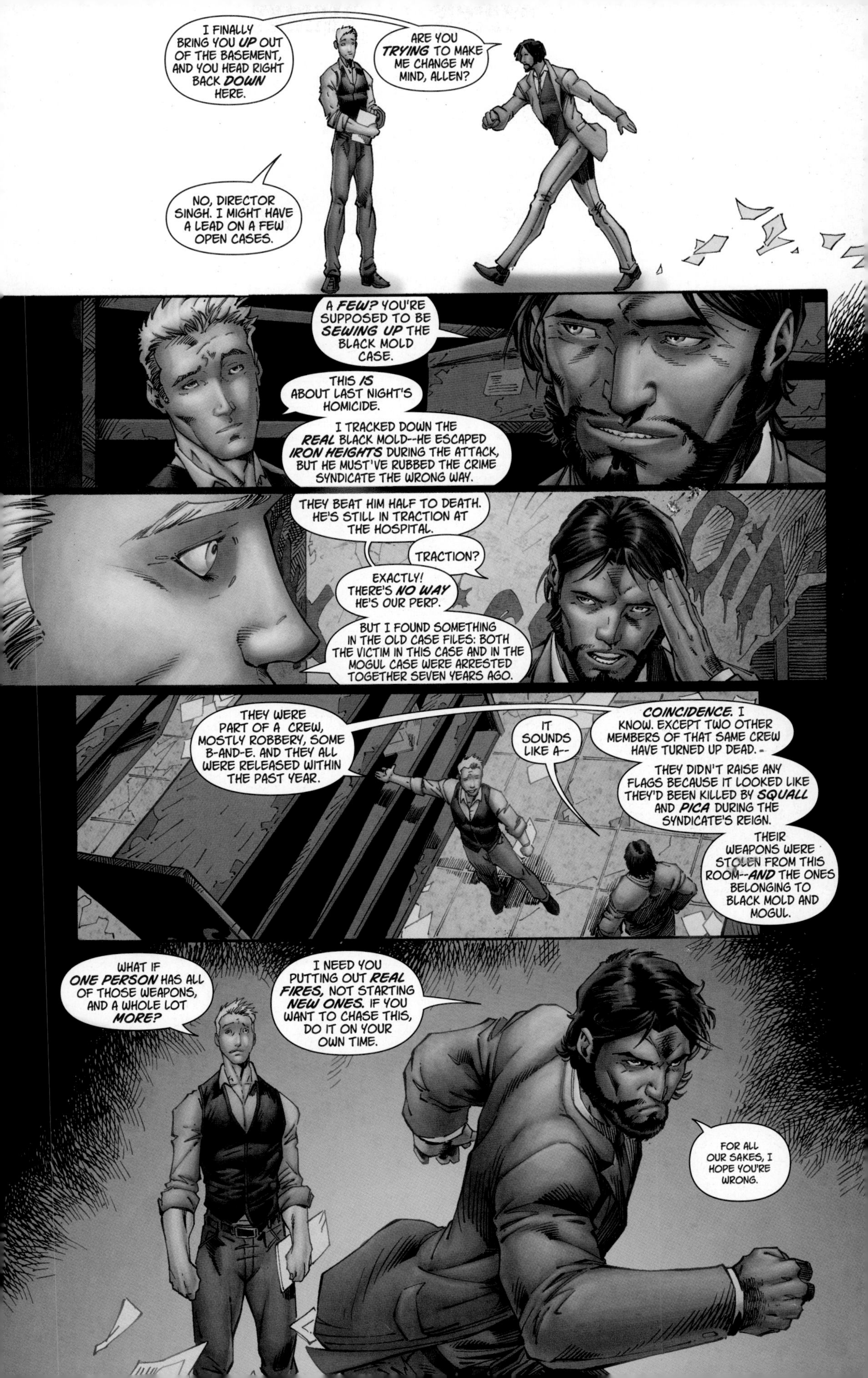
I FINALLY BRING YOU UP OUT OF THE BASEMENT, AND YOU HEAD RIGHT BACK DOWN HERE.
ARE YOU TRYING TO MAKE ME CHANGE MY MIND, ALLEN?
NO, DIRECTOR SINGH. I MIGHT HAVE A LEAD ON A FEW OPEN CASES.
A FEW? YOU'RE SUPPOSED TO BE SEWING UP THE BLACK MOLD CASE.
THIS IS ABOUT LAST NIGHT'S HOMICIDE.
I TRACKED DOWN THE REAL BLACK MOLD--HE ESCAPED IRON HEIGHTS DURING THE ATTACK, BUT HE MUST'VE RUBBED THE CRIME SYNDICATE THE WRONG WAY.
THEY BEAT HIM HALF TO DEATH. HE'S STILL IN TRACTION AT THE HOSPITAL.
TRACTION?
EXACTLY! THERE'S NO WAY HE'S OUR PERP.
BUT I FOUND SOMETHING IN THE OLD CASE FILES: BOTH THE VICTIM IN THIS CASE AND IN THE MOGUL CASE WERE ARRESTED TOGETHER SEVEN YEARS AGO.
THEY WERE PART OF A CREW, MOSTLY ROBBERY, SOME B-AND-E. AND THEY ALL WERE RELEASED WITHIN THE PAST YEAR.
IT SOUNDS LIKE A--
COINCIDENCE. I KNOW. EXCEPT TWO OTHER MEMBERS OF THAT SAME CREW HAVE TURNED UP DEAD.
THEY DIDN'T RAISE ANY FLAGS BECAUSE IT LOOKED LIKE THEY'D BEEN KILLED BY SQUALL AND PICA DURING THE SYNDICATE'S REIGN.
THEIR WEAPONS WERE STOLEN FROM THIS ROOM--AND THE ONES BELONGING TO BLACK MOLD AND MOGUL.
WHAT IF ONE PERSON HAS ALL OF THOSE WEAPONS, AND A WHOLE LOT MORE?
I NEED YOU PUTTING OUT REAL FIRES, NOT STARTING NEW ONES. IF YOU WANT TO CHASE THIS, DO IT ON YOUR OWN TIME.
FOR ALL OUR SAKES, I HOPE YOU'RE WRONG.

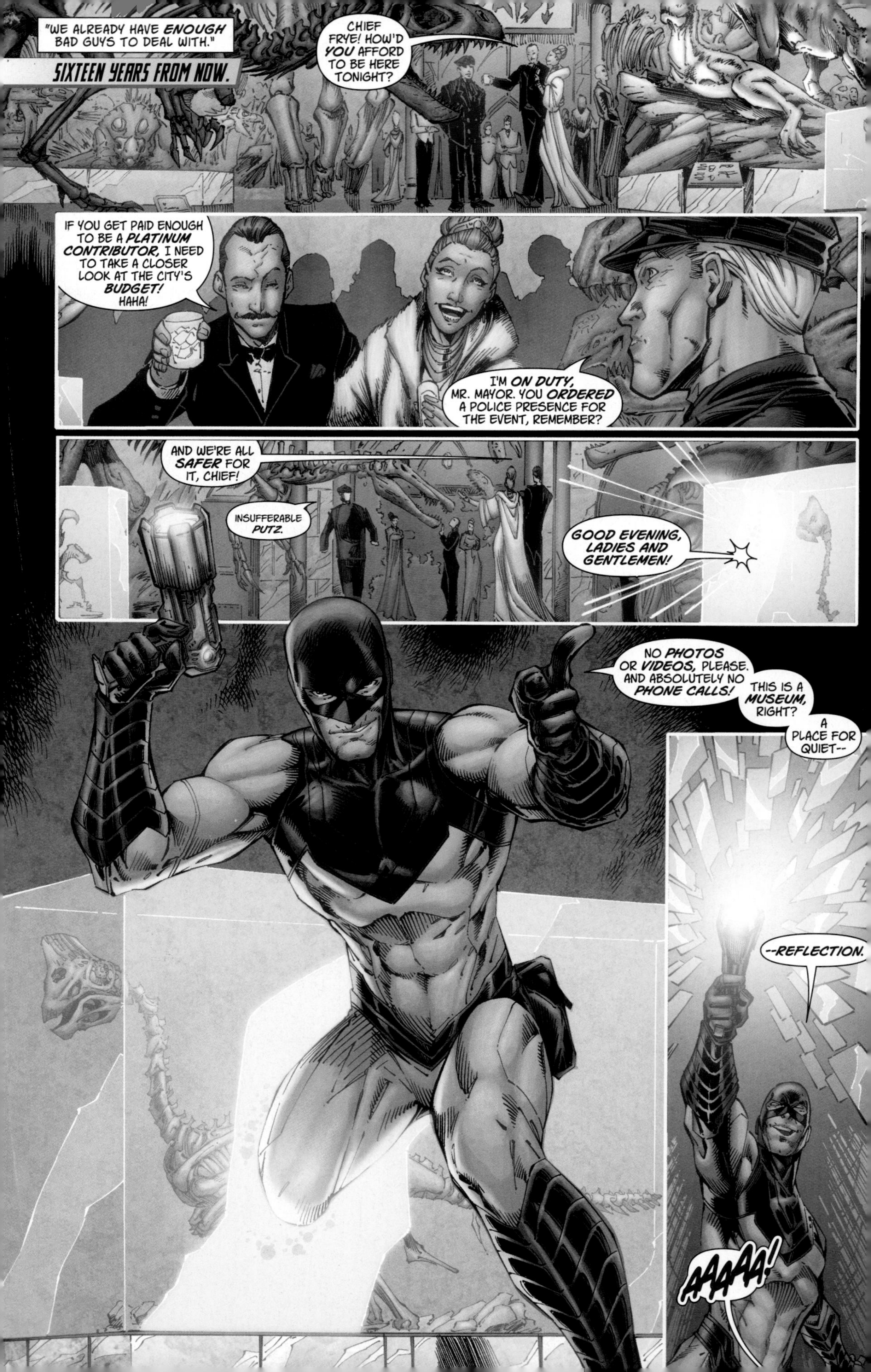
"WE ALREADY HAVE ENOUGH BAD GUYS TO DEAL WITH."
SIXTEEN YEARS FROM NOW.
CHIEF FRYE! HOW'D YOU AFFORD TO BE HERE TONIGHT?
IF YOU GET PAID ENOUGH TO BE A PLATINUM CONTRIBUTOR, I NEED TO TAKE A CLOSER LOOK AT THE CITY'S BUDGET! HAHA!
I'M ON DUTY, MR. MAYOR. YOU ORDERED A POLICE PRESENCE FOR THE EVENT, REMEMBER?
AND WE'RE ALL SAFER FOR IT, CHIEF!
INSUFFERABLE PUTZ.
GOOD EVENING, LADIES AND GENTLEMEN!
NO PHOTOS OR VIDEOS, PLEASE. AND ABSOLUTELY NO PHONE CALLS!
THIS IS A MUSEUM, RIGHT?
A PLACE FOR QUIET--
--REFLECTION.
AAAAA!

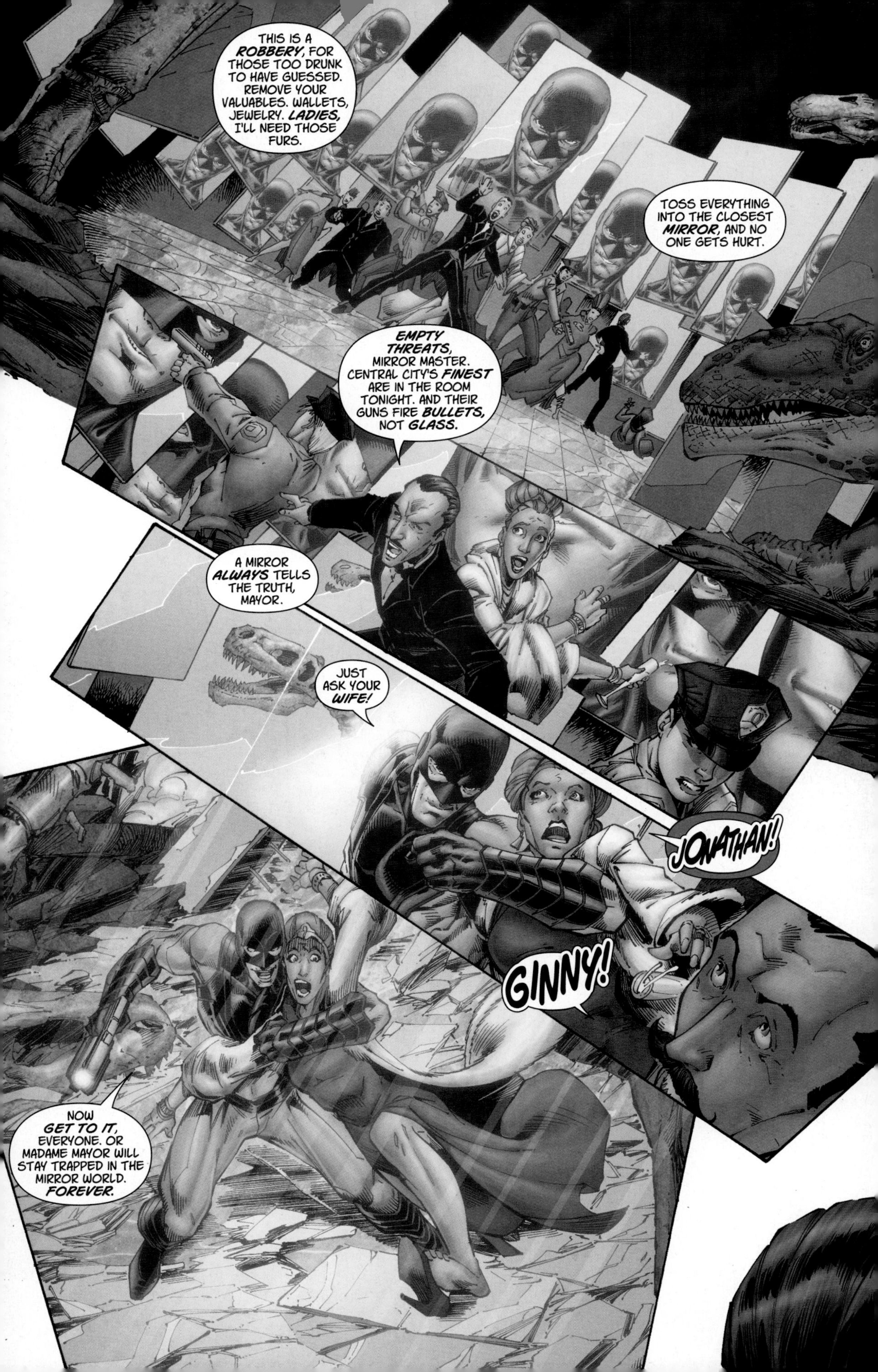
THIS IS A ROBBERY, FOR THOSE TOO DRUNK TO HAVE GUESSED. REMOVE YOUR VALUABLES. WALLETS, JEWELRY. LADIES, I'LL NEED THOSE FURS.
TOSS EVERYTHING INTO THE CLOSEST MIRROR, AND NO ONE GETS HURT.
EMPTY THREATS, MIRROR MASTER. CENTRAL CITY'S FINEST ARE IN THE ROOM TONIGHT. AND THEIR GUNS FIRE BULLETS, NOT GLASS.
A MIRROR ALWAYS TELLS THE TRUTH, MAYOR.
JUST ASK YOUR WIFE!
JONATHAN!
GINNY!
NOW GET TO IT, EVERYONE. OR MADAME MAYOR WILL STAY TRAPPED IN THE MIRROR WORLD. FOREVER.

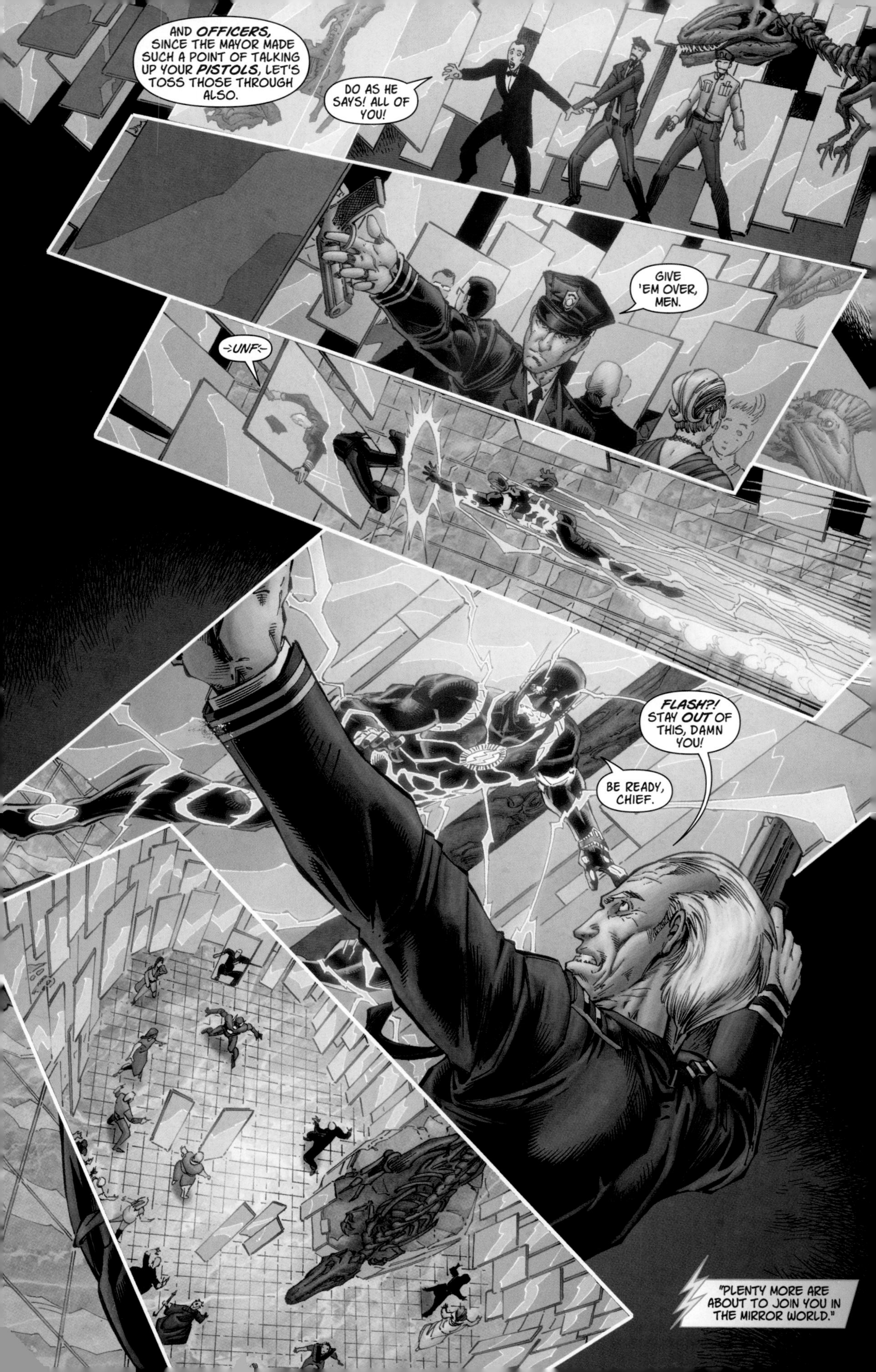
AND OFFICERS, SINCE THE MAYOR MADE SUCH A POINT OF TALKING UP YOUR PISTOLS, LET'S TOSS THOSE THROUGH ALSO.
DO AS HE SAYS! ALL OF YOU!
GIVE 'EM OVER, MEN.
-UNF-
FLASH?! STAY OUT OF THIS, DAMN YOU!
BE READY, CHIEF.
"PLENTY MORE ARE ABOUT TO JOIN YOU IN THE MIRROR WORLD."

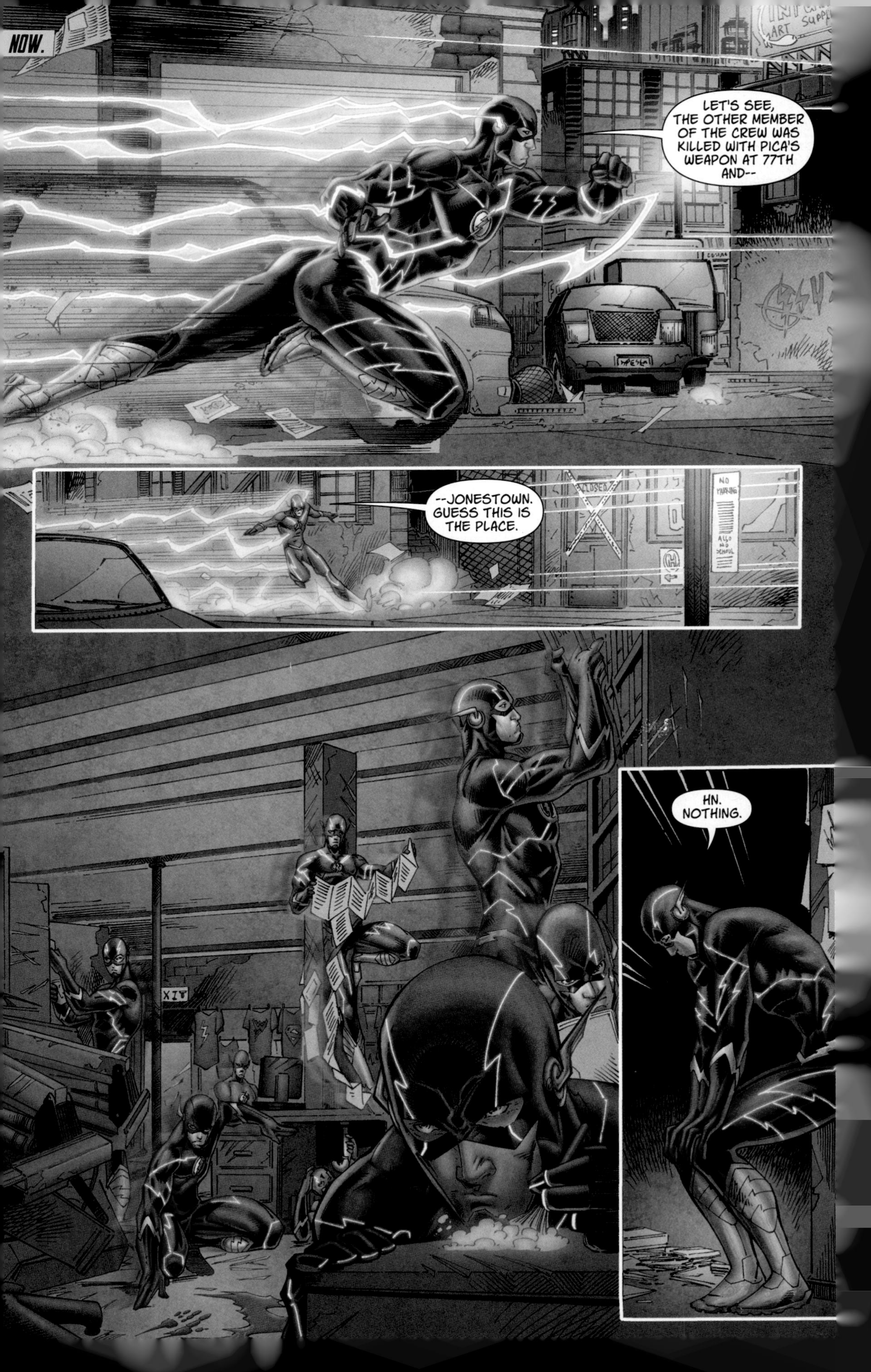
NOW.
LET'S SEE, THE OTHER MEMBER OF THE CREW WAS KILLED WITH PICA'S WEAPON AT 77TH AND--
--JONESTOWN. GUESS THIS IS THE PLACE.
CLOSED
NO PARKING
HN. NOTHING.

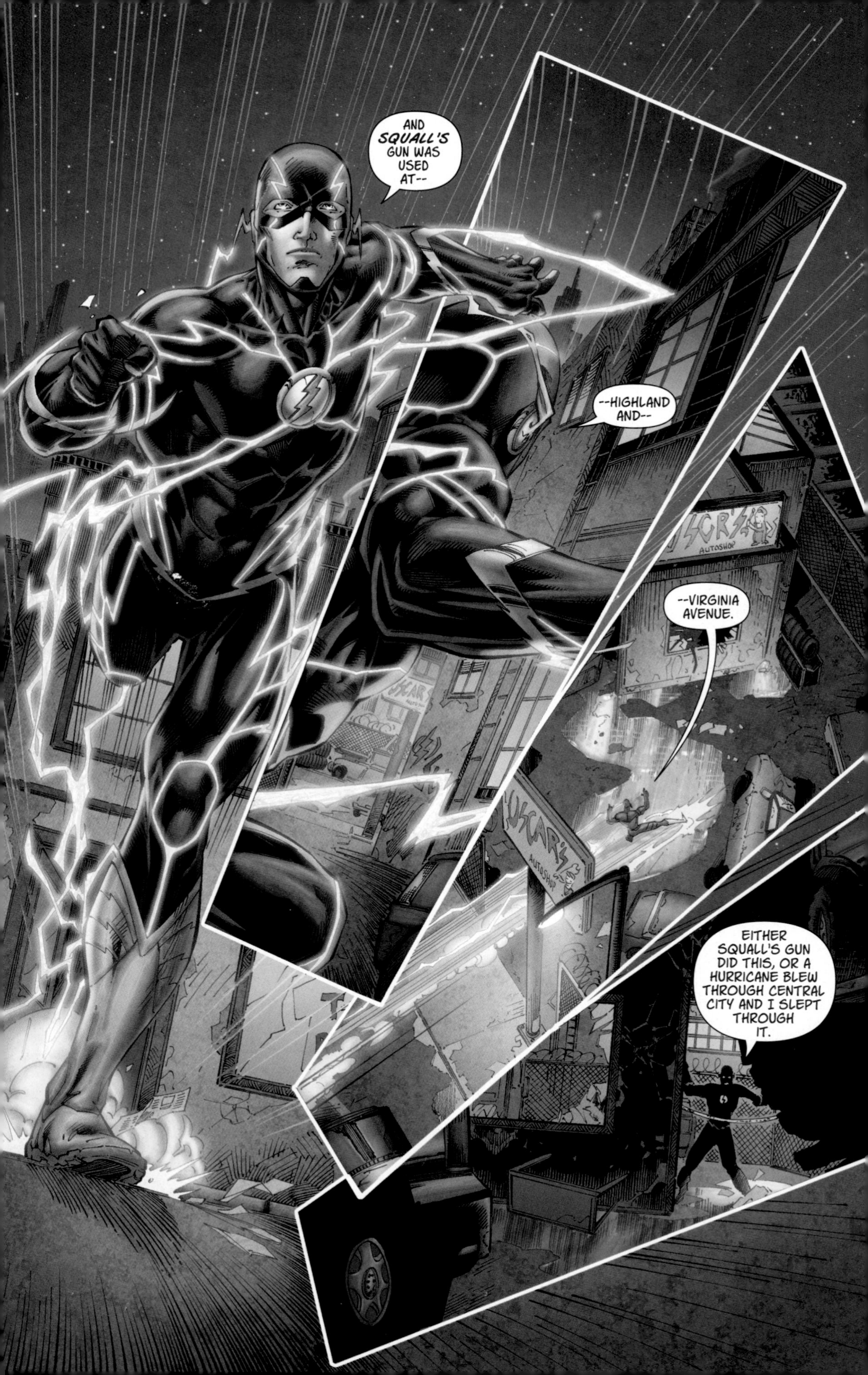
AND SQUALL'S GUN WAS USED AT--
--HIGHLAND AND--
--VIRGINIA AVENUE.
EITHER SQUALL'S GUN DID THIS, OR A HURRICANE BLEW THROUGH CENTRAL CITY AND I SLEPT THROUGH IT.

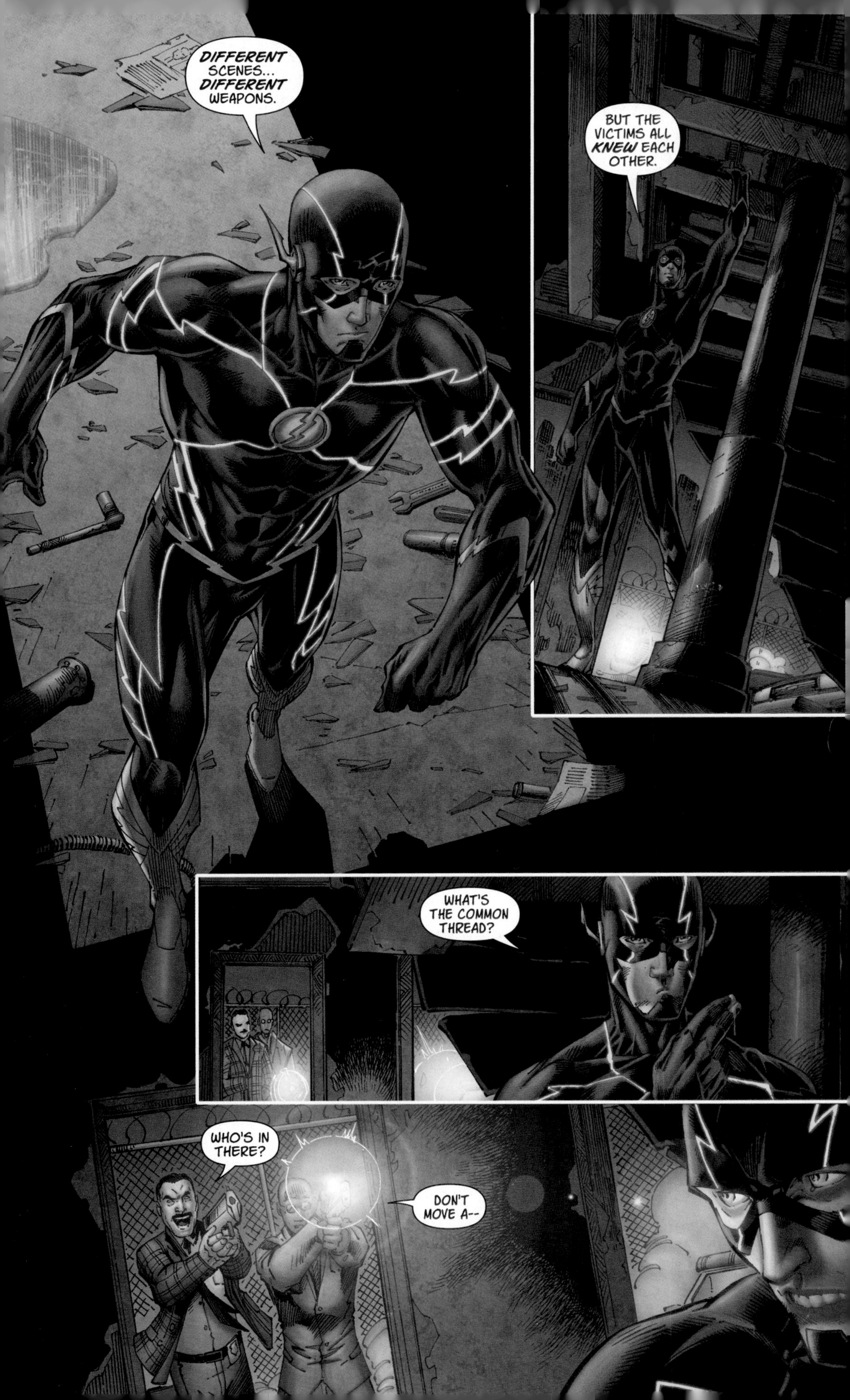
DIFFERENT SCENES... DIFFERENT WEAPONS.
BUT THE VICTIMS ALL KNEW EACH OTHER.
WHAT'S THE COMMON THREAD?
WHO'S IN THERE?
DON'T MOVE A--

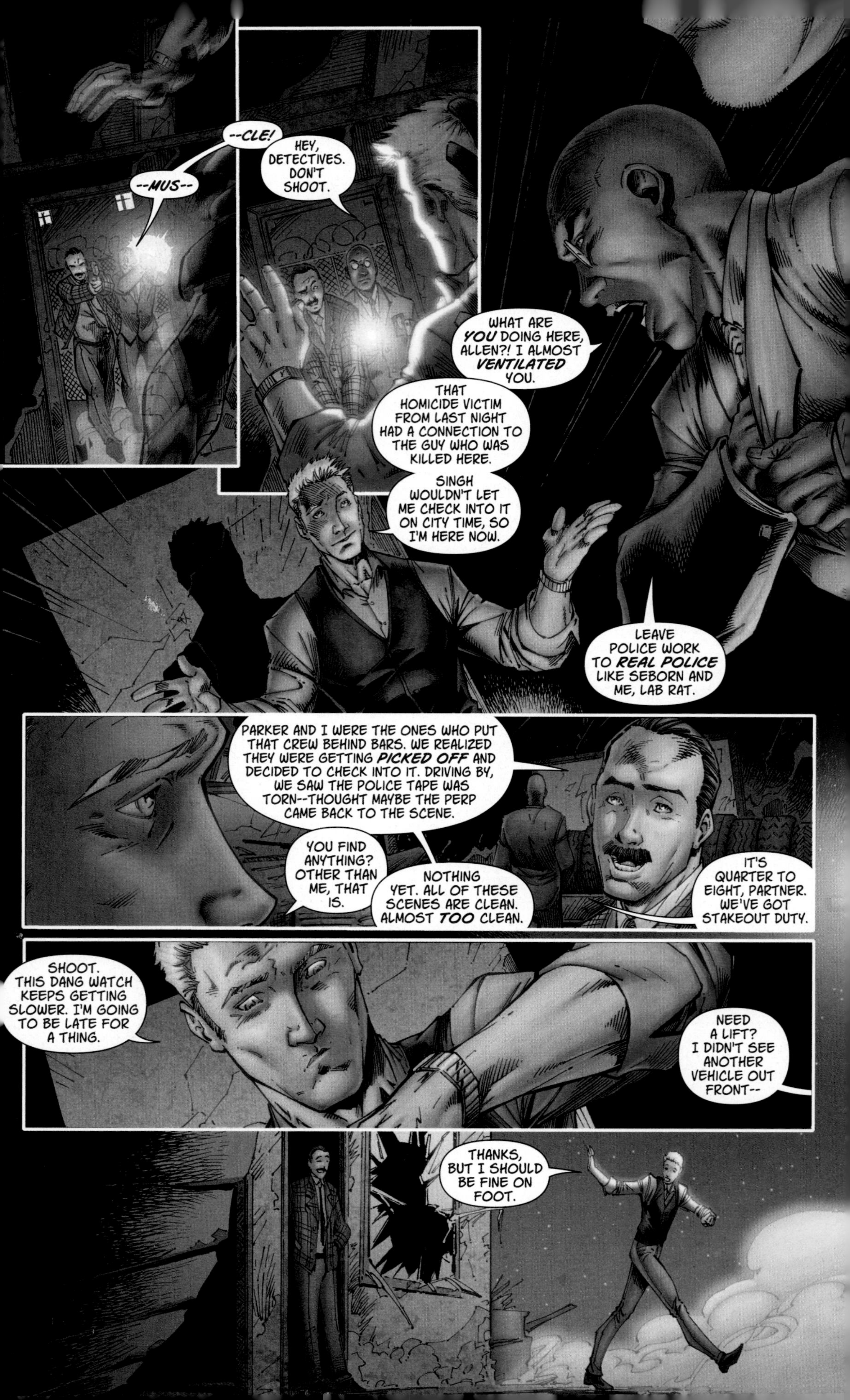
--MUS--
--CLE!
HEY, DETECTIVES. DON'T SHOOT.
WHAT ARE *YOU* DOING HERE, ALLEN?! I ALMOST *VENTILATED* YOU.
THAT HOMICIDE VICTIM FROM LAST NIGHT HAD A CONNECTION TO THE GUY WHO WAS KILLED HERE.
SINGH WOULDN'T LET ME CHECK INTO IT ON CITY TIME, SO I'M HERE NOW.
LEAVE POLICE WORK TO *REAL POLICE* LIKE SEBORN AND ME, LAB RAT.
PARKER AND I WERE THE ONES WHO PUT THAT CREW BEHIND BARS. WE REALIZED THEY WERE GETTING *PICKED OFF* AND DECIDED TO CHECK INTO IT. DRIVING BY, WE SAW THE POLICE TAPE WAS TORN--THOUGHT MAYBE THE PERP CAME BACK TO THE SCENE.
YOU FIND ANYTHING? OTHER THAN ME, THAT IS.
NOTHING YET. ALL OF THESE SCENES ARE CLEAN. ALMOST *TOO* CLEAN.
IT'S QUARTER TO EIGHT, PARTNER. WE'VE GOT STAKEOUT DUTY.
SHOOT. THIS DANG WATCH KEEPS GETTING SLOWER. I'M GOING TO BE LATE FOR A THING.
NEED A LIFT? I DIDN'T SEE ANOTHER VEHICLE OUT FRONT--
THANKS, BUT I SHOULD BE FINE ON FOOT.

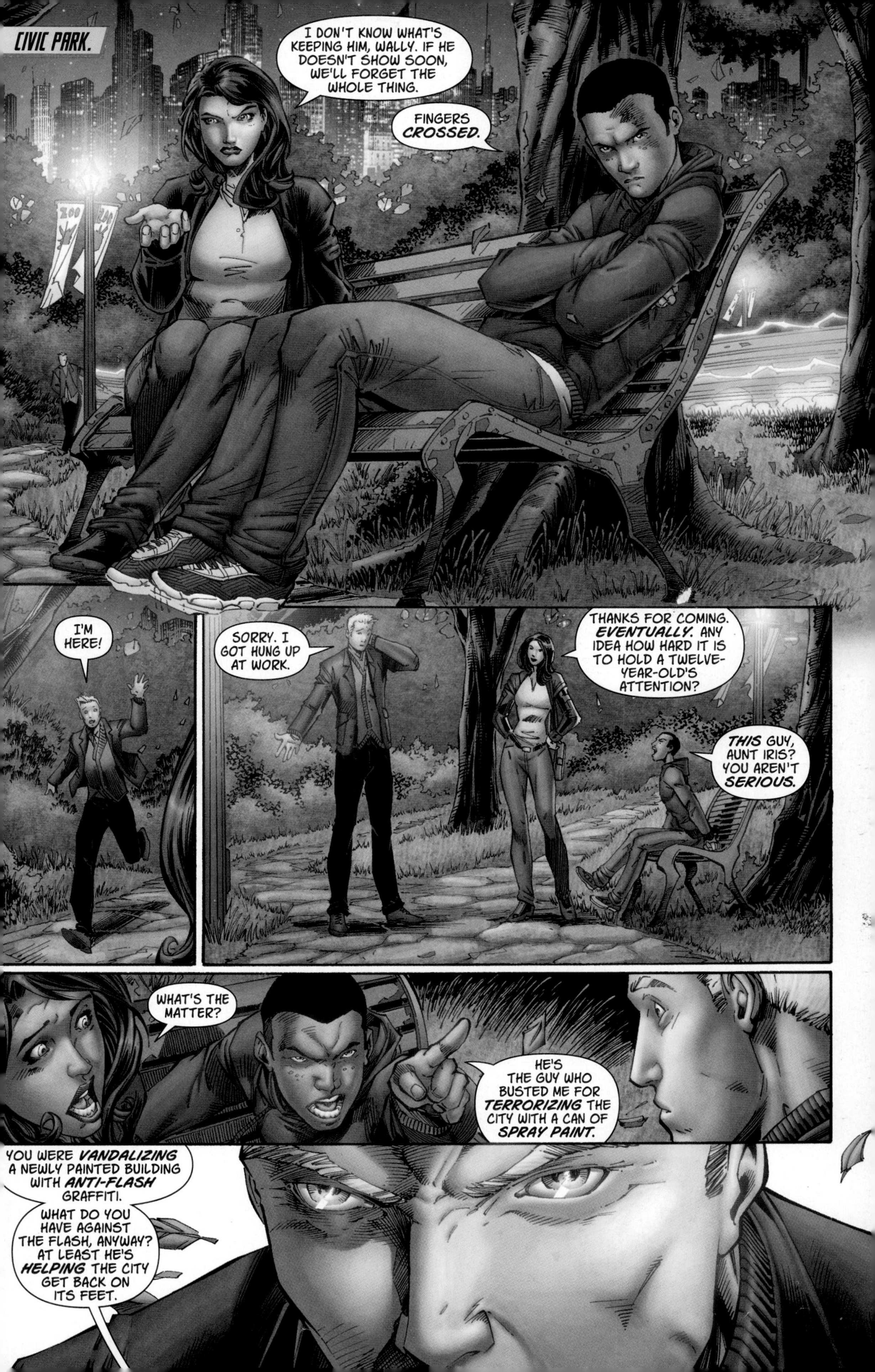
CIVIC PARK.
I DON'T KNOW WHAT'S KEEPING HIM, WALLY. IF HE DOESN'T SHOW SOON, WE'LL FORGET THE WHOLE THING.
FINGERS CROSSED.
I'M HERE!
SORRY. I GOT HUNG UP AT WORK.
THANKS FOR COMING. EVENTUALLY. ANY IDEA HOW HARD IT IS TO HOLD A TWELVE-YEAR-OLD'S ATTENTION?
THIS GUY, AUNT IRIS? YOU AREN'T SERIOUS.
WHAT'S THE MATTER?
HE'S THE GUY WHO BUSTED ME FOR TERRORIZING THE CITY WITH A CAN OF SPRAY PAINT.
YOU WERE VANDALIZING A NEWLY PAINTED BUILDING WITH ANTI-FLASH GRAFFITI.
WHAT DO YOU HAVE AGAINST THE FLASH, ANYWAY? AT LEAST HE'S HELPING THE CITY GET BACK ON ITS FEET.

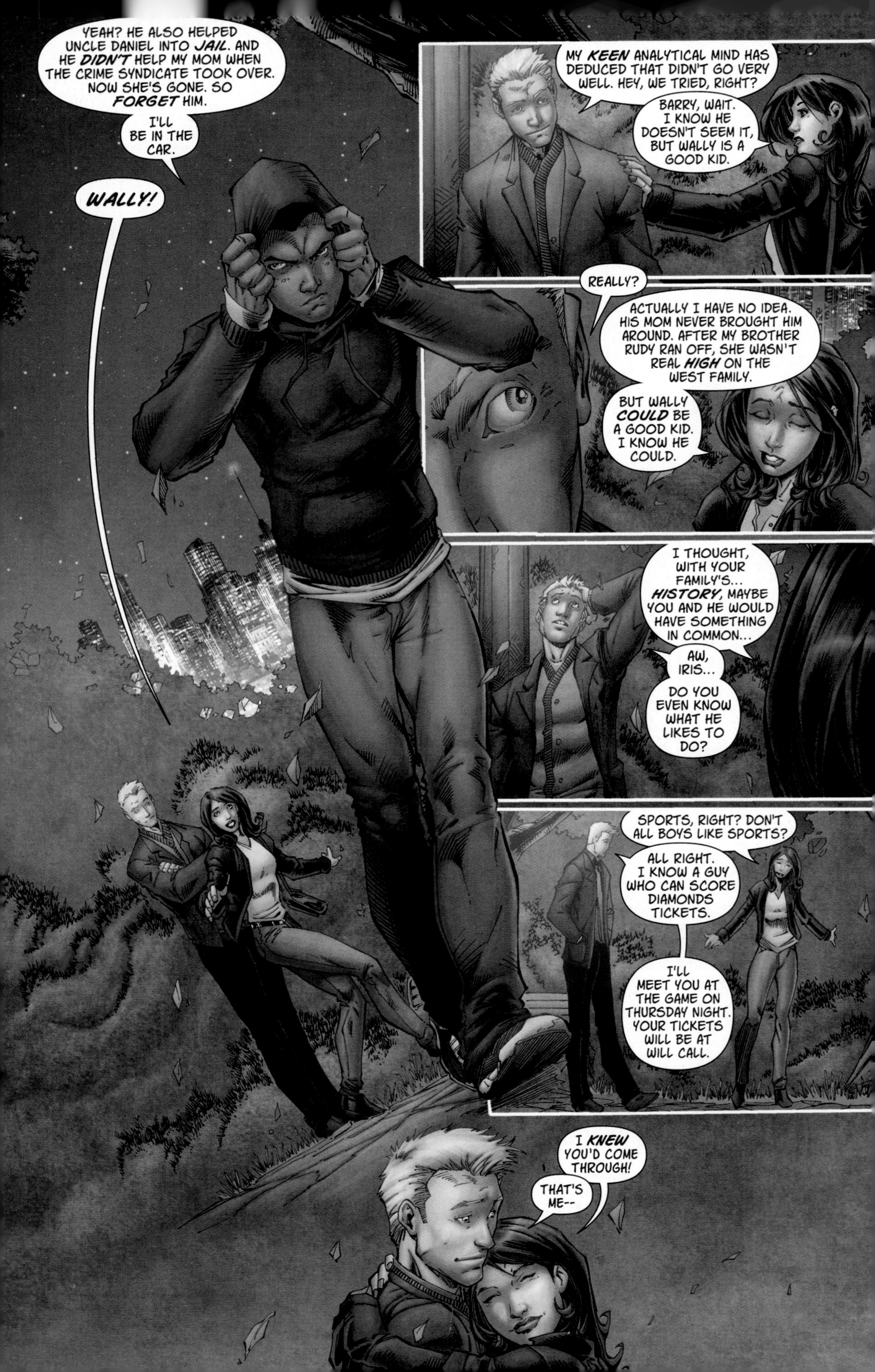
YEAH? HE ALSO HELPED UNCLE DANIEL INTO JAIL. AND HE DIDN'T HELP MY MOM WHEN THE CRIME SYNDICATE TOOK OVER. NOW SHE'S GONE. SO FORGET HIM.
I'LL BE IN THE CAR.
WALLY!
MY KEEN ANALYTICAL MIND HAS DEDUCED THAT DIDN'T GO VERY WELL. HEY, WE TRIED, RIGHT?
BARRY, WAIT. I KNOW HE DOESN'T SEEM IT, BUT WALLY IS A GOOD KID.
REALLY?
ACTUALLY I HAVE NO IDEA. HIS MOM NEVER BROUGHT HIM AROUND. AFTER MY BROTHER RUDY RAN OFF, SHE WASN'T REAL HIGH ON THE WEST FAMILY.
BUT WALLY COULD BE A GOOD KID. I KNOW HE COULD.
I THOUGHT, WITH YOUR FAMILY'S... HISTORY, MAYBE YOU AND HE WOULD HAVE SOMETHING IN COMMON...
AW, IRIS...
DO YOU EVEN KNOW WHAT HE LIKES TO DO?
SPORTS, RIGHT? DON'T ALL BOYS LIKE SPORTS?
ALL RIGHT. I KNOW A GUY WHO CAN SCORE DIAMONDS TICKETS.
I'LL MEET YOU AT THE GAME ON THURSDAY NIGHT. YOUR TICKETS WILL BE AT WILL CALL.
I KNEW YOU'D COME THROUGH!
THAT'S ME--

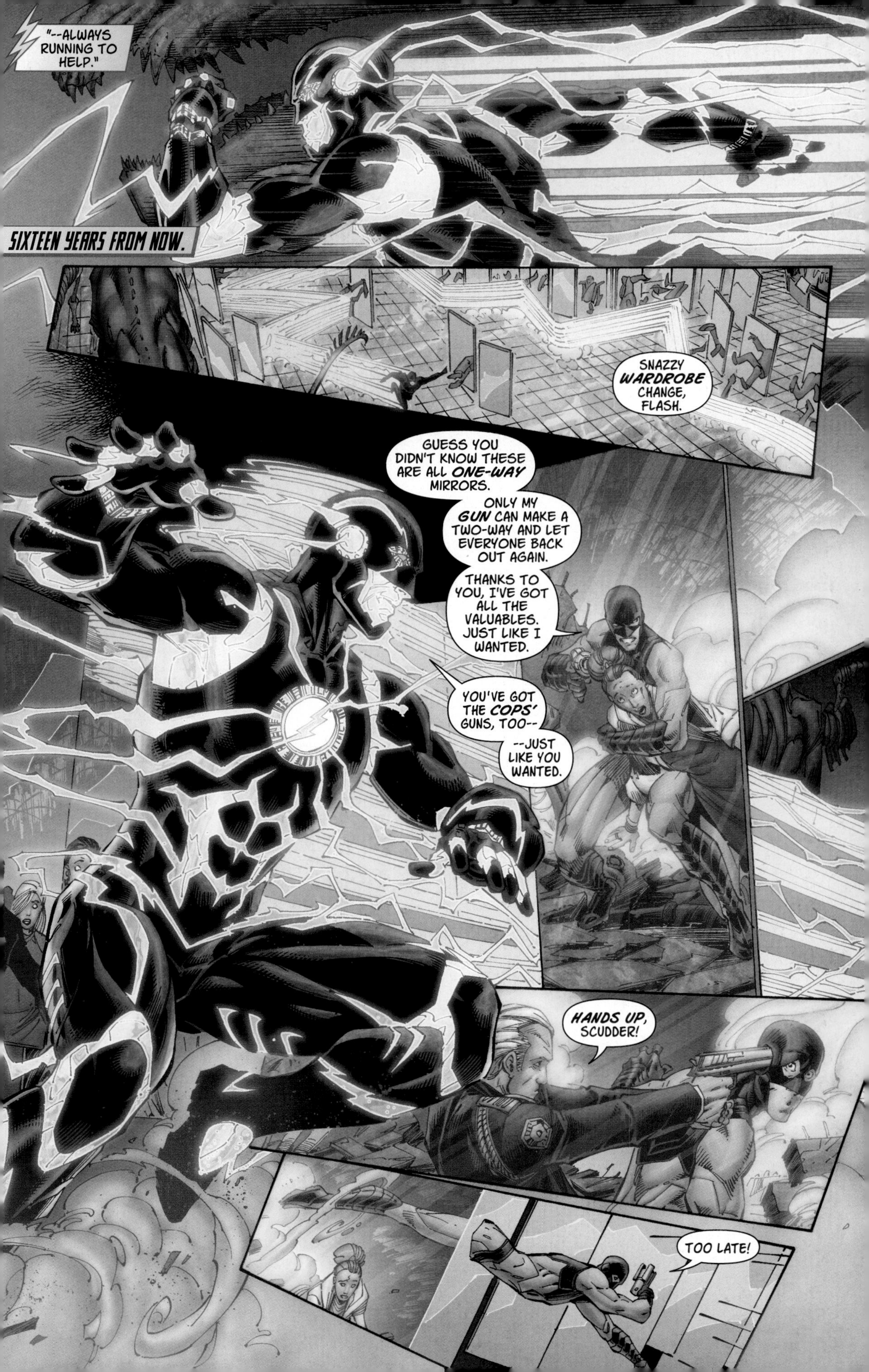
"--ALWAYS RUNNING TO HELP."
SIXTEEN YEARS FROM NOW.
SNAZZY WARDROBE CHANGE, FLASH.
GUESS YOU DIDN'T KNOW THESE ARE ALL ONE-WAY MIRRORS.
ONLY MY GUN CAN MAKE A TWO-WAY AND LET EVERYONE BACK OUT AGAIN.
THANKS TO YOU, I'VE GOT ALL THE VALUABLES. JUST LIKE I WANTED.
YOU'VE GOT THE COPS' GUNS, TOO--
--JUST LIKE YOU WANTED.
HANDS UP, SCUDDER!
TOO LATE!

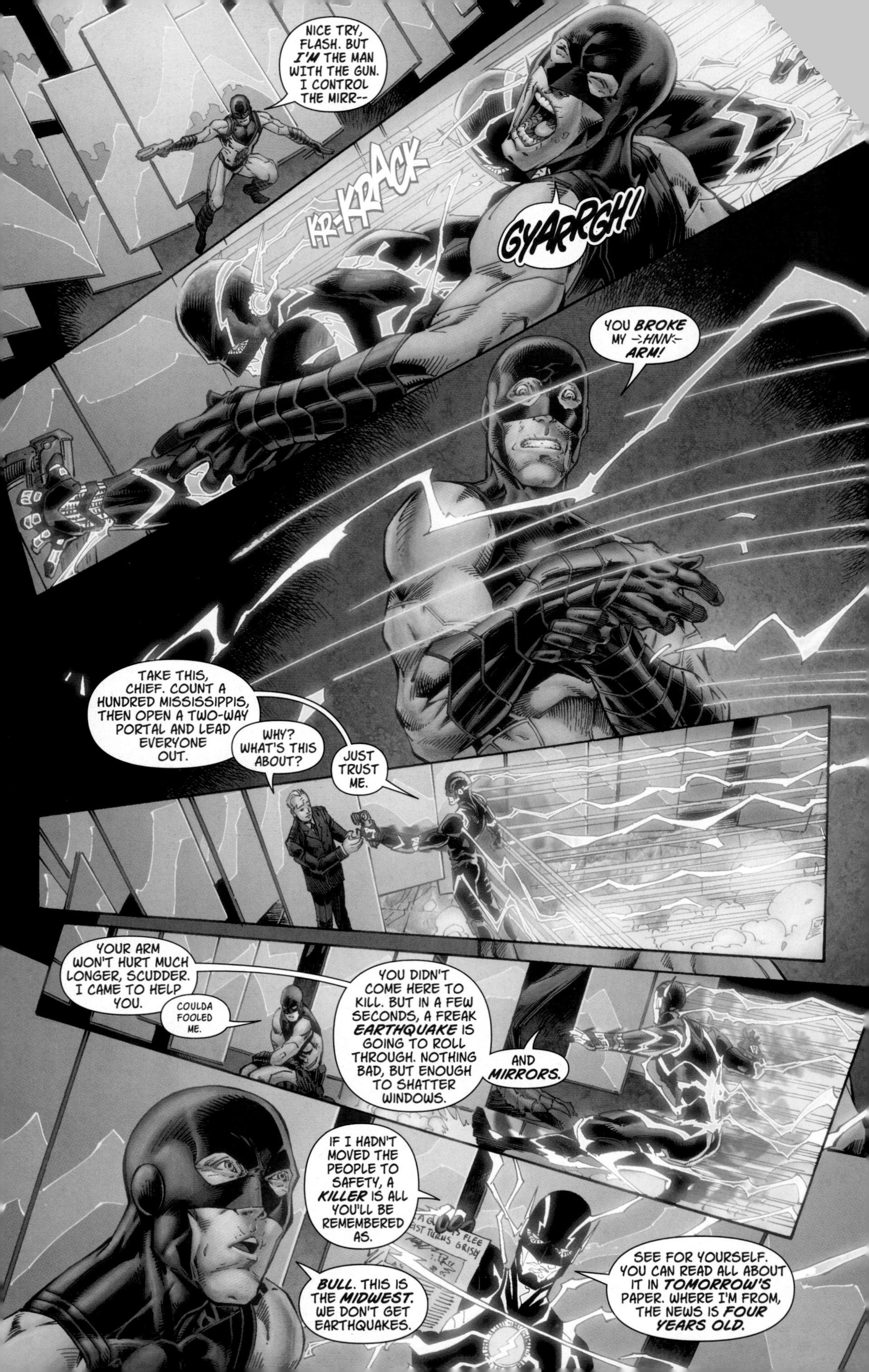
NICE TRY, FLASH. BUT I'M THE MAN WITH THE GUN. I CONTROL THE MIRR--
KR-KRACK
GYARRGH!
YOU BROKE MY -HNN- ARM!
TAKE THIS, CHIEF. COUNT A HUNDRED MISSISSIPPIS, THEN OPEN A TWO-WAY PORTAL AND LEAD EVERYONE OUT.
WHY? WHAT'S THIS ABOUT?
JUST TRUST ME.
YOUR ARM WON'T HURT MUCH LONGER, SCUDDER. I CAME TO HELP YOU.
COULDA FOOLED ME.
YOU DIDN'T COME HERE TO KILL. BUT IN A FEW SECONDS, A FREAK EARTHQUAKE IS GOING TO ROLL THROUGH. NOTHING BAD, BUT ENOUGH TO SHATTER WINDOWS.
AND MIRRORS.
IF I HADN'T MOVED THE PEOPLE TO SAFETY, A KILLER IS ALL YOU'LL BE REMEMBERED AS.
BULL. THIS IS THE MIDWEST. WE DON'T GET EARTHQUAKES.
SEE FOR YOURSELF. YOU CAN READ ALL ABOUT IT IN TOMORROW'S PAPER. WHERE I'M FROM, THE NEWS IS FOUR YEARS OLD.

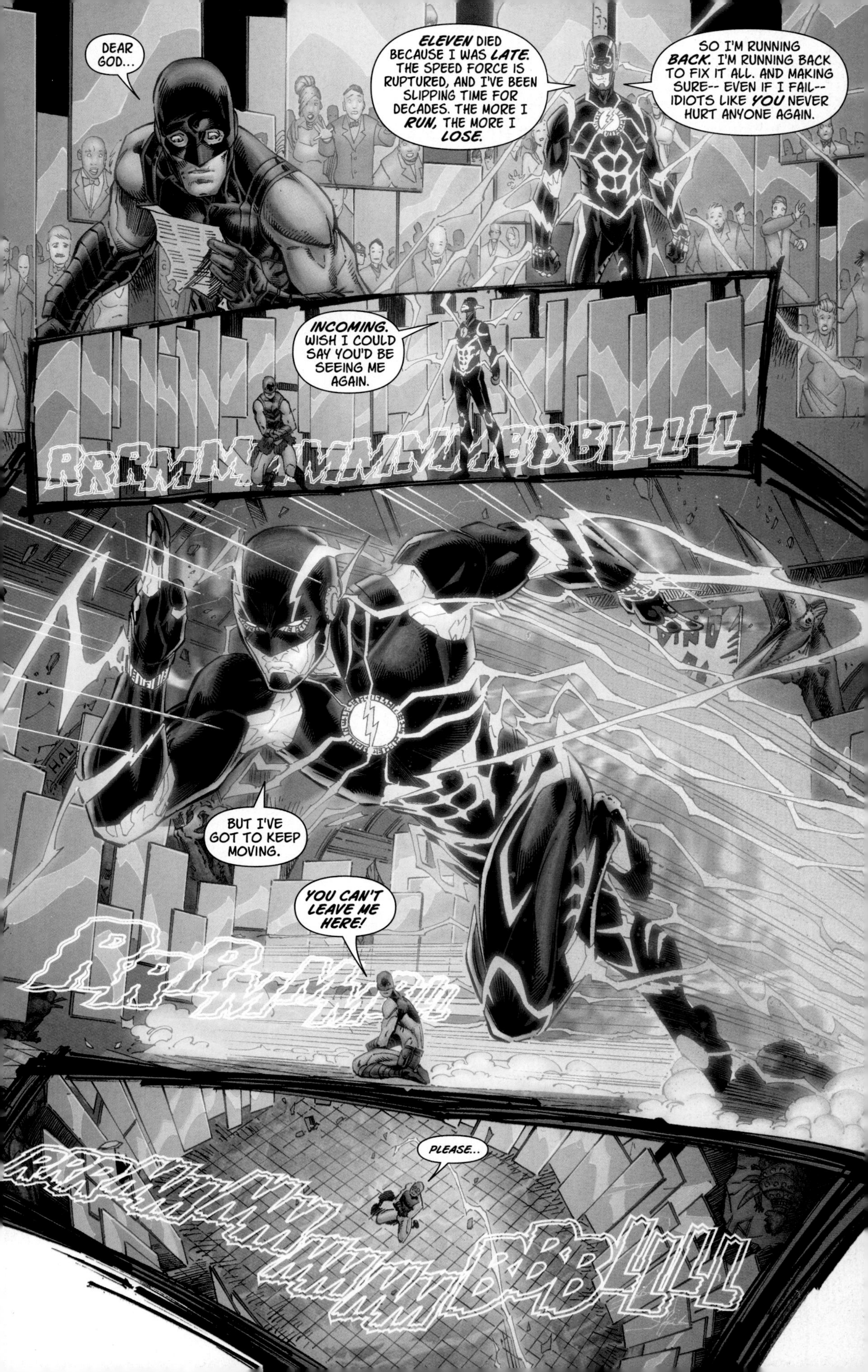
DEAR GOD...
ELEVEN DIED BECAUSE I WAS LATE. THE SPEED FORCE IS RUPTURED, AND I'VE BEEN SLIPPING TIME FOR DECADES. THE MORE I RUN, THE MORE I LOSE.
SO I'M RUNNING BACK. I'M RUNNING BACK TO FIX IT ALL. AND MAKING SURE-- EVEN IF I FAIL-- IDIOTS LIKE YOU NEVER HURT ANYONE AGAIN.
INCOMING. WISH I COULD SAY YOU'D BE SEEING ME AGAIN.
RRRMMMMMMMMBBBLLL-L
BUT I'VE GOT TO KEEP MOVING.
YOU CAN'T LEAVE ME HERE!
PLEASE...

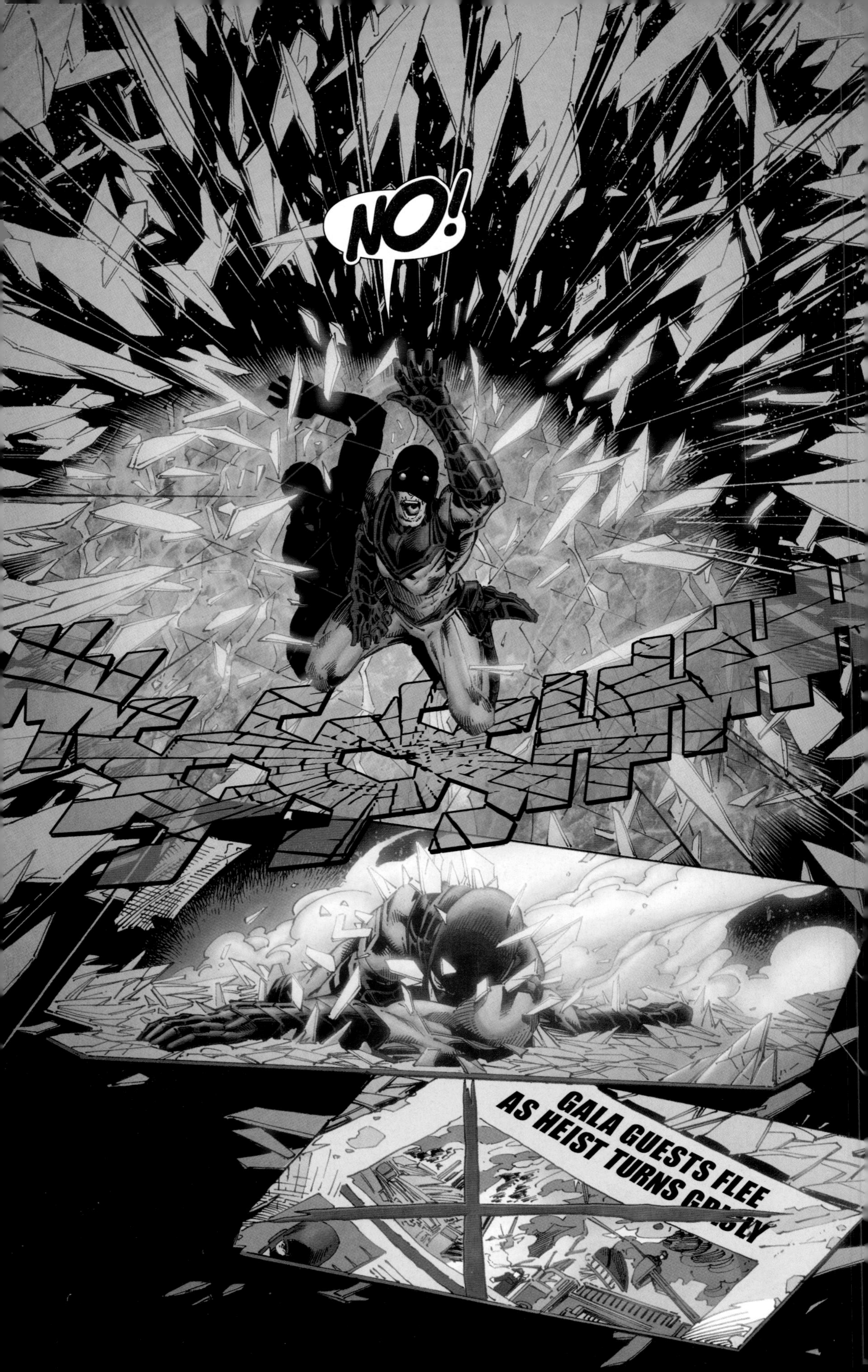
NO!
GALA GUESTS FLEE
AS HEIST TURNS

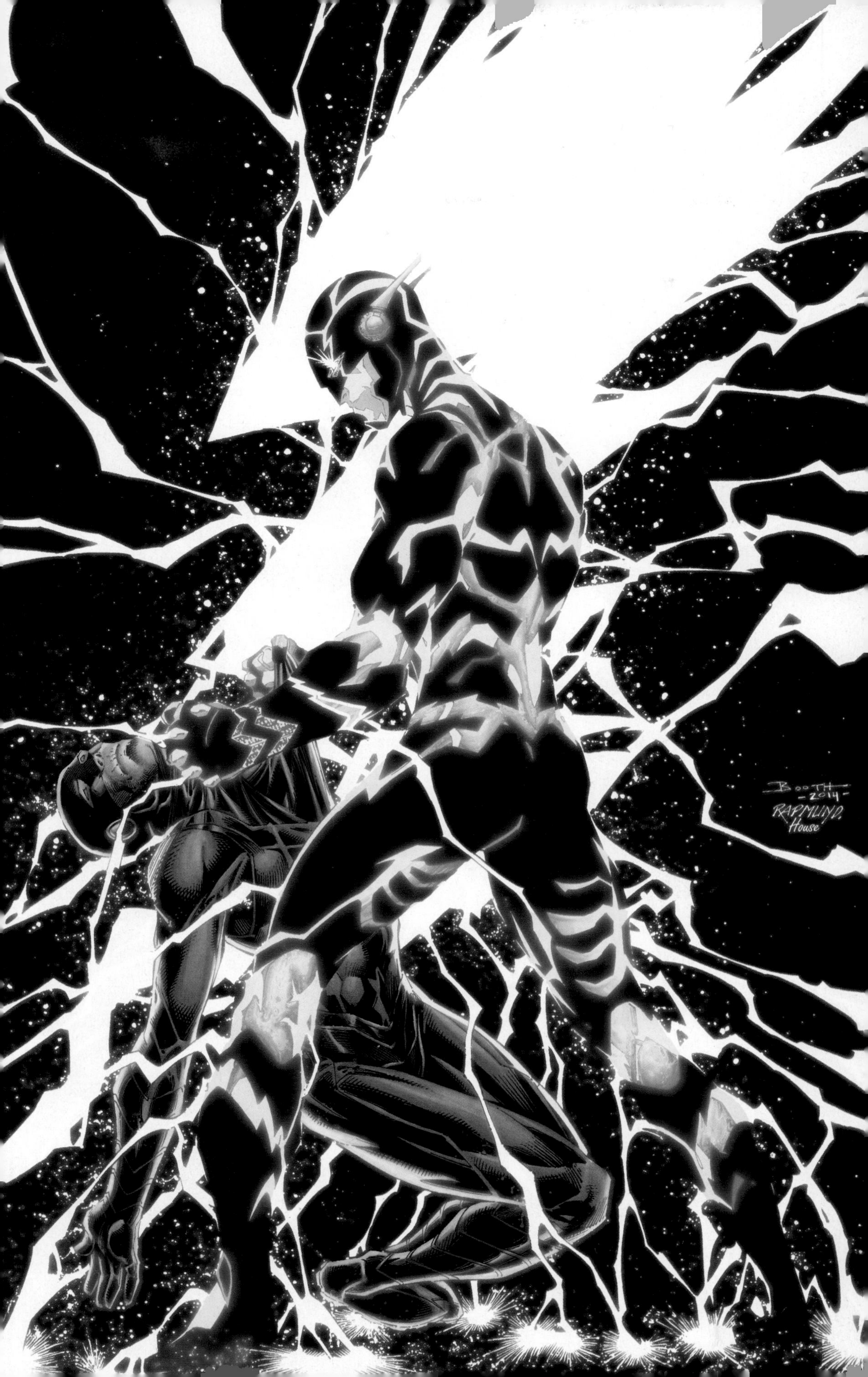
BOOTH
-2014-
RAPMUND
House

COLD CALL

ROBERT VENDITTI & VAN JENSEN writers BRETT BOOTH penciller NORM RAPMUND inker

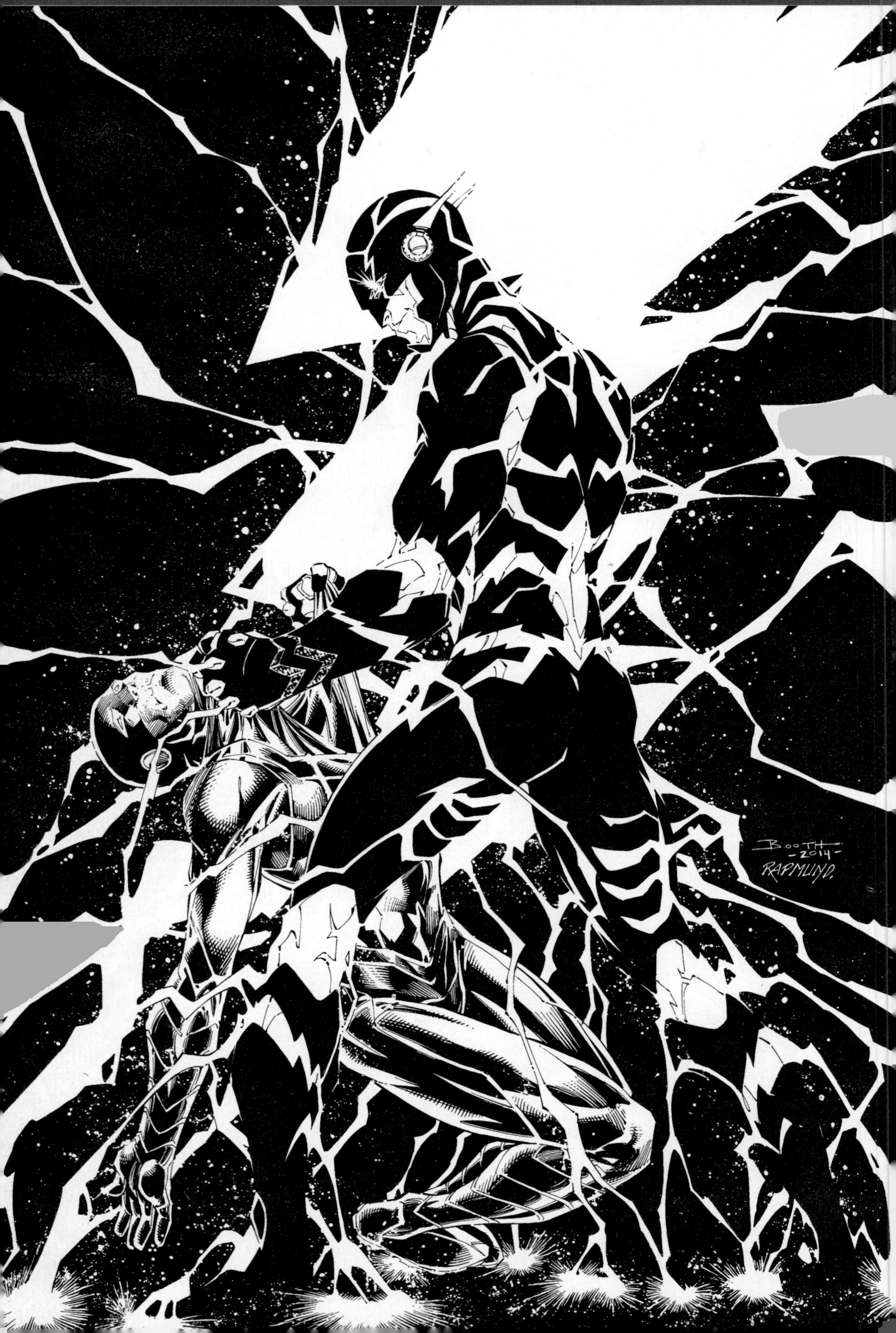
BOOTH -2014-
RAPMUND.

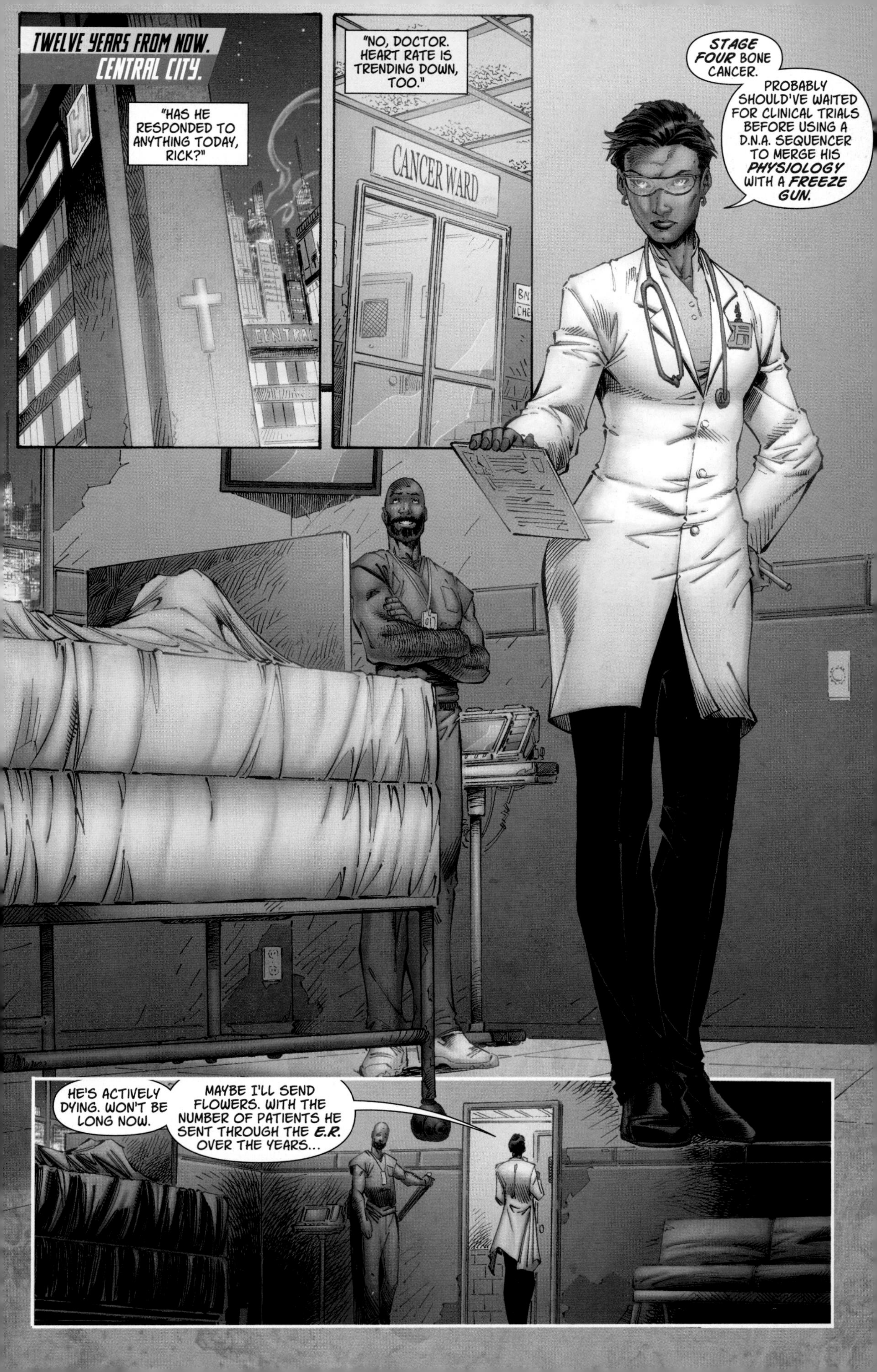
TWELVE YEARS FROM NOW.
CENTRAL CITY.
"HAS HE RESPONDED TO ANYTHING TODAY, RICK?"
CENTRAL
"NO, DOCTOR. HEART RATE IS TRENDING DOWN, TOO."
CANCER WARD
STAGE FOUR BONE CANCER.
PROBABLY SHOULD'VE WAITED FOR CLINICAL TRIALS BEFORE USING A D.N.A. SEQUENCER TO MERGE HIS PHYSIOLOGY WITH A FREEZE GUN.
HE'S ACTIVELY DYING. WON'T BE LONG NOW.
MAYBE I'LL SEND FLOWERS. WITH THE NUMBER OF PATIENTS HE SENT THROUGH THE E.R. OVER THE YEARS...

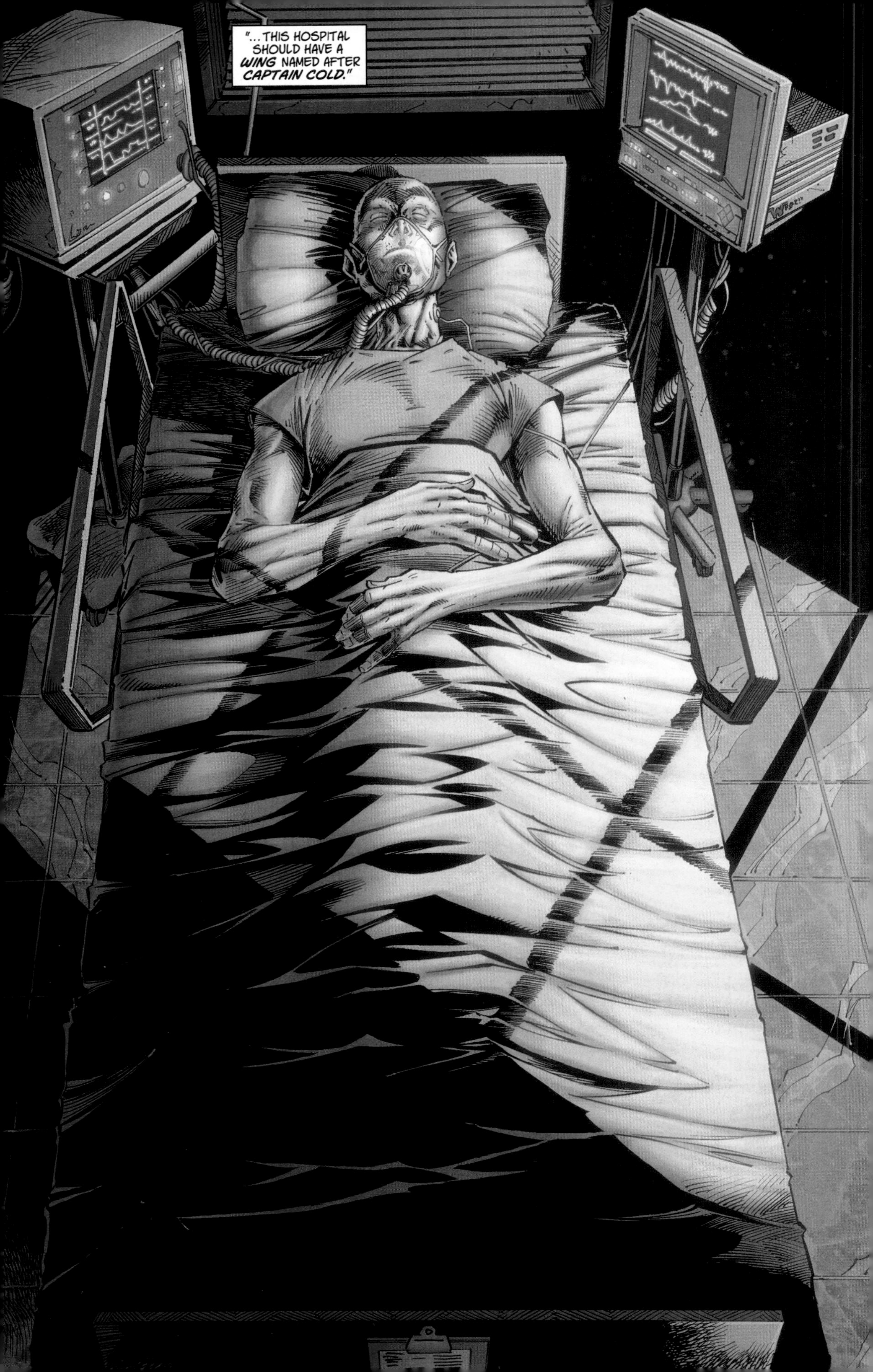
"...THIS HOSPITAL SHOULD HAVE A WING NAMED AFTER CAPTAIN COLD."

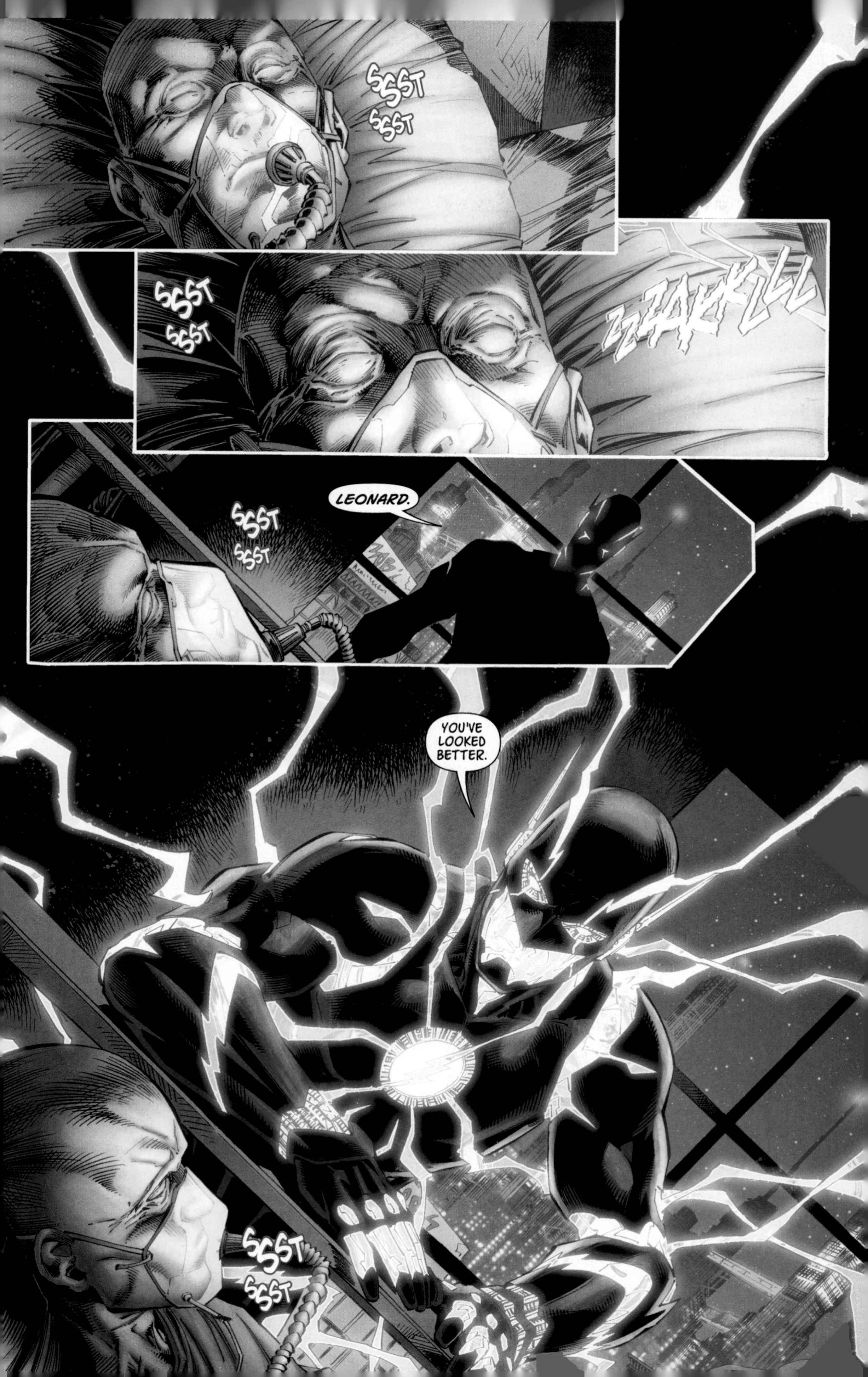
SSST
SSST
SSST
SSST
ZZZAKKLLL
SSST
SSST
LEONARD.
YOU'VE LOOKED BETTER.
SSST
SSST

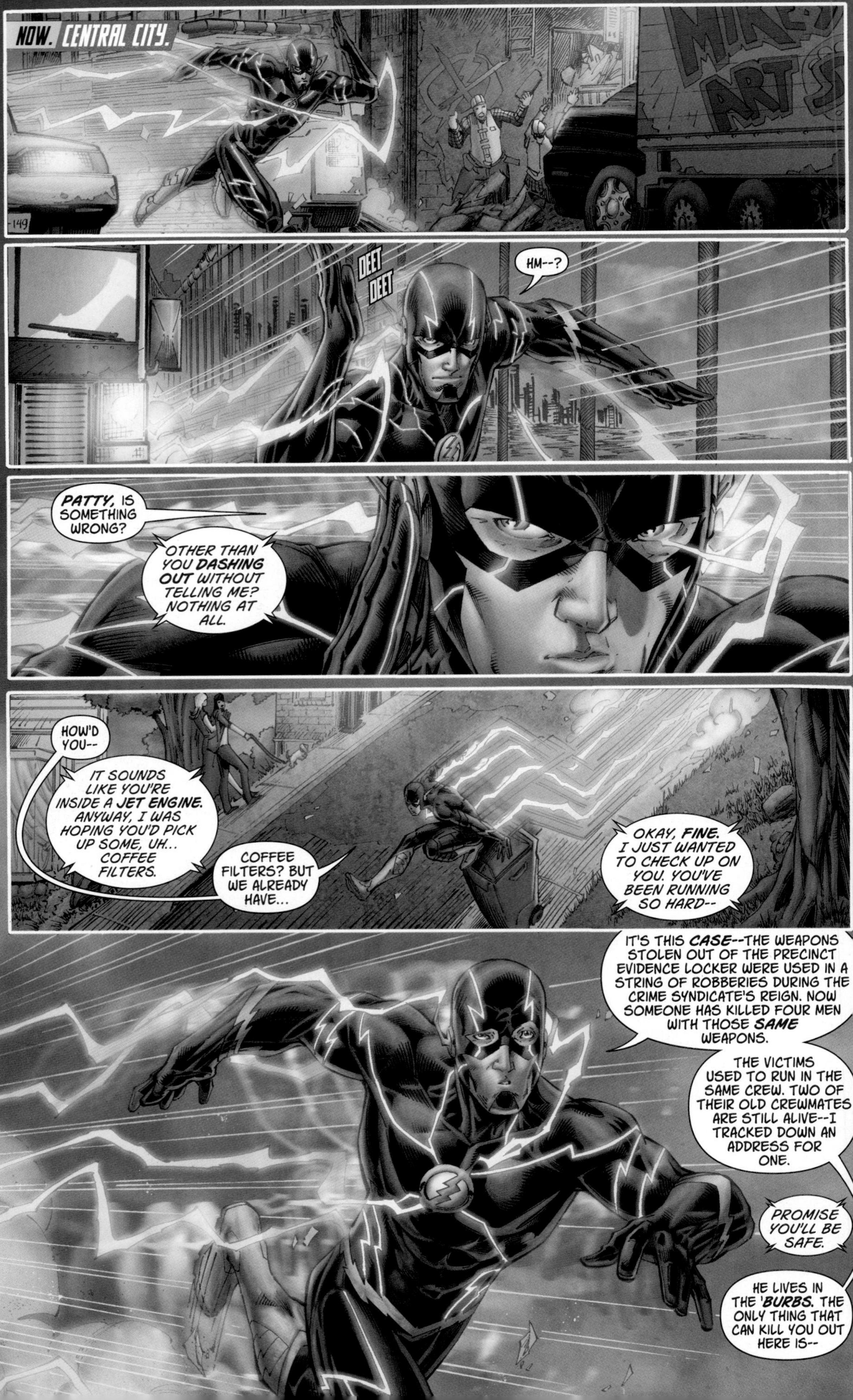
NOW. CENTRAL CITY.
DEET DEET
HM--?
PATTY, IS SOMETHING WRONG?
OTHER THAN YOU DASHING OUT WITHOUT TELLING ME? NOTHING AT ALL.
HOW'D YOU--
IT SOUNDS LIKE YOU'RE INSIDE A JET ENGINE. ANYWAY, I WAS HOPING YOU'D PICK UP SOME, UH... COFFEE FILTERS.
COFFEE FILTERS? BUT WE ALREADY HAVE...
OKAY, FINE. I JUST WANTED TO CHECK UP ON YOU. YOU'VE BEEN RUNNING SO HARD--
IT'S THIS CASE--THE WEAPONS STOLEN OUT OF THE PRECINCT EVIDENCE LOCKER WERE USED IN A STRING OF ROBBERIES DURING THE CRIME SYNDICATE'S REIGN. NOW SOMEONE HAS KILLED FOUR MEN WITH THOSE SAME WEAPONS.
THE VICTIMS USED TO RUN IN THE SAME CREW. TWO OF THEIR OLD CREWMATES ARE STILL ALIVE--I TRACKED DOWN AN ADDRESS FOR ONE.
PROMISE YOU'LL BE SAFE.
HE LIVES IN THE 'BURBS. THE ONLY THING THAT CAN KILL YOU OUT HERE IS--

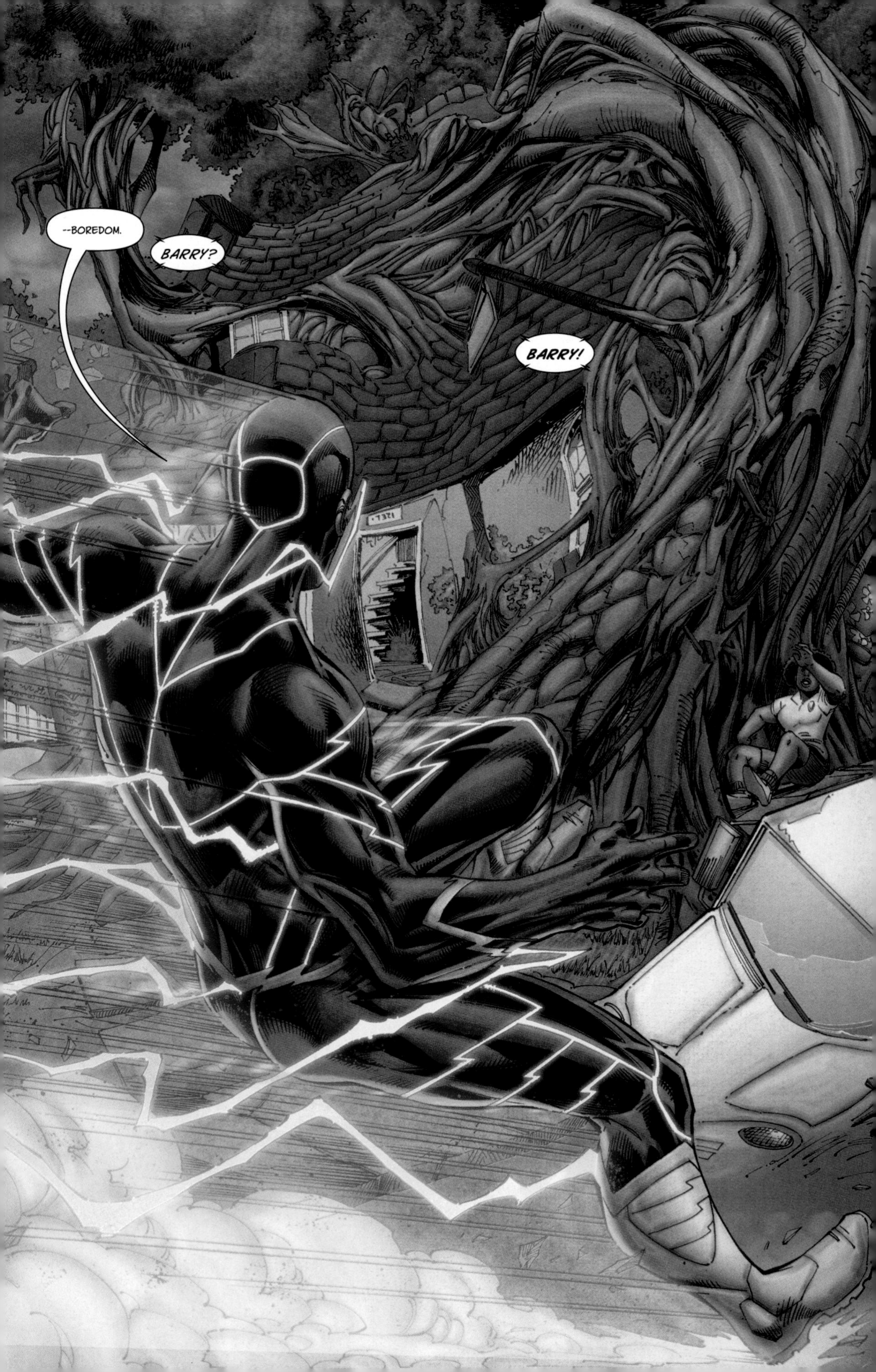
--BOREDOM.
BARRY?
BARRY!

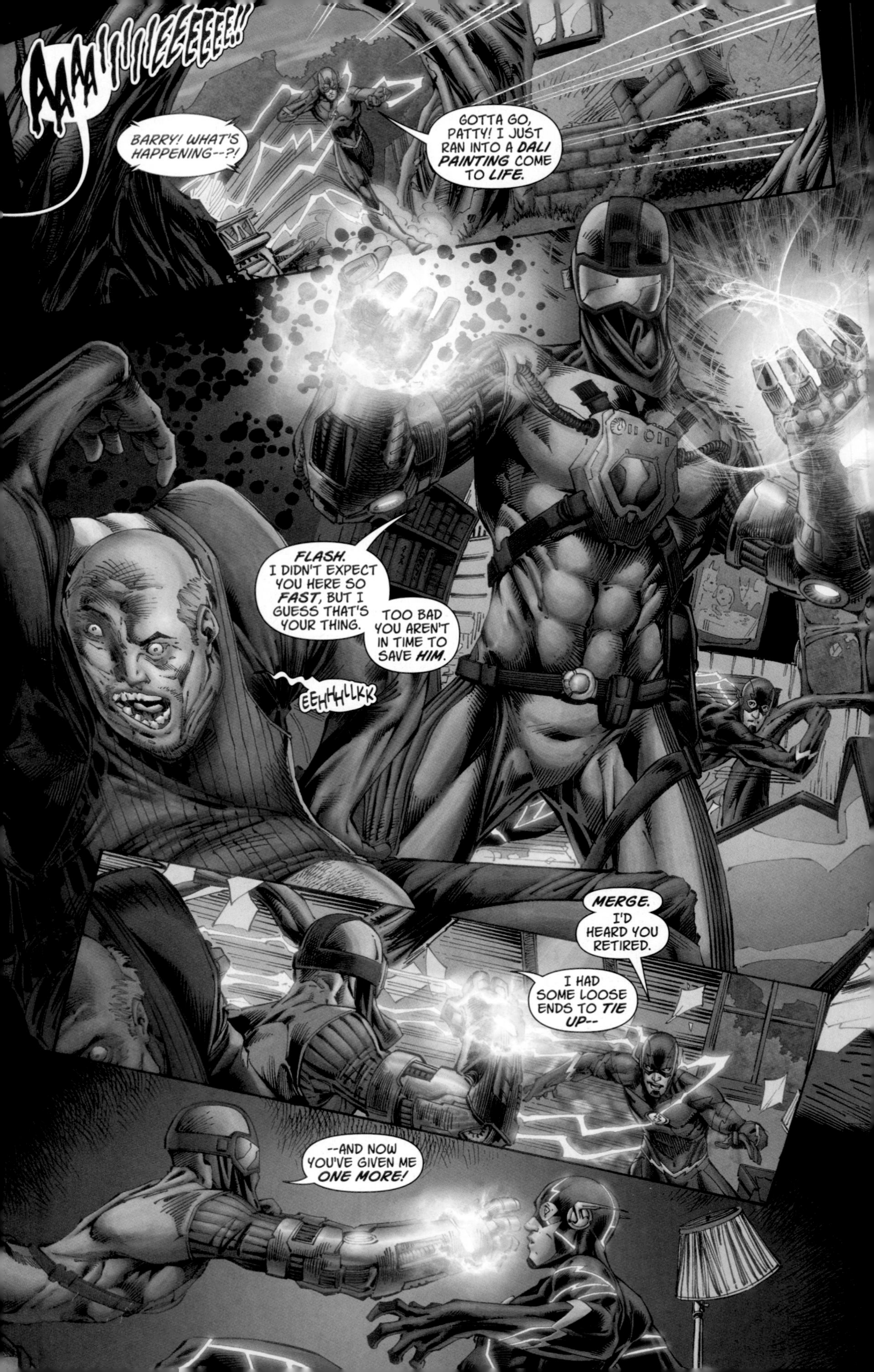
AAAAIIIIIEEEEEE!!
BARRY! WHAT'S HAPPENING--?!
GOTTA GO, PATTY! I JUST RAN INTO A DALI PAINTING COME TO LIFE.
FLASH. I DIDN'T EXPECT YOU HERE SO FAST, BUT I GUESS THAT'S YOUR THING.
TOO BAD YOU AREN'T IN TIME TO SAVE HIM.
EEHHHLLKK
MERGE. I'D HEARD YOU RETIRED.
I HAD SOME LOOSE ENDS TO TIE UP--
--AND NOW YOU'VE GIVEN ME ONE MORE!

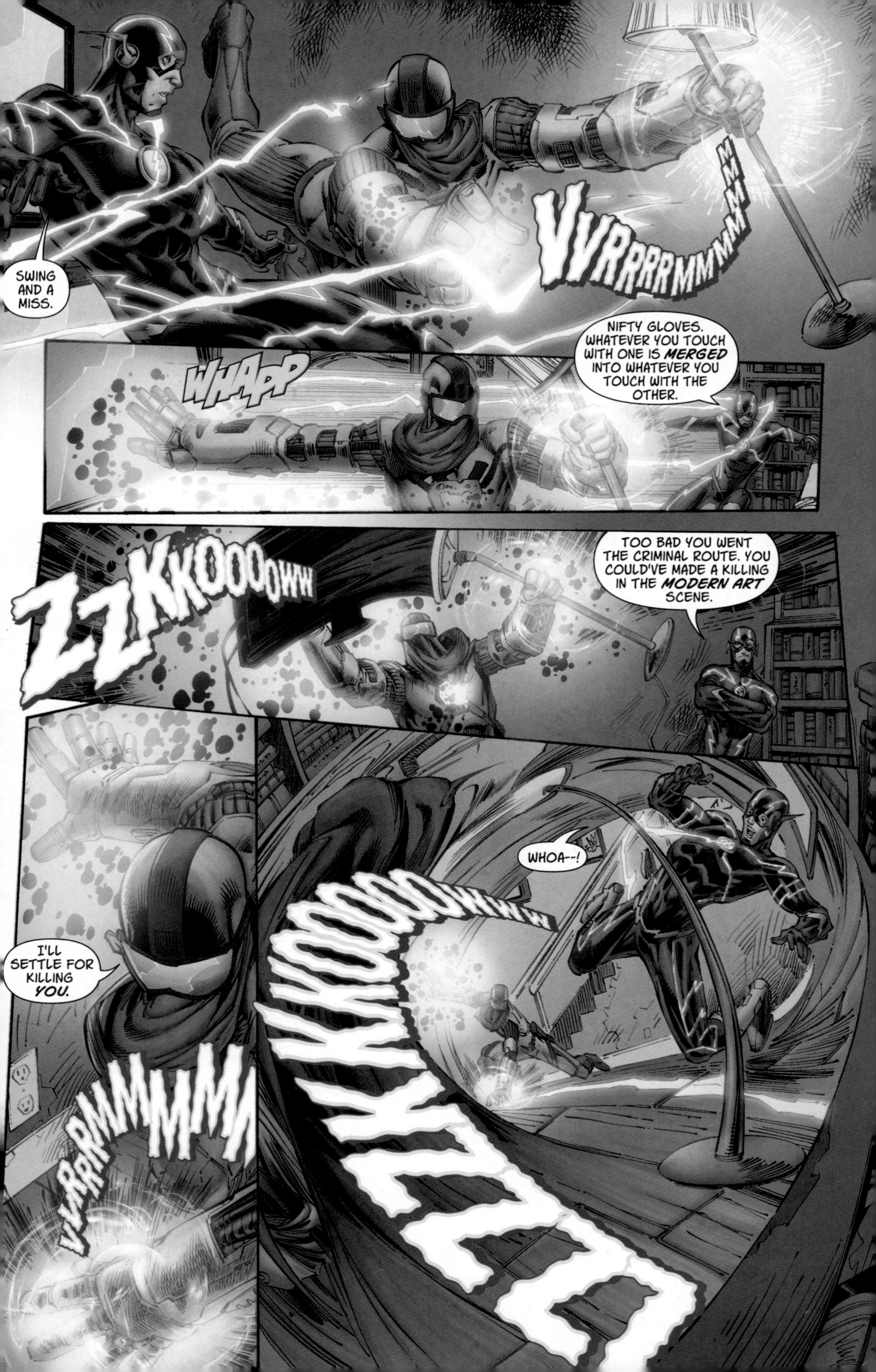
SWING AND A MISS.
VVRRRRMMMMMMMMMM
NIFTY GLOVES. WHATEVER YOU TOUCH WITH ONE IS MERGED INTO WHATEVER YOU TOUCH WITH THE OTHER.
WHAPP
ZZKKOOOOWW
TOO BAD YOU WENT THE CRIMINAL ROUTE. YOU COULD'VE MADE A KILLING IN THE MODERN ART SCENE.
I'LL SETTLE FOR KILLING YOU.
VVRRRMMMMM
WHOA--!
ZZKKOOOOOOWWW

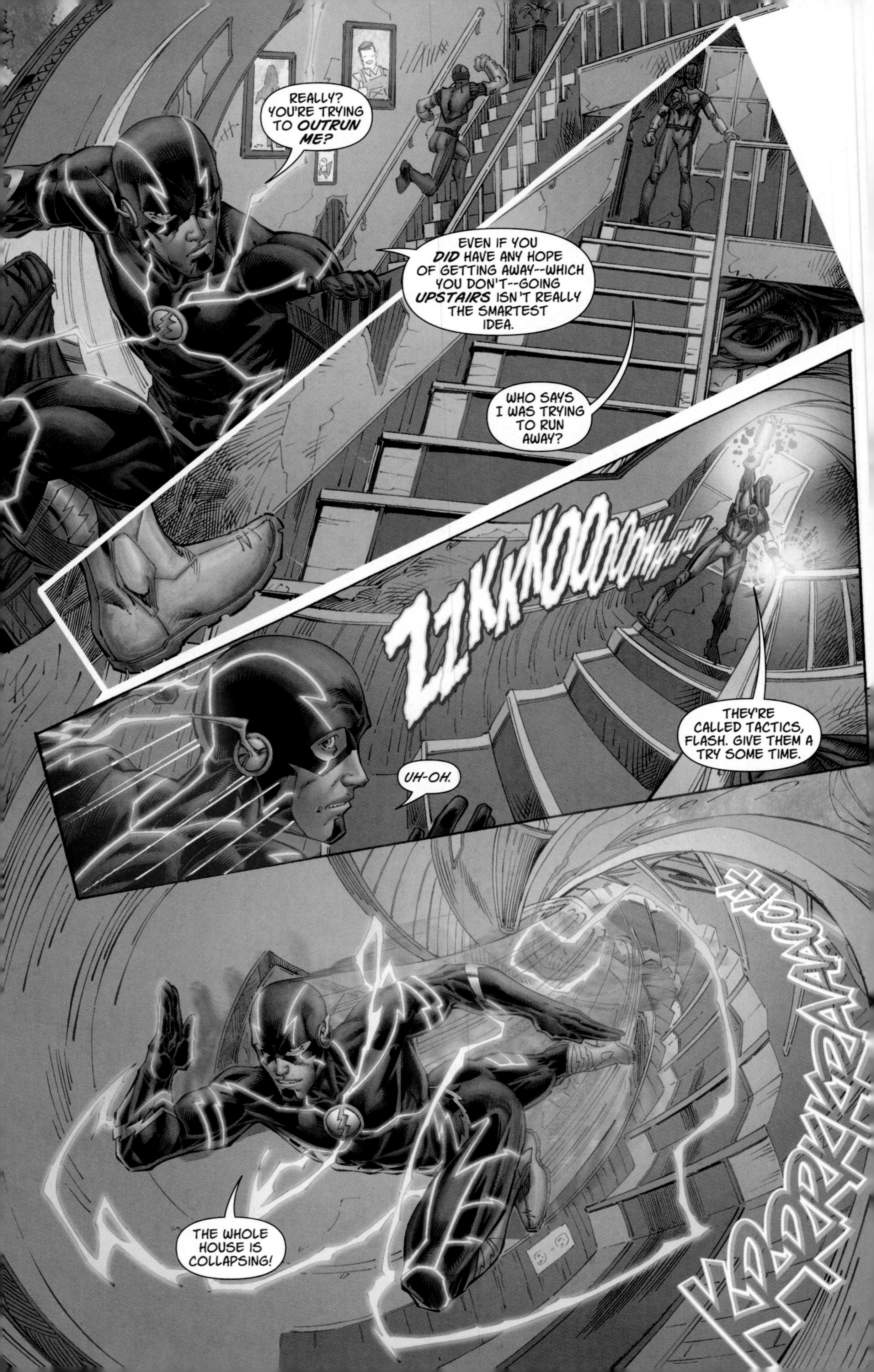
REALLY? YOU'RE TRYING TO OUTRUN ME?
EVEN IF YOU DID HAVE ANY HOPE OF GETTING AWAY--WHICH YOU DON'T--GOING UPSTAIRS ISN'T REALLY THE SMARTEST IDEA.
WHO SAYS I WAS TRYING TO RUN AWAY?
ZZKKKOOOOOHHHH
THEY'RE CALLED TACTICS, FLASH. GIVE THEM A TRY SOME TIME.
UH-OH.
THE WHOLE HOUSE IS COLLAPSING!
KRRRRAAAACKK

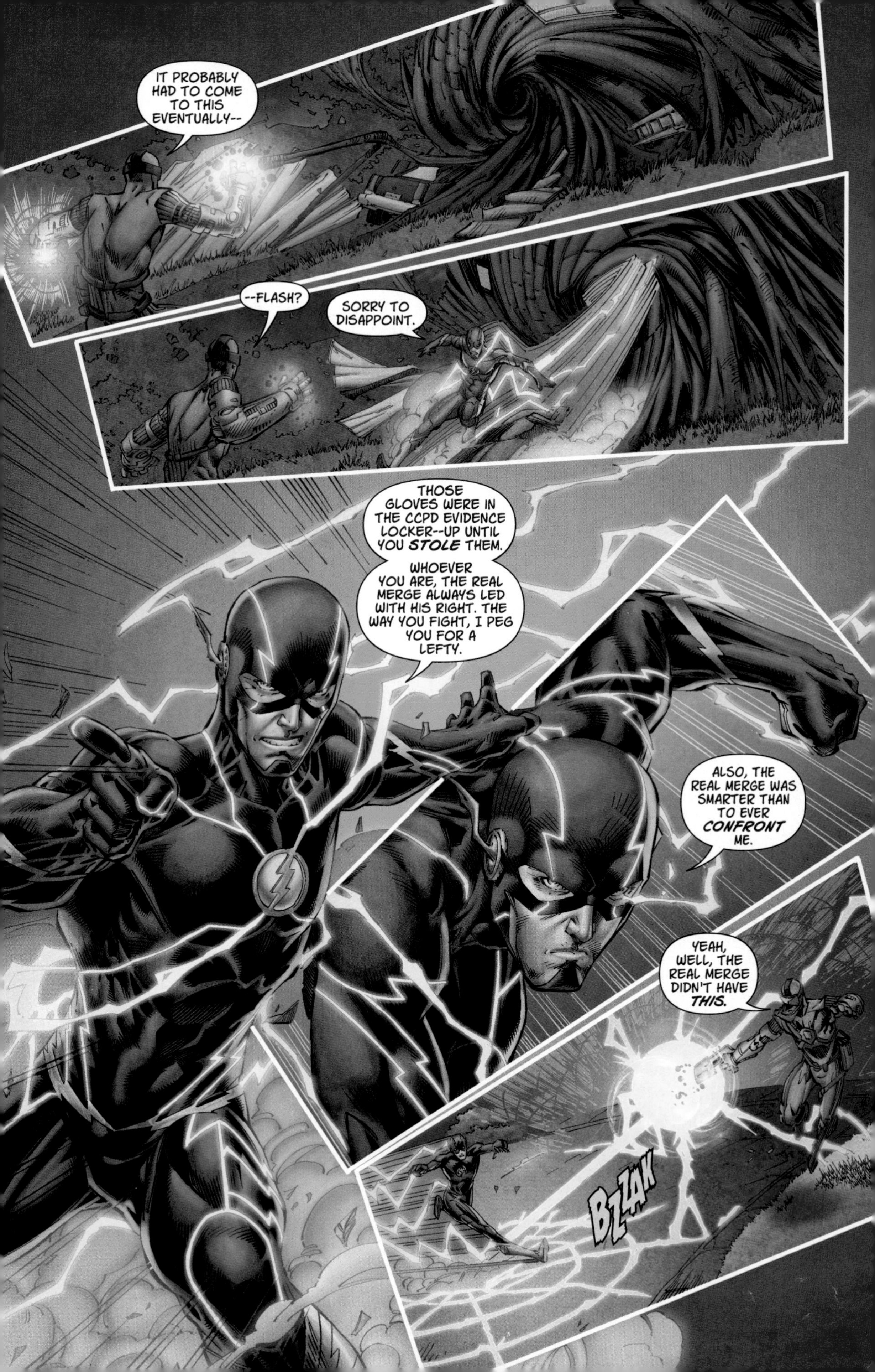
IT PROBABLY HAD TO COME TO THIS EVENTUALLY--
--FLASH?
SORRY TO DISAPPOINT.
THOSE GLOVES WERE IN THE CCPD EVIDENCE LOCKER--UP UNTIL YOU STOLE THEM.
WHOEVER YOU ARE, THE REAL MERGE ALWAYS LED WITH HIS RIGHT. THE WAY YOU FIGHT, I PEG YOU FOR A LEFTY.
ALSO, THE REAL MERGE WAS SMARTER THAN TO EVER CONFRONT ME.
YEAH, WELL, THE REAL MERGE DIDN'T HAVE THIS.
BZZAK

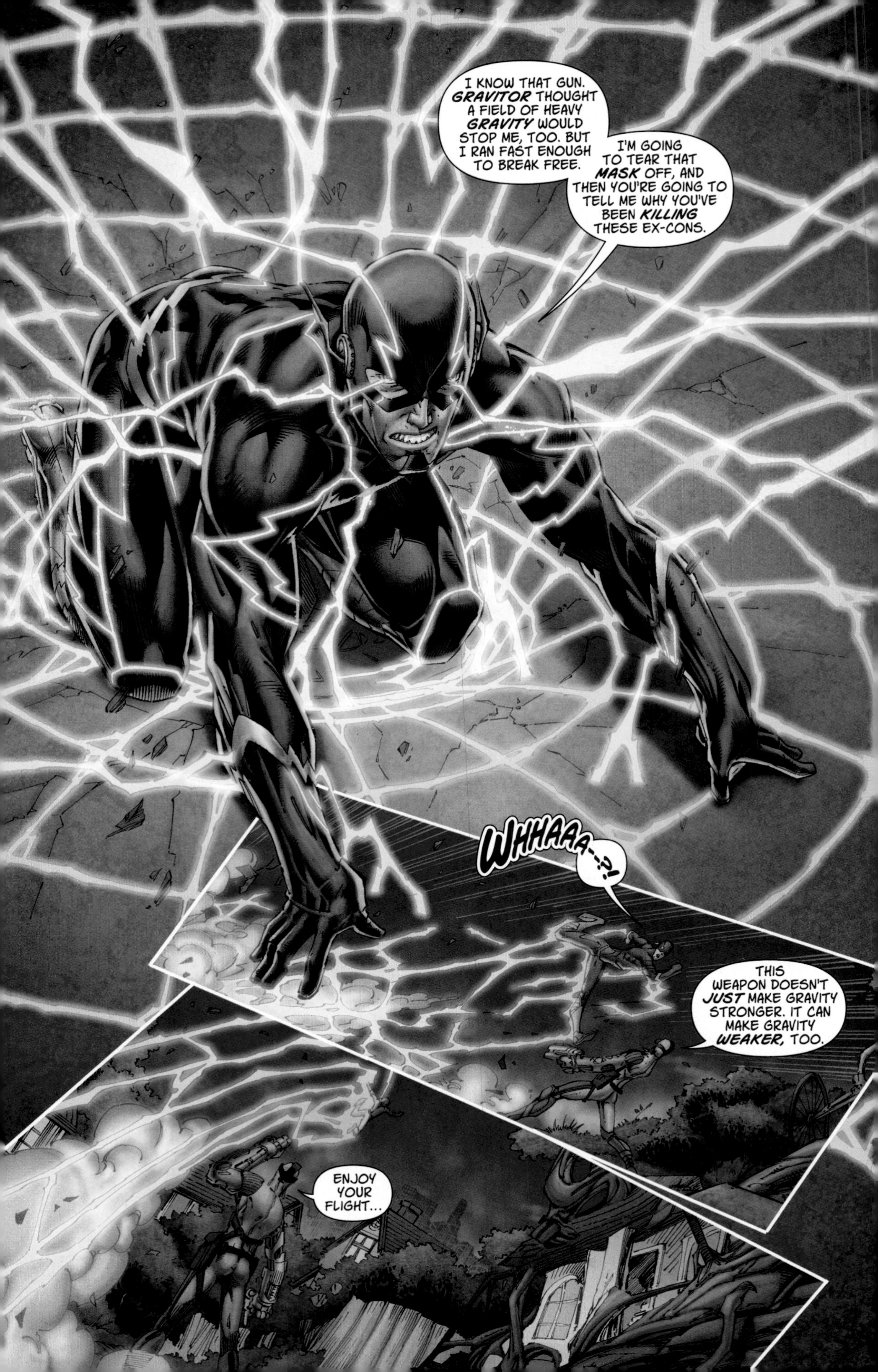
I KNOW THAT GUN. GRAVITOR THOUGHT A FIELD OF HEAVY GRAVITY WOULD STOP ME, TOO. BUT I RAN FAST ENOUGH TO BREAK FREE.
I'M GOING TO TEAR THAT MASK OFF, AND THEN YOU'RE GOING TO TELL ME WHY YOU'VE BEEN KILLING THESE EX-CONS.
WHHAAA--?!
THIS WEAPON DOESN'T JUST MAKE GRAVITY STRONGER. IT CAN MAKE GRAVITY WEAKER, TOO.
ENJOY YOUR FLIGHT...

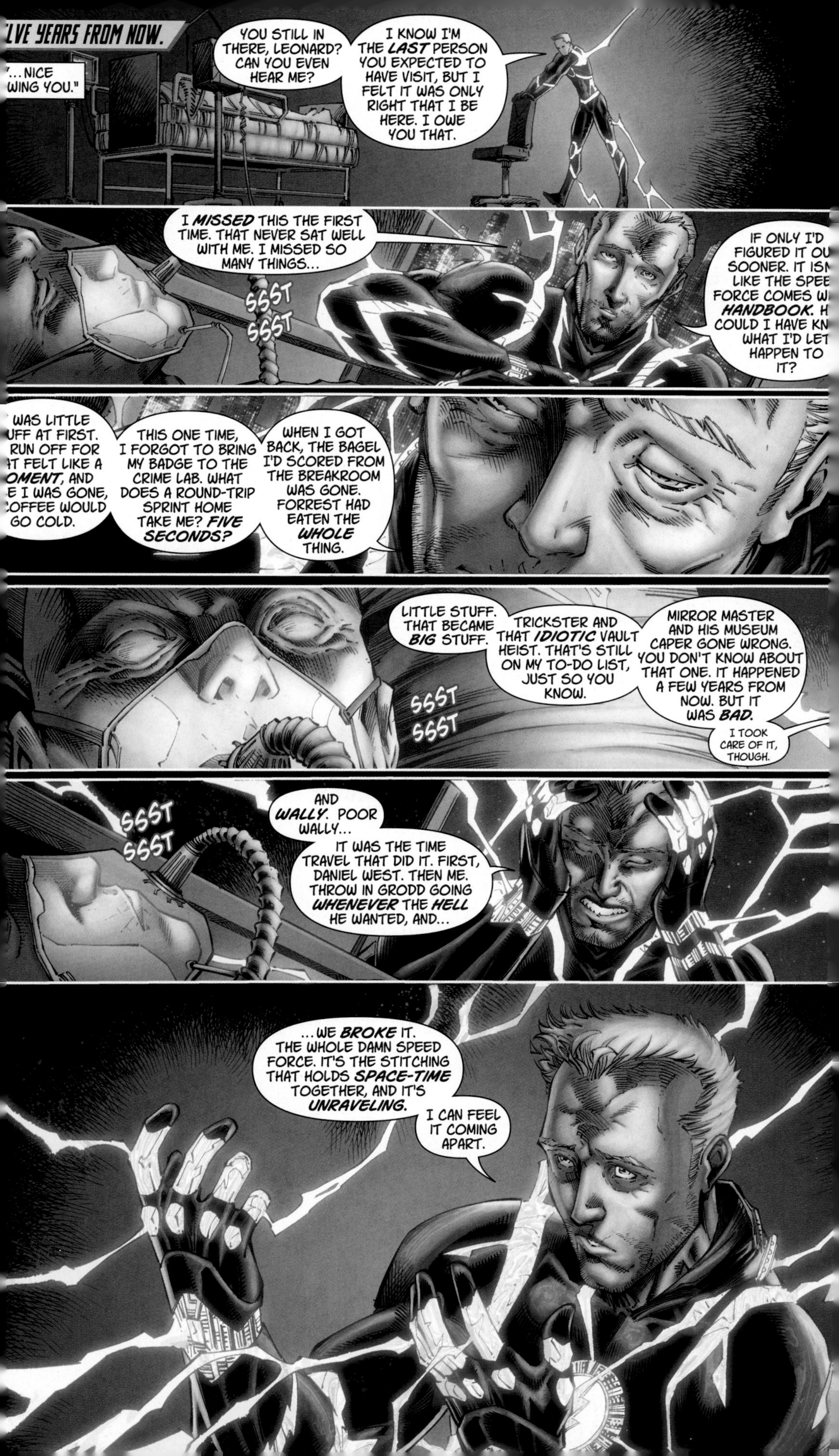

LVE YEARS FROM NOW.
Y... NICE
WING YOU."
YOU STILL IN THERE, LEONARD? CAN YOU EVEN HEAR ME?
I KNOW I'M THE LAST PERSON YOU EXPECTED TO HAVE VISIT, BUT I FELT IT WAS ONLY RIGHT THAT I BE HERE. I OWE YOU THAT.
I MISSED THIS THE FIRST TIME. THAT NEVER SAT WELL WITH ME. I MISSED SO MANY THINGS...
SSST SSST
IF ONLY I'D FIGURED IT OU SOONER. IT ISN LIKE THE SPEE FORCE COMES W HANDBOOK. H COULD I HAVE KN WHAT I'D LET HAPPEN TO IT?
WAS LITTLE UFF AT FIRST. RUN OFF FOR T FELT LIKE A OMENT, AND I WAS GONE, COFFEE WOULD GO COLD.
THIS ONE TIME, I FORGOT TO BRING MY BADGE TO THE CRIME LAB. WHAT DOES A ROUND-TRIP SPRINT HOME TAKE ME? FIVE SECONDS?
WHEN I GOT BACK, THE BAGEL I'D SCORED FROM THE BREAKROOM WAS GONE. FORREST HAD EATEN THE WHOLE THING.
LITTLE STUFF. THAT BECAME BIG STUFF.
TRICKSTER AND THAT IDIOTIC VAULT HEIST. THAT'S STILL ON MY TO-DO LIST, JUST SO YOU KNOW.
MIRROR MASTER AND HIS MUSEUM CAPER GONE WRONG. YOU DON'T KNOW ABOUT THAT ONE. IT HAPPENED A FEW YEARS FROM NOW. BUT IT WAS BAD.
I TOOK CARE OF IT, THOUGH.
SSST SSST
SSST SSST
AND WALLY. POOR WALLY...
IT WAS THE TIME TRAVEL THAT DID IT. FIRST, DANIEL WEST. THEN ME. THROW IN GRODD GOING WHENEVER THE HELL HE WANTED, AND...
...WE BROKE IT. THE WHOLE DAMN SPEED FORCE. IT'S THE STITCHING THAT HOLDS SPACE-TIME TOGETHER, AND IT'S UNRAVELING.
I CAN FEEL IT COMING APART.

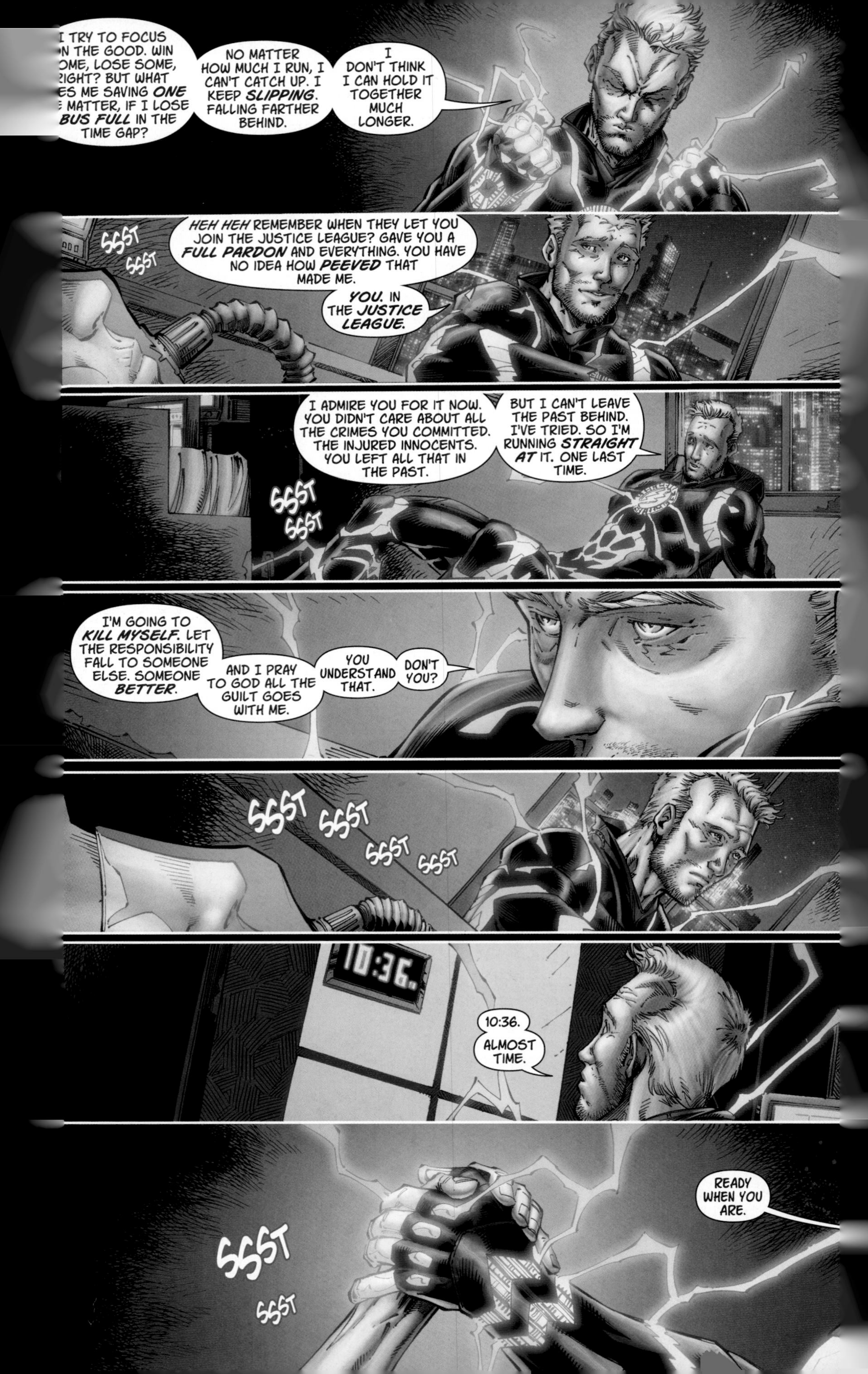
I TRY TO FOCUS ON THE GOOD. WIN OME, LOSE SOME, RIGHT? BUT WHAT ES ME SAVING ONE MATTER, IF I LOSE BUS FULL IN THE TIME GAP?
NO MATTER HOW MUCH I RUN, I CAN'T CATCH UP. I KEEP SLIPPING. FALLING FARTHER BEHIND.
I DON'T THINK I CAN HOLD IT TOGETHER MUCH LONGER.
SSST
SSST
HEH HEH REMEMBER WHEN THEY LET YOU JOIN THE JUSTICE LEAGUE? GAVE YOU A FULL PARDON AND EVERYTHING. YOU HAVE NO IDEA HOW PEEVED THAT MADE ME.
YOU. IN THE JUSTICE LEAGUE.
I ADMIRE YOU FOR IT NOW. YOU DIDN'T CARE ABOUT ALL THE CRIMES YOU COMMITTED. THE INJURED INNOCENTS. YOU LEFT ALL THAT IN THE PAST.
BUT I CAN'T LEAVE THE PAST BEHIND. I'VE TRIED. SO I'M RUNNING STRAIGHT AT IT. ONE LAST TIME.
SSST
SSST
I'M GOING TO KILL MYSELF. LET THE RESPONSIBILITY FALL TO SOMEONE ELSE. SOMEONE BETTER.
AND I PRAY TO GOD ALL THE GUILT GOES WITH ME.
YOU UNDERSTAND THAT.
DON'T YOU?
SSST
SSST
SSST
SSST
10:36.
10:36. ALMOST TIME.
READY WHEN YOU ARE.
SSST
SSST

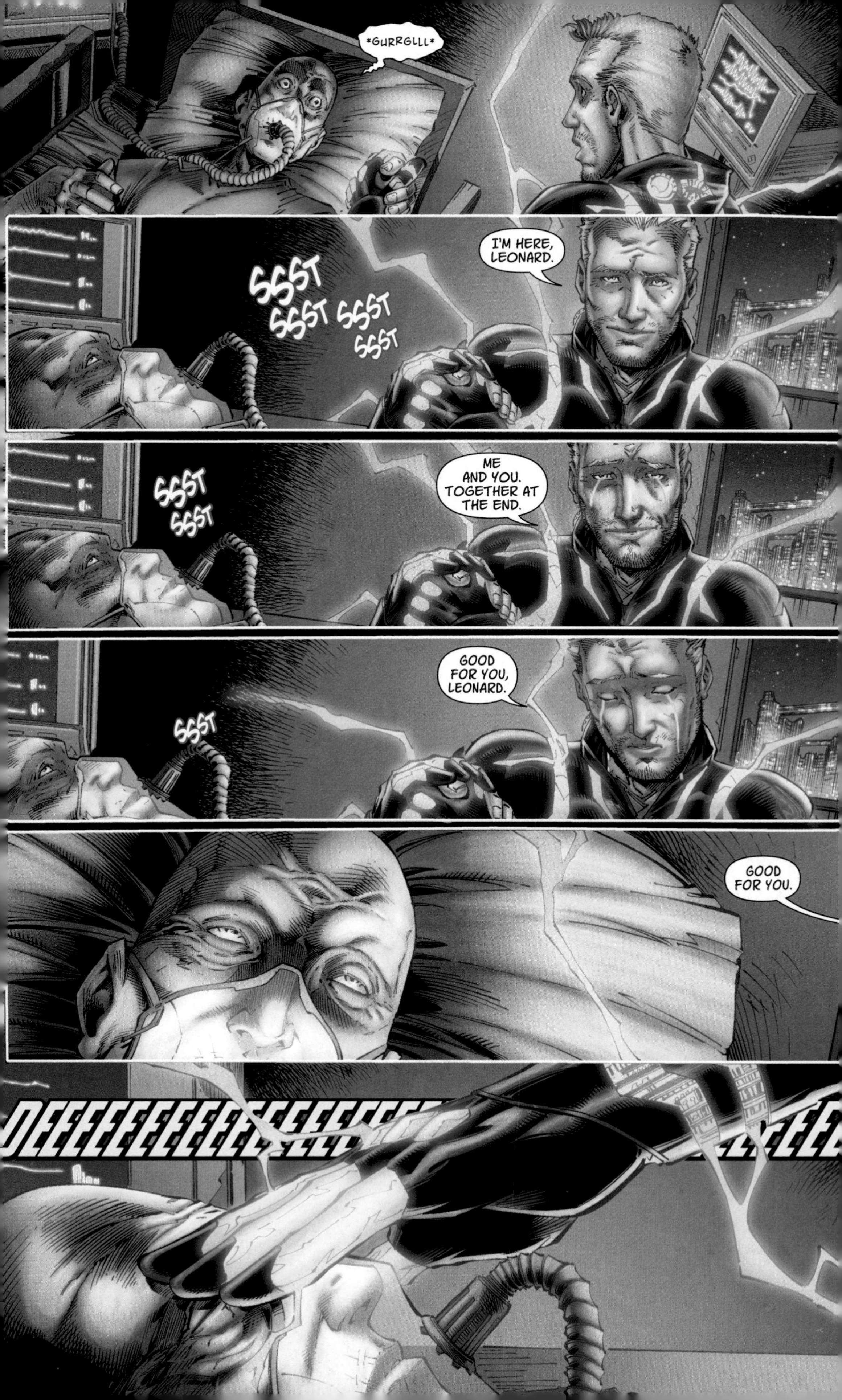
GURRGLLL
I'M HERE, LEONARD.
SSST SSST SSST SSST
ME AND YOU. TOGETHER AT THE END.
SSST SSST
GOOD FOR YOU, LEONARD.
SSST
GOOD FOR YOU.
DEEEEEEEEEEEEEEEEEEEEEEEEEEEEEEEEEE

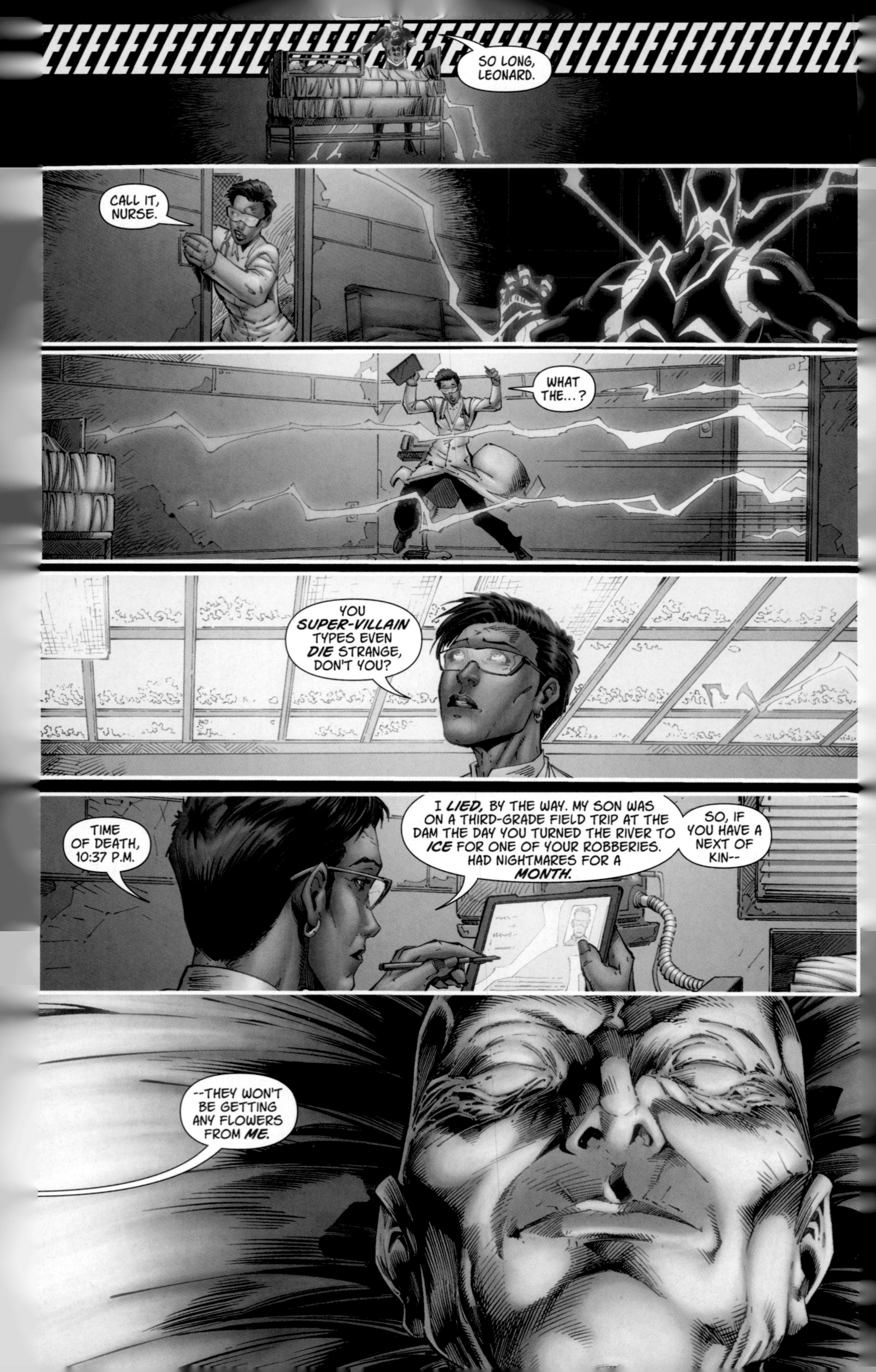
EEEEEEEEEEEEEEEEEEEEEEEEEEEEEEEEEE
SO LONG, LEONARD.
CALL IT, NURSE.
WHAT THE...?
YOU SUPER-VILLAIN TYPES EVEN DIE STRANGE, DON'T YOU?
TIME OF DEATH, 10:37 P.M.
I LIED, BY THE WAY. MY SON WAS ON A THIRD-GRADE FIELD TRIP AT THE DAM THE DAY YOU TURNED THE RIVER TO ICE FOR ONE OF YOUR ROBBERIES. HAD NIGHTMARES FOR A MONTH.
SO, IF YOU HAVE A NEXT OF KIN--
--THEY WON'T BE GETTING ANY FLOWERS FROM ME.

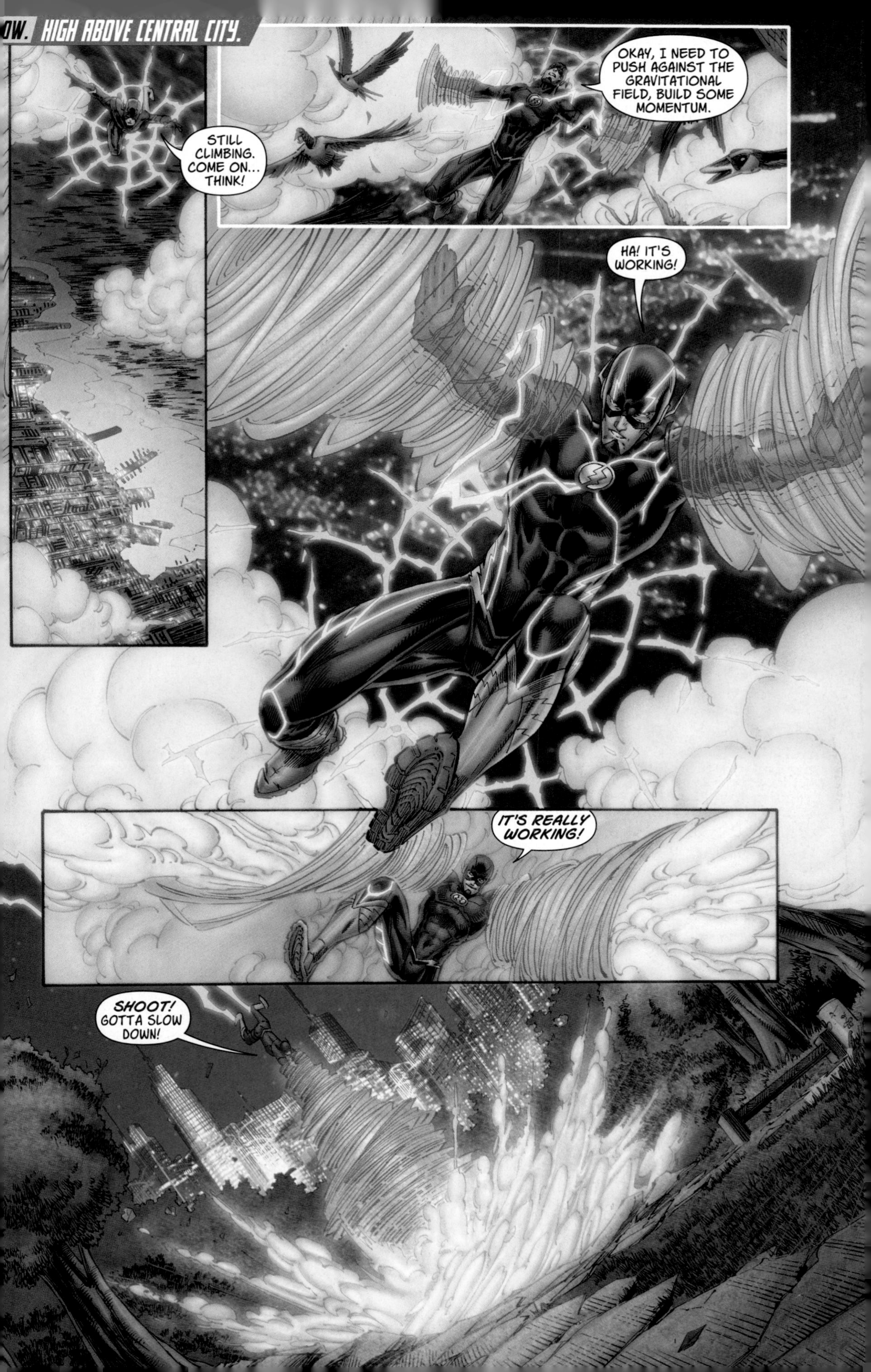
OW. HIGH ABOVE CENTRAL CITY.
STILL CLIMBING. COME ON... THINK!
OKAY, I NEED TO PUSH AGAINST THE GRAVITATIONAL FIELD, BUILD SOME MOMENTUM.
HA! IT'S WORKING!
IT'S REALLY WORKING!
SHOOT! GOTTA SLOW DOWN!

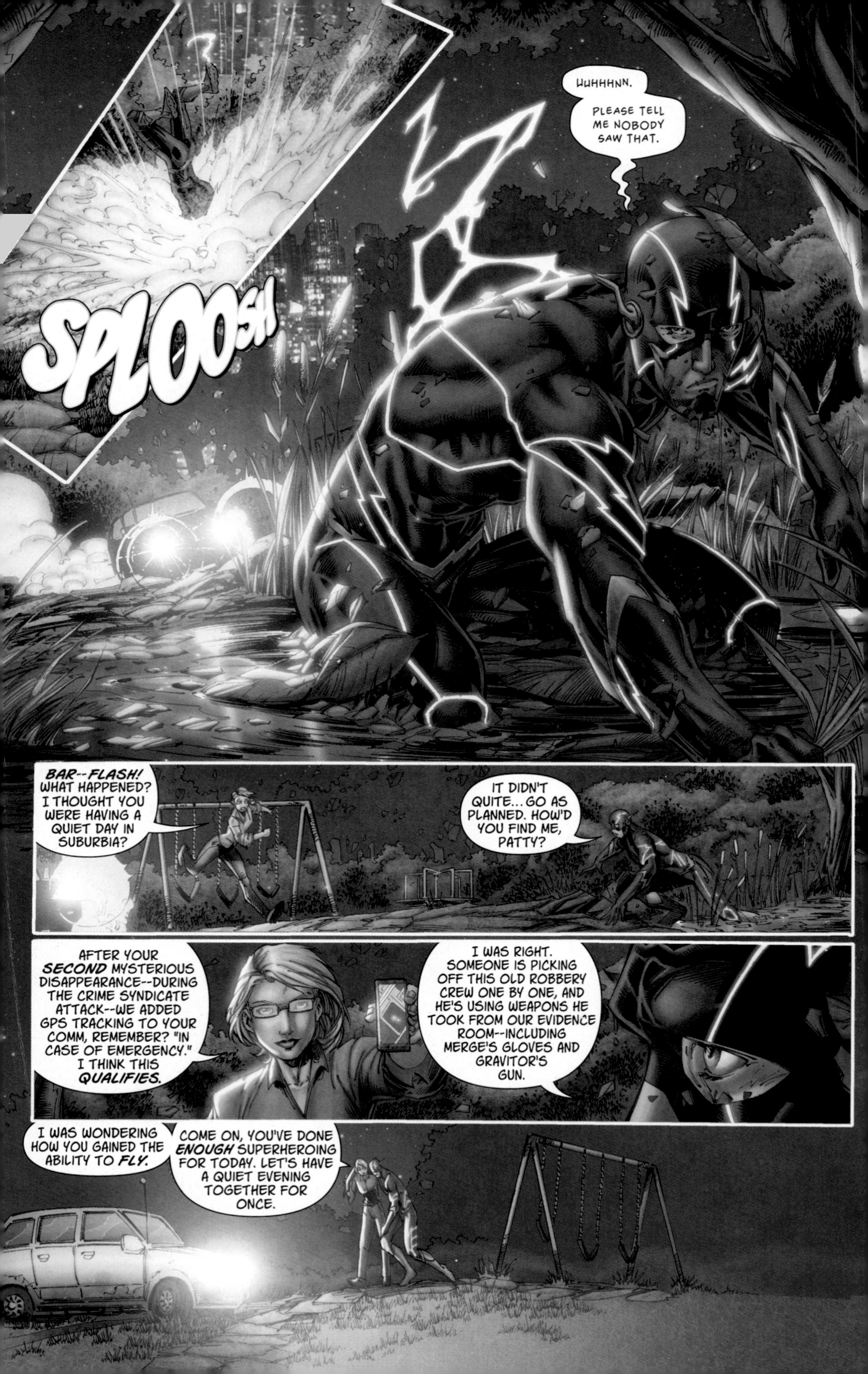
SPLOOSH
UHHHHNN.
PLEASE TELL ME NOBODY SAW THAT.
BAR--FLASH! WHAT HAPPENED? I THOUGHT YOU WERE HAVING A QUIET DAY IN SUBURBIA?
IT DIDN'T QUITE... GO AS PLANNED. HOW'D YOU FIND ME, PATTY?
AFTER YOUR SECOND MYSTERIOUS DISAPPEARANCE--DURING THE CRIME SYNDICATE ATTACK--WE ADDED GPS TRACKING TO YOUR COMM, REMEMBER? "IN CASE OF EMERGENCY." I THINK THIS QUALIFIES.
I WAS RIGHT. SOMEONE IS PICKING OFF THIS OLD ROBBERY CREW ONE BY ONE, AND HE'S USING WEAPONS HE TOOK FROM OUR EVIDENCE ROOM--INCLUDING MERGE'S GLOVES AND GRAVITOR'S GUN.
I WAS WONDERING HOW YOU GAINED THE ABILITY TO FLY.
COME ON, YOU'VE DONE ENOUGH SUPERHEROING FOR TODAY. LET'S HAVE A QUIET EVENING TOGETHER FOR ONCE.

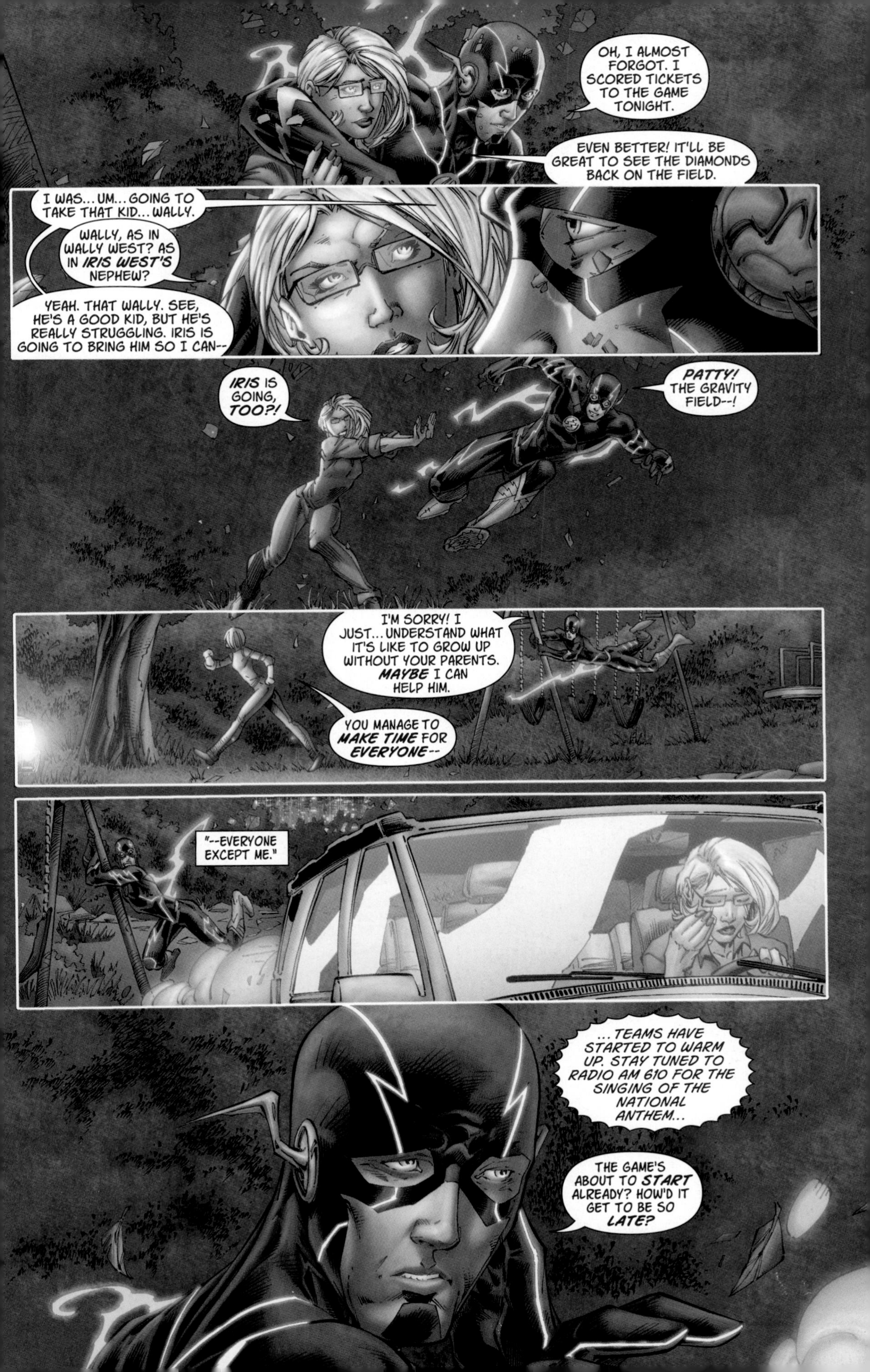
OH, I ALMOST FORGOT. I SCORED TICKETS TO THE GAME TONIGHT.
EVEN BETTER! IT'LL BE GREAT TO SEE THE DIAMONDS BACK ON THE FIELD.
I WAS... UM... GOING TO TAKE THAT KID... WALLY.
WALLY, AS IN WALLY WEST? AS IN IRIS WEST'S NEPHEW?
YEAH. THAT WALLY. SEE, HE'S A GOOD KID, BUT HE'S REALLY STRUGGLING. IRIS IS GOING TO BRING HIM SO I CAN--
IRIS IS GOING, TOO?!
PATTY! THE GRAVITY FIELD--!
I'M SORRY! I JUST... UNDERSTAND WHAT IT'S LIKE TO GROW UP WITHOUT YOUR PARENTS. MAYBE I CAN HELP HIM.
YOU MANAGE TO MAKE TIME FOR EVERYONE--
"--EVERYONE EXCEPT ME."
...TEAMS HAVE STARTED TO WARM UP. STAY TUNED TO RADIO AM 610 FOR THE SINGING OF THE NATIONAL ANTHEM...
THE GAME'S ABOUT TO START ALREADY? HOW'D IT GET TO BE SO LATE?

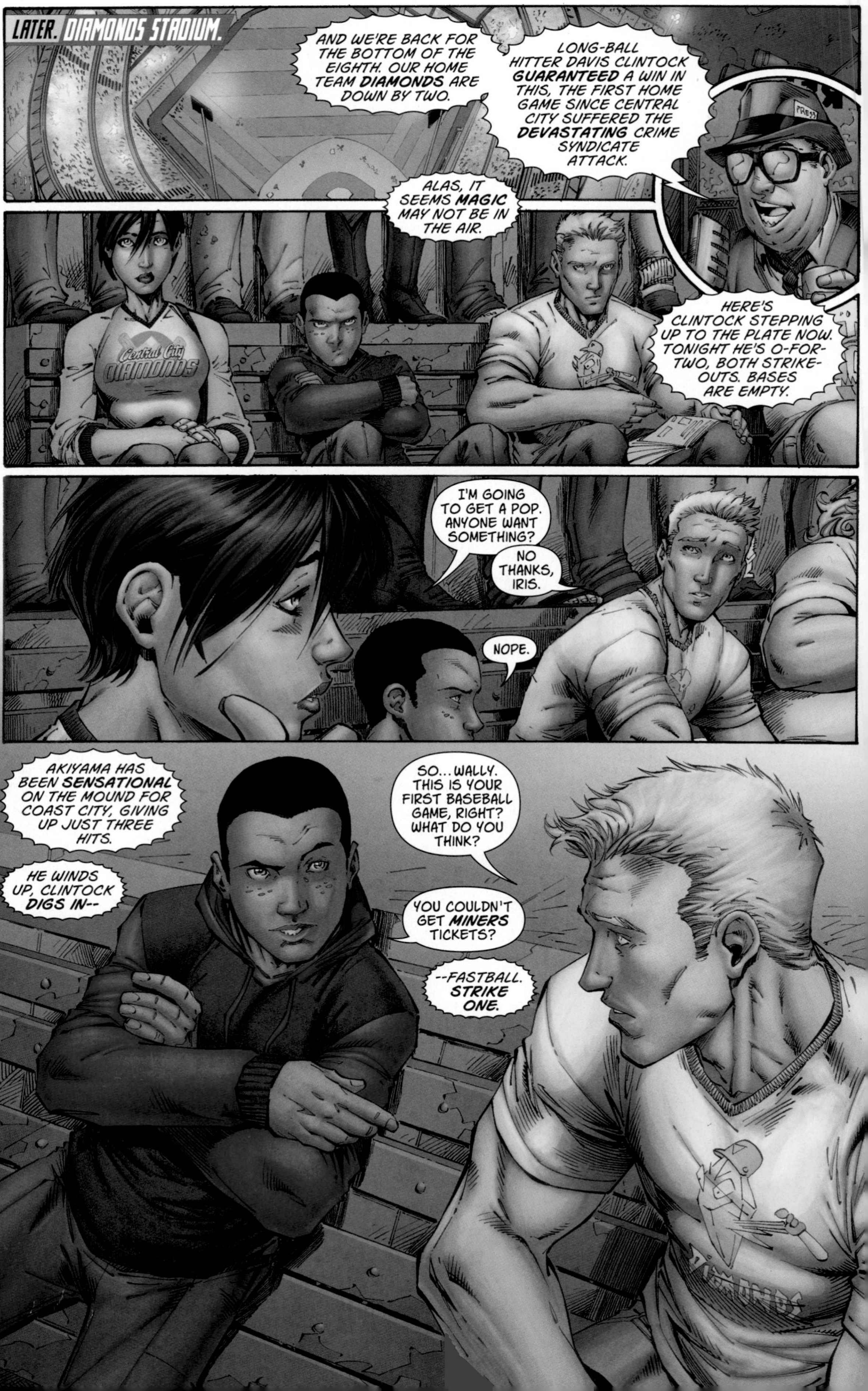
LATER. DIAMONDS STADIUM.
AND WE'RE BACK FOR THE BOTTOM OF THE EIGHTH. OUR HOME TEAM DIAMONDS ARE DOWN BY TWO.
LONG-BALL HITTER DAVIS CLINTOCK GUARANTEED A WIN IN THIS, THE FIRST HOME GAME SINCE CENTRAL CITY SUFFERED THE DEVASTATING CRIME SYNDICATE ATTACK.
ALAS, IT SEEMS MAGIC MAY NOT BE IN THE AIR.
PRESS
Central City DIAMONDS
HERE'S CLINTOCK STEPPING UP TO THE PLATE NOW. TONIGHT HE'S O-FOR-TWO, BOTH STRIKE-OUTS. BASES ARE EMPTY.
I'M GOING TO GET A POP. ANYONE WANT SOMETHING?
NO THANKS, IRIS.
NOPE.
AKIYAMA HAS BEEN SENSATIONAL ON THE MOUND FOR COAST CITY, GIVING UP JUST THREE HITS.
HE WINDS UP, CLINTOCK DIGS IN--
SO... WALLY. THIS IS YOUR FIRST BASEBALL GAME, RIGHT? WHAT DO YOU THINK?
YOU COULDN'T GET MINERS TICKETS?
--FASTBALL. STRIKE ONE.

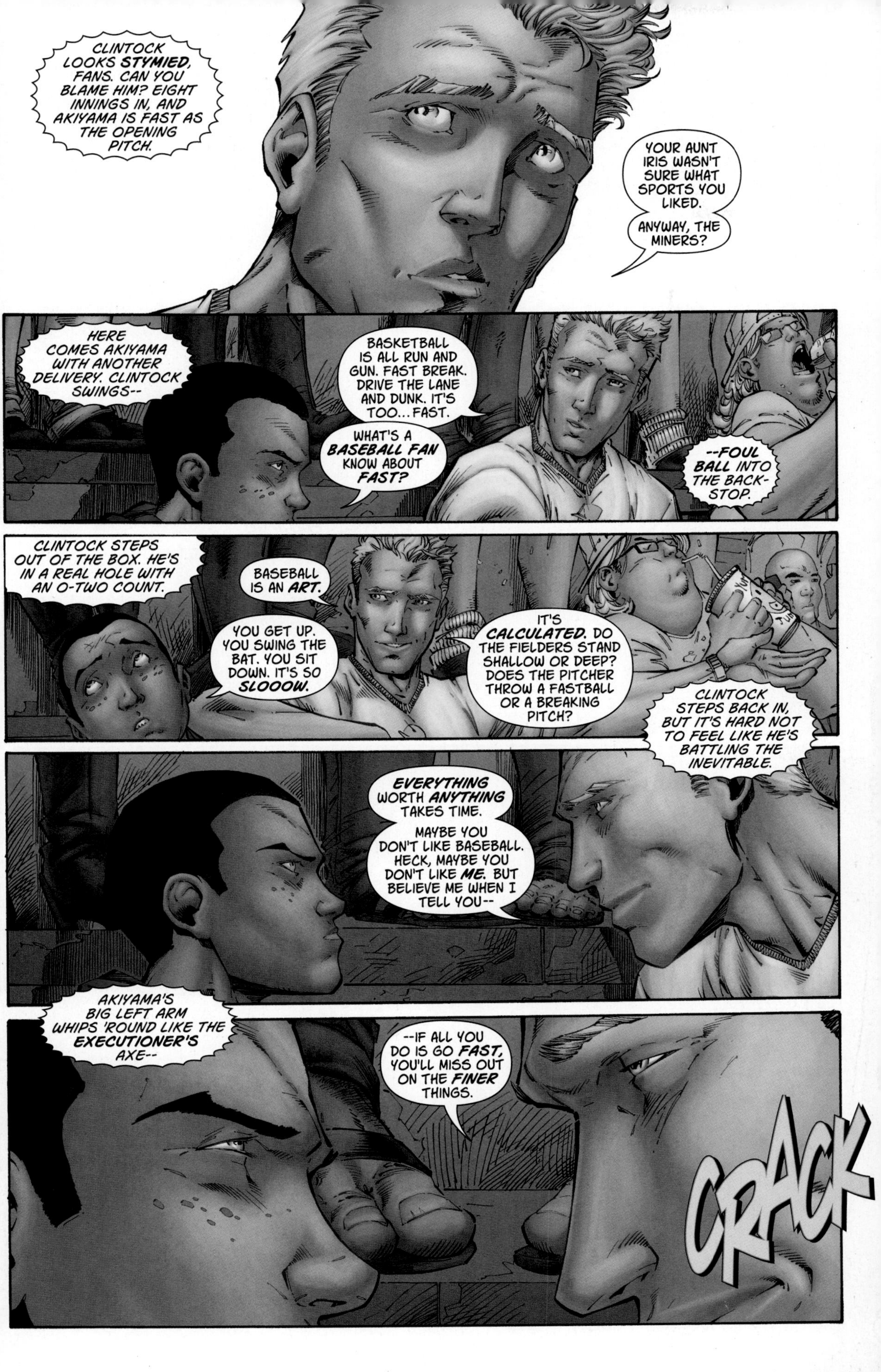

CLINTOCK LOOKS STYMIED, FANS. CAN YOU BLAME HIM? EIGHT INNINGS IN, AND AKIYAMA IS FAST AS THE OPENING PITCH.
YOUR AUNT IRIS WASN'T SURE WHAT SPORTS YOU LIKED.
ANYWAY, THE MINERS?
HERE COMES AKIYAMA WITH ANOTHER DELIVERY. CLINTOCK SWINGS--
BASKETBALL IS ALL RUN AND GUN. FAST BREAK. DRIVE THE LANE AND DUNK. IT'S TOO... FAST.
WHAT'S A BASEBALL FAN KNOW ABOUT FAST?
--FOUL BALL INTO THE BACK-STOP.
CLINTOCK STEPS OUT OF THE BOX. HE'S IN A REAL HOLE WITH AN O-TWO COUNT.
BASEBALL IS AN ART.
YOU GET UP. YOU SWING THE BAT. YOU SIT DOWN. IT'S SO SLOOOW.
IT'S CALCULATED. DO THE FIELDERS STAND SHALLOW OR DEEP? DOES THE PITCHER THROW A FASTBALL OR A BREAKING PITCH?
CLINTOCK STEPS BACK IN, BUT IT'S HARD NOT TO FEEL LIKE HE'S BATTLING THE INEVITABLE.
EVERYTHING WORTH ANYTHING TAKES TIME.
MAYBE YOU DON'T LIKE BASEBALL. HECK, MAYBE YOU DON'T LIKE ME. BUT BELIEVE ME WHEN I TELL YOU--
AKIYAMA'S BIG LEFT ARM WHIPS 'ROUND LIKE THE EXECUTIONER'S AXE--
--IF ALL YOU DO IS GO FAST, YOU'LL MISS OUT ON THE FINER THINGS.
CRACK

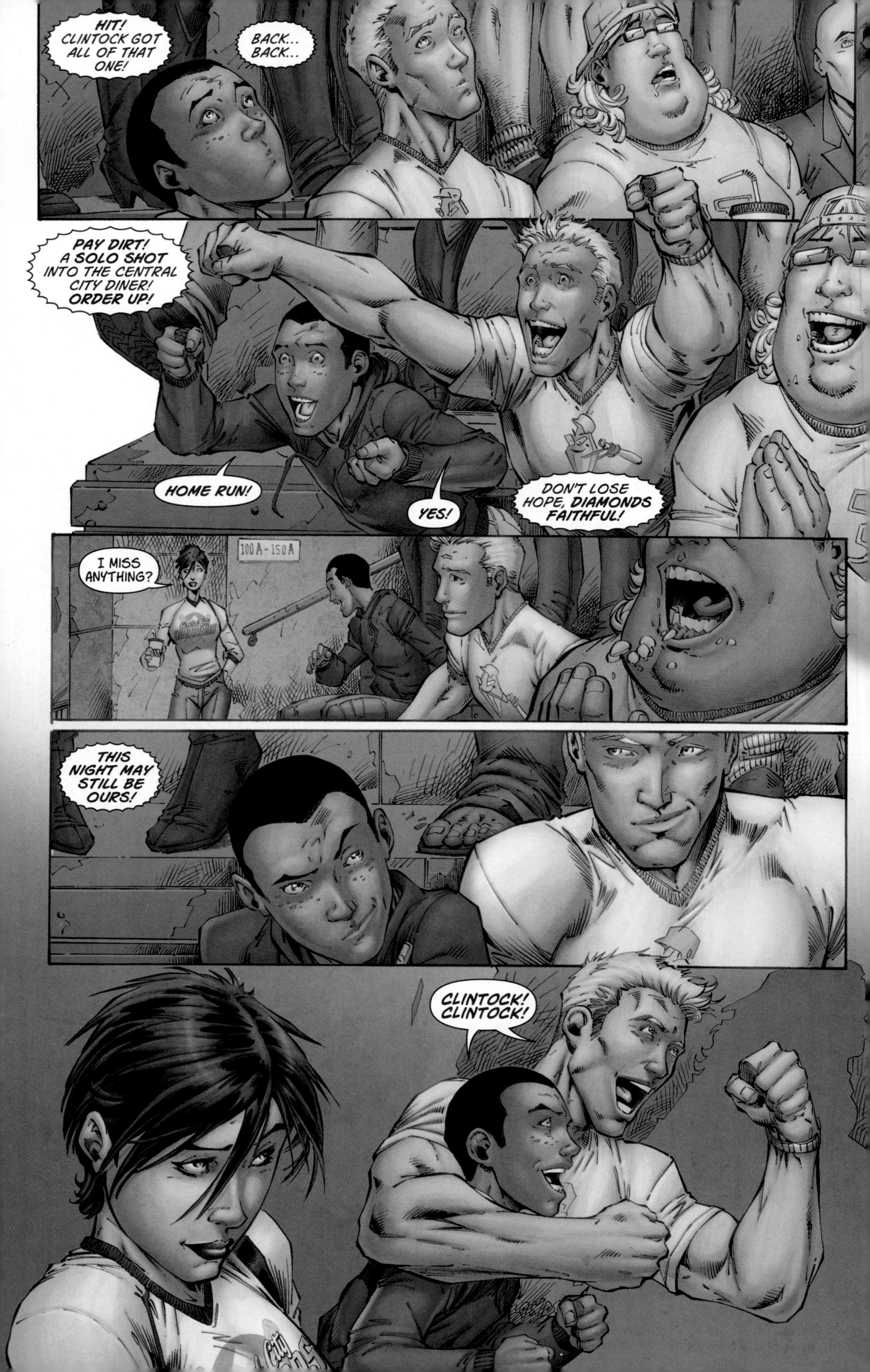
HIT! CLINTOCK GOT ALL OF THAT ONE!
BACK... BACK...
PAY DIRT! A SOLO SHOT INTO THE CENTRAL CITY DINER! ORDER UP!
HOME RUN!
YES!
DON'T LOSE HOPE, DIAMONDS FAITHFUL!
I MISS ANYTHING?
100 A - 150 A
THIS NIGHT MAY STILL BE OURS!
CLINTOCK! CLINTOCK!

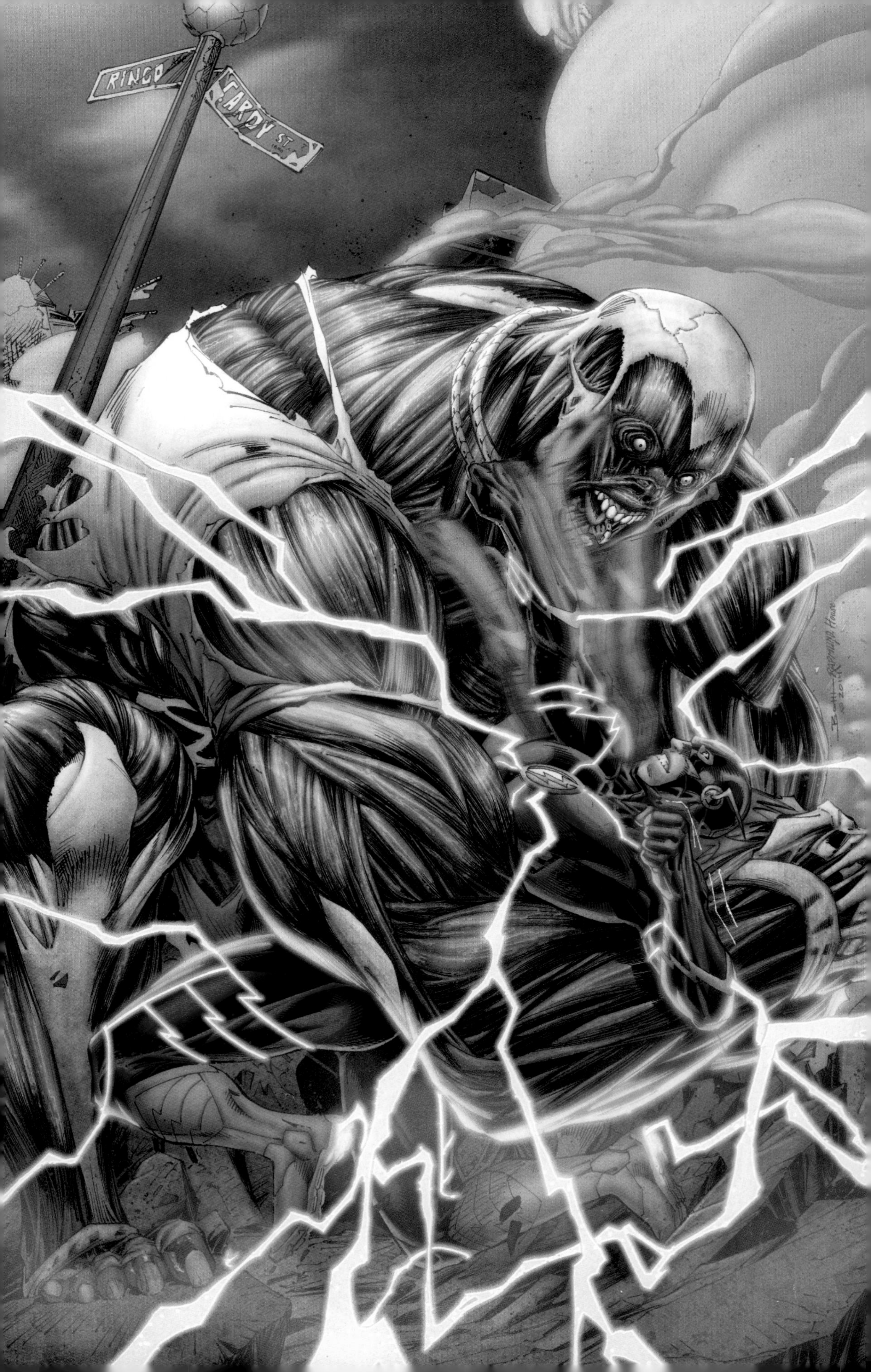
RINGO
ARDY ST.

A STEP BEHIND

ROBERT VENDITTI & VAN JENSEN writers **BRETT BOOTH** penciller **NORM RAPMUND** inker

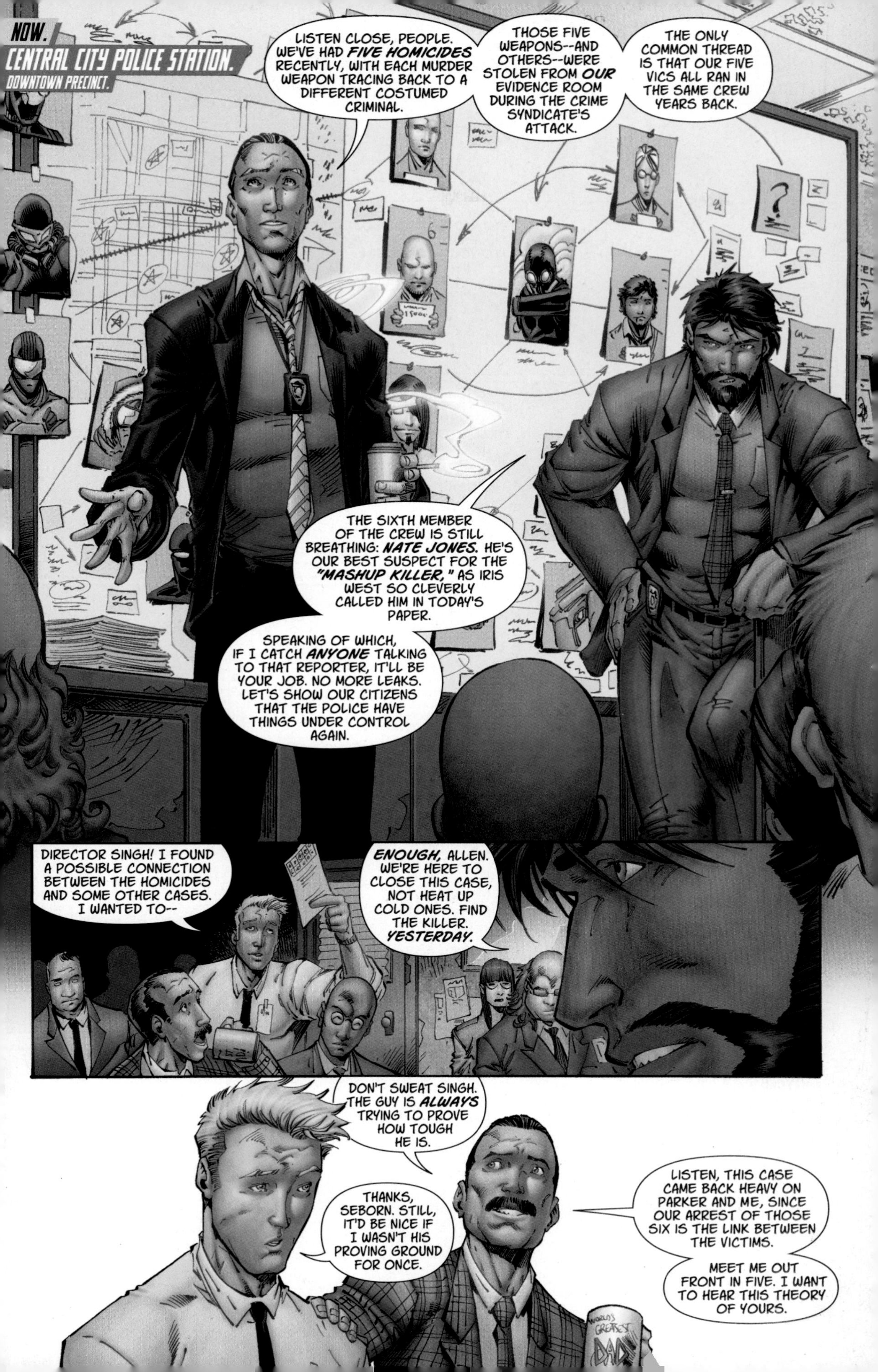
NOW.
CENTRAL CITY POLICE STATION.
DOWNTOWN PRECINCT.
LISTEN CLOSE, PEOPLE. WE'VE HAD FIVE HOMICIDES RECENTLY, WITH EACH MURDER WEAPON TRACING BACK TO A DIFFERENT COSTUMED CRIMINAL.
THOSE FIVE WEAPONS--AND OTHERS--WERE STOLEN FROM OUR EVIDENCE ROOM DURING THE CRIME SYNDICATE'S ATTACK.
THE ONLY COMMON THREAD IS THAT OUR FIVE VICS ALL RAN IN THE SAME CREW YEARS BACK.
THE SIXTH MEMBER OF THE CREW IS STILL BREATHING: NATE JONES. HE'S OUR BEST SUSPECT FOR THE "MASHUP KILLER," AS IRIS WEST SO CLEVERLY CALLED HIM IN TODAY'S PAPER.
SPEAKING OF WHICH, IF I CATCH ANYONE TALKING TO THAT REPORTER, IT'LL BE YOUR JOB. NO MORE LEAKS. LET'S SHOW OUR CITIZENS THAT THE POLICE HAVE THINGS UNDER CONTROL AGAIN.
DIRECTOR SINGH! I FOUND A POSSIBLE CONNECTION BETWEEN THE HOMICIDES AND SOME OTHER CASES. I WANTED TO--
ENOUGH, ALLEN. WE'RE HERE TO CLOSE THIS CASE, NOT HEAT UP COLD ONES. FIND THE KILLER. YESTERDAY.
DON'T SWEAT SINGH. THE GUY IS ALWAYS TRYING TO PROVE HOW TOUGH HE IS.
THANKS, SEBORN. STILL, IT'D BE NICE IF I WASN'T HIS PROVING GROUND FOR ONCE.
LISTEN, THIS CASE CAME BACK HEAVY ON PARKER AND ME, SINCE OUR ARREST OF THOSE SIX IS THE LINK BETWEEN THE VICTIMS.
MEET ME OUT FRONT IN FIVE. I WANT TO HEAR THIS THEORY OF YOURS.
WORLD'S GREATEST DAD

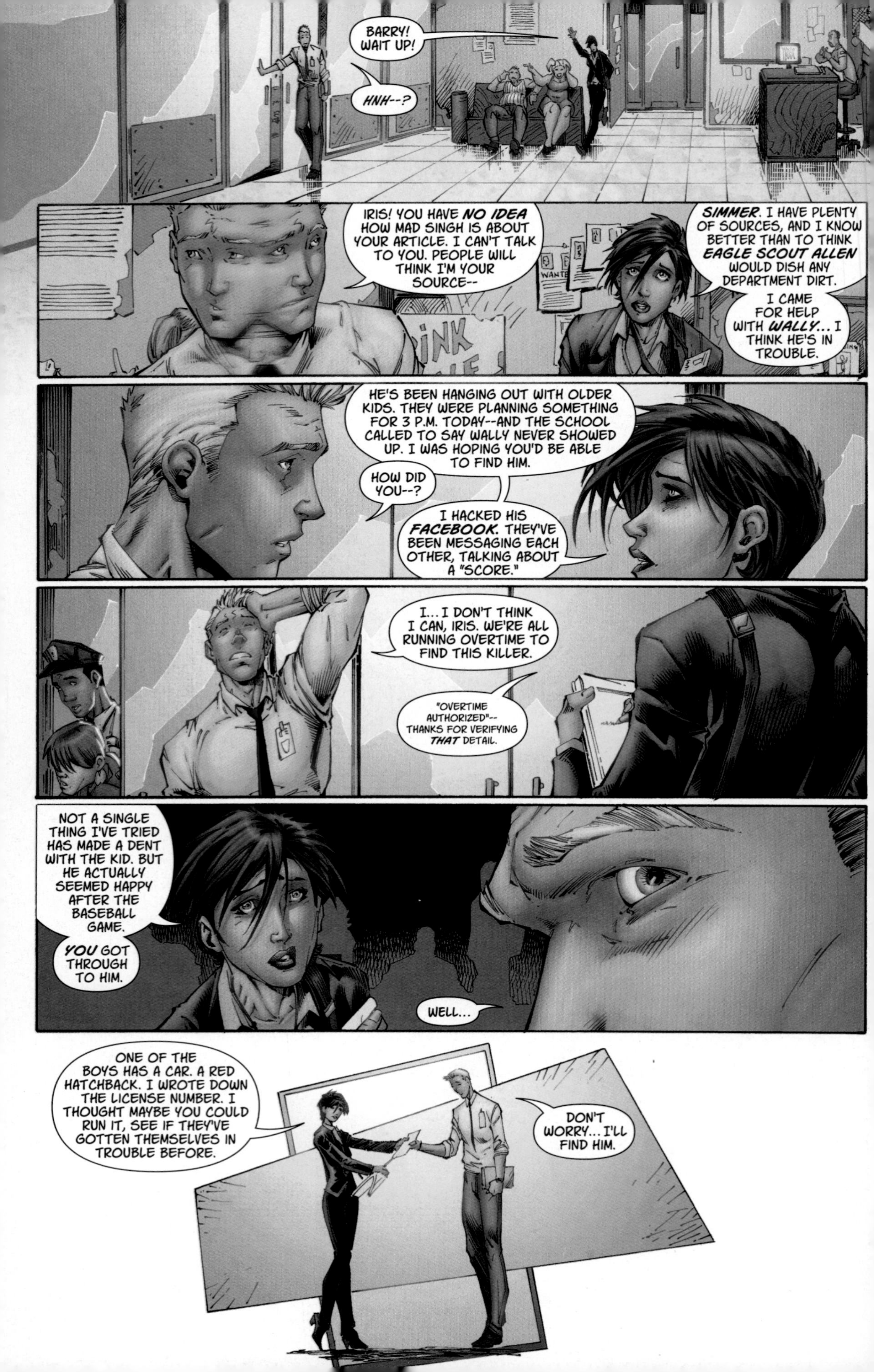
BARRY! WAIT UP!
HNH--?
IRIS! YOU HAVE **NO IDEA** HOW MAD SINGH IS ABOUT YOUR ARTICLE. I CAN'T TALK TO YOU. PEOPLE WILL THINK I'M YOUR SOURCE--
SIMMER. I HAVE PLENTY OF SOURCES, AND I KNOW BETTER THAN TO THINK **EAGLE SCOUT ALLEN** WOULD DISH ANY DEPARTMENT DIRT.
I CAME FOR HELP WITH **WALLY**... I THINK HE'S IN TROUBLE.
HE'S BEEN HANGING OUT WITH OLDER KIDS. THEY WERE PLANNING SOMETHING FOR 3 P.M. TODAY--AND THE SCHOOL CALLED TO SAY WALLY NEVER SHOWED UP. I WAS HOPING YOU'D BE ABLE TO FIND HIM.
HOW DID YOU--?
I HACKED HIS **FACEBOOK**. THEY'VE BEEN MESSAGING EACH OTHER, TALKING ABOUT A "SCORE."
I... I DON'T THINK I CAN, IRIS. WE'RE ALL RUNNING OVERTIME TO FIND THIS KILLER.
"OVERTIME AUTHORIZED"-- THANKS FOR VERIFYING **THAT** DETAIL.
NOT A SINGLE THING I'VE TRIED HAS MADE A DENT WITH THE KID. BUT HE ACTUALLY SEEMED HAPPY AFTER THE BASEBALL GAME.
YOU GOT THROUGH TO HIM.
WELL...
ONE OF THE BOYS HAS A CAR. A RED HATCHBACK. I WROTE DOWN THE LICENSE NUMBER. I THOUGHT MAYBE YOU COULD RUN IT, SEE IF THEY'VE GOTTEN THEMSELVES IN TROUBLE BEFORE.
DON'T WORRY... I'LL FIND HIM.

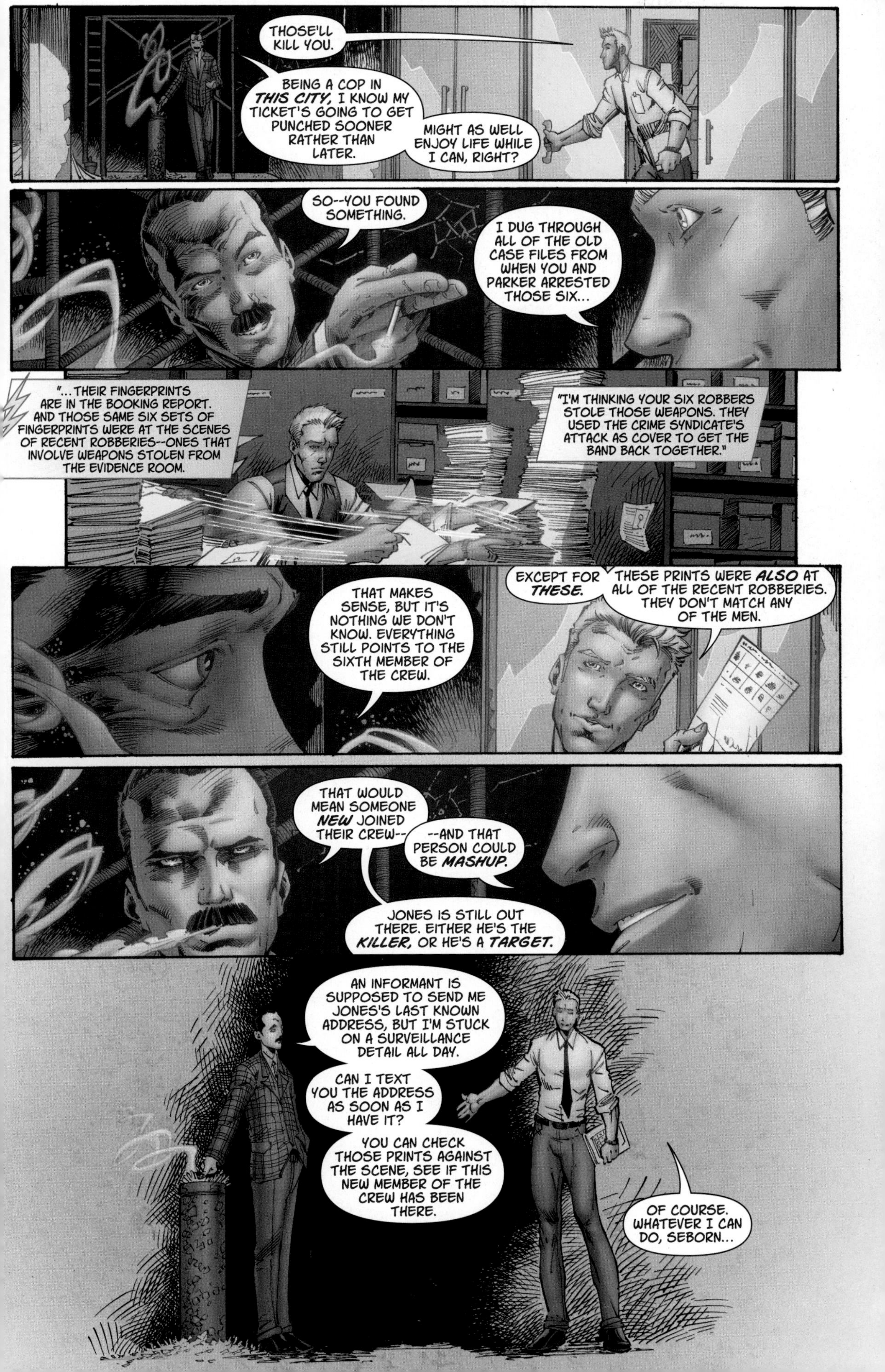
THOSE'LL KILL YOU.
BEING A COP IN THIS CITY, I KNOW MY TICKET'S GOING TO GET PUNCHED SOONER RATHER THAN LATER.
MIGHT AS WELL ENJOY LIFE WHILE I CAN, RIGHT?
SO--YOU FOUND SOMETHING.
I DUG THROUGH ALL OF THE OLD CASE FILES FROM WHEN YOU AND PARKER ARRESTED THOSE SIX...
"...THEIR FINGERPRINTS ARE IN THE BOOKING REPORT. AND THOSE SAME SIX SETS OF FINGERPRINTS WERE AT THE SCENES OF RECENT ROBBERIES--ONES THAT INVOLVE WEAPONS STOLEN FROM THE EVIDENCE ROOM.
"I'M THINKING YOUR SIX ROBBERS STOLE THOSE WEAPONS. THEY USED THE CRIME SYNDICATE'S ATTACK AS COVER TO GET THE BAND BACK TOGETHER."
THAT MAKES SENSE, BUT IT'S NOTHING WE DON'T KNOW. EVERYTHING STILL POINTS TO THE SIXTH MEMBER OF THE CREW.
EXCEPT FOR THESE.
THESE PRINTS WERE ALSO AT ALL OF THE RECENT ROBBERIES. THEY DON'T MATCH ANY OF THE MEN.
THAT WOULD MEAN SOMEONE NEW JOINED THEIR CREW--
--AND THAT PERSON COULD BE MASHUP.
JONES IS STILL OUT THERE. EITHER HE'S THE KILLER, OR HE'S A TARGET.
AN INFORMANT IS SUPPOSED TO SEND ME JONES'S LAST KNOWN ADDRESS, BUT I'M STUCK ON A SURVEILLANCE DETAIL ALL DAY.
CAN I TEXT YOU THE ADDRESS AS SOON AS I HAVE IT?
YOU CAN CHECK THOSE PRINTS AGAINST THE SCENE, SEE IF THIS NEW MEMBER OF THE CREW HAS BEEN THERE.
OF COURSE. WHATEVER I CAN DO, SEBORN...

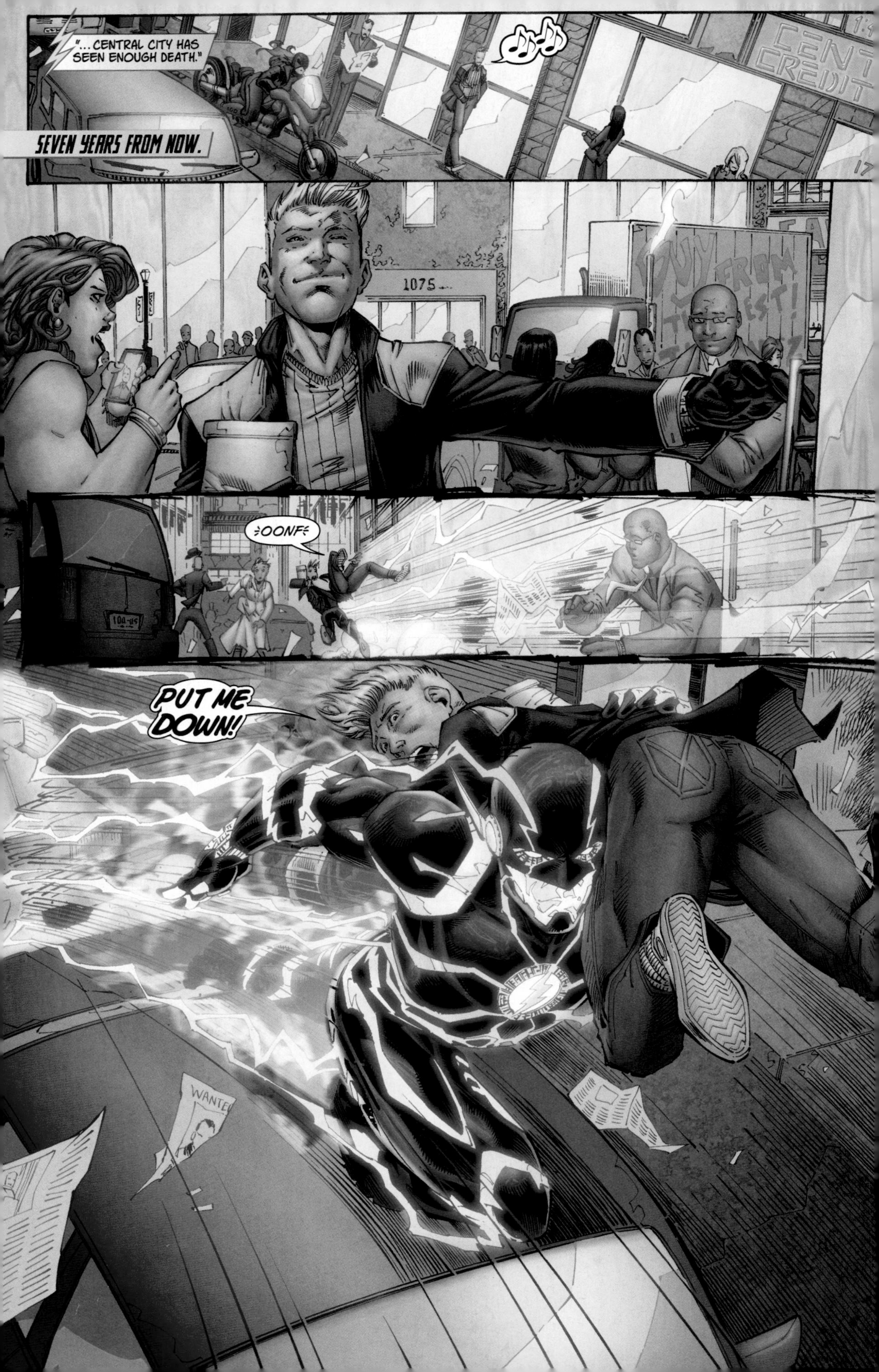

"...CENTRAL CITY HAS SEEN ENOUGH DEATH."
SEVEN YEARS FROM NOW.
1075
OONF
PUT ME DOWN!

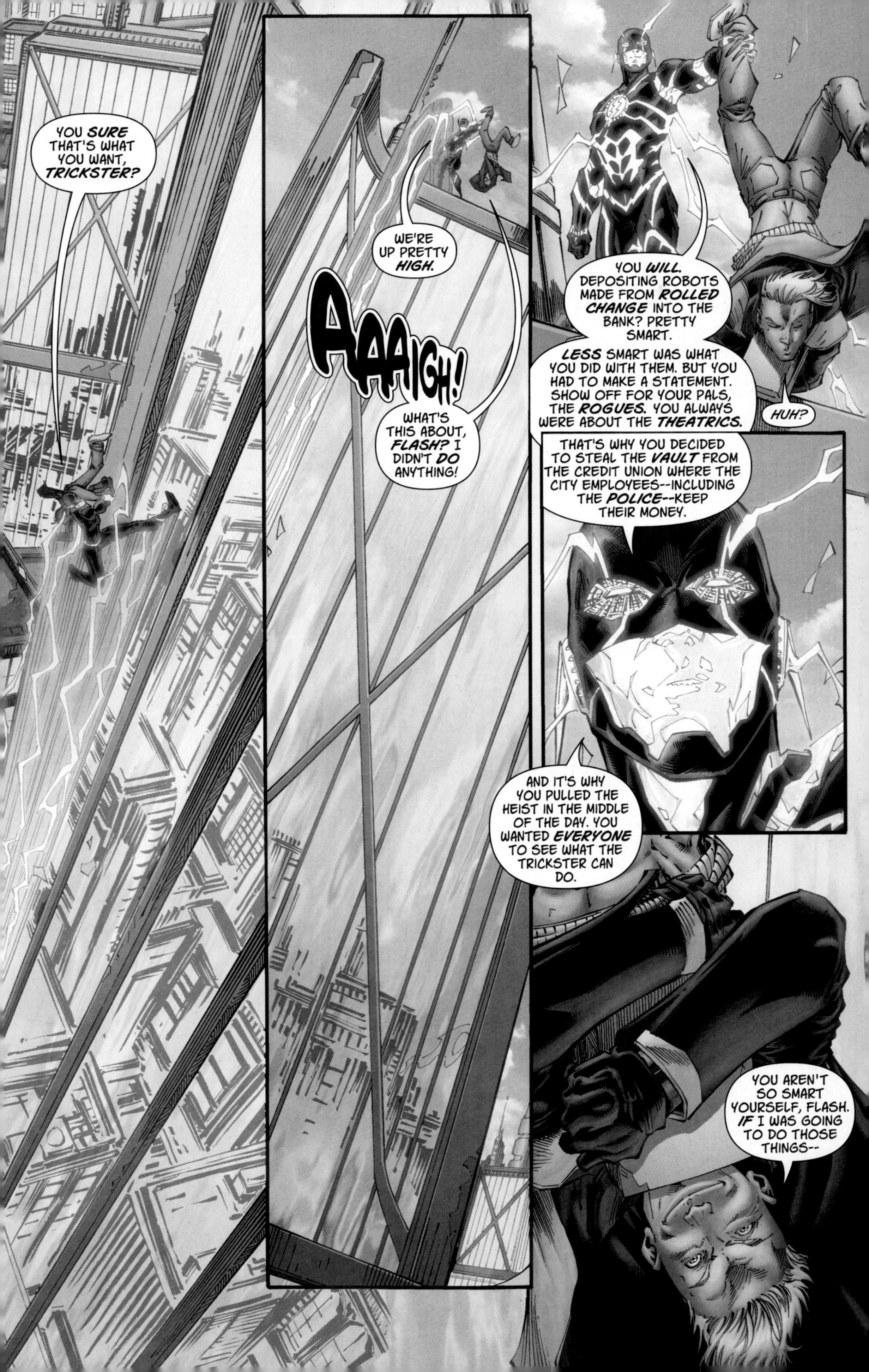
YOU SURE THAT'S WHAT YOU WANT, TRICKSTER?
WE'RE UP PRETTY HIGH.
AAAIGH!
WHAT'S THIS ABOUT, FLASH? I DIDN'T DO ANYTHING!
YOU WILL. DEPOSITING ROBOTS MADE FROM ROLLED CHANGE INTO THE BANK? PRETTY SMART.
LESS SMART WAS WHAT YOU DID WITH THEM. BUT YOU HAD TO MAKE A STATEMENT. SHOW OFF FOR YOUR PALS, THE ROGUES. YOU ALWAYS WERE ABOUT THE THEATRICS.
HUH?
THAT'S WHY YOU DECIDED TO STEAL THE VAULT FROM THE CREDIT UNION WHERE THE CITY EMPLOYEES--INCLUDING THE POLICE--KEEP THEIR MONEY.
AND IT'S WHY YOU PULLED THE HEIST IN THE MIDDLE OF THE DAY. YOU WANTED EVERYONE TO SEE WHAT THE TRICKSTER CAN DO.
YOU AREN'T SO SMART YOURSELF, FLASH. IF I WAS GOING TO DO THOSE THINGS--

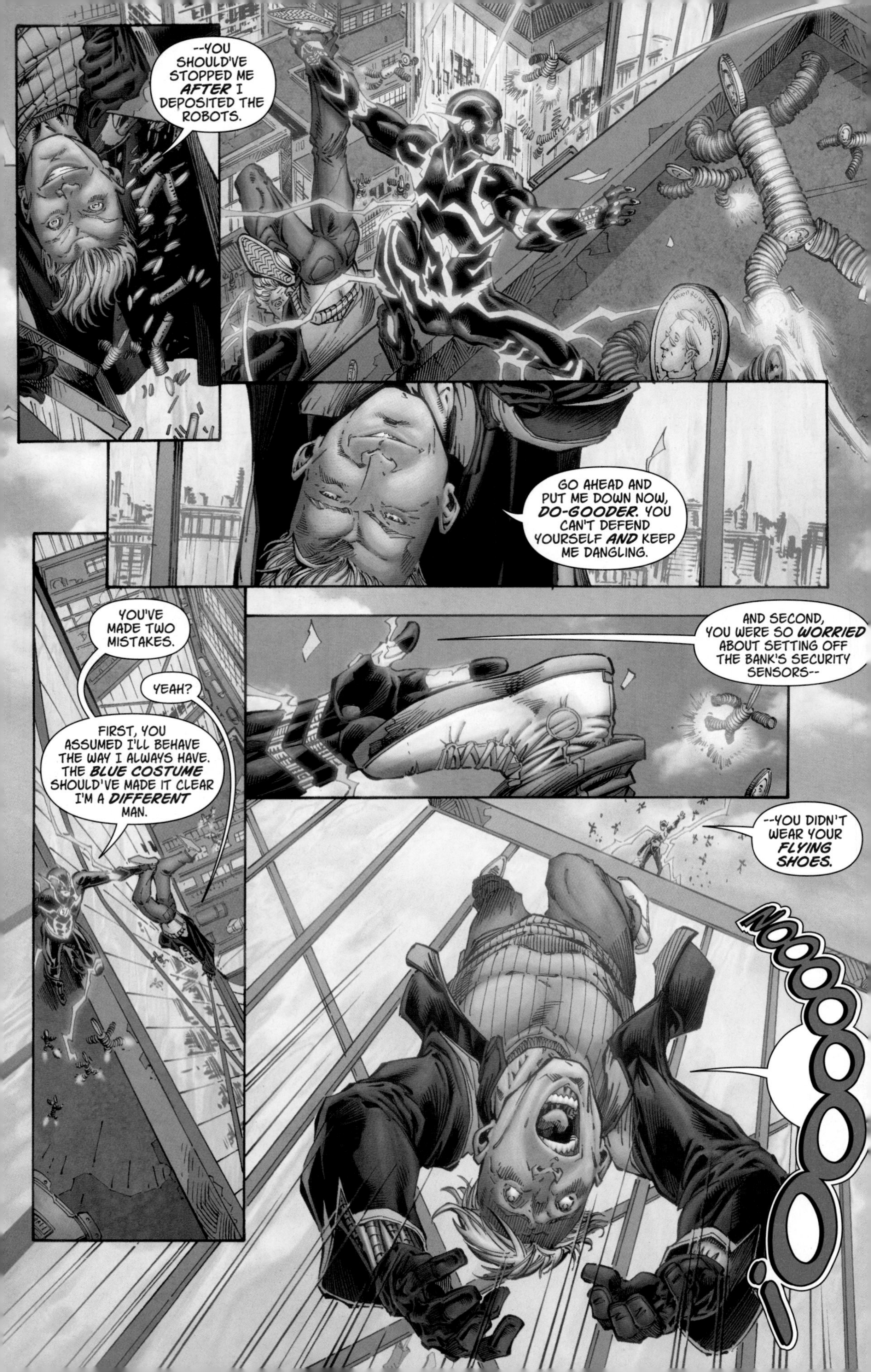
--YOU SHOULD'VE STOPPED ME AFTER I DEPOSITED THE ROBOTS.
GO AHEAD AND PUT ME DOWN NOW, DO-GOODER. YOU CAN'T DEFEND YOURSELF AND KEEP ME DANGLING.
YOU'VE MADE TWO MISTAKES.
YEAH?
FIRST, YOU ASSUMED I'LL BEHAVE THE WAY I ALWAYS HAVE. THE BLUE COSTUME SHOULD'VE MADE IT CLEAR I'M A DIFFERENT MAN.
AND SECOND, YOU WERE SO WORRIED ABOUT SETTING OFF THE BANK'S SECURITY SENSORS--
--YOU DIDN'T WEAR YOUR FLYING SHOES.
NOOOOOOOO!

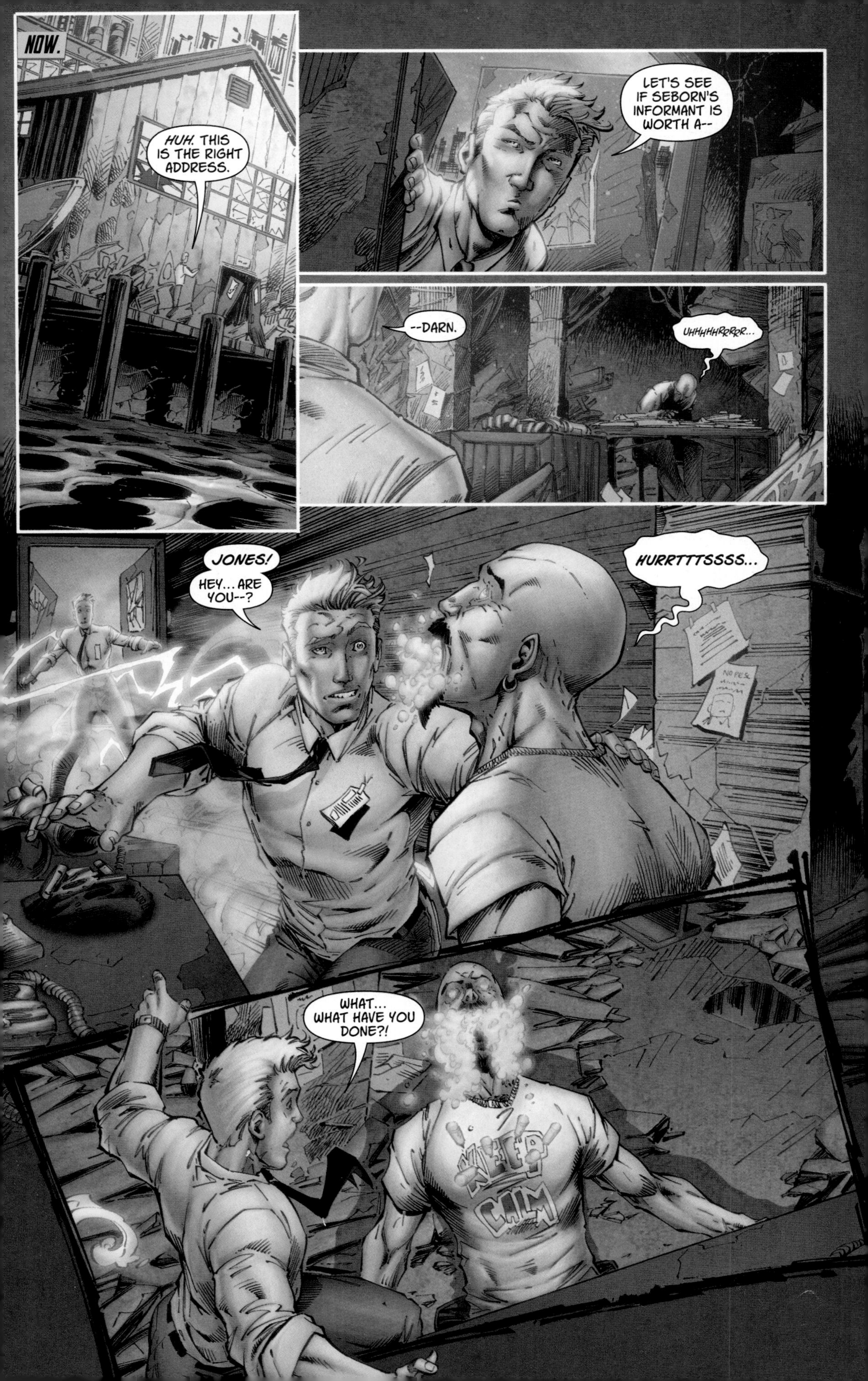
NOW.
HUH. THIS IS THE RIGHT ADDRESS.
LET'S SEE IF SEBORN'S INFORMANT IS WORTH A--
--DARN.
UHHHHRRRRR...
JONES! HEY... ARE YOU--?
HURRTTTSSSS...
WHAT... WHAT HAVE YOU DONE?!

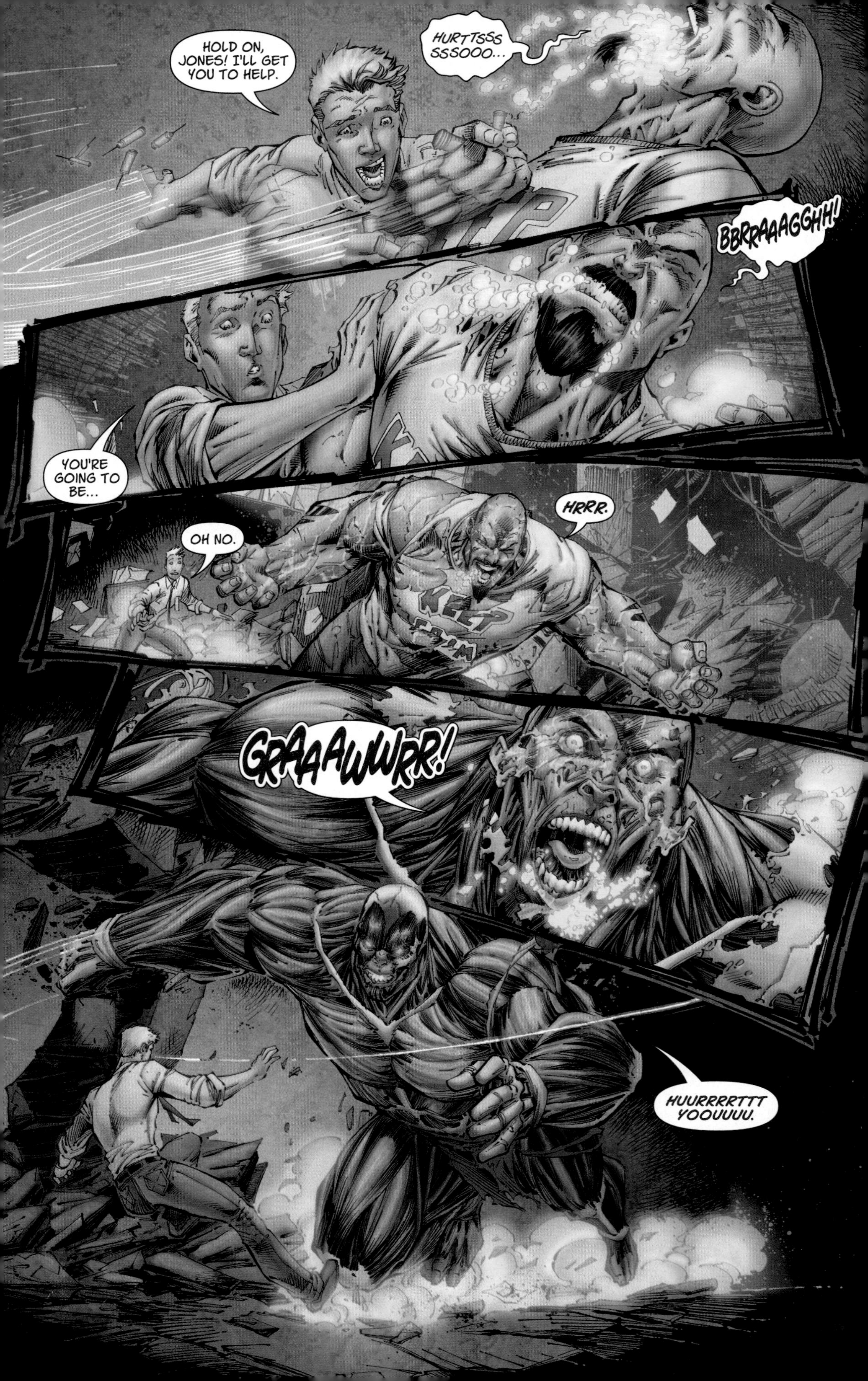
HOLD ON, JONES! I'LL GET YOU TO HELP.
HURTTSSS SSSOOO...
BBRRAAAGGHH!
YOU'RE GOING TO BE...
OH NO.
HRRR.
GRAAAWWRR!
HUURRRRTTT YOOUUUU.

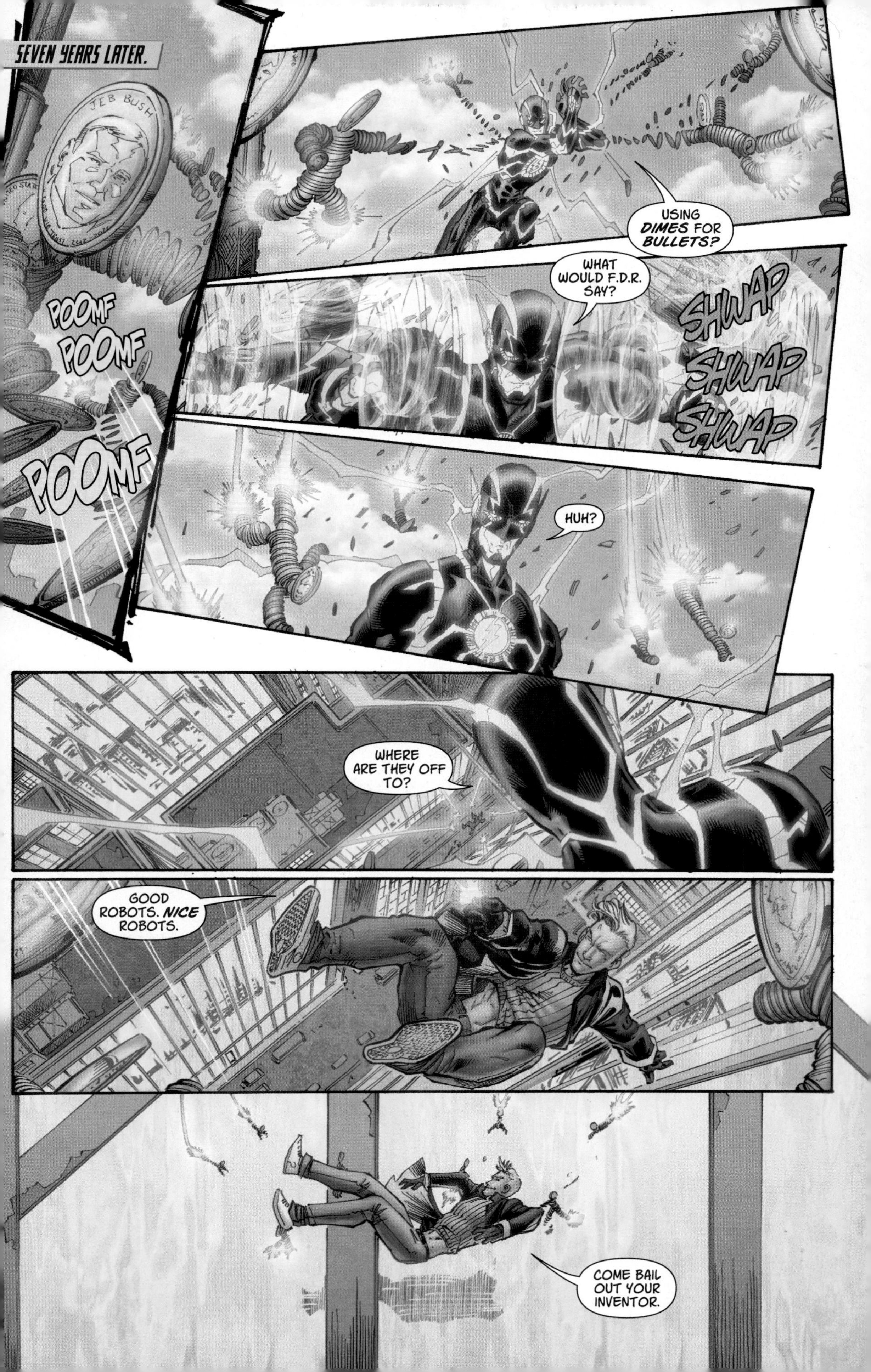
SEVEN YEARS LATER.
JEB BUSH
POOMF
POOMF
POOMF
USING DIMES FOR BULLETS?
WHAT WOULD F.D.R. SAY?
SHWAP
SHWAP
SHWAP
HUH?
WHERE ARE THEY OFF TO?
GOOD ROBOTS. NICE ROBOTS.
COME BAIL OUT YOUR INVENTOR.

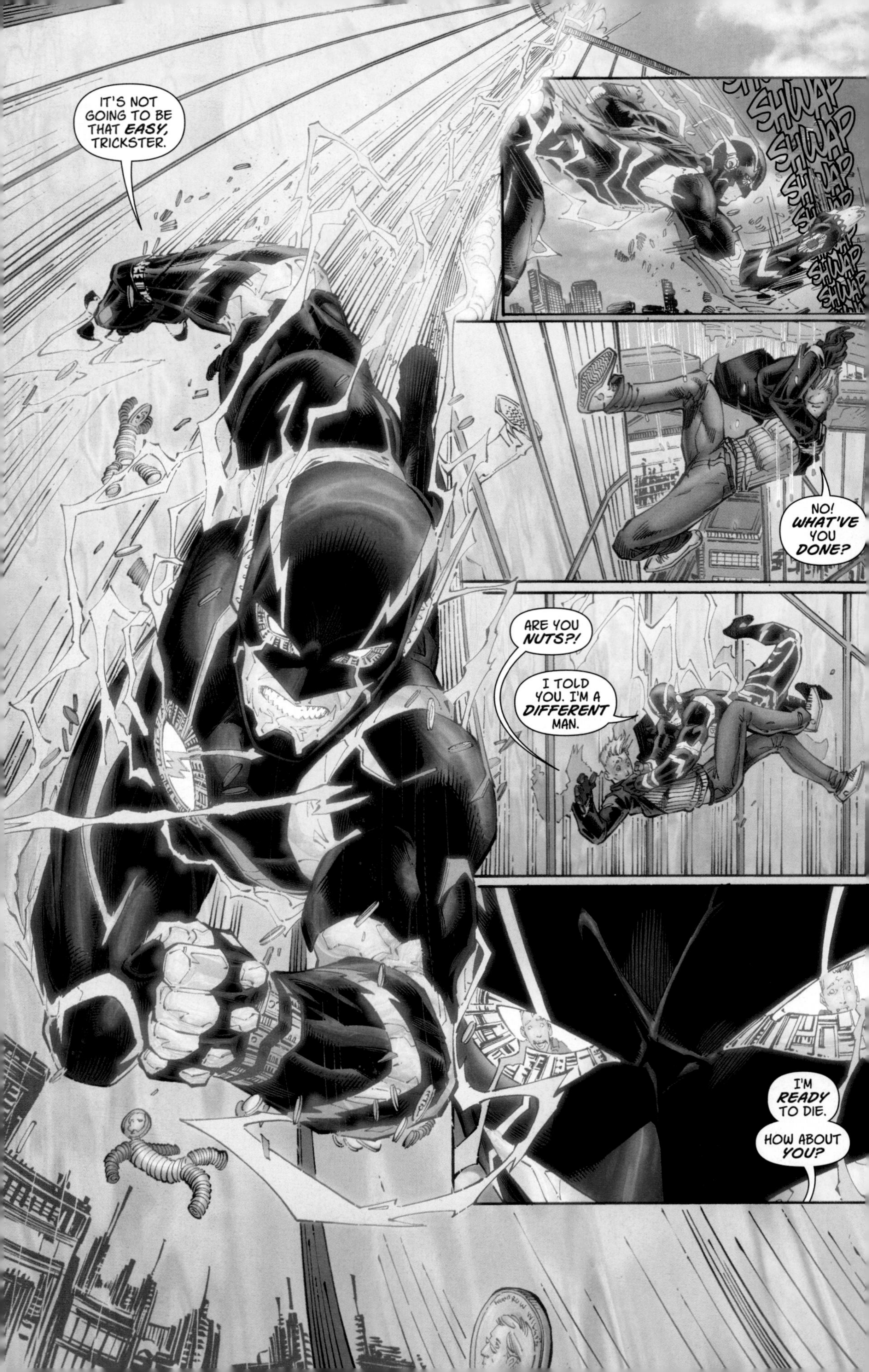
IT'S NOT GOING TO BE THAT *EASY,* TRICKSTER.
SHWAP SHWAP SHWAP SHWAP SHWAP SHWAP
NO! *WHAT'VE* YOU *DONE?*
ARE YOU *NUTS?!*
I TOLD YOU. I'M A *DIFFERENT* MAN.
I'M *READY* TO DIE.
HOW ABOUT *YOU?*

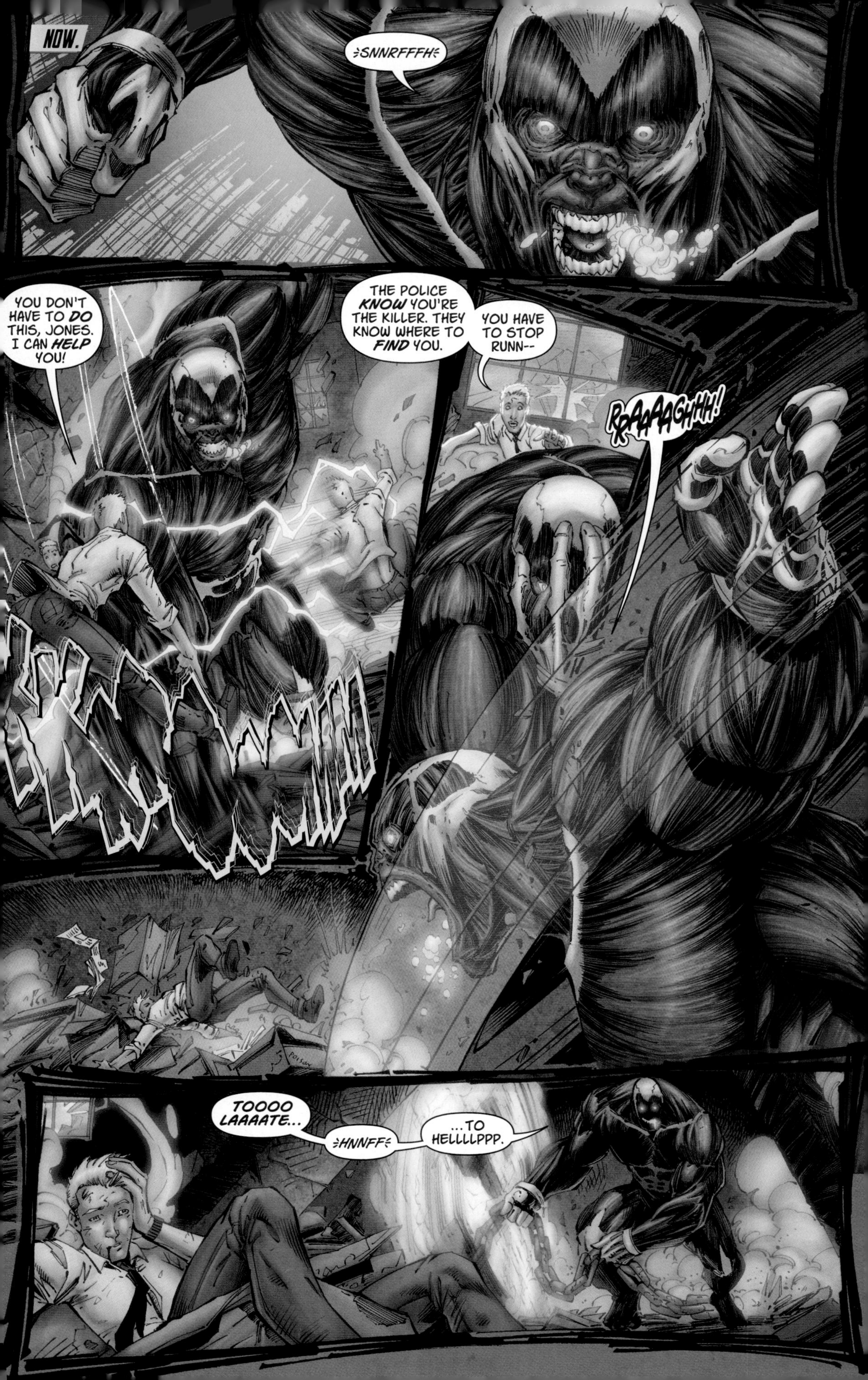
NOW.
SNNRFFFH
YOU DON'T HAVE TO DO THIS, JONES. I CAN HELP YOU!
THE POLICE KNOW YOU'RE THE KILLER. THEY KNOW WHERE TO FIND YOU.
YOU HAVE TO STOP RUNN--
RRAAAAGHHH!
TOOOO LAAAATE...
HNNFF
...TO HELLLLPPP.

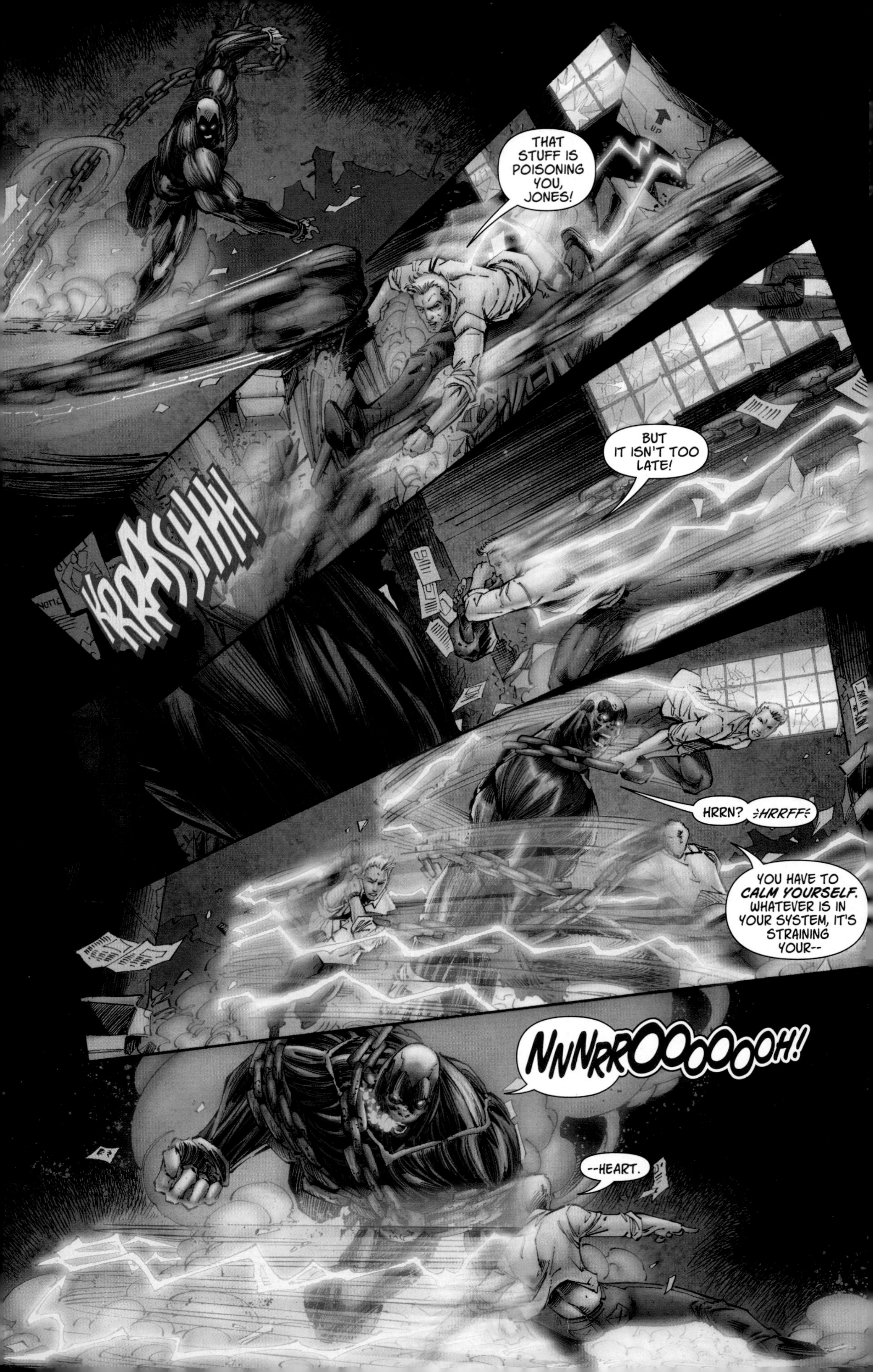
THAT STUFF IS POISONING YOU, JONES!
KRRASHH
BUT IT ISN'T TOO LATE!
HRRN? HRRFF
YOU HAVE TO CALM YOURSELF. WHATEVER IS IN YOUR SYSTEM, IT'S STRAINING YOUR--
NNNRROOOOOOOH!
--HEART.

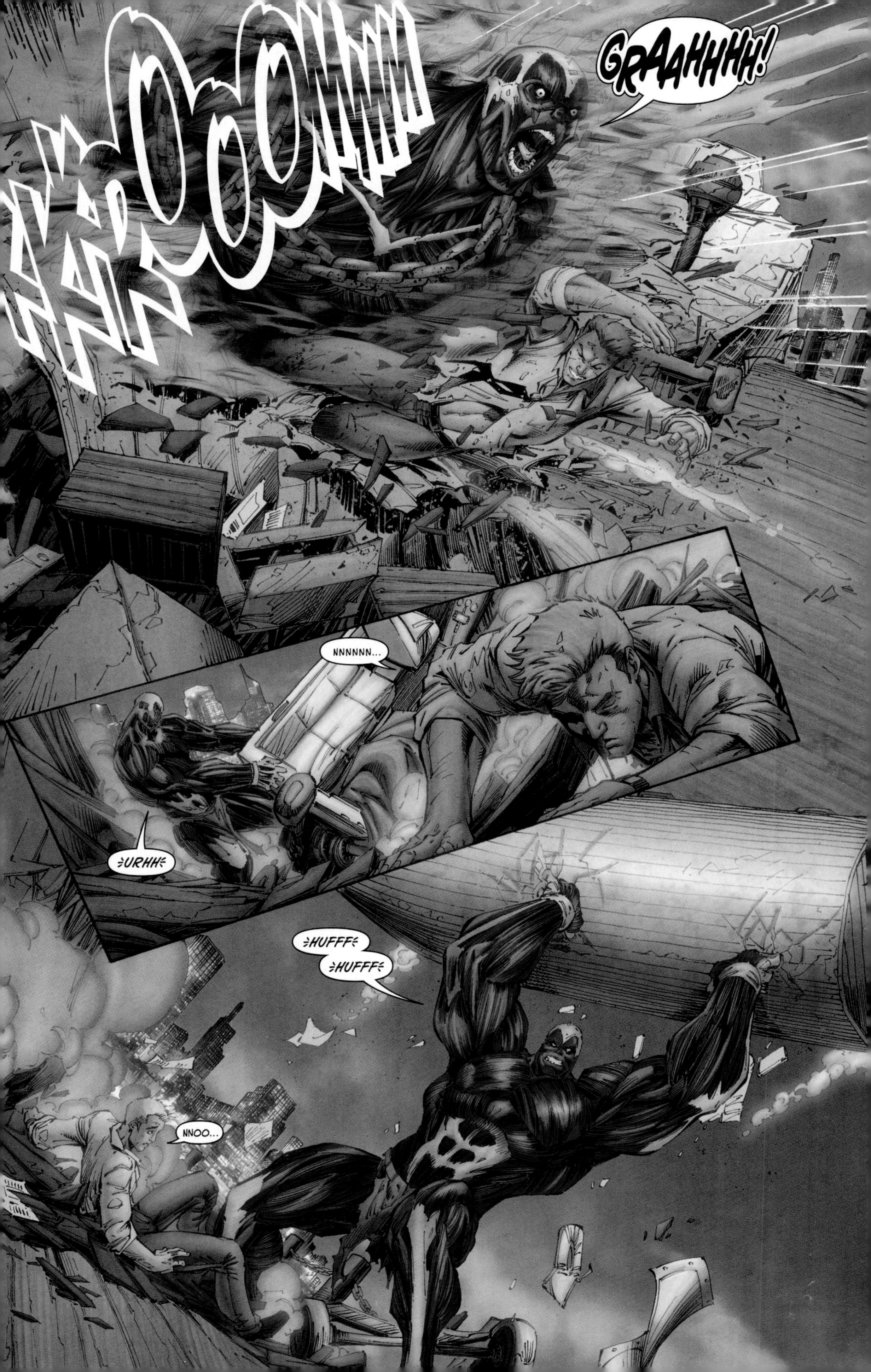
KA-BOOOMMM
GRAAHHHH!
NNNNNN...
URHH
HUFFF
HUFFF
NNOO...

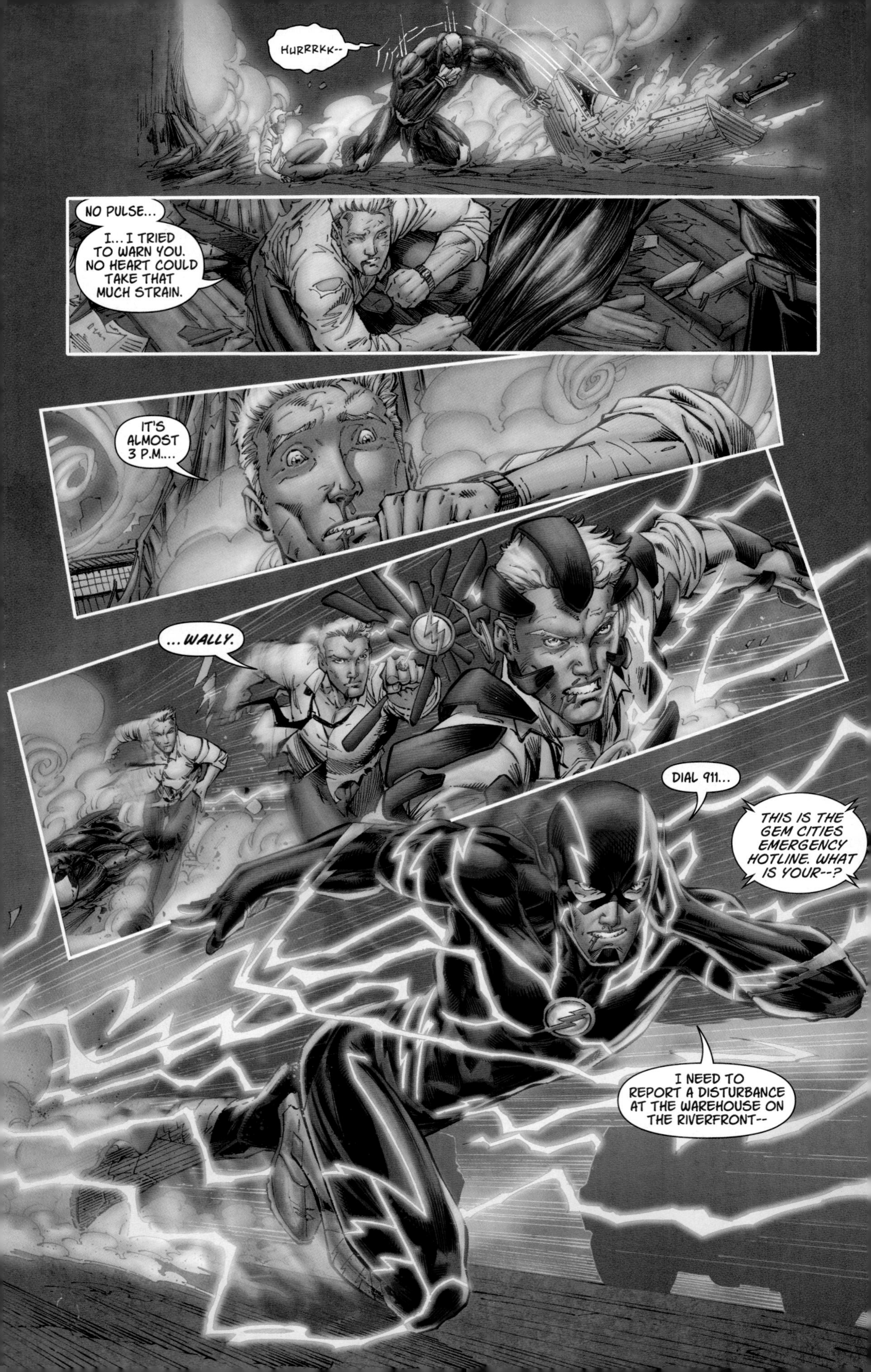
HURRRKK--
NO PULSE...
I... I TRIED TO WARN YOU. NO HEART COULD TAKE THAT MUCH STRAIN.
IT'S ALMOST 3 P.M....
...WALLY.
DIAL 911...
THIS IS THE GEM CITIES EMERGENCY HOTLINE. WHAT IS YOUR--?
I NEED TO REPORT A DISTURBANCE AT THE WAREHOUSE ON THE RIVERFRONT--

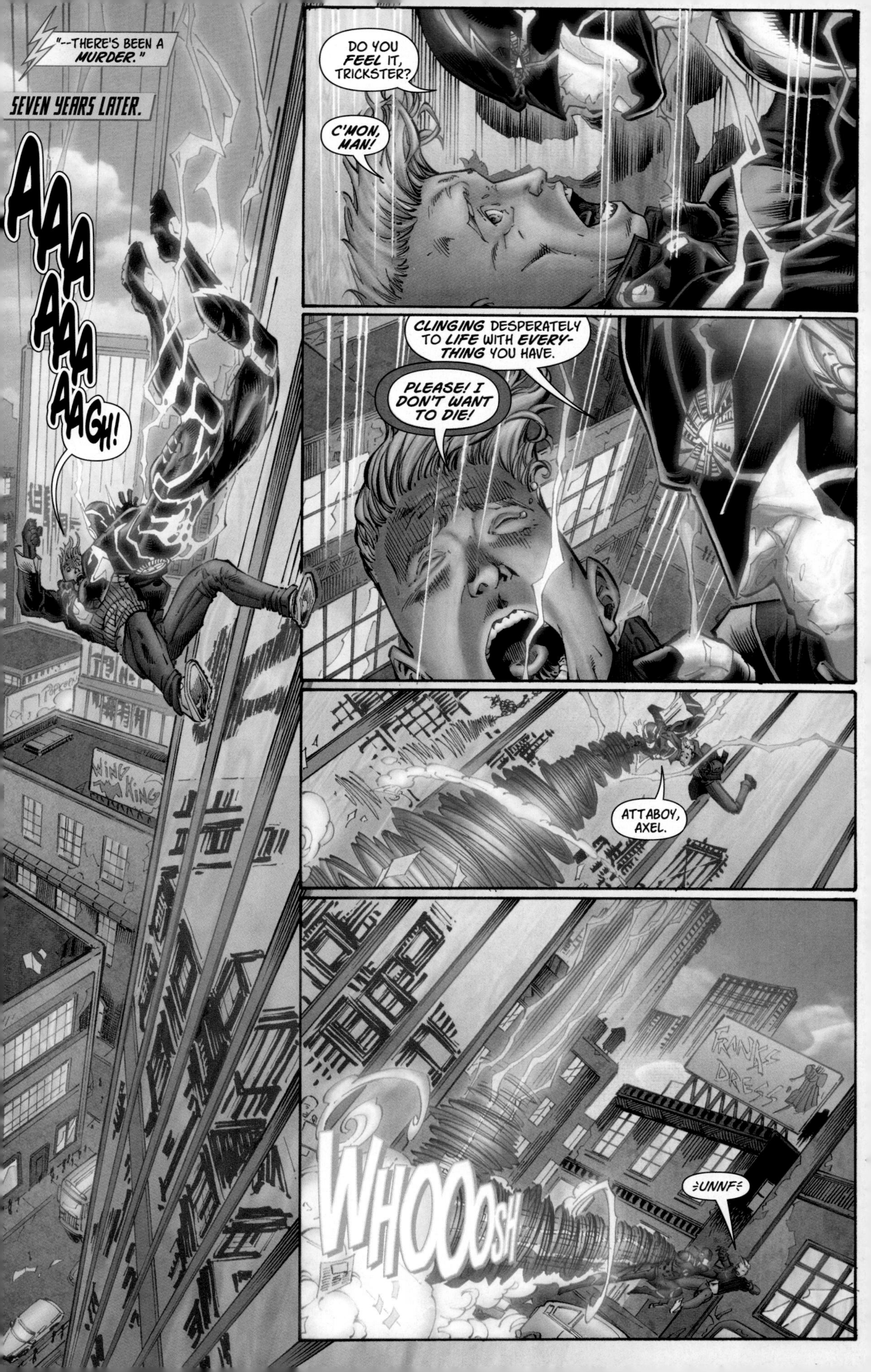
"--THERE'S BEEN A MURDER."
SEVEN YEARS LATER.
AAAAAAAAAAGH!
DO YOU FEEL IT, TRICKSTER?
C'MON, MAN!
CLINGING DESPERATELY TO LIFE WITH EVERY-THING YOU HAVE.
PLEASE! I DON'T WANT TO DIE!
ATTABOY, AXEL.
WHOOOSH
UNNF

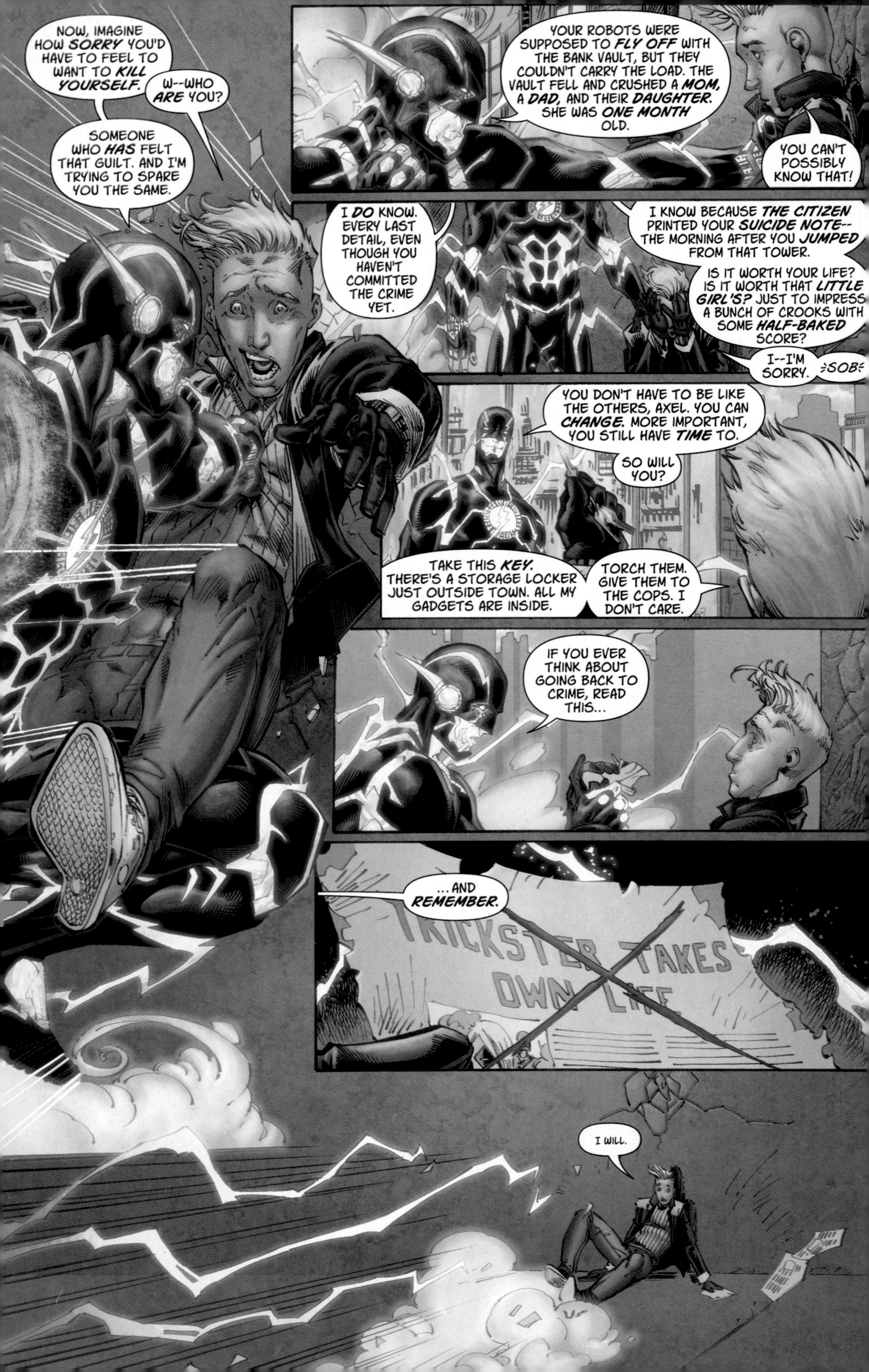
NOW, IMAGINE HOW SORRY YOU'D HAVE TO FEEL TO WANT TO KILL YOURSELF.
W--WHO ARE YOU?
SOMEONE WHO HAS FELT THAT GUILT. AND I'M TRYING TO SPARE YOU THE SAME.
YOUR ROBOTS WERE SUPPOSED TO FLY OFF WITH THE BANK VAULT, BUT THEY COULDN'T CARRY THE LOAD. THE VAULT FELL AND CRUSHED A MOM, A DAD, AND THEIR DAUGHTER. SHE WAS ONE MONTH OLD.
YOU CAN'T POSSIBLY KNOW THAT!
I DO KNOW. EVERY LAST DETAIL, EVEN THOUGH YOU HAVEN'T COMMITTED THE CRIME YET.
I KNOW BECAUSE THE CITIZEN PRINTED YOUR SUICIDE NOTE-- THE MORNING AFTER YOU JUMPED FROM THAT TOWER.
IS IT WORTH YOUR LIFE? IS IT WORTH THAT LITTLE GIRL'S? JUST TO IMPRESS A BUNCH OF CROOKS WITH SOME HALF-BAKED SCORE?
I--I'M SORRY.
<SOB>
YOU DON'T HAVE TO BE LIKE THE OTHERS, AXEL. YOU CAN CHANGE. MORE IMPORTANT, YOU STILL HAVE TIME TO.
SO WILL YOU?
TAKE THIS KEY. THERE'S A STORAGE LOCKER JUST OUTSIDE TOWN. ALL MY GADGETS ARE INSIDE.
TORCH THEM. GIVE THEM TO THE COPS. I DON'T CARE.
IF YOU EVER THINK ABOUT GOING BACK TO CRIME, READ THIS...
...AND REMEMBER.
TAKES
I WILL.

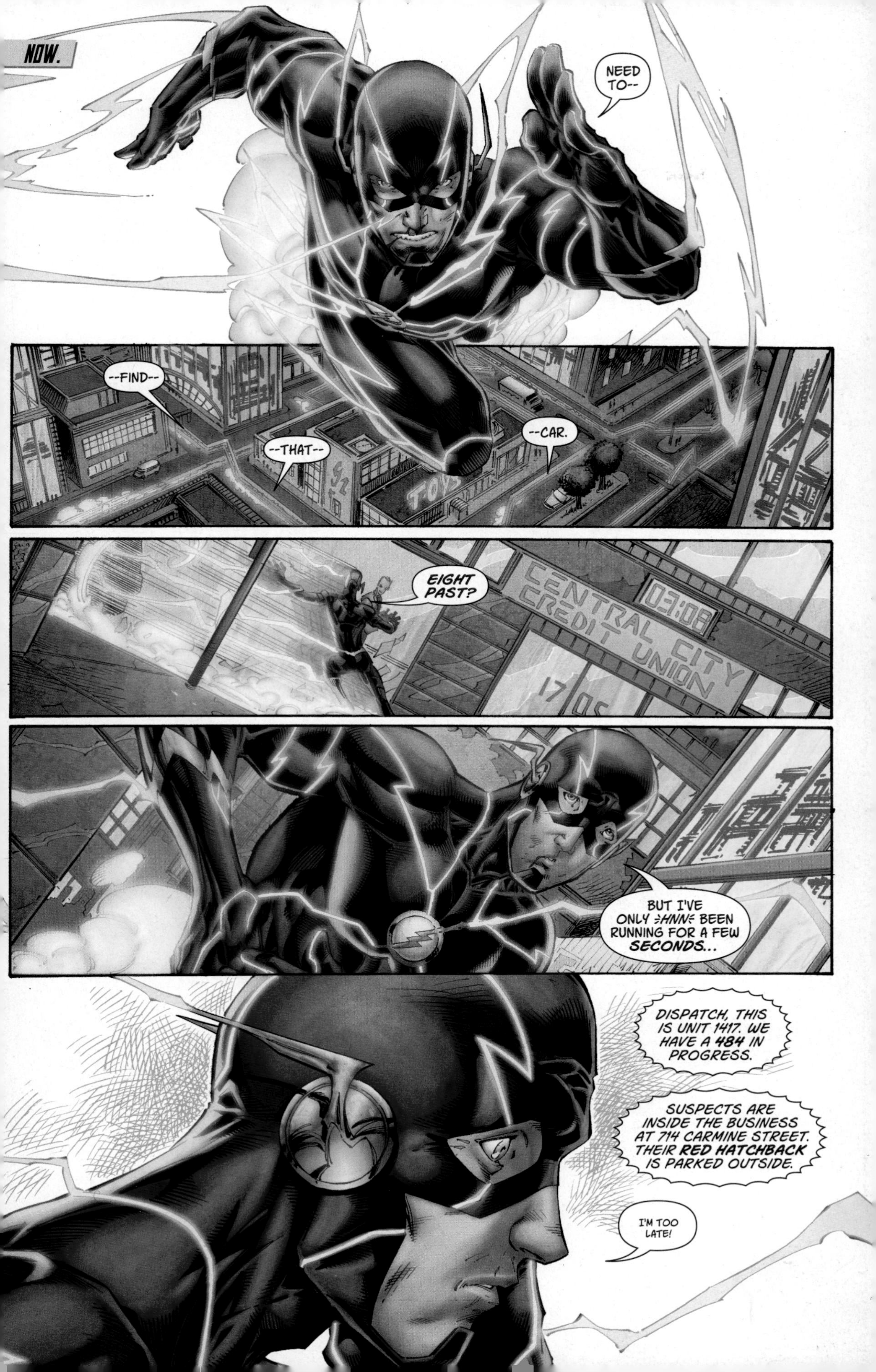
NOW.
NEED TO--
--FIND--
--THAT--
--CAR.
EIGHT PAST?
CENTRAL CITY CREDIT UNION
03:08
BUT I'VE ONLY HNN BEEN RUNNING FOR A FEW SECONDS...
DISPATCH, THIS IS UNIT 1417. WE HAVE A 484 IN PROGRESS.
SUSPECTS ARE INSIDE THE BUSINESS AT 714 CARMINE STREET. THEIR RED HATCHBACK IS PARKED OUTSIDE.
I'M TOO LATE!

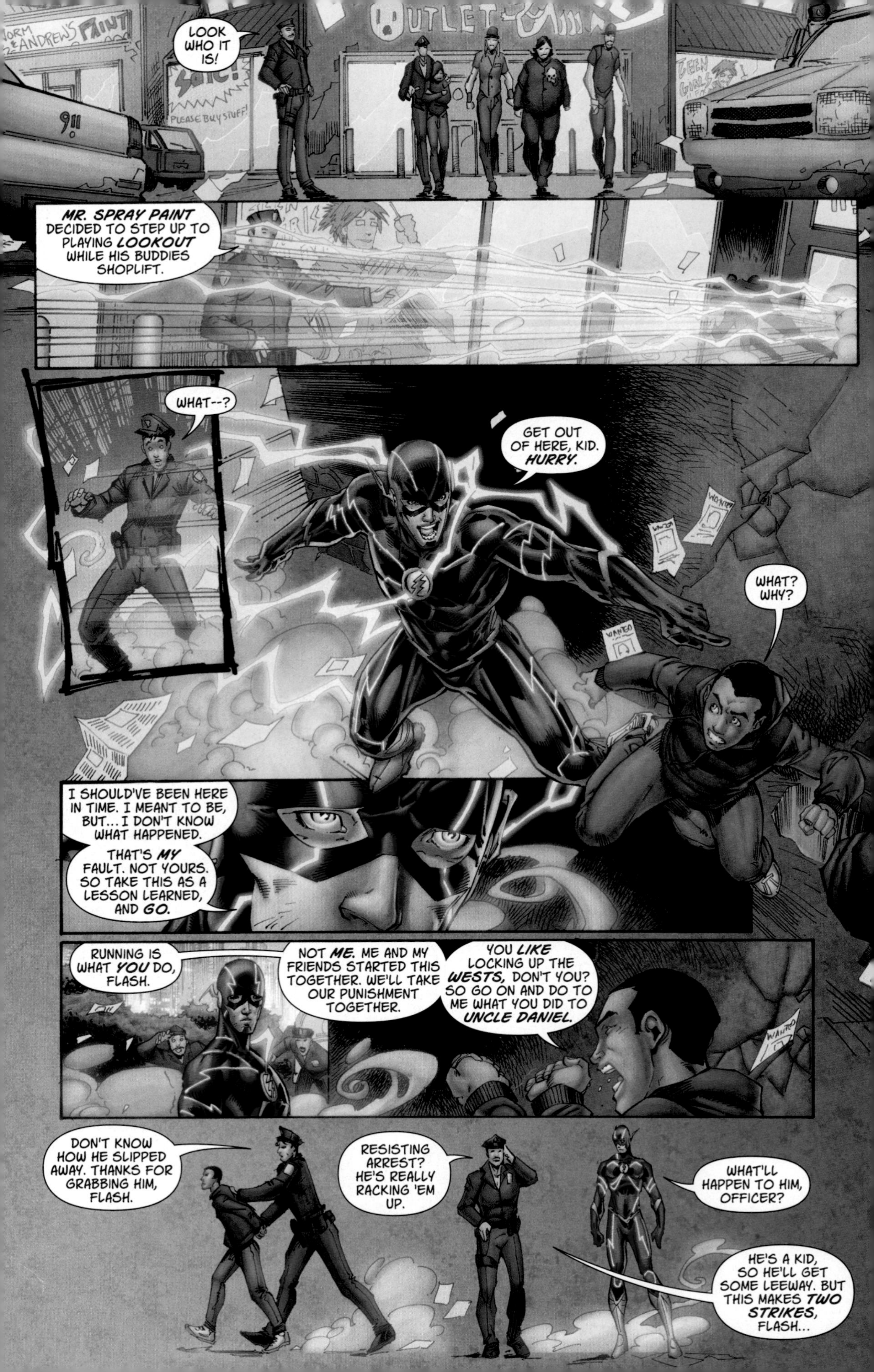
NORM & ANDREW'S PAINT
OUTLET
SALE! PLEASE BUY STUFF!
LOOK WHO IT IS!
MR. SPRAY PAINT DECIDED TO STEP UP TO PLAYING LOOKOUT WHILE HIS BUDDIES SHOPLIFT.
WHAT--?
GET OUT OF HERE, KID. HURRY.
WHAT? WHY?
I SHOULD'VE BEEN HERE IN TIME. I MEANT TO BE, BUT... I DON'T KNOW WHAT HAPPENED.
THAT'S MY FAULT. NOT YOURS. SO TAKE THIS AS A LESSON LEARNED, AND GO.
RUNNING IS WHAT YOU DO, FLASH.
NOT ME. ME AND MY FRIENDS STARTED THIS TOGETHER. WE'LL TAKE OUR PUNISHMENT TOGETHER.
YOU LIKE LOCKING UP THE WESTS, DON'T YOU? SO GO ON AND DO TO ME WHAT YOU DID TO UNCLE DANIEL.
DON'T KNOW HOW HE SLIPPED AWAY. THANKS FOR GRABBING HIM, FLASH.
RESISTING ARREST? HE'S REALLY RACKING 'EM UP.
WHAT'LL HAPPEN TO HIM, OFFICER?
HE'S A KID, SO HE'LL GET SOME LEEWAY. BUT THIS MAKES TWO STRIKES, FLASH...

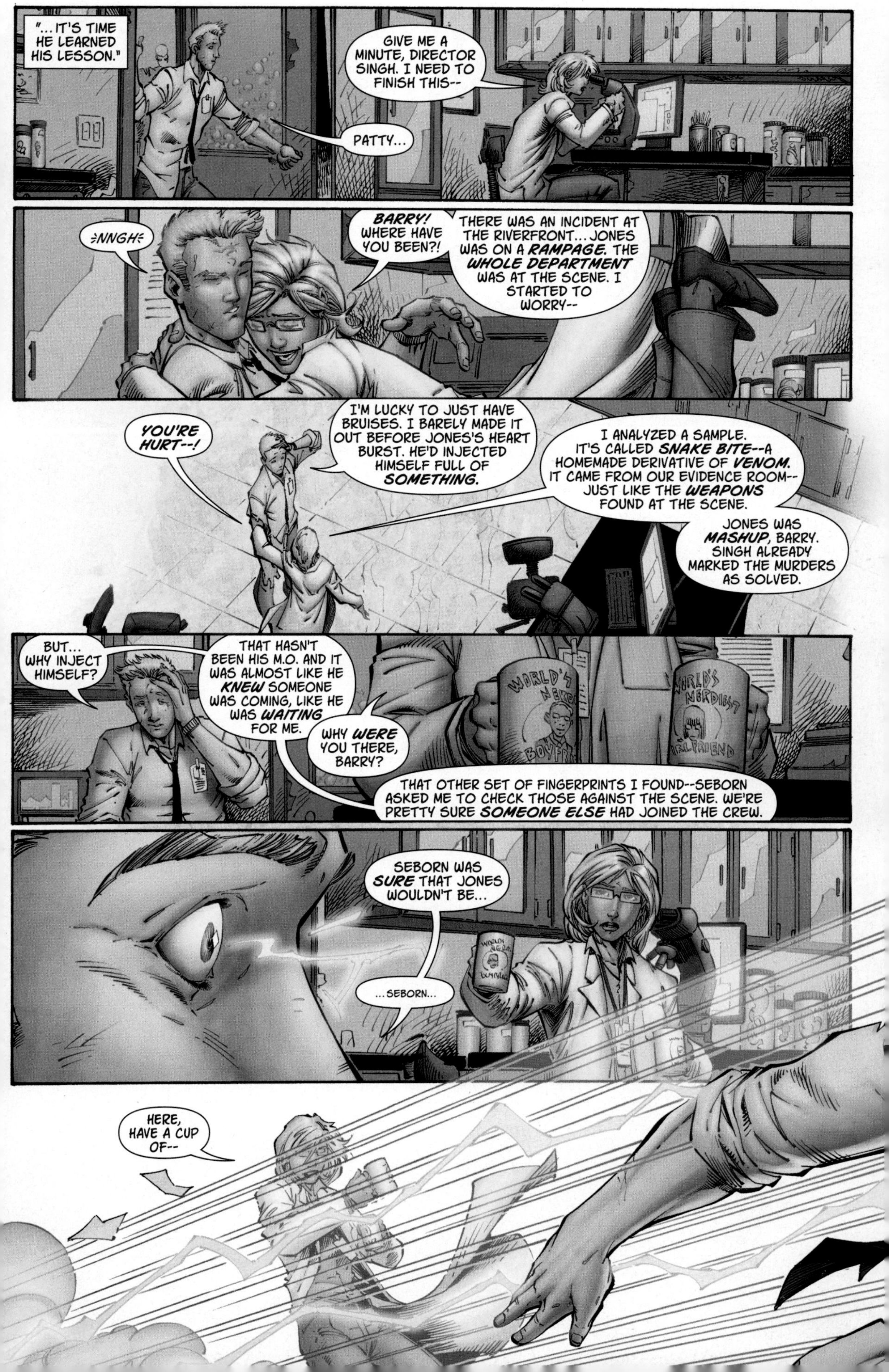
"...IT'S TIME HE LEARNED HIS LESSON."
GIVE ME A MINUTE, DIRECTOR SINGH. I NEED TO FINISH THIS--
PATTY...
NNGH
BARRY! WHERE HAVE YOU BEEN?!
THERE WAS AN INCIDENT AT THE RIVERFRONT... JONES WAS ON A RAMPAGE. THE WHOLE DEPARTMENT WAS AT THE SCENE. I STARTED TO WORRY--
YOU'RE HURT--!
I'M LUCKY TO JUST HAVE BRUISES. I BARELY MADE IT OUT BEFORE JONES'S HEART BURST. HE'D INJECTED HIMSELF FULL OF SOMETHING.
I ANALYZED A SAMPLE. IT'S CALLED SNAKE BITE--A HOMEMADE DERIVATIVE OF VENOM. IT CAME FROM OUR EVIDENCE ROOM--JUST LIKE THE WEAPONS FOUND AT THE SCENE.
JONES WAS MASHUP, BARRY. SINGH ALREADY MARKED THE MURDERS AS SOLVED.
BUT... WHY INJECT HIMSELF?
THAT HASN'T BEEN HIS M.O. AND IT WAS ALMOST LIKE HE KNEW SOMEONE WAS COMING, LIKE HE WAS WAITING FOR ME.
WORLD'S NERDIEST GIRLFRIEND
WHY WERE YOU THERE, BARRY?
THAT OTHER SET OF FINGERPRINTS I FOUND--SEBORN ASKED ME TO CHECK THOSE AGAINST THE SCENE. WE'RE PRETTY SURE SOMEONE ELSE HAD JOINED THE CREW.
SEBORN WAS SURE THAT JONES WOULDN'T BE...
...SEBORN...
HERE, HAVE A CUP OF--

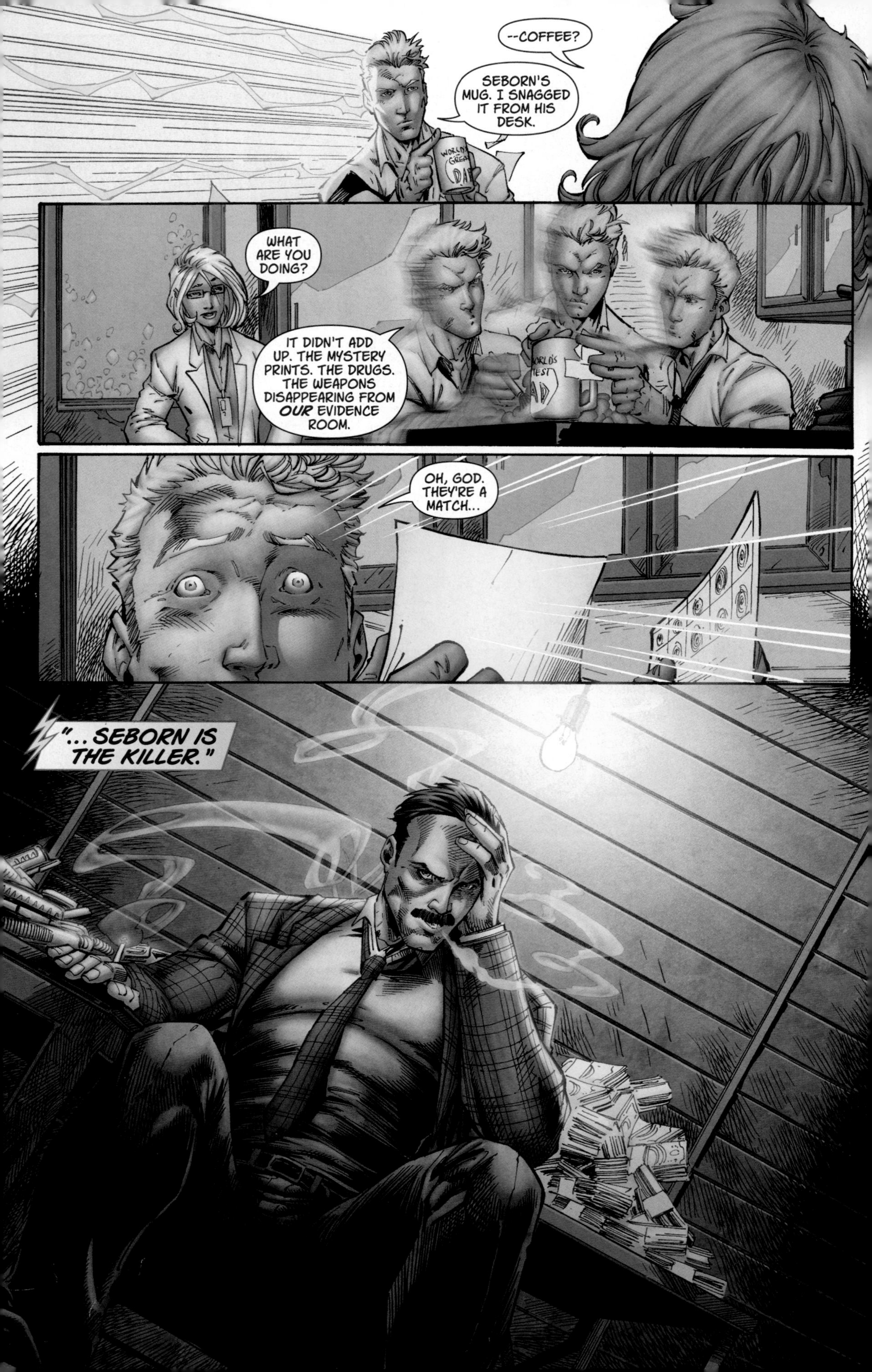
--COFFEE?
SEBORN'S MUG. I SNAGGED IT FROM HIS DESK.
WHAT ARE YOU DOING?
IT DIDN'T ADD UP. THE MYSTERY PRINTS. THE DRUGS. THE WEAPONS DISAPPEARING FROM OUR EVIDENCE ROOM.
OH, GOD. THEY'RE A MATCH...
"...SEBORN IS THE KILLER."

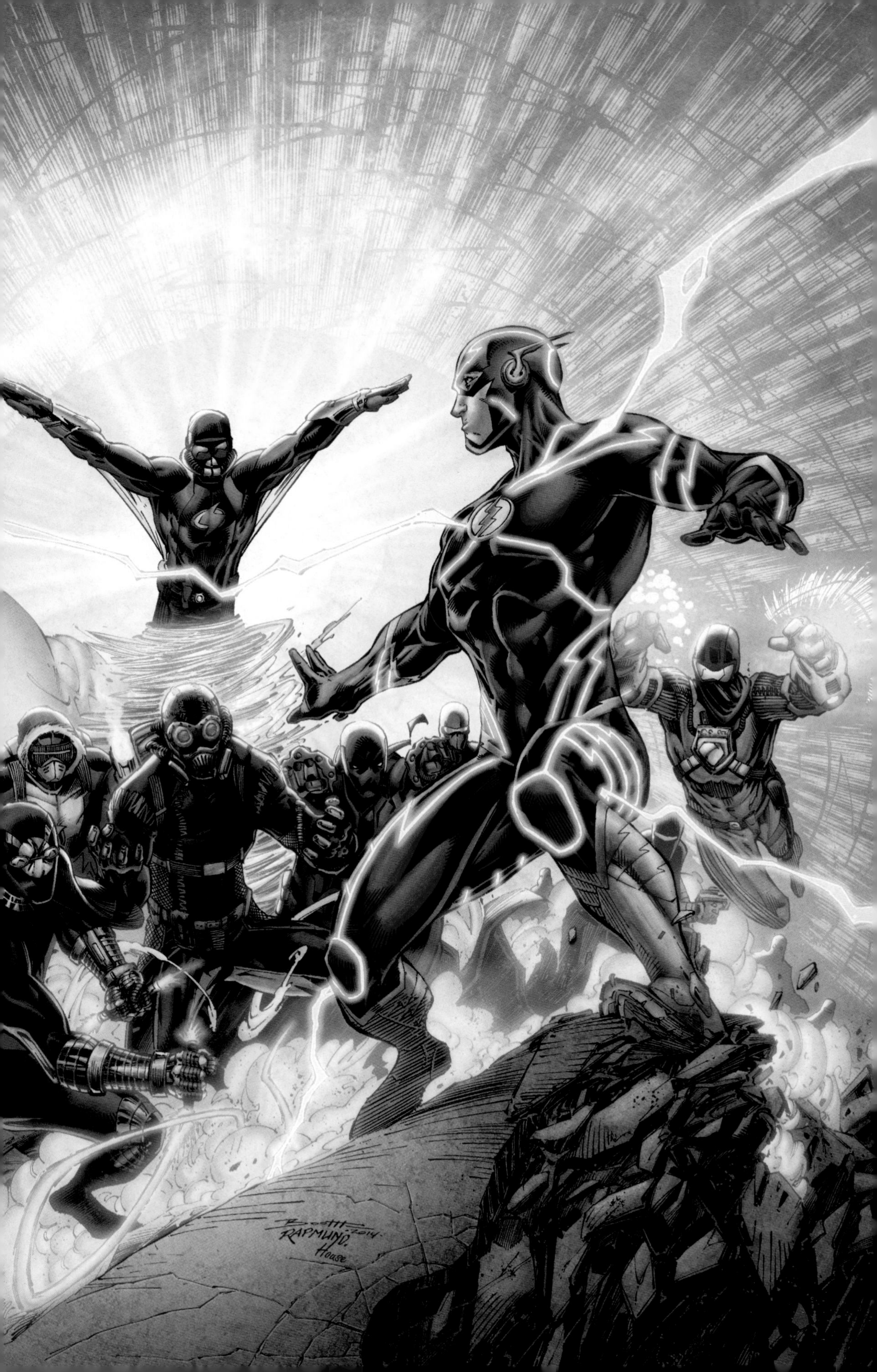
BOOTH 2014
RAPMUND.
House

COLLISION COURSE

ROBERT VENDITTI & VAN JENSEN writers **BRETT BOOTH** penciller **NORM RAPMUND** inker

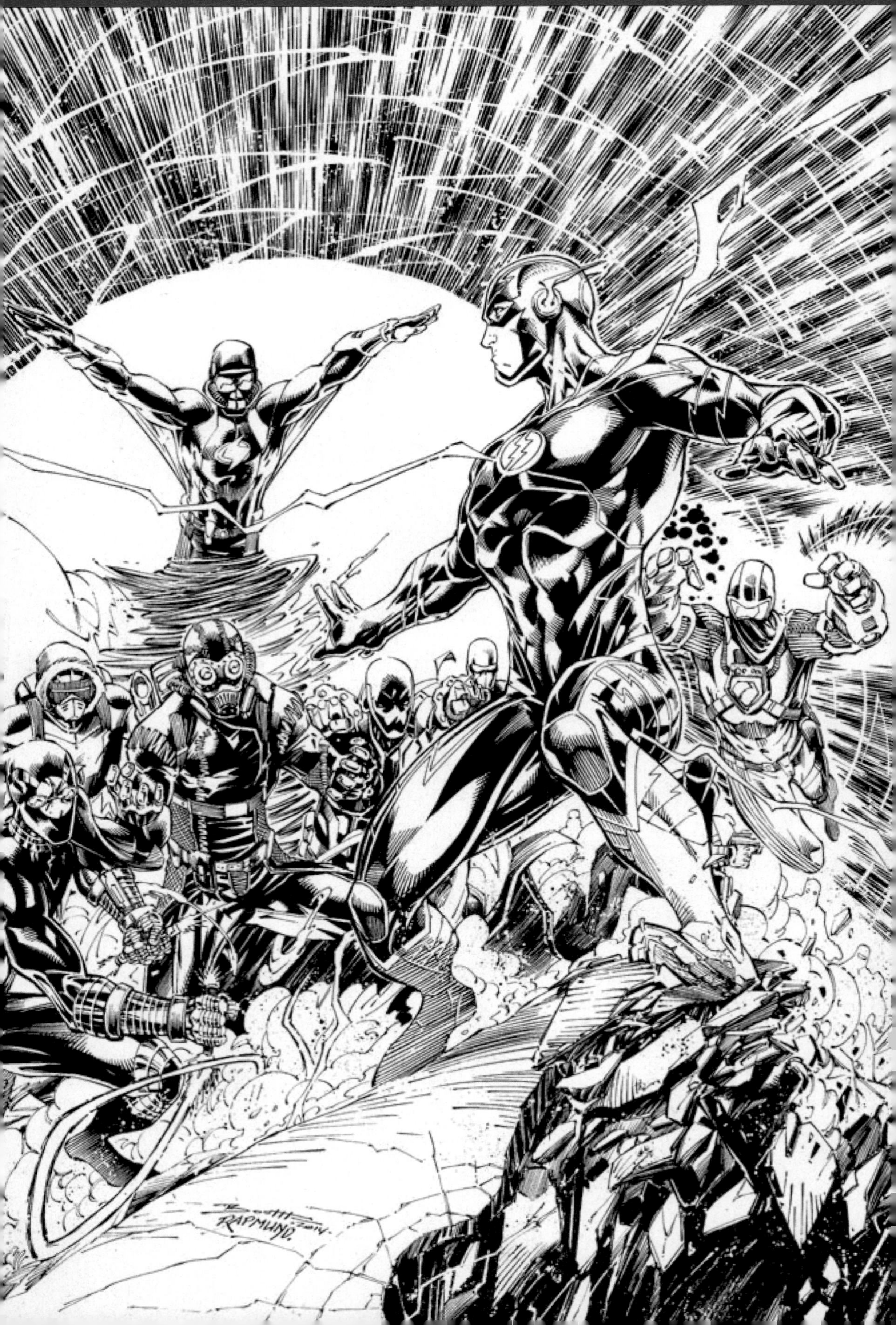

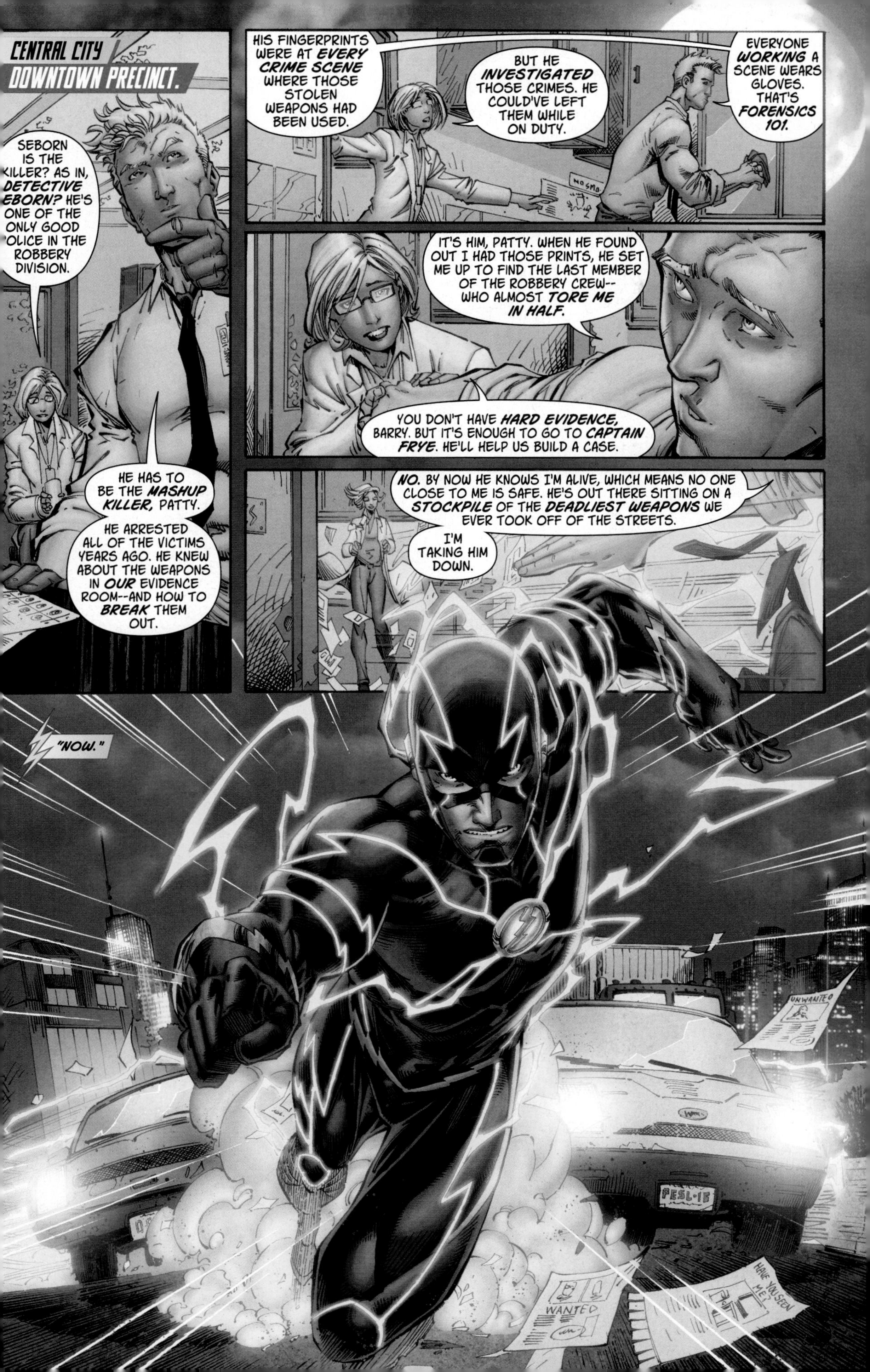
CENTRAL CITY
DOWNTOWN PRECINCT.
SEBORN IS THE KILLER? AS IN, DETECTIVE SEBORN? HE'S ONE OF THE ONLY GOOD POLICE IN THE ROBBERY DIVISION.
HE HAS TO BE THE MASHUP KILLER, PATTY.
HE ARRESTED ALL OF THE VICTIMS YEARS AGO. HE KNEW ABOUT THE WEAPONS IN OUR EVIDENCE ROOM--AND HOW TO BREAK THEM OUT.
HIS FINGERPRINTS WERE AT EVERY CRIME SCENE WHERE THOSE STOLEN WEAPONS HAD BEEN USED.
BUT HE INVESTIGATED THOSE CRIMES. HE COULD'VE LEFT THEM WHILE ON DUTY.
EVERYONE WORKING A SCENE WEARS GLOVES. THAT'S FORENSICS 101.
IT'S HIM, PATTY. WHEN HE FOUND OUT I HAD THOSE PRINTS, HE SET ME UP TO FIND THE LAST MEMBER OF THE ROBBERY CREW-- WHO ALMOST TORE ME IN HALF.
YOU DON'T HAVE HARD EVIDENCE, BARRY. BUT IT'S ENOUGH TO GO TO CAPTAIN FRYE. HE'LL HELP US BUILD A CASE.
NO. BY NOW HE KNOWS I'M ALIVE, WHICH MEANS NO ONE CLOSE TO ME IS SAFE. HE'S OUT THERE SITTING ON A STOCKPILE OF THE DEADLIEST WEAPONS WE EVER TOOK OFF OF THE STREETS.
I'M TAKING HIM DOWN.
"NOW."
UNWANTED
FESL-15
WANTED
HAVE YOU SEEN ME?

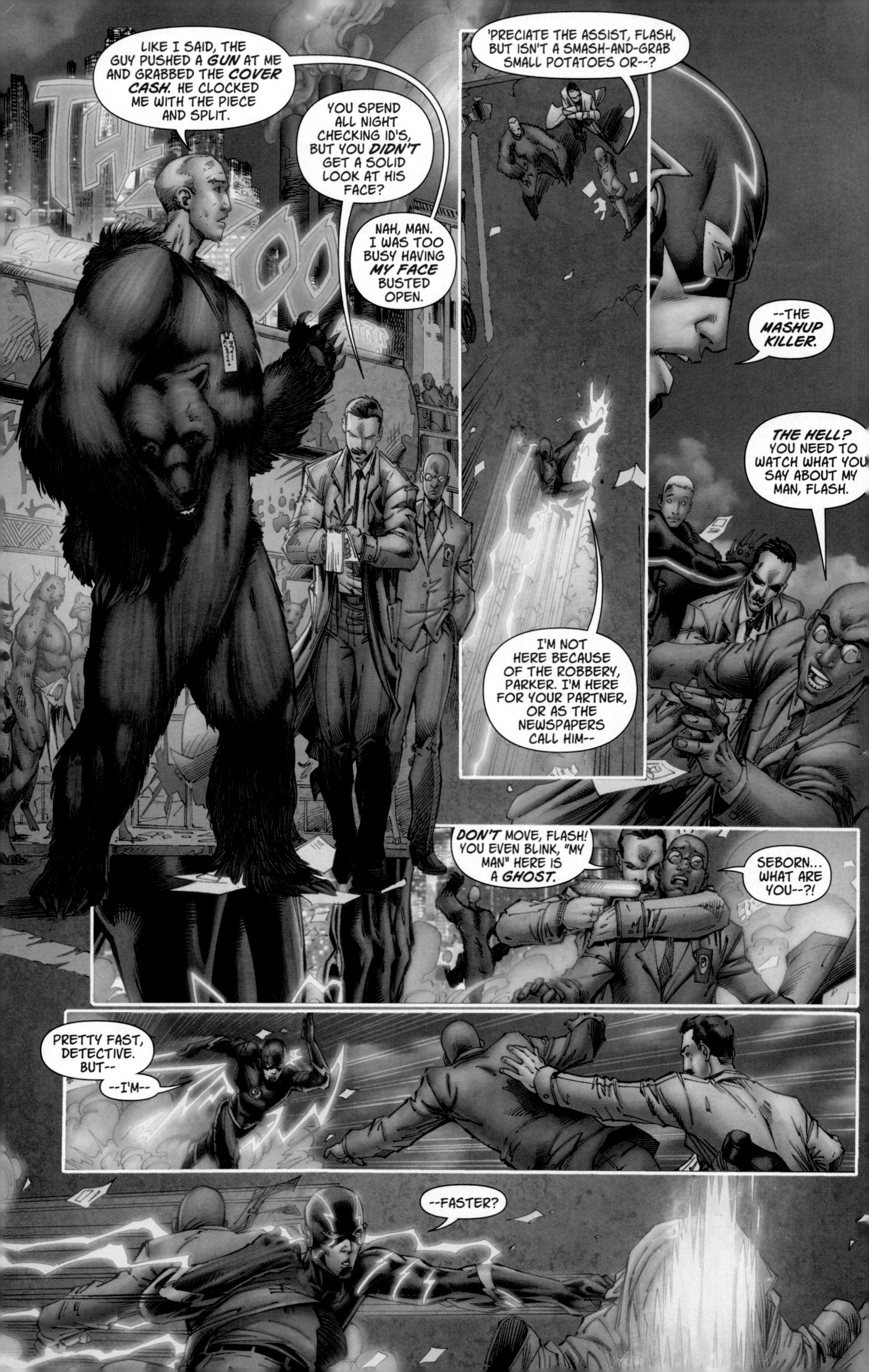
LIKE I SAID, THE GUY PUSHED A GUN AT ME AND GRABBED THE COVER CASH. HE CLOCKED ME WITH THE PIECE AND SPLIT.
YOU SPEND ALL NIGHT CHECKING ID'S, BUT YOU DIDN'T GET A SOLID LOOK AT HIS FACE?
NAH, MAN. I WAS TOO BUSY HAVING MY FACE BUSTED OPEN.
'PRECIATE THE ASSIST, FLASH, BUT ISN'T A SMASH-AND-GRAB SMALL POTATOES OR--?
I'M NOT HERE BECAUSE OF THE ROBBERY, PARKER. I'M HERE FOR YOUR PARTNER, OR AS THE NEWSPAPERS CALL HIM--
--THE MASHUP KILLER.
THE HELL? YOU NEED TO WATCH WHAT YOU SAY ABOUT MY MAN, FLASH.
DON'T MOVE, FLASH! YOU EVEN BLINK, "MY MAN" HERE IS A GHOST.
SEBORN... WHAT ARE YOU--?!
PRETTY FAST, DETECTIVE. BUT--
--I'M--
--FASTER?

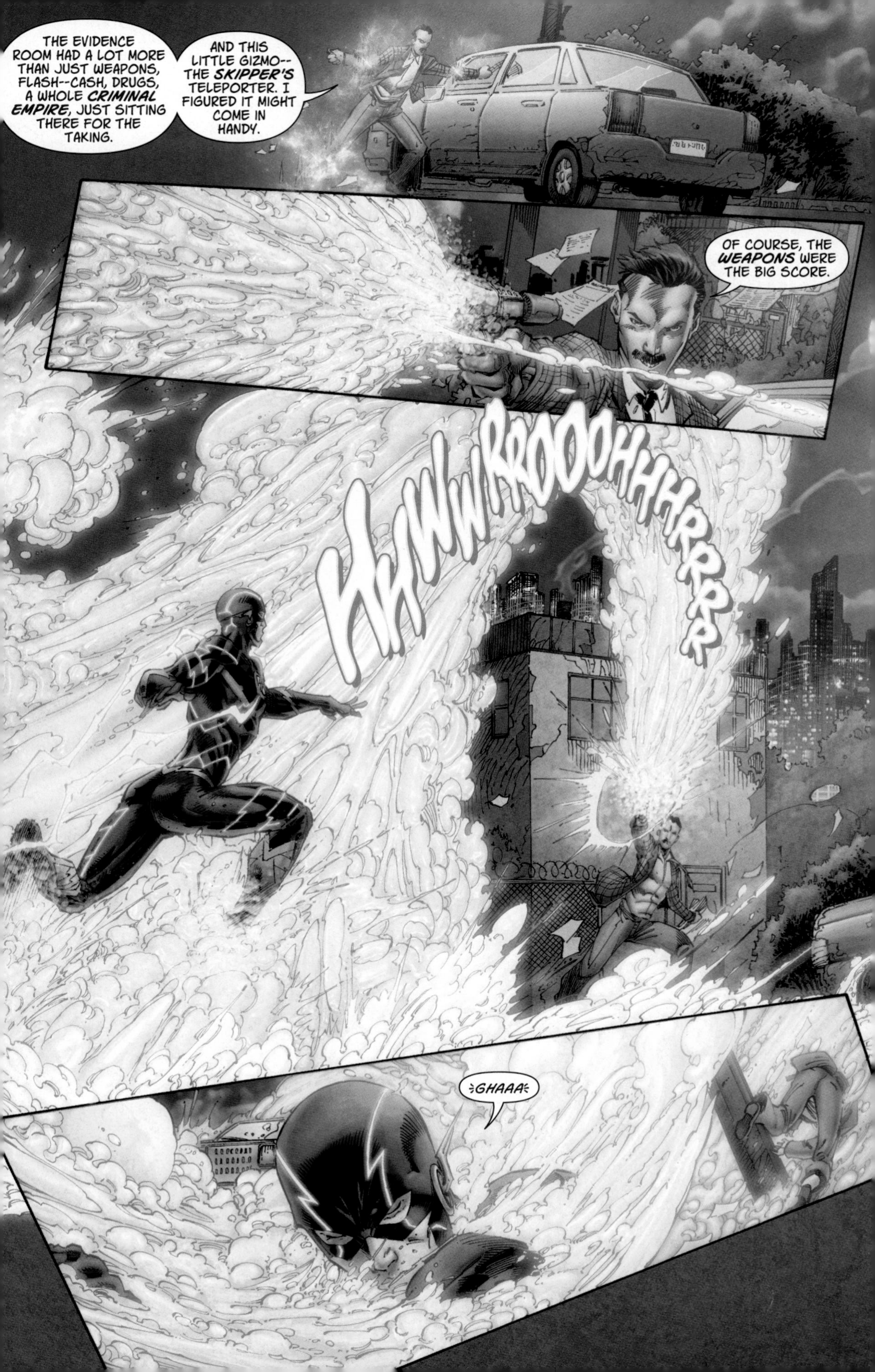

THE EVIDENCE ROOM HAD A LOT MORE THAN JUST WEAPONS, FLASH--CASH, DRUGS, A WHOLE CRIMINAL EMPIRE, JUST SITTING THERE FOR THE TAKING.
AND THIS LITTLE GIZMO--THE SKIPPER'S TELEPORTER. I FIGURED IT MIGHT COME IN HANDY.
OF COURSE, THE WEAPONS WERE THE BIG SCORE.
HHWWRROOOHHHRRRR
GHAAA

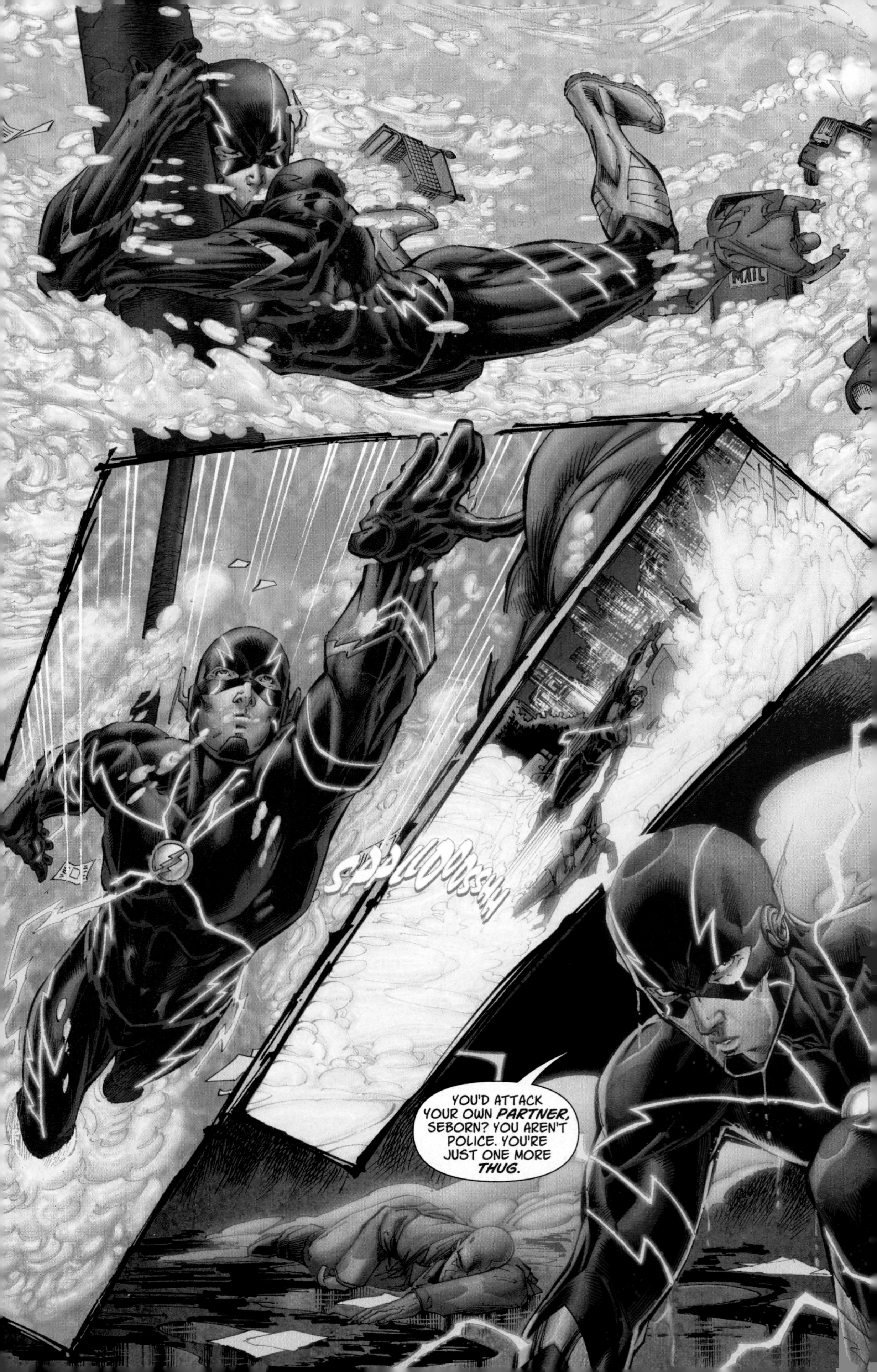
SPPLUUUSSHH
YOU'D ATTACK YOUR OWN PARTNER, SEBORN? YOU AREN'T POLICE. YOU'RE JUST ONE MORE THUG.

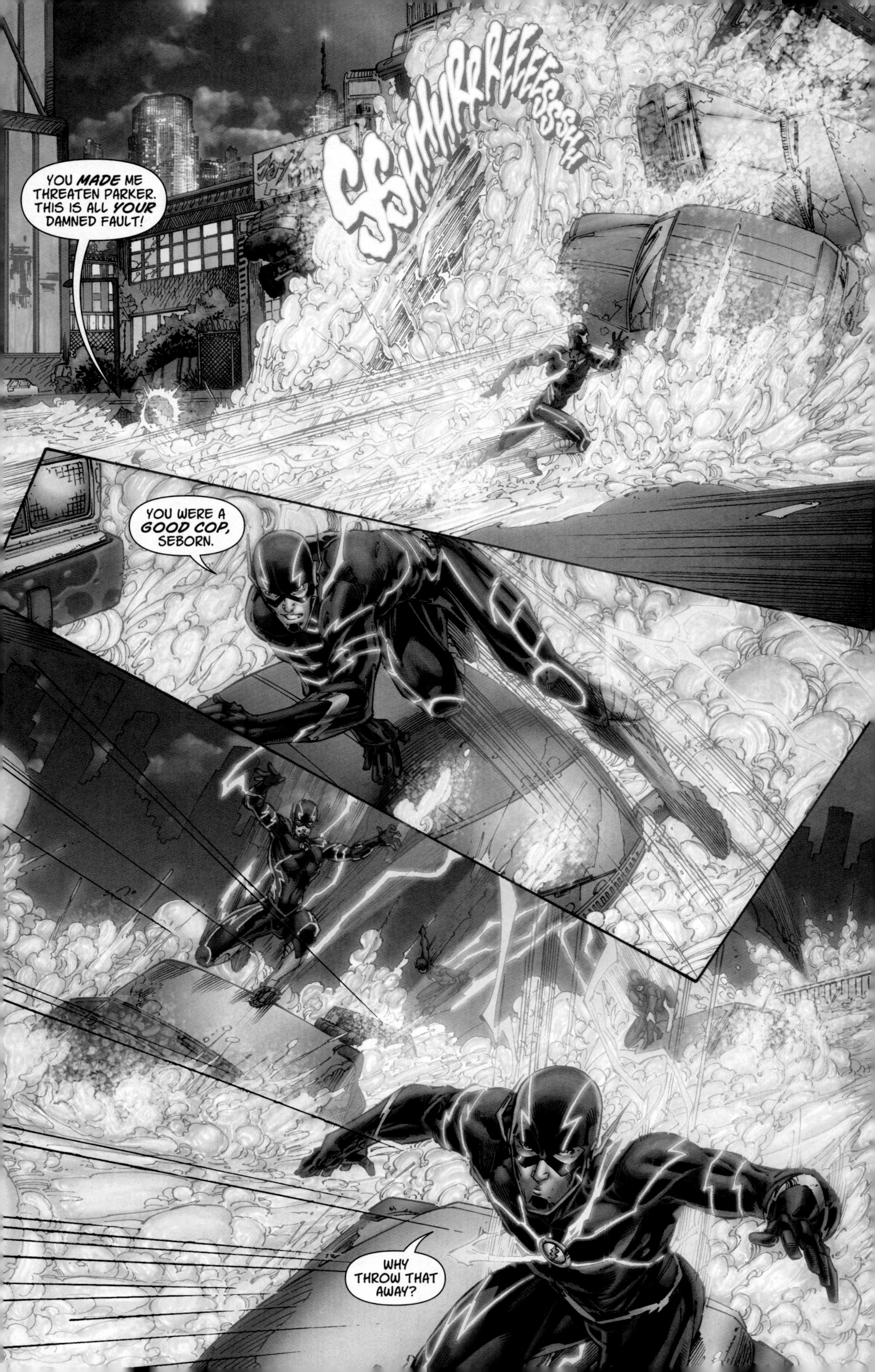
CSHHHRRREEEESSSH
YOU MADE ME THREATEN PARKER. THIS IS ALL YOUR DAMNED FAULT!
YOU WERE A GOOD COP, SEBORN.
WHY THROW THAT AWAY?

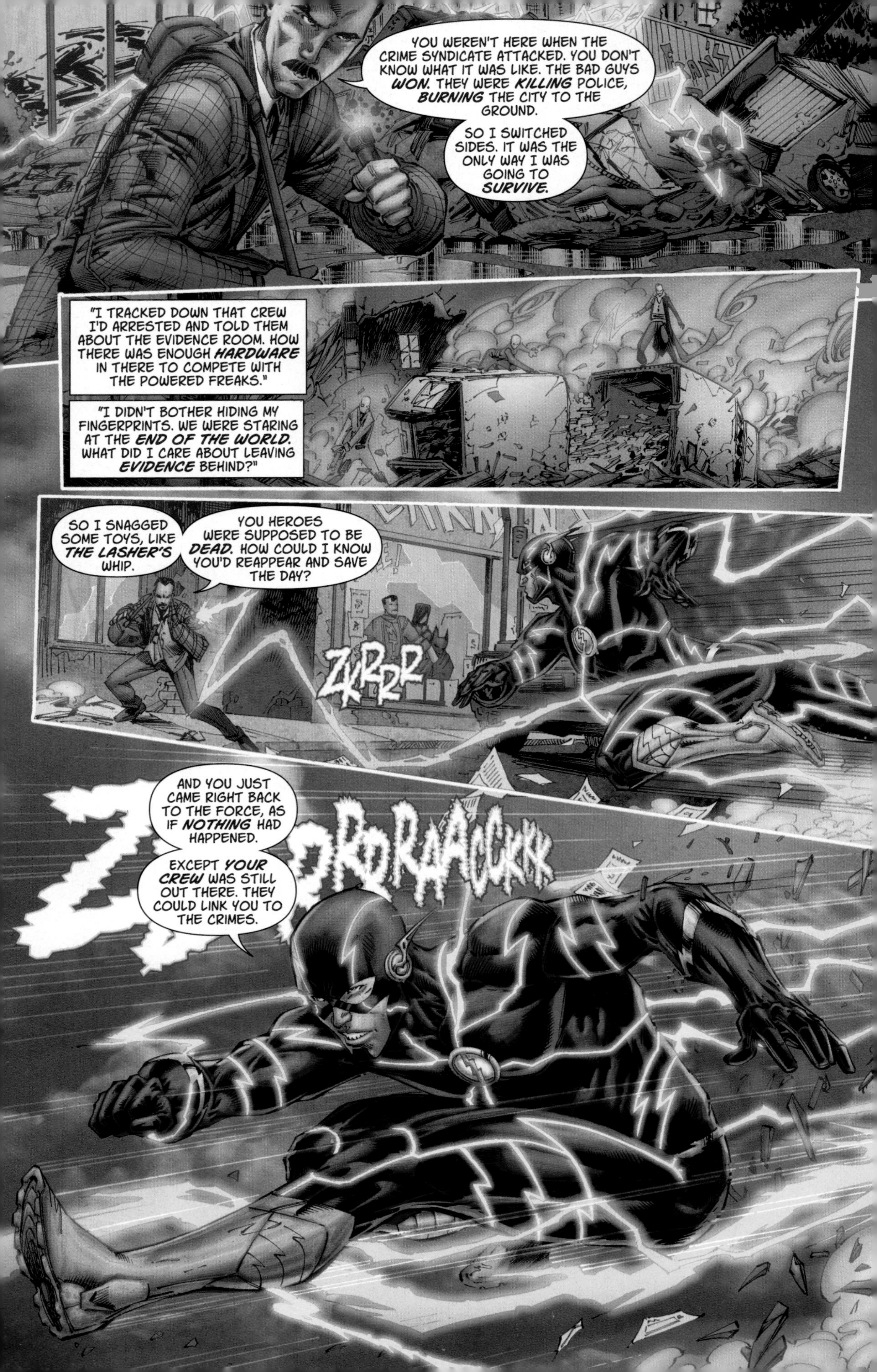

YOU WEREN'T HERE WHEN THE CRIME SYNDICATE ATTACKED. YOU DON'T KNOW WHAT IT WAS LIKE. THE BAD GUYS WON. THEY WERE KILLING POLICE, BURNING THE CITY TO THE GROUND.
SO I SWITCHED SIDES. IT WAS THE ONLY WAY I WAS GOING TO SURVIVE.
"I TRACKED DOWN THAT CREW I'D ARRESTED AND TOLD THEM ABOUT THE EVIDENCE ROOM. HOW THERE WAS ENOUGH HARDWARE IN THERE TO COMPETE WITH THE POWERED FREAKS."
"I DIDN'T BOTHER HIDING MY FINGERPRINTS. WE WERE STARING AT THE END OF THE WORLD. WHAT DID I CARE ABOUT LEAVING EVIDENCE BEHIND?"
SO I SNAGGED SOME TOYS, LIKE THE LASHER'S WHIP.
YOU HEROES WERE SUPPOSED TO BE DEAD. HOW COULD I KNOW YOU'D REAPPEAR AND SAVE THE DAY?
ZKRRR
AND YOU JUST CAME RIGHT BACK TO THE FORCE, AS IF NOTHING HAD HAPPENED.
EXCEPT YOUR CREW WAS STILL OUT THERE. THEY COULD LINK YOU TO THE CRIMES.

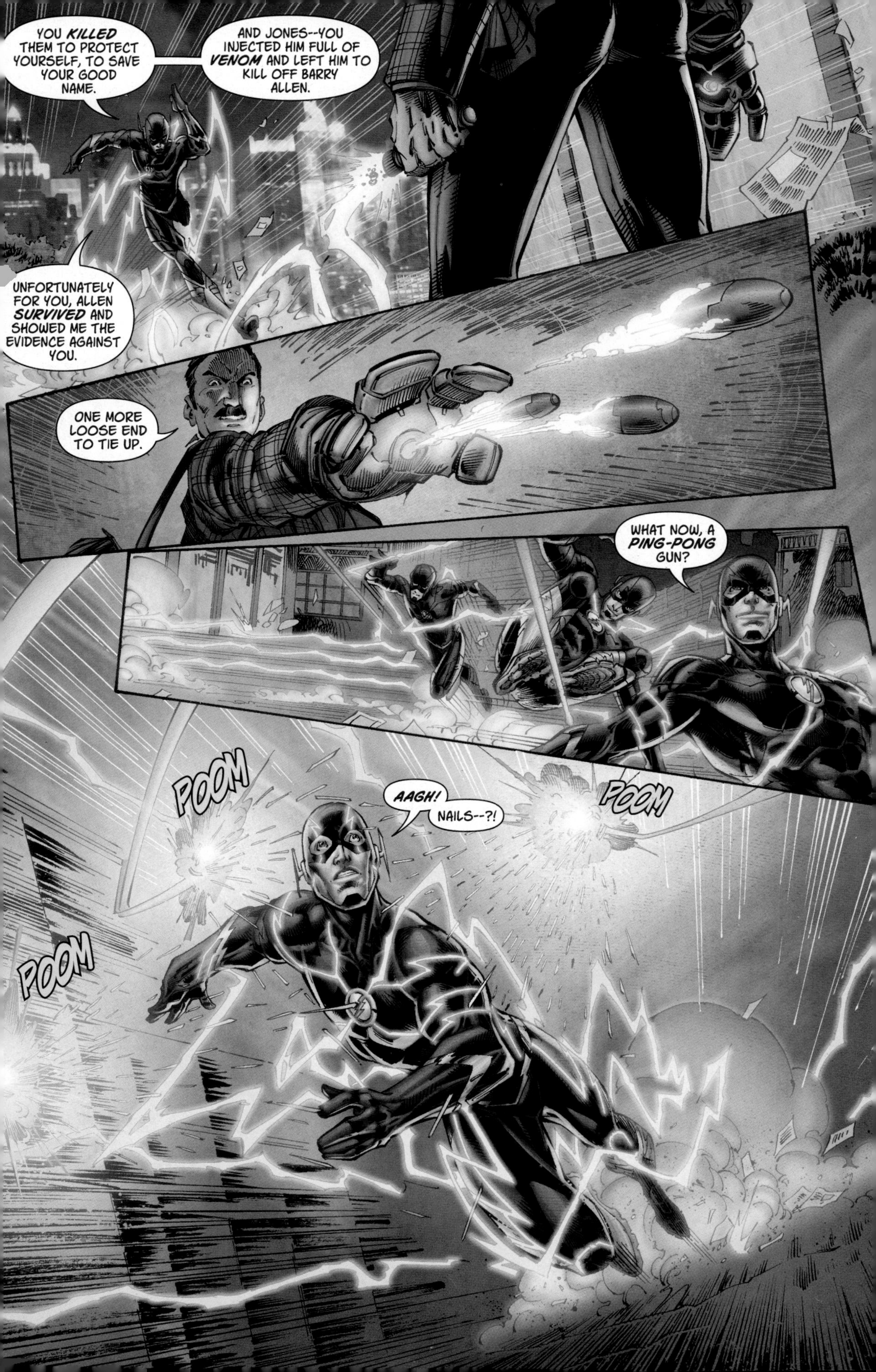
YOU KILLED THEM TO PROTECT YOURSELF, TO SAVE YOUR GOOD NAME.
AND JONES--YOU INJECTED HIM FULL OF VENOM AND LEFT HIM TO KILL OFF BARRY ALLEN.
UNFORTUNATELY FOR YOU, ALLEN SURVIVED AND SHOWED ME THE EVIDENCE AGAINST YOU.
ONE MORE LOOSE END TO TIE UP.
WHAT NOW, A PING-PONG GUN?
POOM
AAGH!
NAILS--?!
POOM
POOM

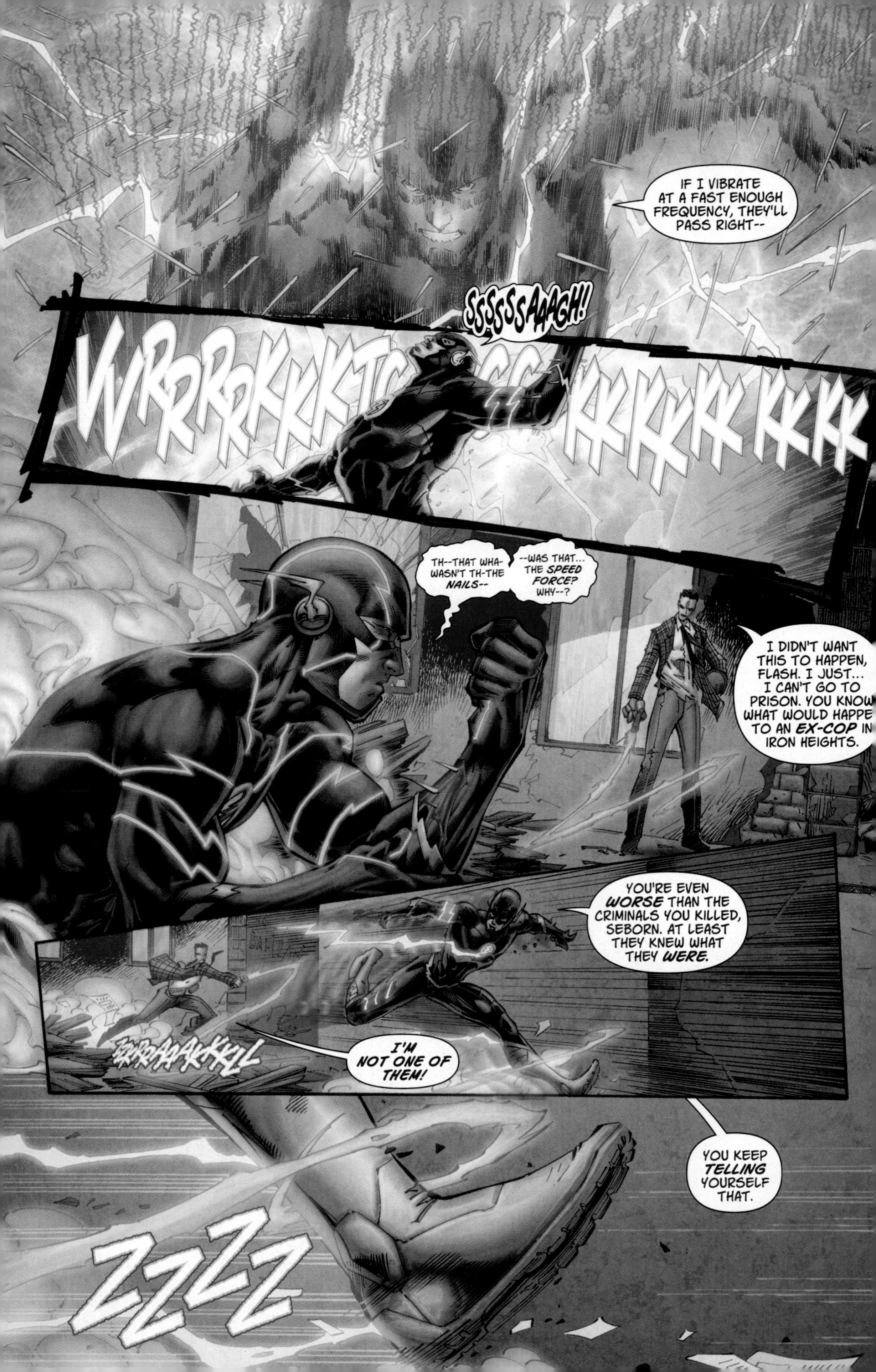
IF I VIBRATE AT A FAST ENOUGH FREQUENCY, THEY'LL PASS RIGHT--
SSSSSSAAAGH!
VVRRRRKKKKT
KKKKKKKKKKK
TH--THAT WHA-WASN'T TH-THE NAILS--
--WAS THAT... THE SPEED FORCE? WHY--?
I DIDN'T WANT THIS TO HAPPEN, FLASH. I JUST... I CAN'T GO TO PRISON. YOU KNOW WHAT WOULD HAPPE TO AN EX-COP IN IRON HEIGHTS.
YOU'RE EVEN WORSE THAN THE CRIMINALS YOU KILLED, SEBORN. AT LEAST THEY KNEW WHAT THEY WERE.
I'M NOT ONE OF THEM!
YOU KEEP TELLING YOURSELF THAT.
ZZZZ

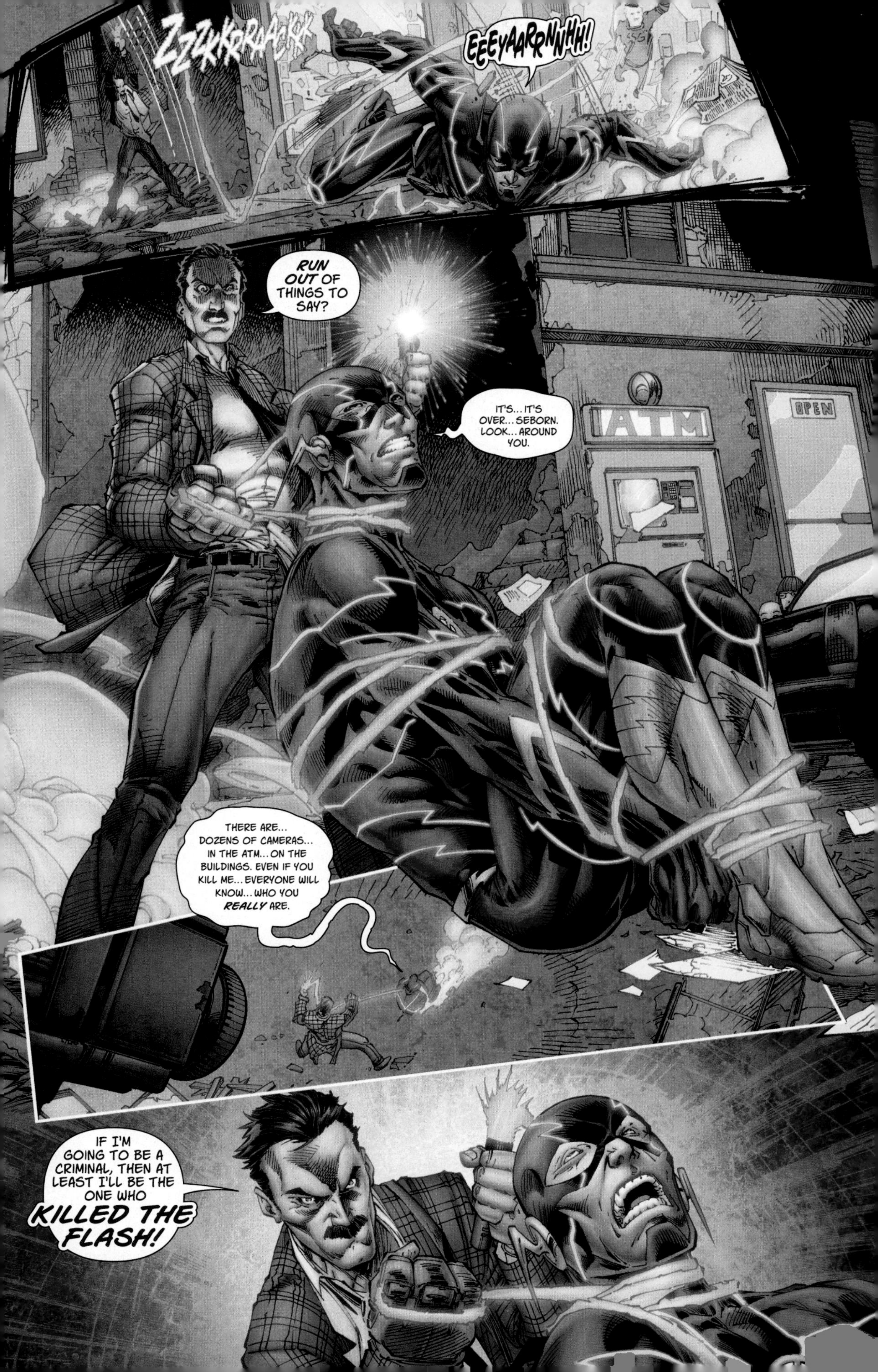
ZZZKKRRAACKKK
EEEYAARRNNHH!
RUN OUT OF THINGS TO SAY?
IT'S... IT'S OVER... SEBORN. LOOK... AROUND YOU.
ATM
OPEN
THERE ARE... DOZENS OF CAMERAS... IN THE ATM... ON THE BUILDINGS. EVEN IF YOU KILL ME... EVERYONE WILL KNOW... WHO YOU REALLY ARE.
IF I'M GOING TO BE A CRIMINAL, THEN AT LEAST I'LL BE THE ONE WHO KILLED THE FLASH!

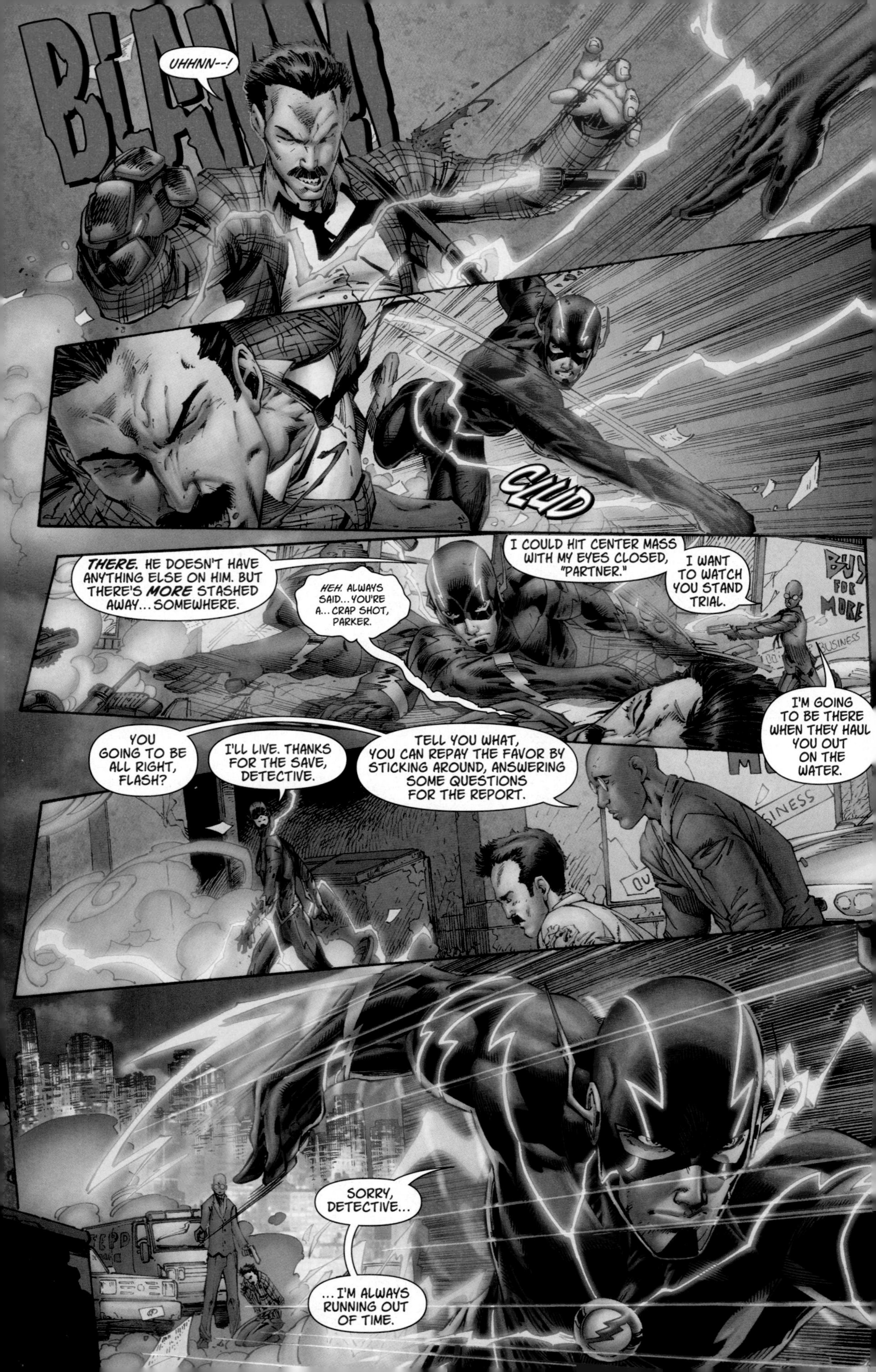
BLAMM
UHHNN--!
CLUD
THERE. HE DOESN'T HAVE ANYTHING ELSE ON HIM. BUT THERE'S MORE STASHED AWAY... SOMEWHERE.
HEH. ALWAYS SAID... YOU'RE A... CRAP SHOT, PARKER.
I COULD HIT CENTER MASS WITH MY EYES CLOSED, "PARTNER."
I WANT TO WATCH YOU STAND TRIAL.
I'M GOING TO BE THERE WHEN THEY HAUL YOU OUT ON THE WATER.
YOU GOING TO BE ALL RIGHT, FLASH?
I'LL LIVE. THANKS FOR THE SAVE, DETECTIVE.
TELL YOU WHAT, YOU CAN REPAY THE FAVOR BY STICKING AROUND, ANSWERING SOME QUESTIONS FOR THE REPORT.
SORRY, DETECTIVE...
...I'M ALWAYS RUNNING OUT OF TIME.

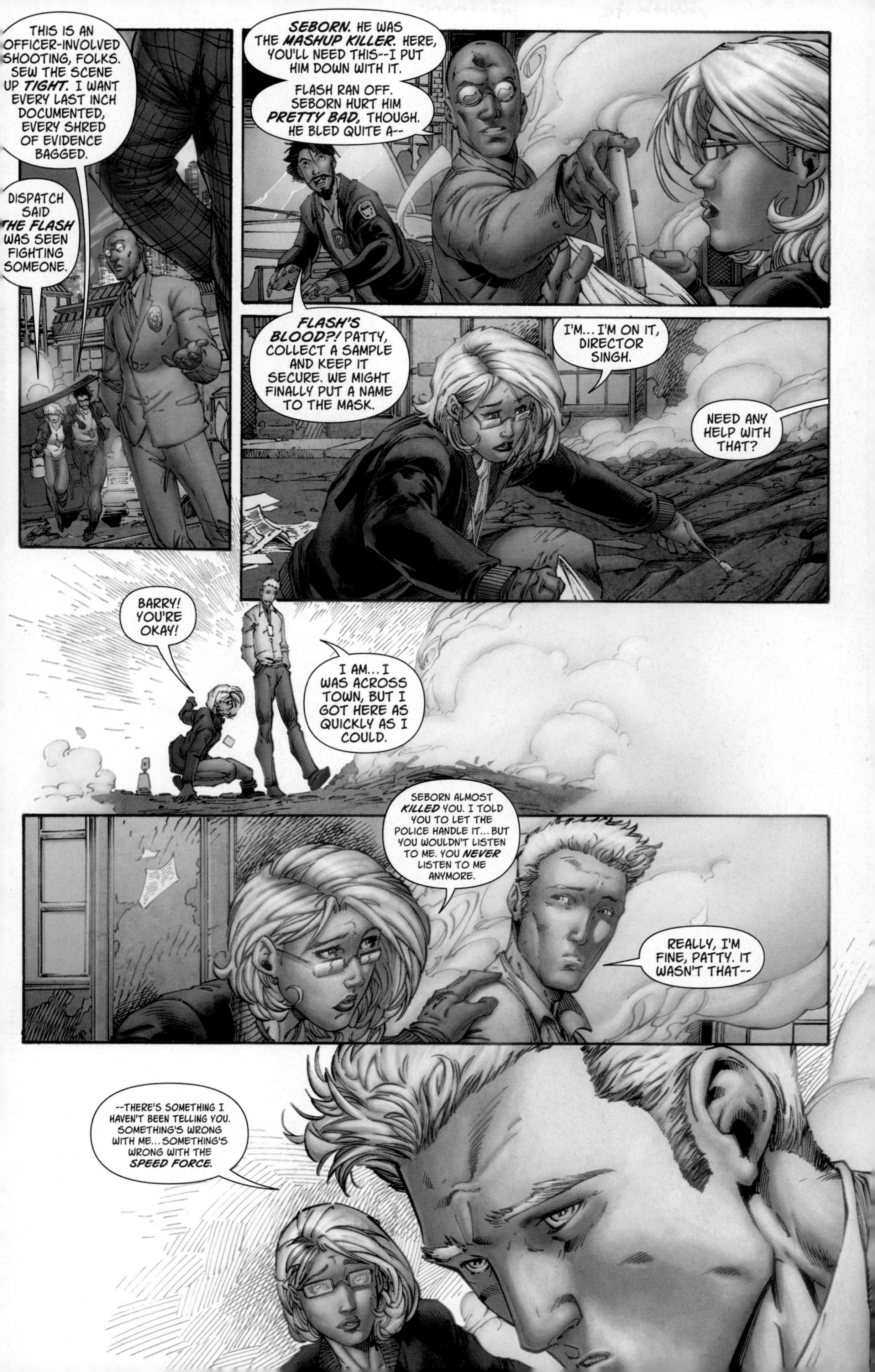
THIS IS AN OFFICER-INVOLVED SHOOTING, FOLKS. SEW THE SCENE UP TIGHT. I WANT EVERY LAST INCH DOCUMENTED, EVERY SHRED OF EVIDENCE BAGGED.
DISPATCH SAID THE FLASH WAS SEEN FIGHTING SOMEONE.
SEBORN. HE WAS THE MASHUP KILLER. HERE, YOU'LL NEED THIS--I PUT HIM DOWN WITH IT.
FLASH RAN OFF. SEBORN HURT HIM PRETTY BAD, THOUGH. HE BLED QUITE A--
FLASH'S BLOOD?! PATTY, COLLECT A SAMPLE AND KEEP IT SECURE. WE MIGHT FINALLY PUT A NAME TO THE MASK.
I'M... I'M ON IT, DIRECTOR SINGH.
NEED ANY HELP WITH THAT?
BARRY! YOU'RE OKAY!
I AM... I WAS ACROSS TOWN, BUT I GOT HERE AS QUICKLY AS I COULD.
SEBORN ALMOST KILLED YOU. I TOLD YOU TO LET THE POLICE HANDLE IT... BUT YOU WOULDN'T LISTEN TO ME. YOU NEVER LISTEN TO ME ANYMORE.
REALLY, I'M FINE, PATTY. IT WASN'T THAT--
--THERE'S SOMETHING I HAVEN'T BEEN TELLING YOU. SOMETHING'S WRONG WITH ME... SOMETHING'S WRONG WITH THE SPEED FORCE.

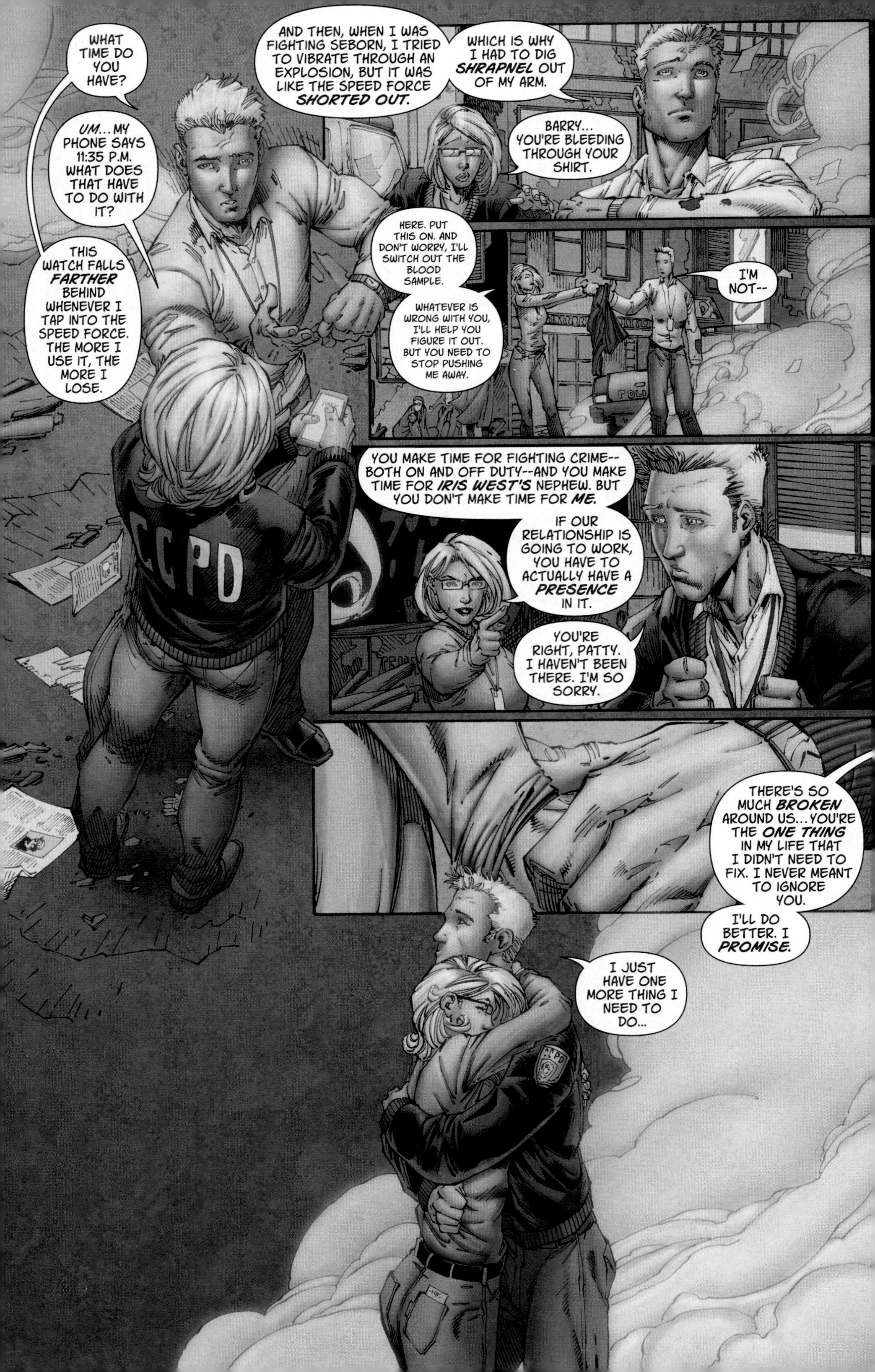
WHAT TIME DO YOU HAVE?
UM... MY PHONE SAYS 11:35 P.M. WHAT DOES THAT HAVE TO DO WITH IT?
THIS WATCH FALLS FARTHER BEHIND WHENEVER I TAP INTO THE SPEED FORCE. THE MORE I USE IT, THE MORE I LOSE.
AND THEN, WHEN I WAS FIGHTING SEBORN, I TRIED TO VIBRATE THROUGH AN EXPLOSION, BUT IT WAS LIKE THE SPEED FORCE SHORTED OUT.
WHICH IS WHY I HAD TO DIG SHRAPNEL OUT OF MY ARM.
BARRY... YOU'RE BLEEDING THROUGH YOUR SHIRT.
HERE. PUT THIS ON. AND DON'T WORRY, I'LL SWITCH OUT THE BLOOD SAMPLE.
WHATEVER IS WRONG WITH YOU, I'LL HELP YOU FIGURE IT OUT. BUT YOU NEED TO STOP PUSHING ME AWAY.
I'M NOT--
YOU MAKE TIME FOR FIGHTING CRIME--BOTH ON AND OFF DUTY--AND YOU MAKE TIME FOR IRIS WEST'S NEPHEW. BUT YOU DON'T MAKE TIME FOR ME.
IF OUR RELATIONSHIP IS GOING TO WORK, YOU HAVE TO ACTUALLY HAVE A PRESENCE IN IT.
YOU'RE RIGHT, PATTY. I HAVEN'T BEEN THERE. I'M SO SORRY.
THERE'S SO MUCH BROKEN AROUND US... YOU'RE THE ONE THING IN MY LIFE THAT I DIDN'T NEED TO FIX. I NEVER MEANT TO IGNORE YOU.
I'LL DO BETTER. I PROMISE.
I JUST HAVE ONE MORE THING I NEED TO DO...

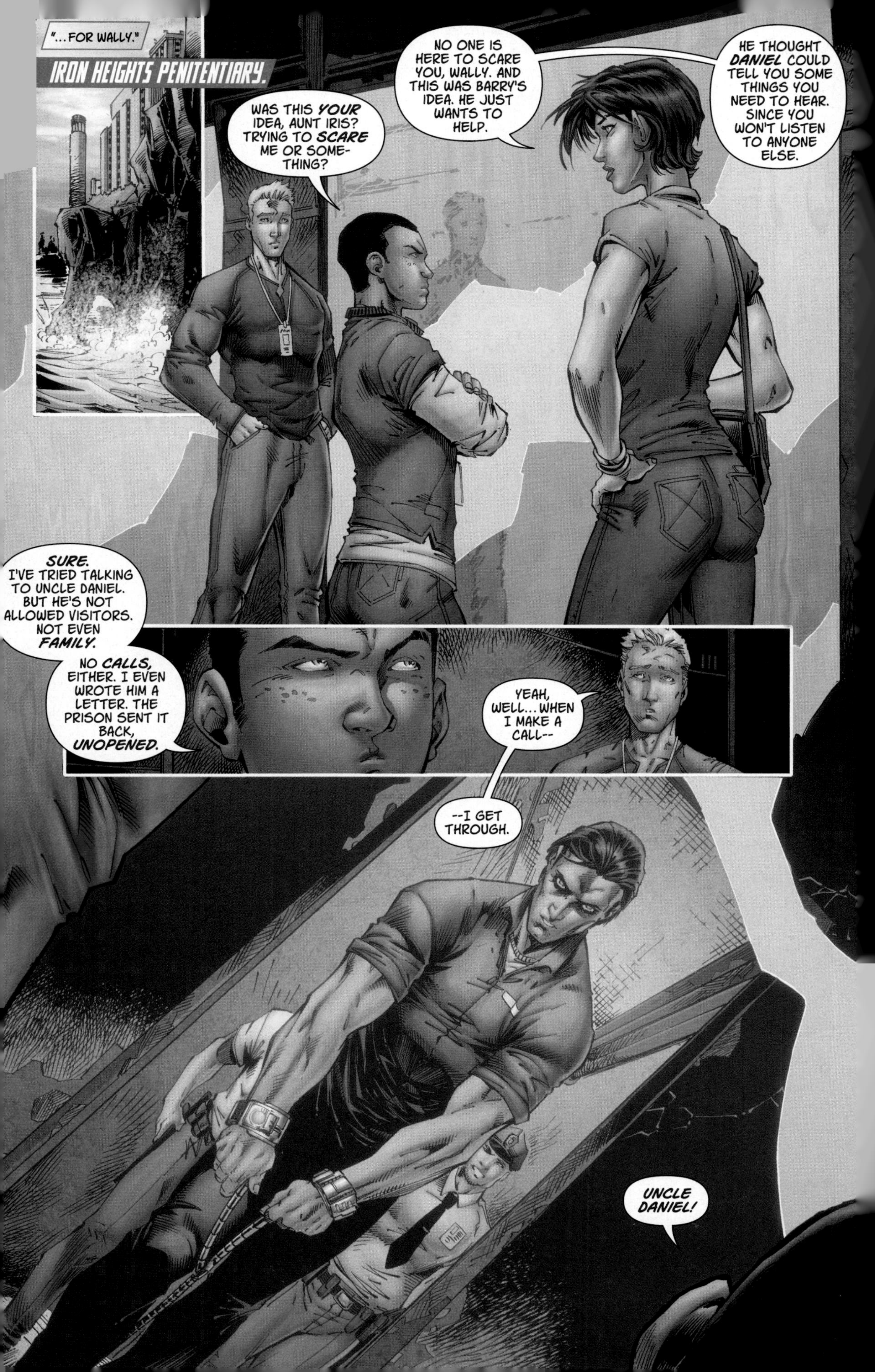
"...FOR WALLY."
IRON HEIGHTS PENITENTIARY.
WAS THIS YOUR IDEA, AUNT IRIS? TRYING TO SCARE ME OR SOME-THING?
NO ONE IS HERE TO SCARE YOU, WALLY. AND THIS WAS BARRY'S IDEA. HE JUST WANTS TO HELP.
HE THOUGHT DANIEL COULD TELL YOU SOME THINGS YOU NEED TO HEAR. SINCE YOU WON'T LISTEN TO ANYONE ELSE.
SURE. I'VE TRIED TALKING TO UNCLE DANIEL. BUT HE'S NOT ALLOWED VISITORS. NOT EVEN FAMILY.
NO CALLS, EITHER. I EVEN WROTE HIM A LETTER. THE PRISON SENT IT BACK, UNOPENED.
YEAH, WELL... WHEN I MAKE A CALL--
--I GET THROUGH.
UNCLE DANIEL!

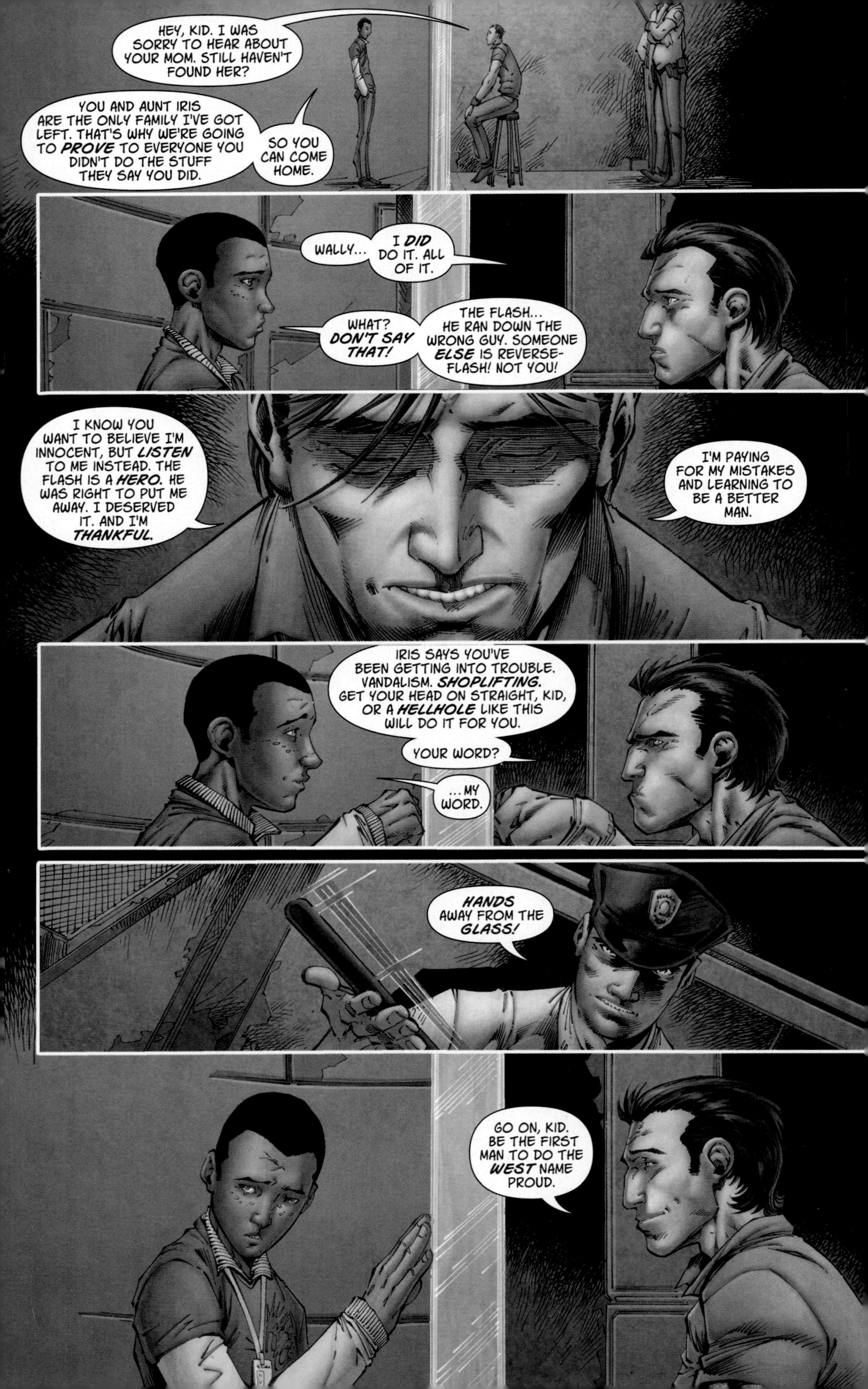

HEY, KID. I WAS SORRY TO HEAR ABOUT YOUR MOM. STILL HAVEN'T FOUND HER?
YOU AND AUNT IRIS ARE THE ONLY FAMILY I'VE GOT LEFT. THAT'S WHY WE'RE GOING TO PROVE TO EVERYONE YOU DIDN'T DO THE STUFF THEY SAY YOU DID.
SO YOU CAN COME HOME.
WALLY...
I DID DO IT. ALL OF IT.
WHAT? DON'T SAY THAT!
THE FLASH... HE RAN DOWN THE WRONG GUY. SOMEONE ELSE IS REVERSE-FLASH! NOT YOU!
I KNOW YOU WANT TO BELIEVE I'M INNOCENT, BUT LISTEN TO ME INSTEAD. THE FLASH IS A HERO. HE WAS RIGHT TO PUT ME AWAY. I DESERVED IT. AND I'M THANKFUL.
I'M PAYING FOR MY MISTAKES AND LEARNING TO BE A BETTER MAN.
IRIS SAYS YOU'VE BEEN GETTING INTO TROUBLE. VANDALISM. SHOPLIFTING. GET YOUR HEAD ON STRAIGHT, KID, OR A HELLHOLE LIKE THIS WILL DO IT FOR YOU.
YOUR WORD?
...MY WORD.
HANDS AWAY FROM THE GLASS!
GO ON, KID. BE THE FIRST MAN TO DO THE WEST NAME PROUD.

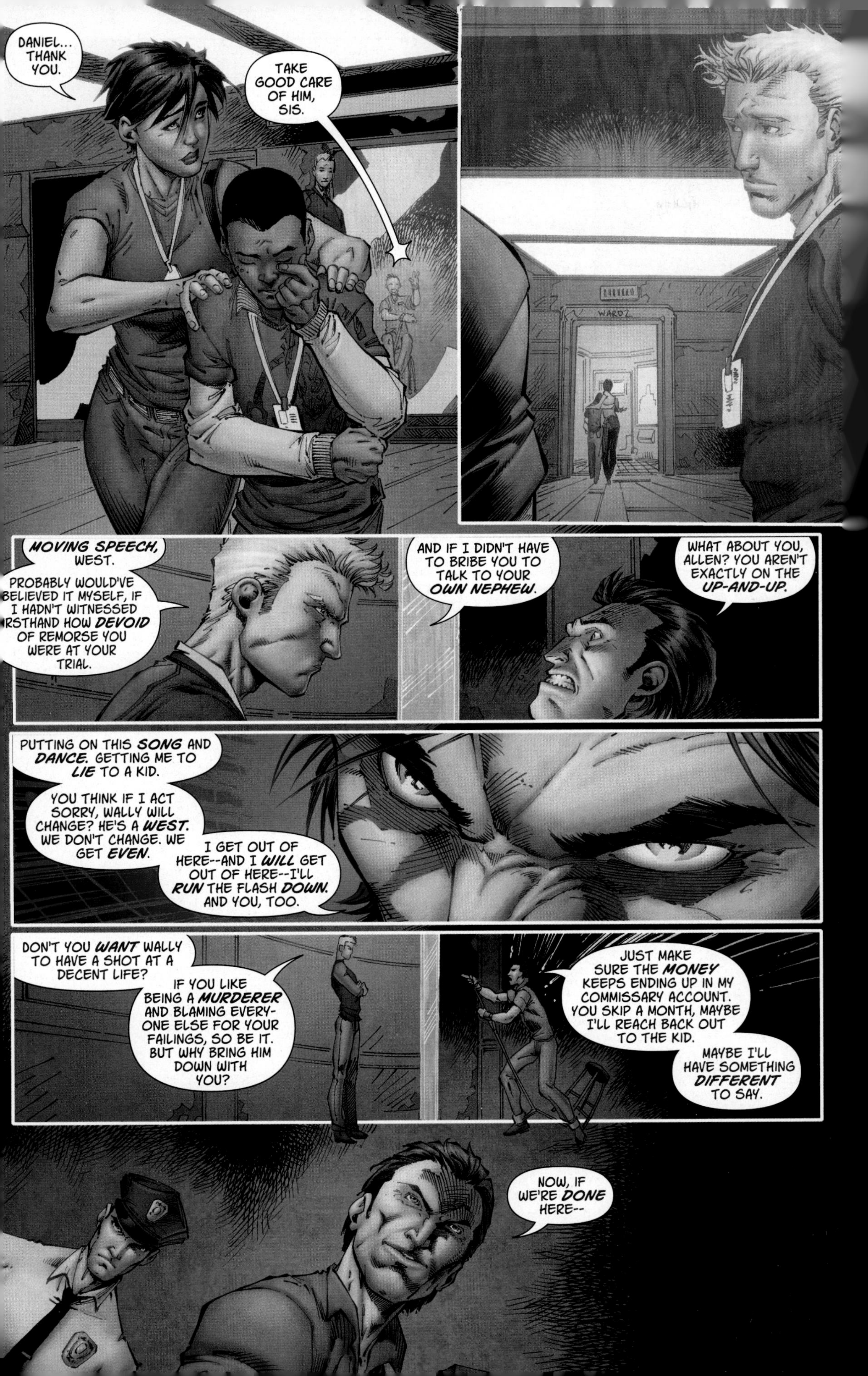
DANIEL... THANK YOU.
TAKE GOOD CARE OF HIM, SIS.
WARD 2
MOVING SPEECH, WEST.
PROBABLY WOULD'VE BELIEVED IT MYSELF, IF I HADN'T WITNESSED RSTHAND HOW DEVOID OF REMORSE YOU WERE AT YOUR TRIAL.
AND IF I DIDN'T HAVE TO BRIBE YOU TO TALK TO YOUR OWN NEPHEW.
WHAT ABOUT YOU, ALLEN? YOU AREN'T EXACTLY ON THE UP-AND-UP.
PUTTING ON THIS SONG AND DANCE. GETTING ME TO LIE TO A KID.
YOU THINK IF I ACT SORRY, WALLY WILL CHANGE? HE'S A WEST. WE DON'T CHANGE. WE GET EVEN.
I GET OUT OF HERE--AND I WILL GET OUT OF HERE--I'LL RUN THE FLASH DOWN. AND YOU, TOO.
DON'T YOU WANT WALLY TO HAVE A SHOT AT A DECENT LIFE?
IF YOU LIKE BEING A MURDERER AND BLAMING EVERY-ONE ELSE FOR YOUR FAILINGS, SO BE IT. BUT WHY BRING HIM DOWN WITH YOU?
JUST MAKE SURE THE MONEY KEEPS ENDING UP IN MY COMMISSARY ACCOUNT. YOU SKIP A MONTH, MAYBE I'LL REACH BACK OUT TO THE KID.
MAYBE I'LL HAVE SOMETHING DIFFERENT TO SAY.
NOW, IF WE'RE DONE HERE--

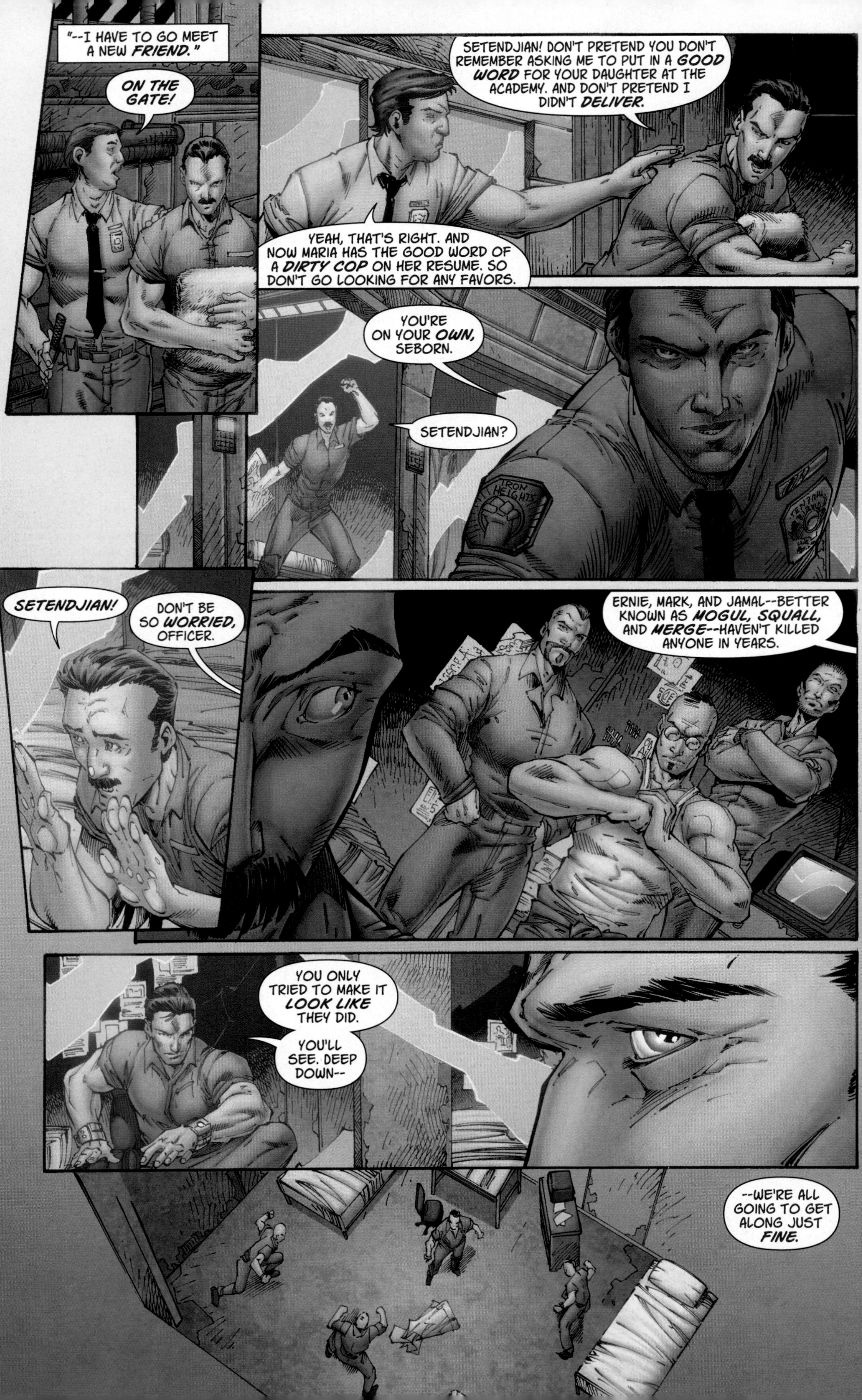
"--I HAVE TO GO MEET A NEW FRIEND."
ON THE GATE!
SETENDJIAN! DON'T PRETEND YOU DON'T REMEMBER ASKING ME TO PUT IN A GOOD WORD FOR YOUR DAUGHTER AT THE ACADEMY. AND DON'T PRETEND I DIDN'T DELIVER.
YEAH, THAT'S RIGHT. AND NOW MARIA HAS THE GOOD WORD OF A DIRTY COP ON HER RESUME. SO DON'T GO LOOKING FOR ANY FAVORS.
YOU'RE ON YOUR OWN, SEBORN.
SETENDJIAN?
SETENDJIAN!
DON'T BE SO WORRIED, OFFICER.
ERNIE, MARK, AND JAMAL--BETTER KNOWN AS MOGUL, SQUALL, AND MERGE--HAVEN'T KILLED ANYONE IN YEARS.
YOU ONLY TRIED TO MAKE IT LOOK LIKE THEY DID.
YOU'LL SEE. DEEP DOWN--
--WE'RE ALL GOING TO GET ALONG JUST FINE.

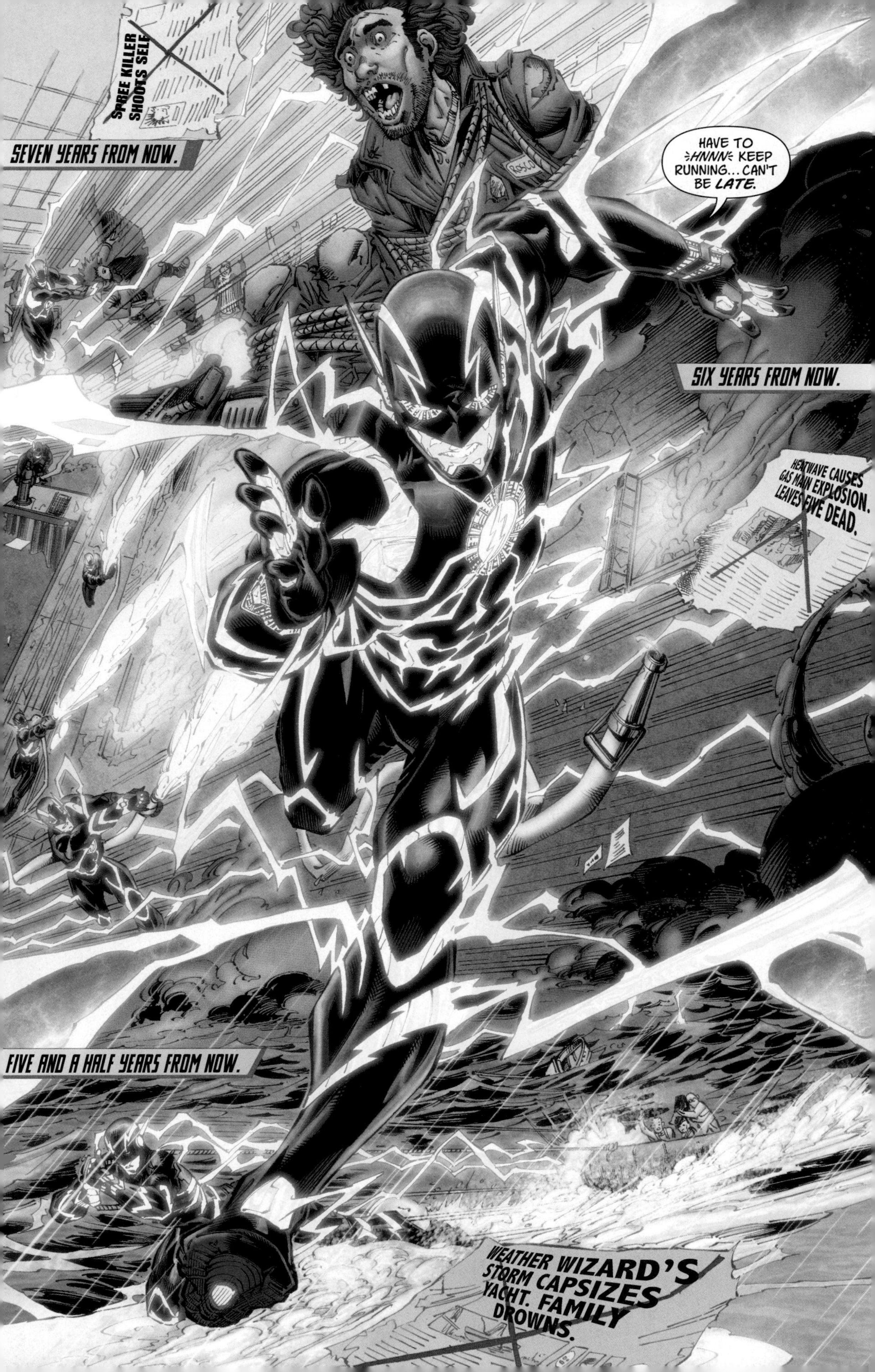
SPREE KILLER SHOOTS SELF
SEVEN YEARS FROM NOW.
HAVE TO HNNN KEEP RUNNING... CAN'T BE LATE.
SIX YEARS FROM NOW.
HEATWAVE CAUSES GAS MAIN EXPLOSION. LEAVES FIVE DEAD.
FIVE AND A HALF YEARS FROM NOW.
WEATHER WIZARD'S STORM CAPSIZES YACHT. FAMILY DROWNS.

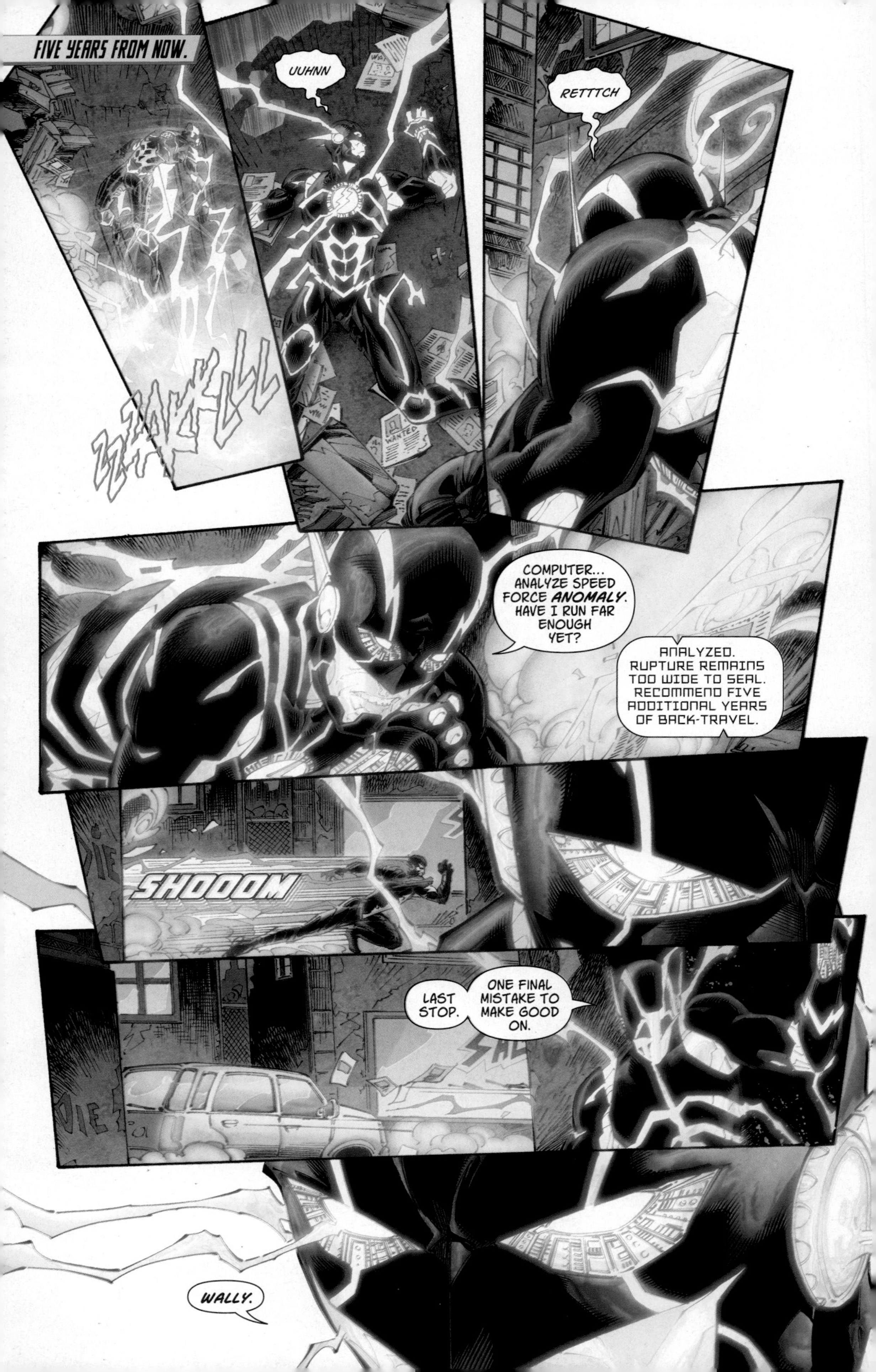
FIVE YEARS FROM NOW.
UUHNN
RETTTCH
ZZZAKKLL
COMPUTER... ANALYZE SPEED FORCE ANOMALY. HAVE I RUN FAR ENOUGH YET?
ANALYZED. RUPTURE REMAINS TOO WIDE TO SEAL. RECOMMEND FIVE ADDITIONAL YEARS OF BACK-TRAVEL.
SHOOOM
LAST STOP.
ONE FINAL MISTAKE TO MAKE GOOD ON.
WALLY.

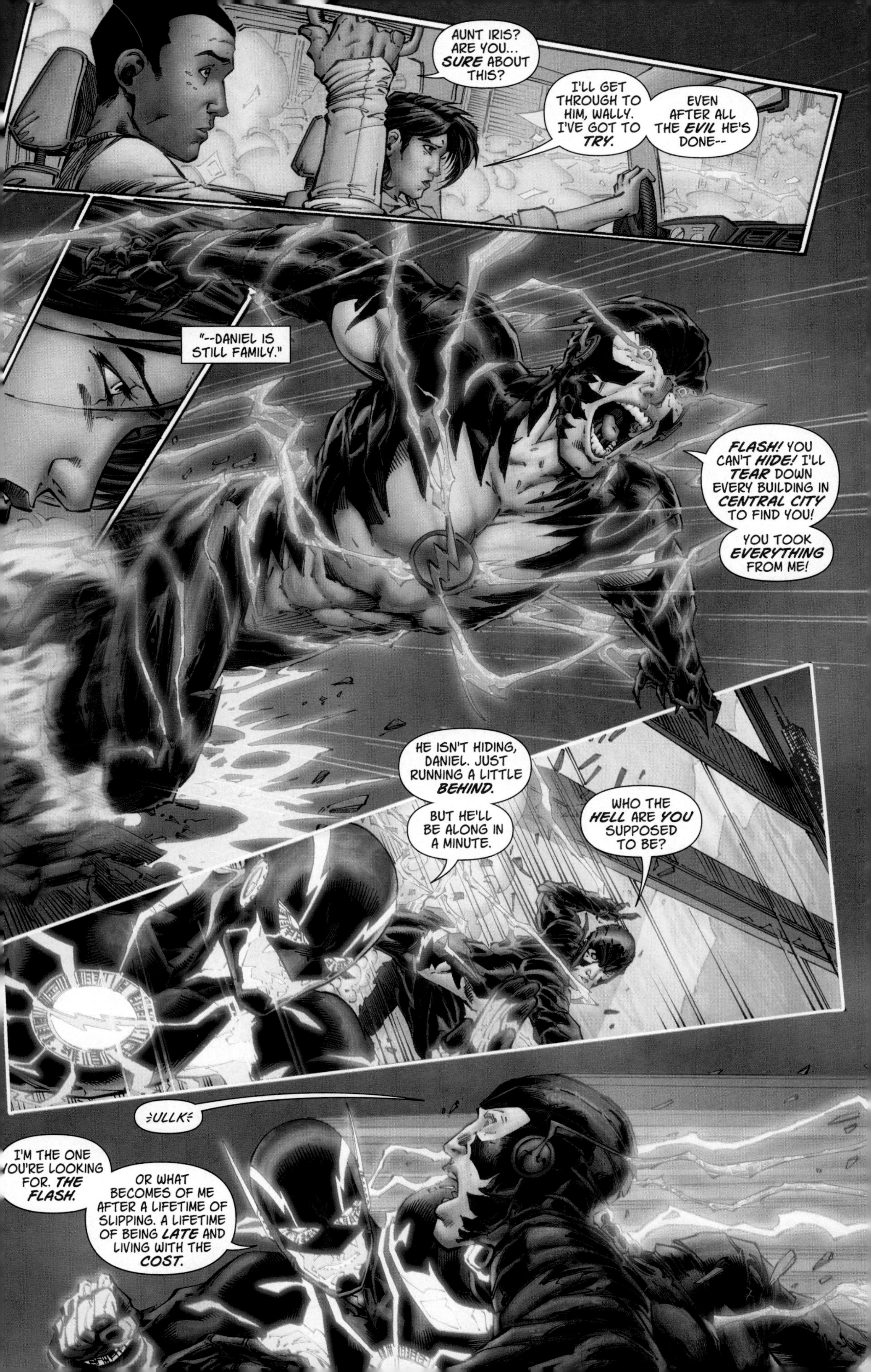
AUNT IRIS? ARE YOU... SURE ABOUT THIS?
I'LL GET THROUGH TO HIM, WALLY. I'VE GOT TO TRY.
EVEN AFTER ALL THE EVIL HE'S DONE--
"--DANIEL IS STILL FAMILY."
FLASH! YOU CAN'T HIDE! I'LL TEAR DOWN EVERY BUILDING IN CENTRAL CITY TO FIND YOU!
YOU TOOK EVERYTHING FROM ME!
HE ISN'T HIDING, DANIEL. JUST RUNNING A LITTLE BEHIND.
BUT HE'LL BE ALONG IN A MINUTE.
WHO THE HELL ARE YOU SUPPOSED TO BE?
ULLK
I'M THE ONE YOU'RE LOOKING FOR. THE FLASH.
OR WHAT BECOMES OF ME AFTER A LIFETIME OF SLIPPING. A LIFETIME OF BEING LATE AND LIVING WITH THE COST.

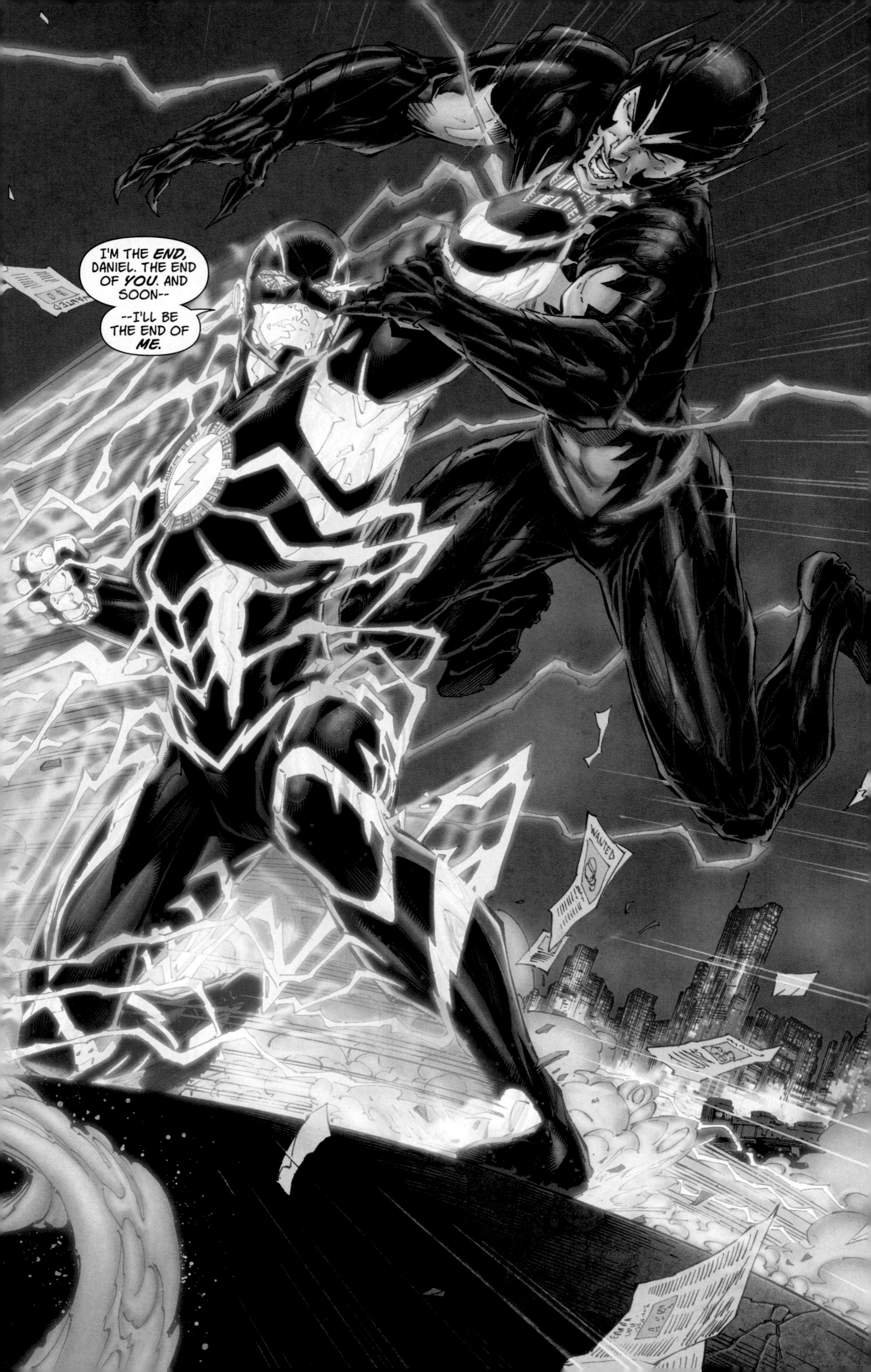
I'M THE END, DANIEL. THE END OF YOU. AND SOON--
--I'LL BE THE END OF ME.

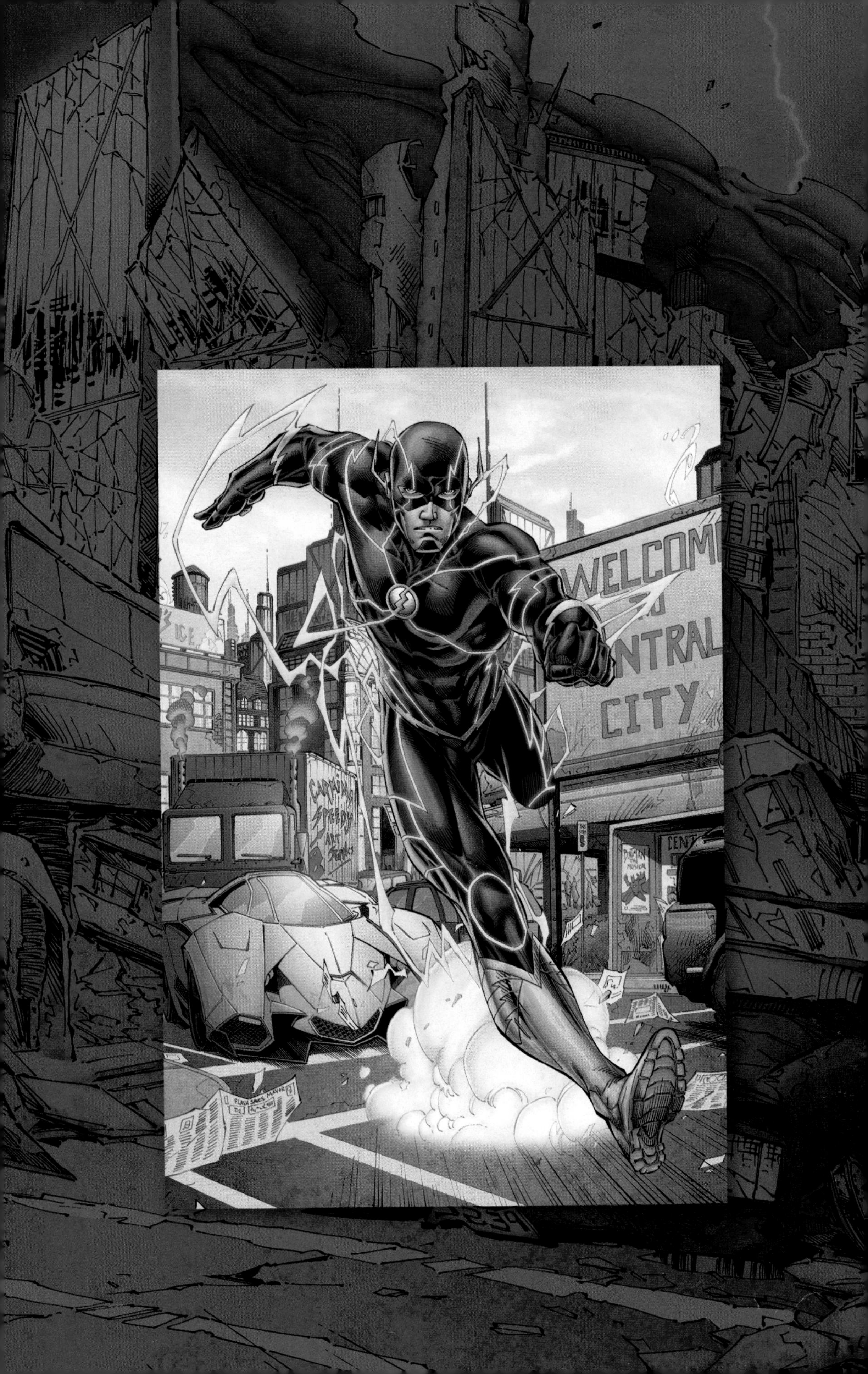
WELCOM
NTRAL
CITY
ICE
SPEEDY
ART
BATMAN THE MUSICAL
FLASH SAVES MAYOR

IMPACT VELOCITY

ROBERT VENDITTI & VAN JENSEN writers **BRETT BOOTH** penciller **NORM RAPMUND** inker

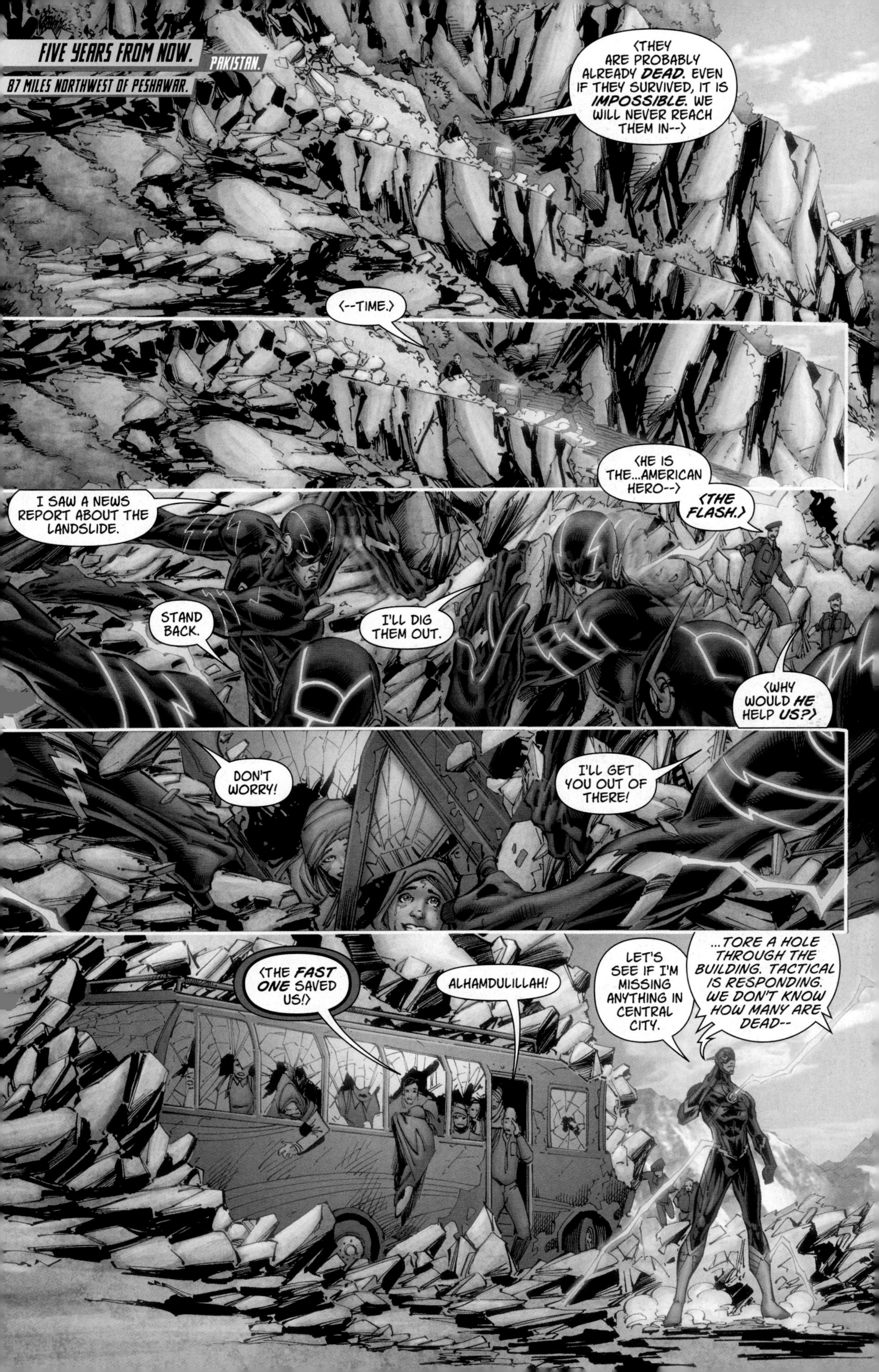
FIVE YEARS FROM NOW.
PAKISTAN.
87 MILES NORTHWEST OF PESHAWAR.
‹THEY ARE PROBABLY ALREADY DEAD. EVEN IF THEY SURVIVED, IT IS IMPOSSIBLE. WE WILL NEVER REACH THEM IN--›
‹--TIME.›
‹HE IS THE...AMERICAN HERO--›
‹THE FLASH.›
I SAW A NEWS REPORT ABOUT THE LANDSLIDE.
STAND BACK.
I'LL DIG THEM OUT.
‹WHY WOULD HE HELP US?›
DON'T WORRY!
I'LL GET YOU OUT OF THERE!
‹THE FAST ONE SAVED US!›
ALHAMDULILLAH!
LET'S SEE IF I'M MISSING ANYTHING IN CENTRAL CITY.
...TORE A HOLE THROUGH THE BUILDING. TACTICAL IS RESPONDING. WE DON'T KNOW HOW MANY ARE DEAD--

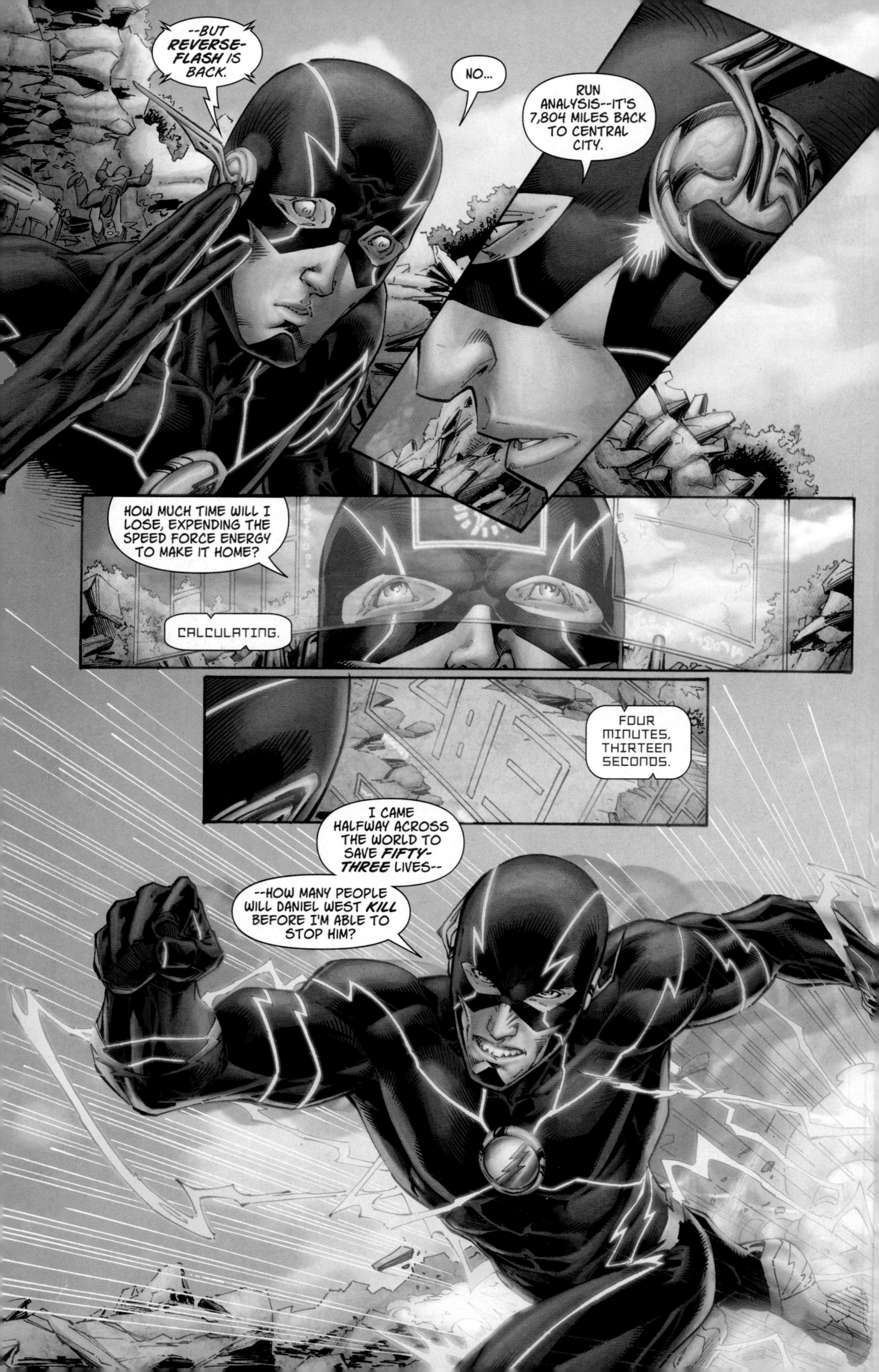
--BUT REVERSE-FLASH IS BACK.
NO...
RUN ANALYSIS--IT'S 7,804 MILES BACK TO CENTRAL CITY.
HOW MUCH TIME WILL I LOSE, EXPENDING THE SPEED FORCE ENERGY TO MAKE IT HOME?
CALCULATING.
FOUR MINUTES, THIRTEEN SECONDS.
I CAME HALFWAY ACROSS THE WORLD TO SAVE FIFTY-THREE LIVES--
--HOW MANY PEOPLE WILL DANIEL WEST KILL BEFORE I'M ABLE TO STOP HIM?

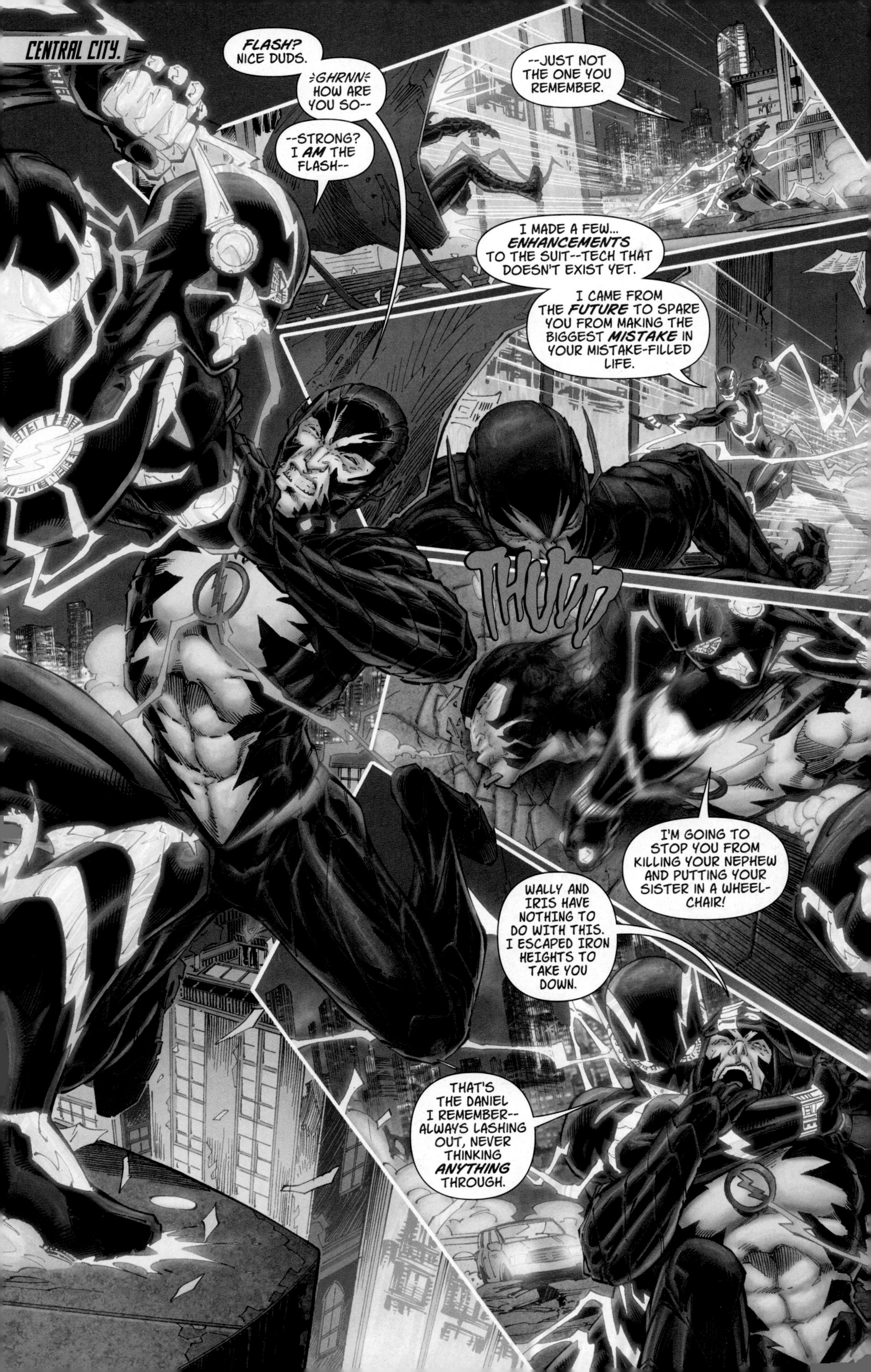
CENTRAL CITY.
FLASH? NICE DUDS.
GHRNN HOW ARE YOU SO--
--STRONG? I AM THE FLASH--
--JUST NOT THE ONE YOU REMEMBER.
I MADE A FEW... ENHANCEMENTS TO THE SUIT--TECH THAT DOESN'T EXIST YET.
I CAME FROM THE FUTURE TO SPARE YOU FROM MAKING THE BIGGEST MISTAKE IN YOUR MISTAKE-FILLED LIFE.
THUDD
I'M GOING TO STOP YOU FROM KILLING YOUR NEPHEW AND PUTTING YOUR SISTER IN A WHEEL-CHAIR!
WALLY AND IRIS HAVE NOTHING TO DO WITH THIS. I ESCAPED IRON HEIGHTS TO TAKE YOU DOWN.
THAT'S THE DANIEL I REMEMBER-- ALWAYS LASHING OUT, NEVER THINKING ANYTHING THROUGH.

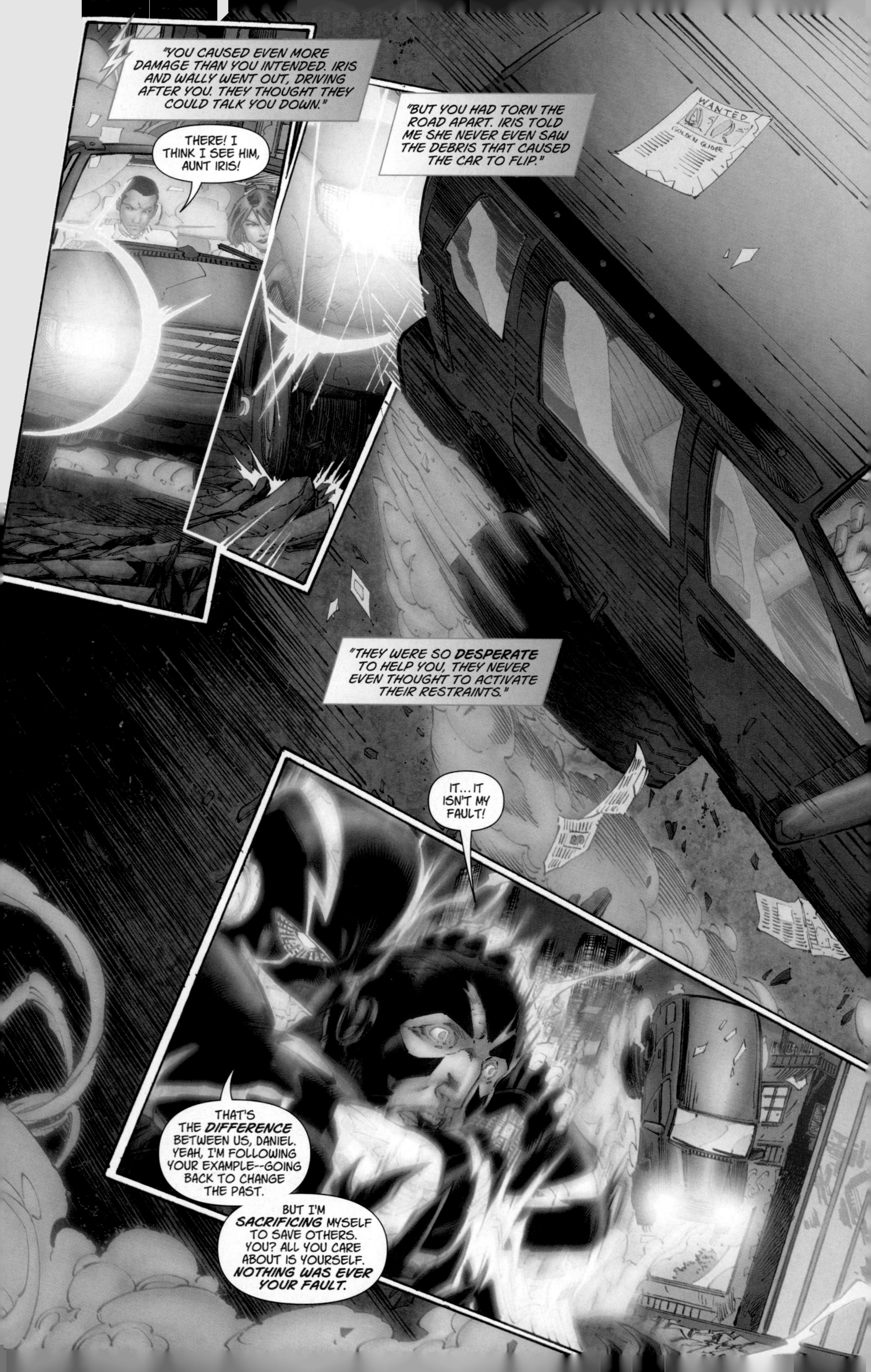
"YOU CAUSED EVEN MORE DAMAGE THAN YOU INTENDED. IRIS AND WALLY WENT OUT, DRIVING AFTER YOU. THEY THOUGHT THEY COULD TALK YOU DOWN."
THERE! I THINK I SEE HIM, AUNT IRIS!
"BUT YOU HAD TORN THE ROAD APART. IRIS TOLD ME SHE NEVER EVEN SAW THE DEBRIS THAT CAUSED THE CAR TO FLIP."
WANTED
"THEY WERE SO DESPERATE TO HELP YOU, THEY NEVER EVEN THOUGHT TO ACTIVATE THEIR RESTRAINTS."
IT... IT ISN'T MY FAULT!
THAT'S THE DIFFERENCE BETWEEN US, DANIEL. YEAH, I'M FOLLOWING YOUR EXAMPLE--GOING BACK TO CHANGE THE PAST.
BUT I'M SACRIFICING MYSELF TO SAVE OTHERS. YOU? ALL YOU CARE ABOUT IS YOURSELF. NOTHING WAS EVER YOUR FAULT.

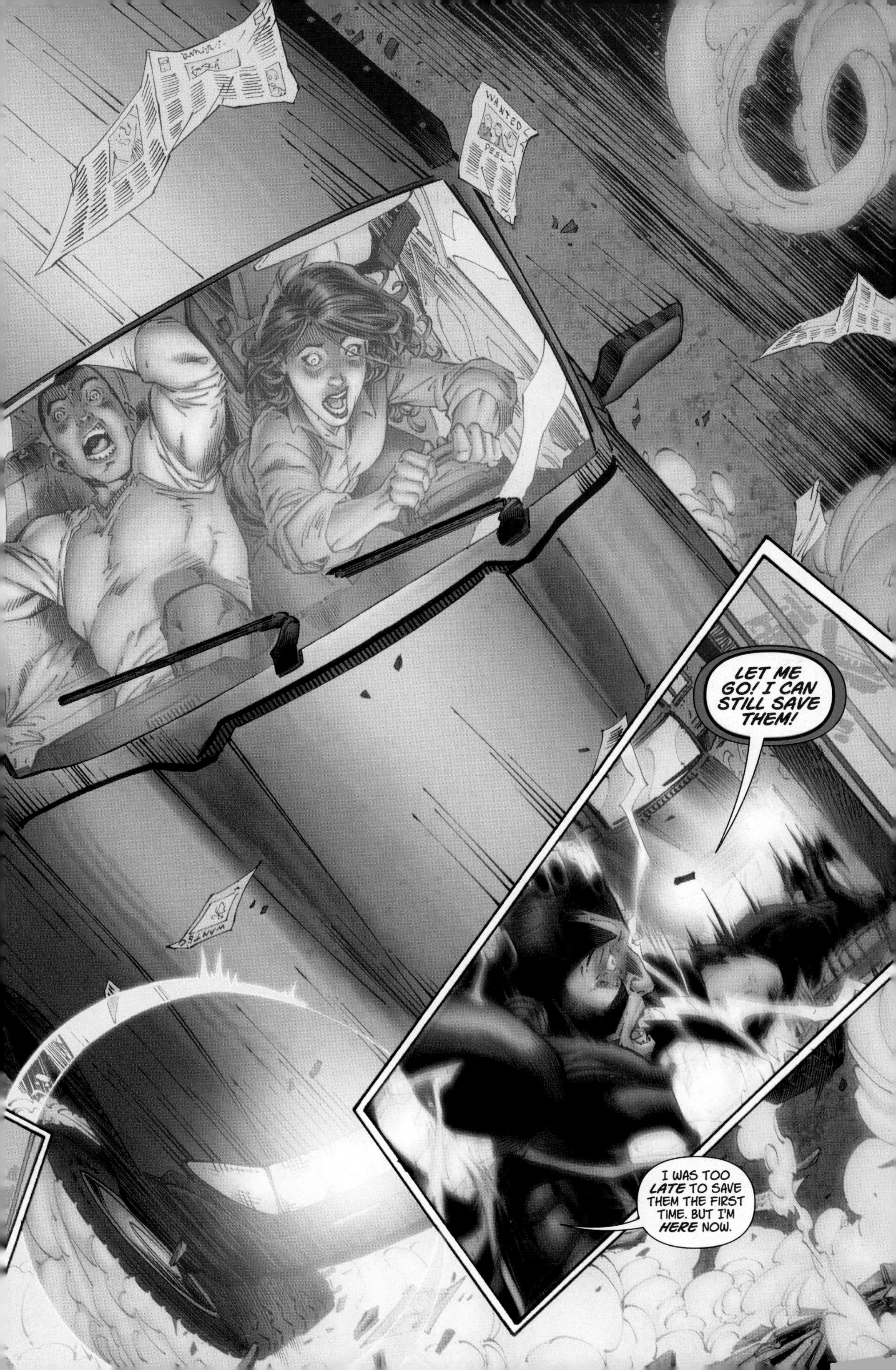
LET ME GO! I CAN STILL SAVE THEM!
I WAS TOO LATE TO SAVE THEM THE FIRST TIME. BUT I'M HERE NOW.

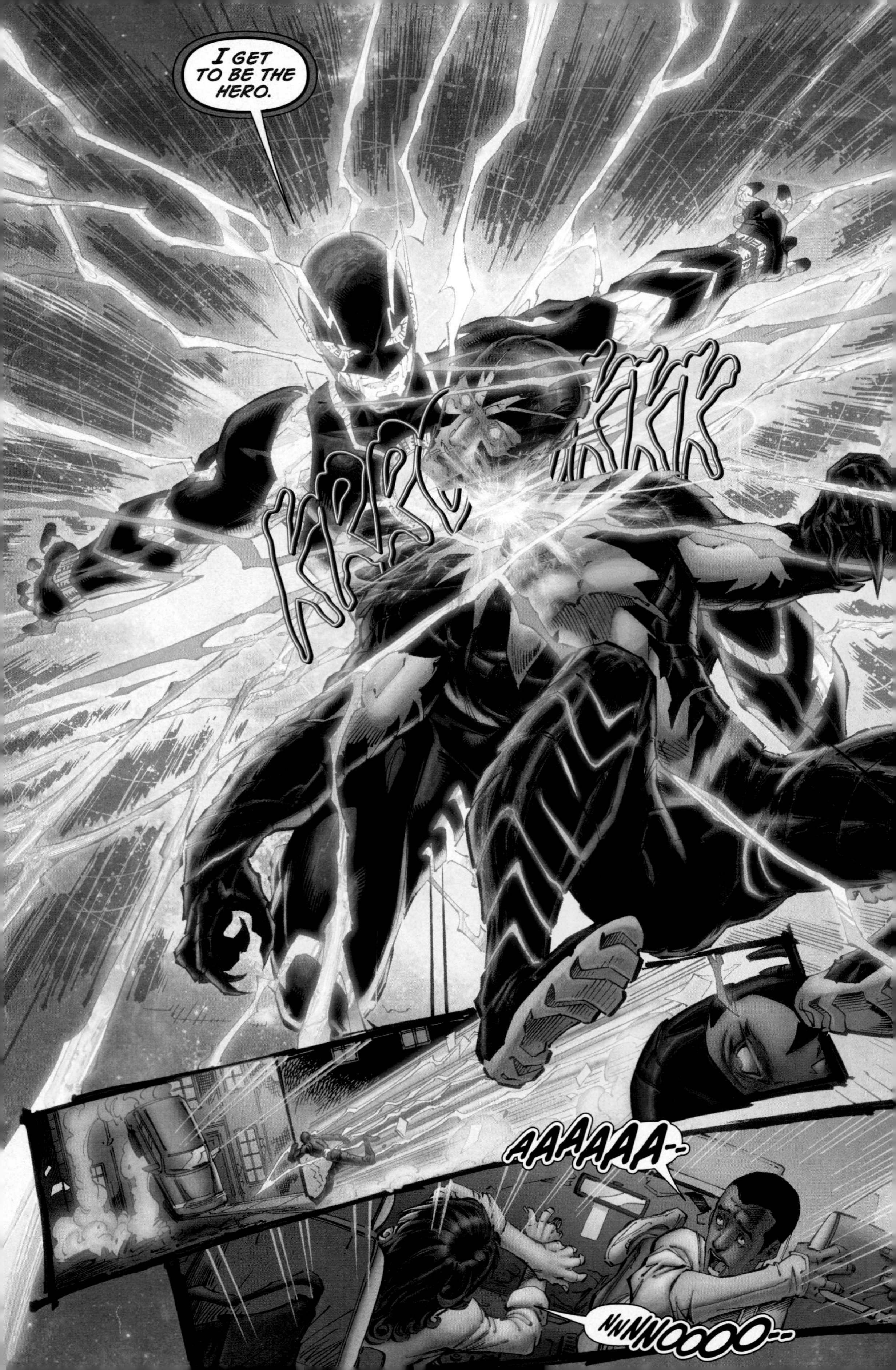
I GET TO BE THE HERO.
AAAAAA--
NNNNOOOO--

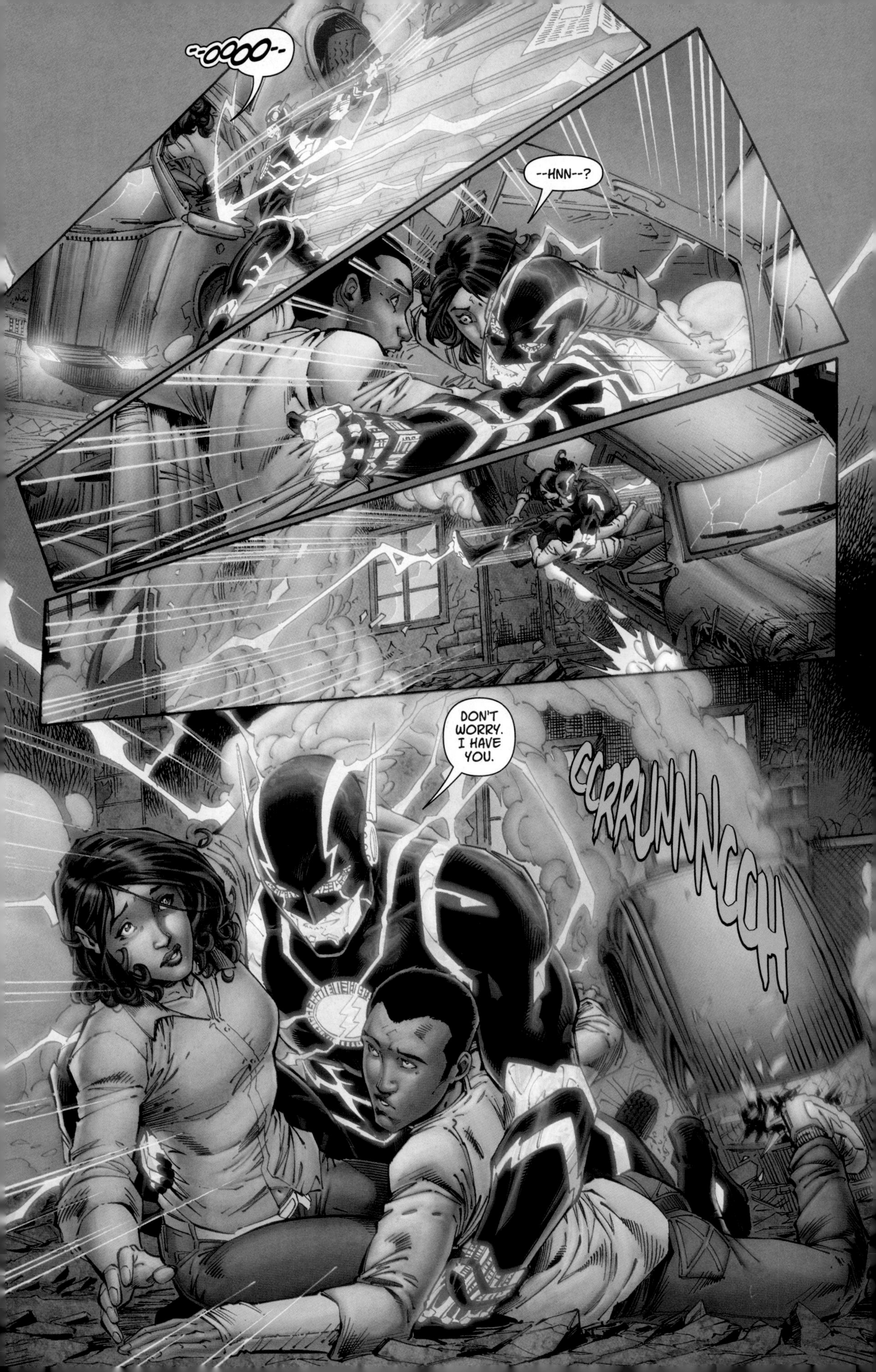
--OOOO--
--HNN--?
DON'T WORRY. I HAVE YOU.
CCRRUNNNCCCH

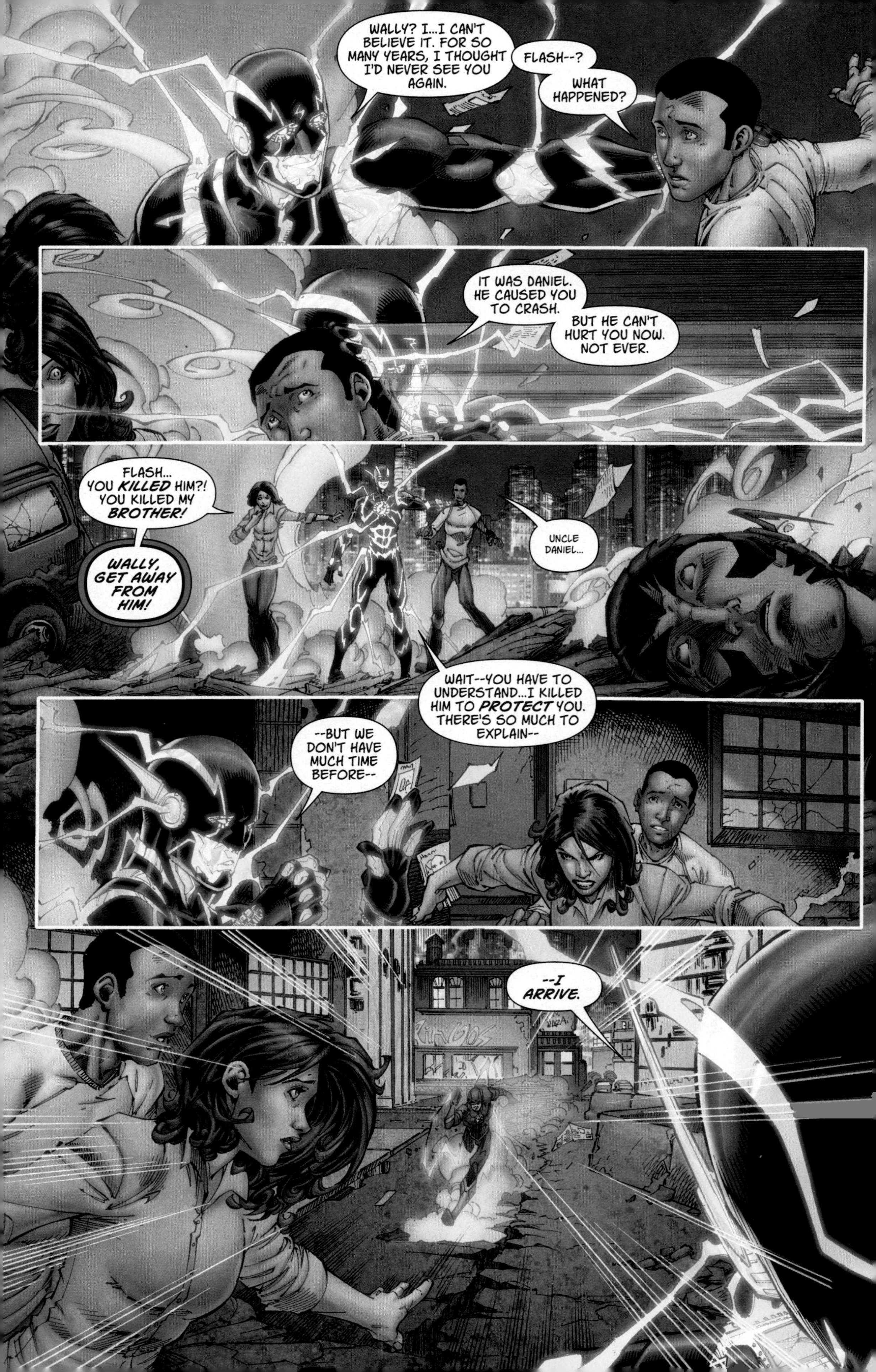

WALLY? I...I CAN'T BELIEVE IT. FOR SO MANY YEARS, I THOUGHT I'D NEVER SEE YOU AGAIN.
FLASH--?
WHAT HAPPENED?
IT WAS DANIEL. HE CAUSED YOU TO CRASH.
BUT HE CAN'T HURT YOU NOW. NOT EVER.
FLASH... YOU *KILLED* HIM?! YOU KILLED MY *BROTHER!*
WALLY, GET AWAY FROM HIM!
UNCLE DANIEL...
WAIT--YOU HAVE TO UNDERSTAND...I KILLED HIM TO *PROTECT* YOU. THERE'S SO MUCH TO EXPLAIN--
--BUT WE DON'T HAVE MUCH TIME BEFORE--
--I ARRIVE.

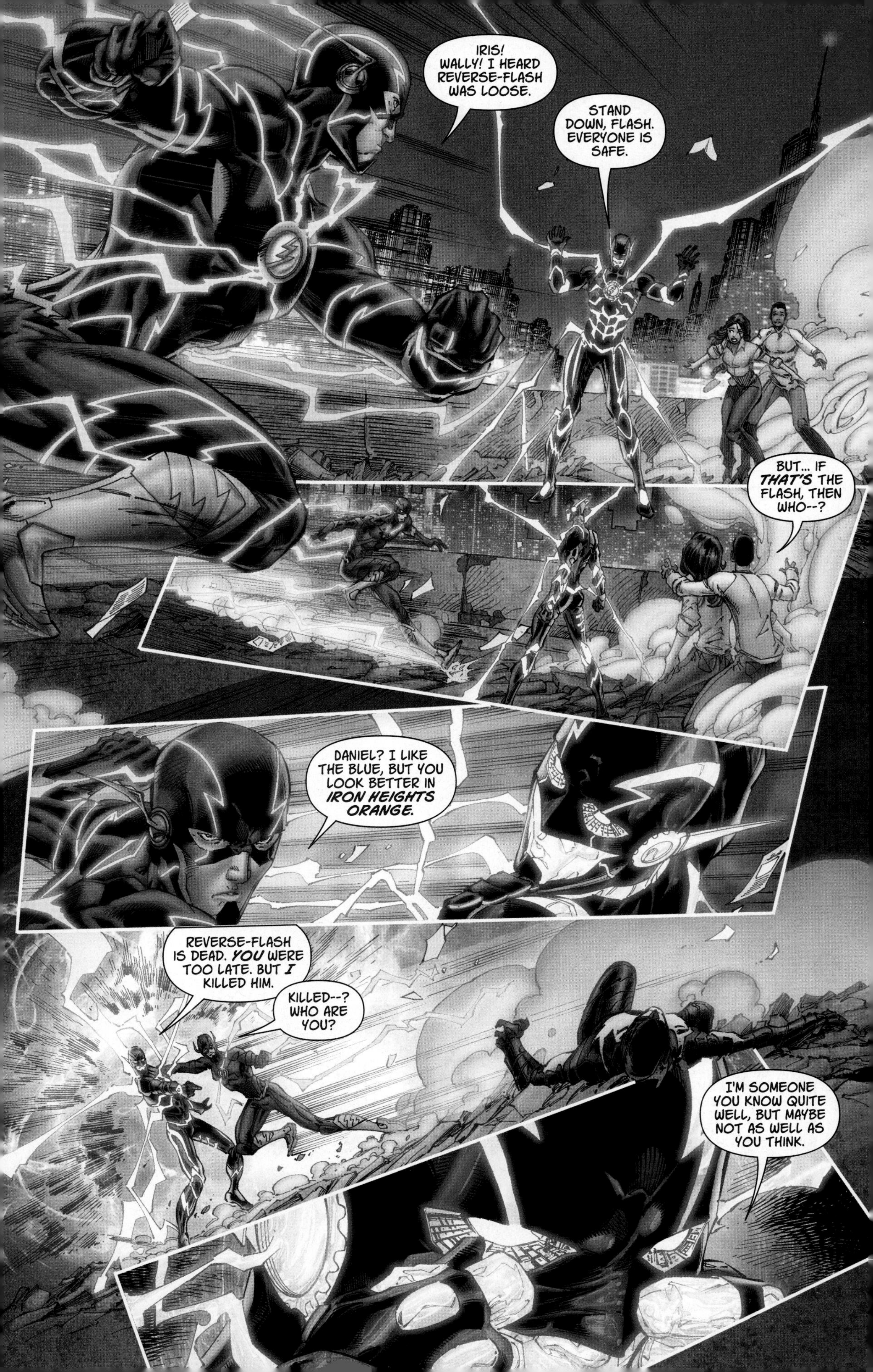
IRIS! WALLY! I HEARD REVERSE-FLASH WAS LOOSE.
STAND DOWN, FLASH. EVERYONE IS SAFE.
BUT... IF THAT'S THE FLASH, THEN WHO--?
DANIEL? I LIKE THE BLUE, BUT YOU LOOK BETTER IN IRON HEIGHTS ORANGE.
REVERSE-FLASH IS DEAD. YOU WERE TOO LATE. BUT I KILLED HIM.
KILLED--? WHO ARE YOU?
I'M SOMEONE YOU KNOW QUITE WELL, BUT MAYBE NOT AS WELL AS YOU THINK.

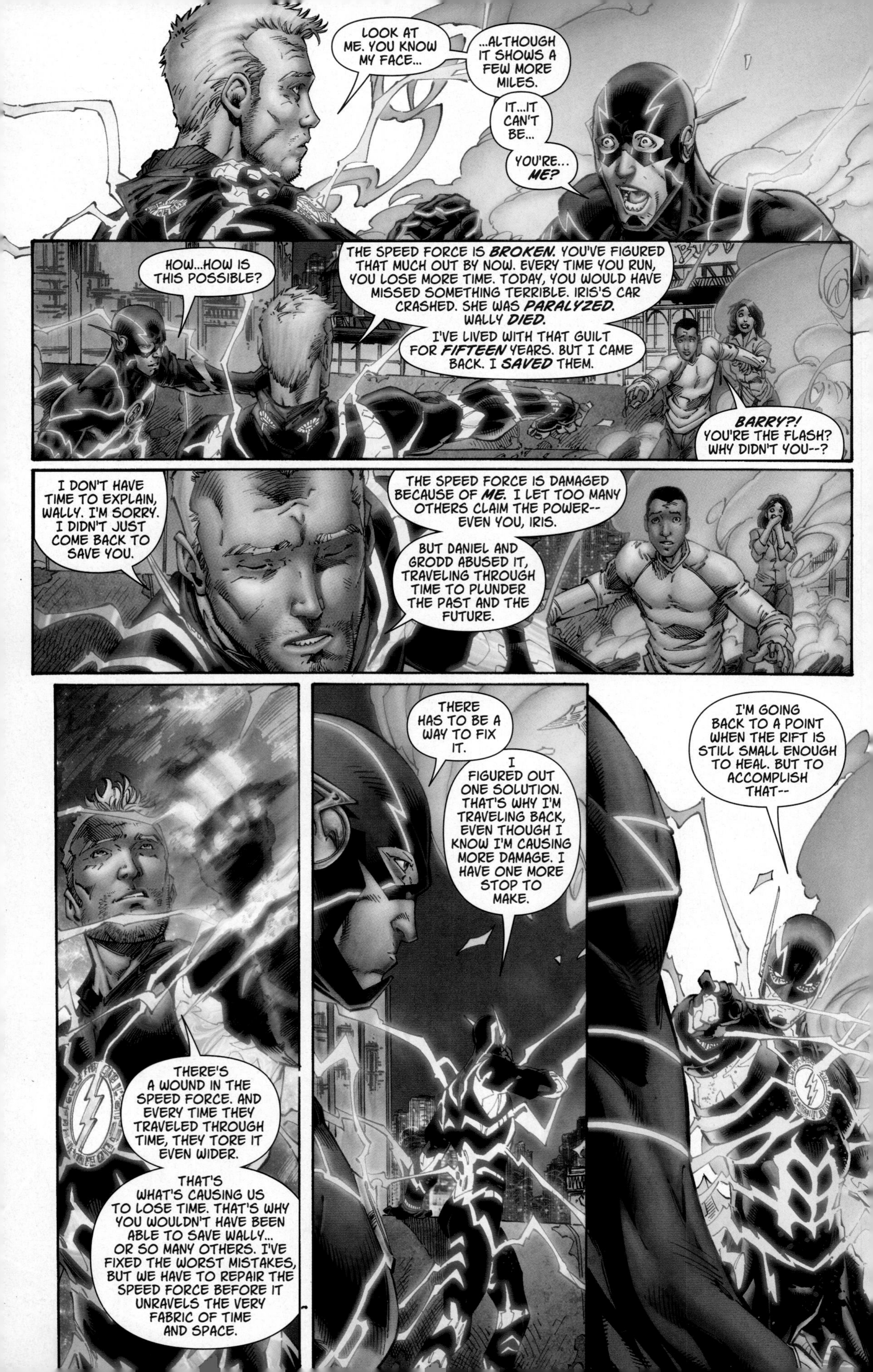
LOOK AT ME. YOU KNOW MY FACE...
...ALTHOUGH IT SHOWS A FEW MORE MILES.
IT...IT CAN'T BE...
YOU'RE... ME?
HOW...HOW IS THIS POSSIBLE?
THE SPEED FORCE IS BROKEN. YOU'VE FIGURED THAT MUCH OUT BY NOW. EVERY TIME YOU RUN, YOU LOSE MORE TIME. TODAY, YOU WOULD HAVE MISSED SOMETHING TERRIBLE. IRIS'S CAR CRASHED. SHE WAS PARALYZED. WALLY DIED.
I'VE LIVED WITH THAT GUILT FOR FIFTEEN YEARS. BUT I CAME BACK. I SAVED THEM.
BARRY?! YOU'RE THE FLASH? WHY DIDN'T YOU--?
I DON'T HAVE TIME TO EXPLAIN, WALLY. I'M SORRY. I DIDN'T JUST COME BACK TO SAVE YOU.
THE SPEED FORCE IS DAMAGED BECAUSE OF ME. I LET TOO MANY OTHERS CLAIM THE POWER-- EVEN YOU, IRIS.
BUT DANIEL AND GRODD ABUSED IT, TRAVELING THROUGH TIME TO PLUNDER THE PAST AND THE FUTURE.
THERE'S A WOUND IN THE SPEED FORCE. AND EVERY TIME THEY TRAVELED THROUGH TIME, THEY TORE IT EVEN WIDER.
THAT'S WHAT'S CAUSING US TO LOSE TIME. THAT'S WHY YOU WOULDN'T HAVE BEEN ABLE TO SAVE WALLY... OR SO MANY OTHERS. I'VE FIXED THE WORST MISTAKES, BUT WE HAVE TO REPAIR THE SPEED FORCE BEFORE IT UNRAVELS THE VERY FABRIC OF TIME AND SPACE.
THERE HAS TO BE A WAY TO FIX IT.
I FIGURED OUT ONE SOLUTION. THAT'S WHY I'M TRAVELING BACK, EVEN THOUGH I KNOW I'M CAUSING MORE DAMAGE. I HAVE ONE MORE STOP TO MAKE.
I'M GOING BACK TO A POINT WHEN THE RIFT IS STILL SMALL ENOUGH TO HEAL. BUT TO ACCOMPLISH THAT--

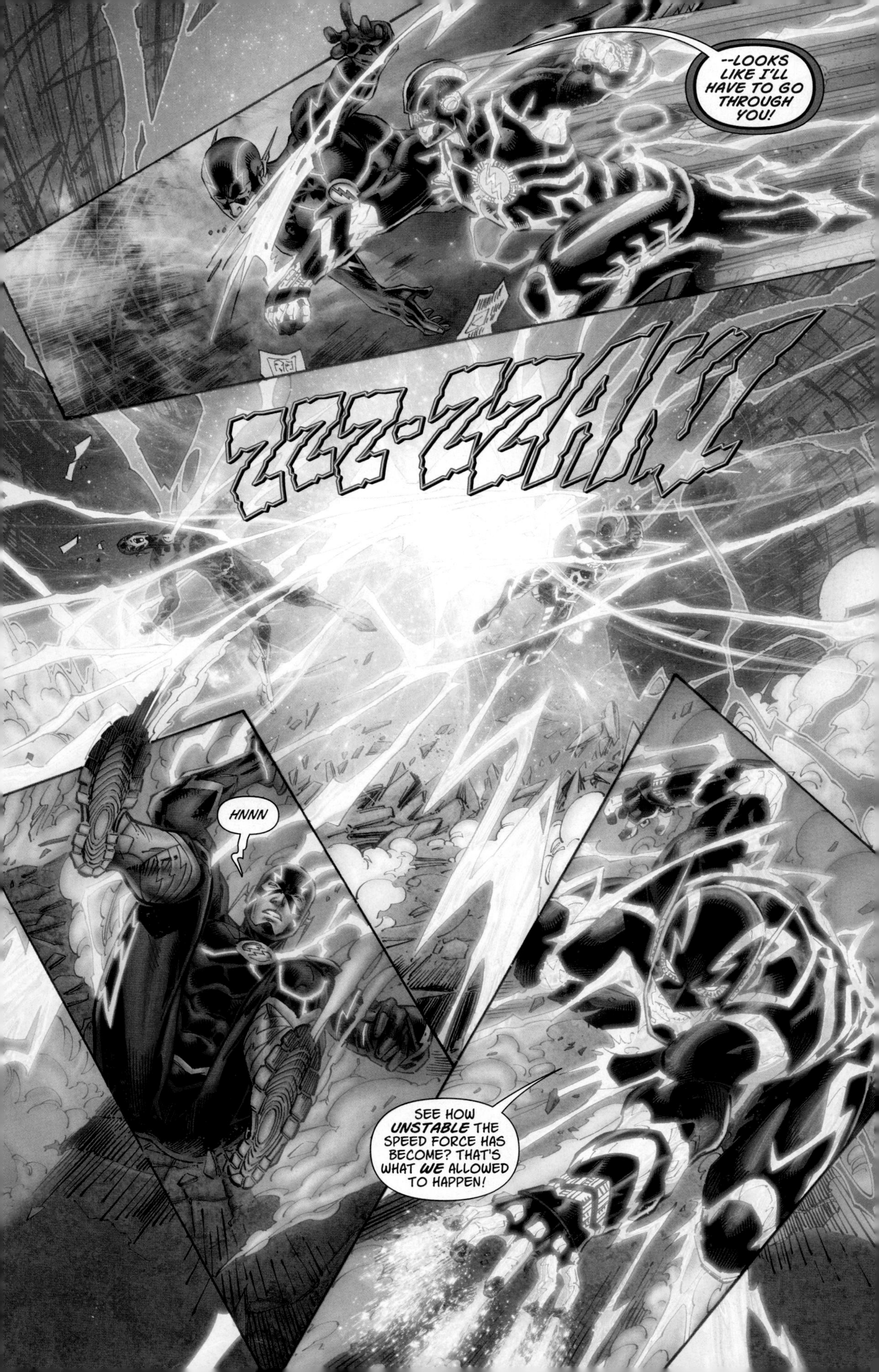
--LOOKS LIKE I'LL HAVE TO GO THROUGH YOU!
ZZZ-ZZAKK
HNNN
SEE HOW UNSTABLE THE SPEED FORCE HAS BECOME? THAT'S WHAT WE ALLOWED TO HAPPEN!

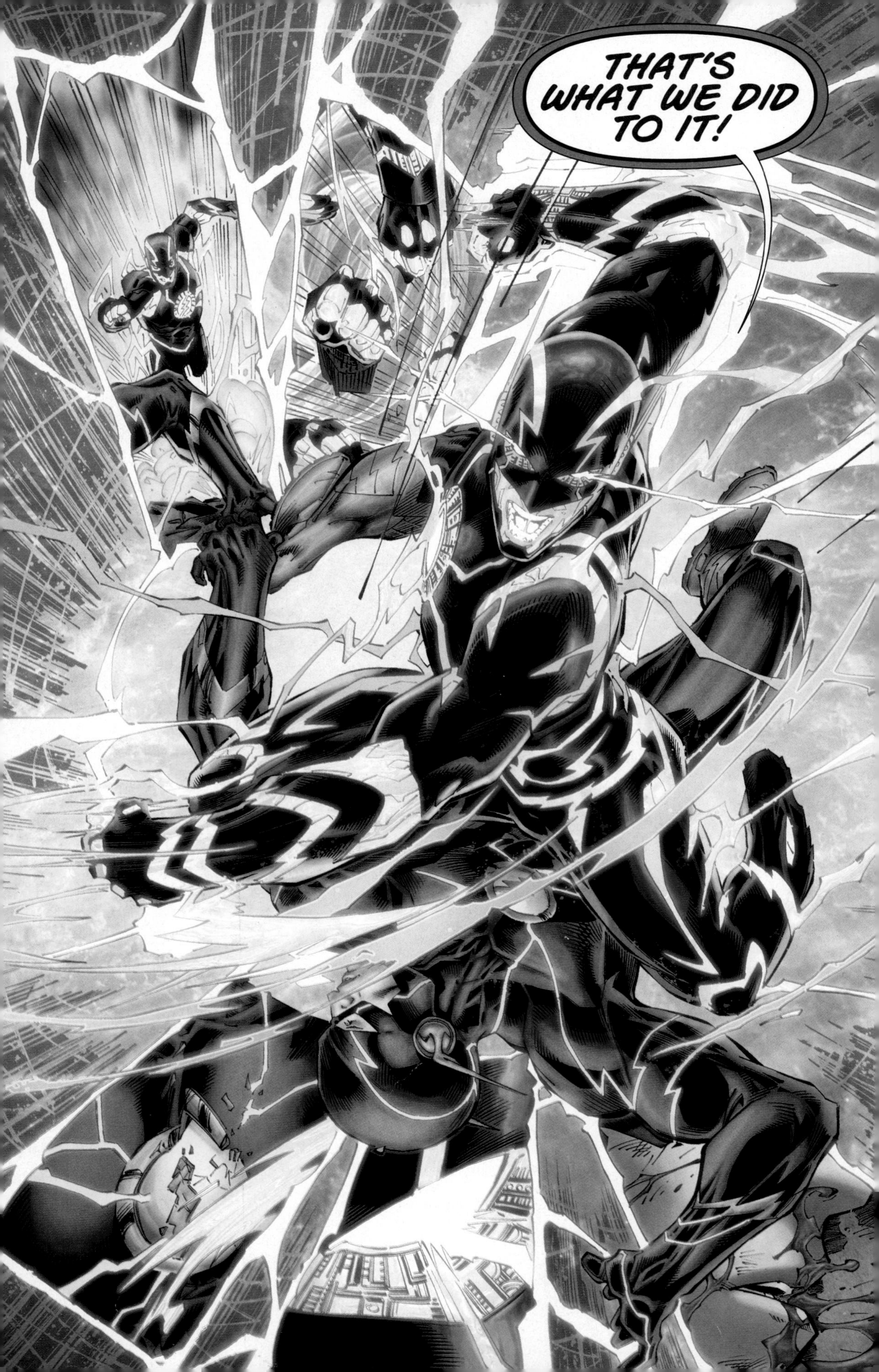
THAT'S WHAT WE DID TO IT!

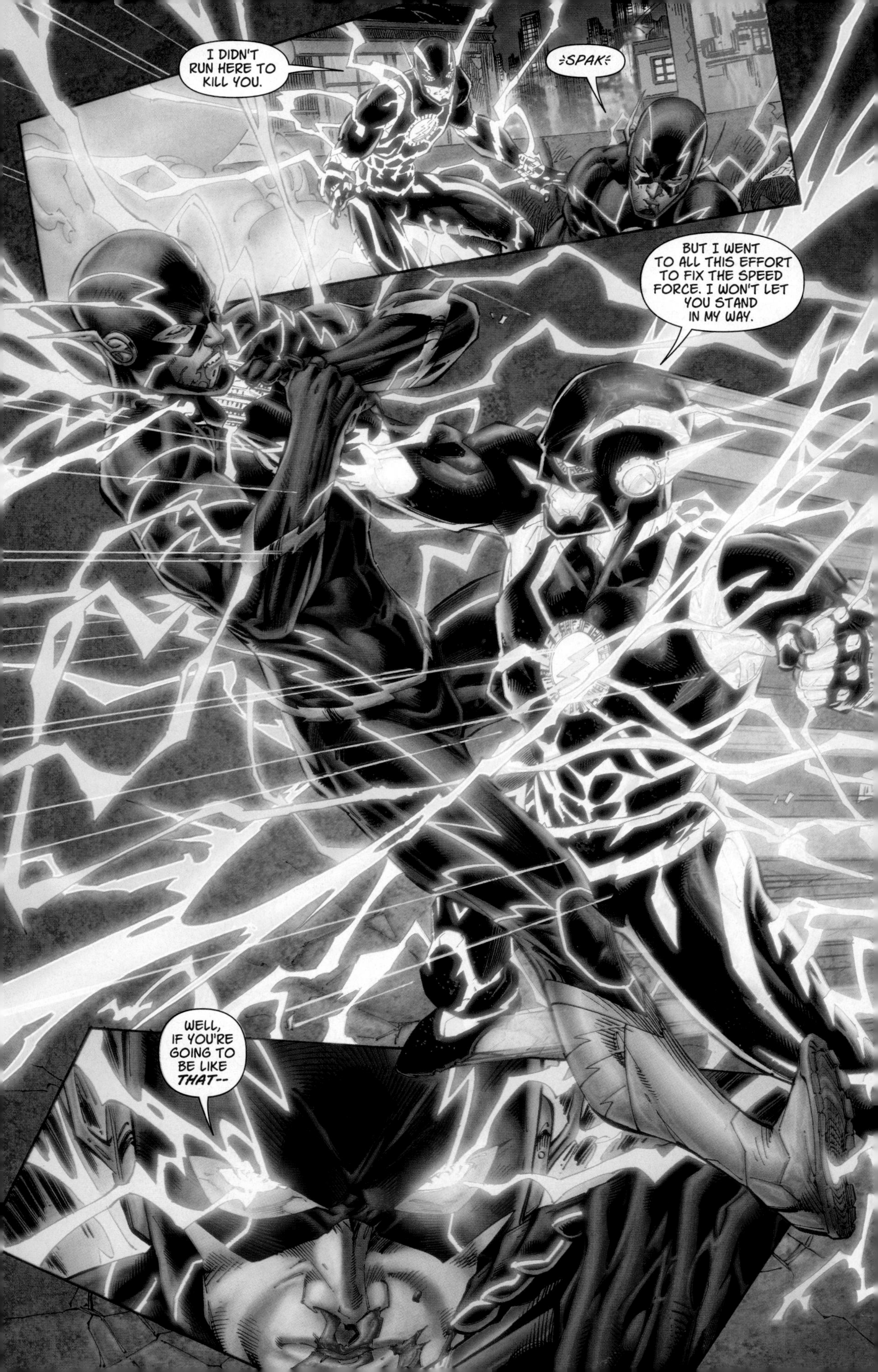
I DIDN'T RUN HERE TO KILL YOU.
SPAK
BUT I WENT TO ALL THIS EFFORT TO FIX THE SPEED FORCE. I WON'T LET YOU STAND IN MY WAY.
WELL, IF YOU'RE GOING TO BE LIKE *THAT*--

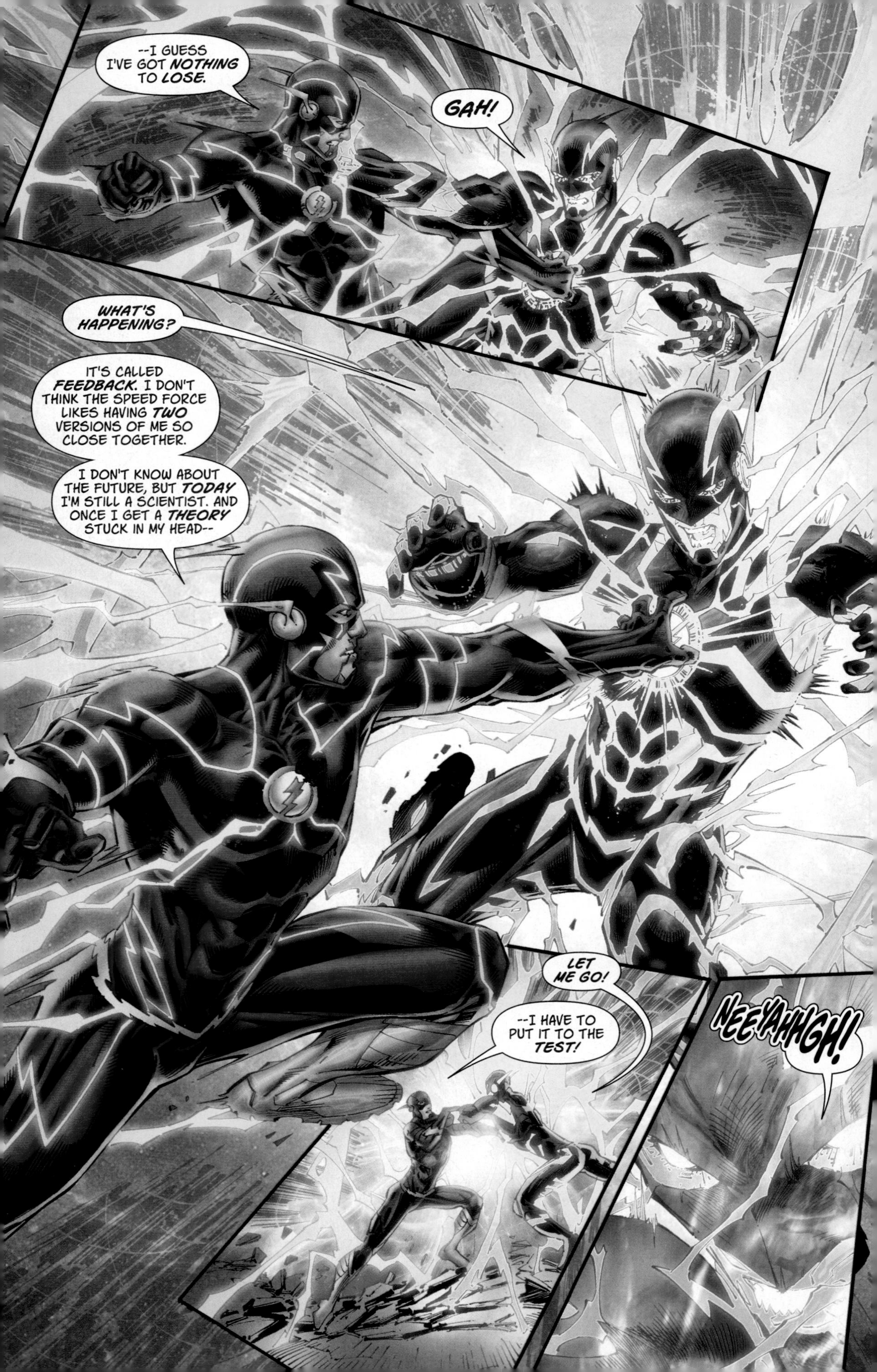
--I GUESS I'VE GOT NOTHING TO LOSE.
GAH!
WHAT'S HAPPENING?
IT'S CALLED FEEDBACK. I DON'T THINK THE SPEED FORCE LIKES HAVING TWO VERSIONS OF ME SO CLOSE TOGETHER.
I DON'T KNOW ABOUT THE FUTURE, BUT TODAY I'M STILL A SCIENTIST. AND ONCE I GET A THEORY STUCK IN MY HEAD--
LET ME GO!
--I HAVE TO PUT IT TO THE TEST!
NEEYAHHGH!

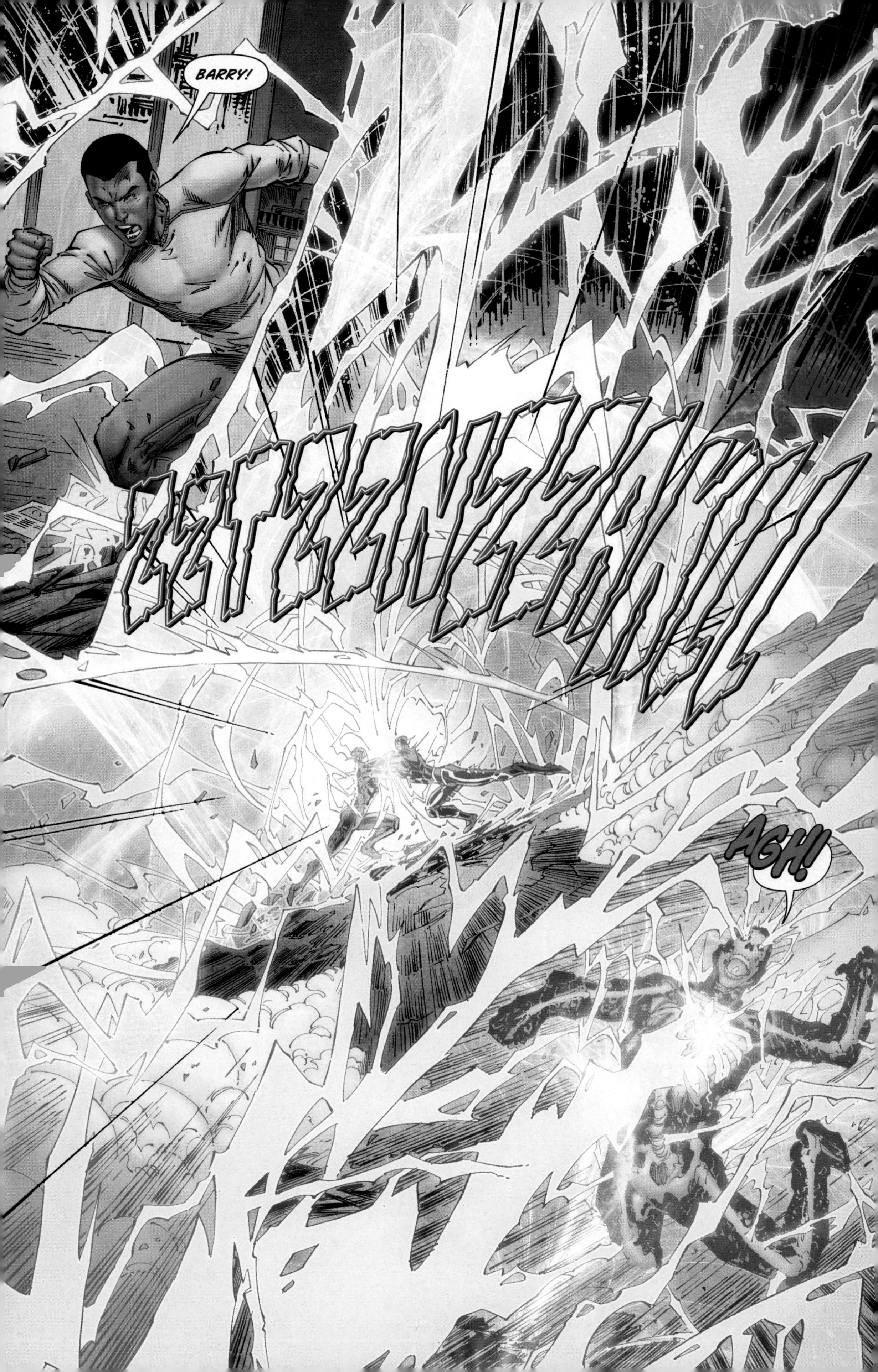
BARRY!
AGH!

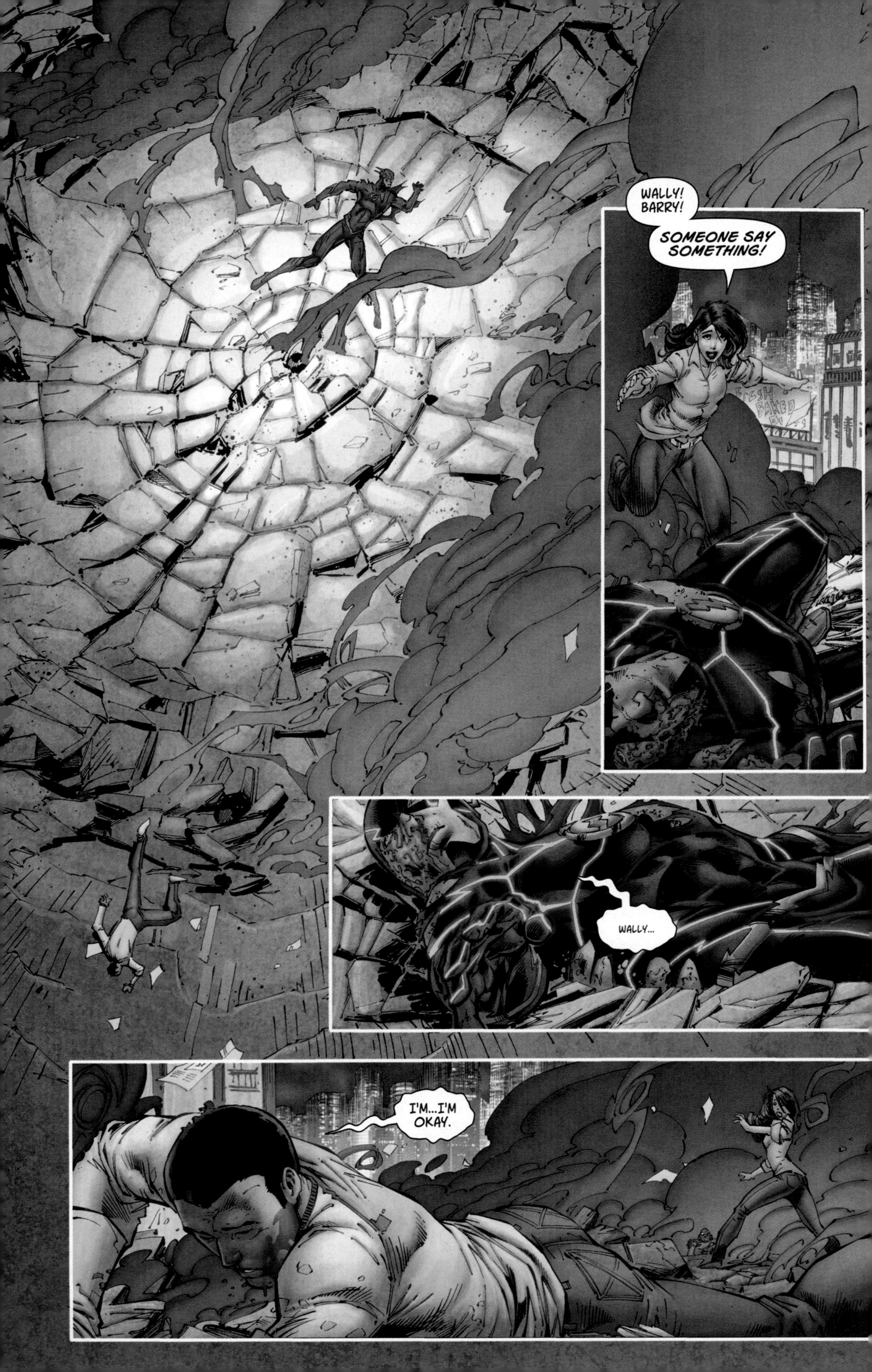
WALLY! BARRY!
SOMEONE SAY SOMETHING!
FRESH BAKED
WALLY...
I'M...I'M OKAY.

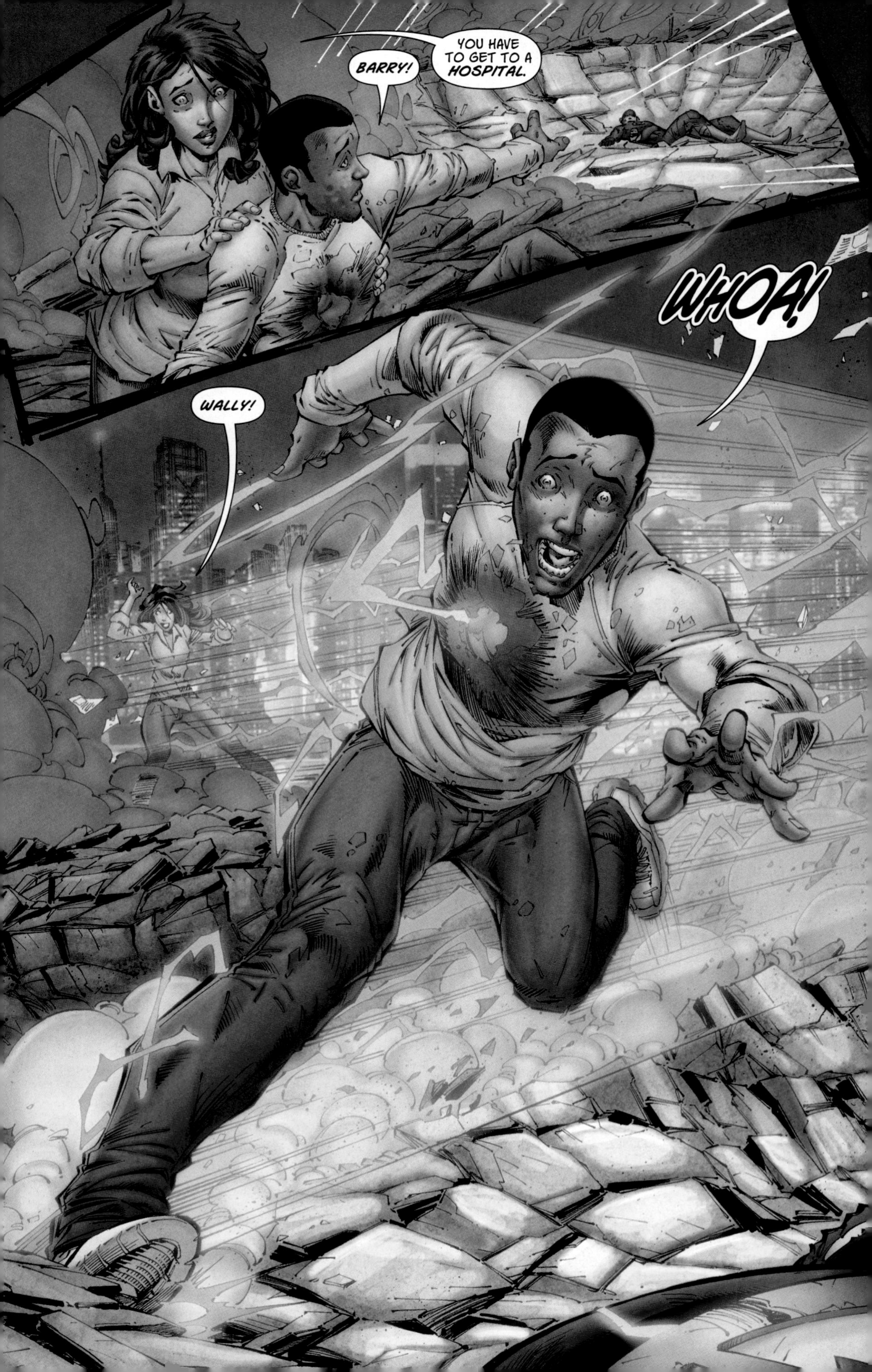
BARRY!
YOU HAVE TO GET TO A HOSPITAL.
WHOA!
WALLY!

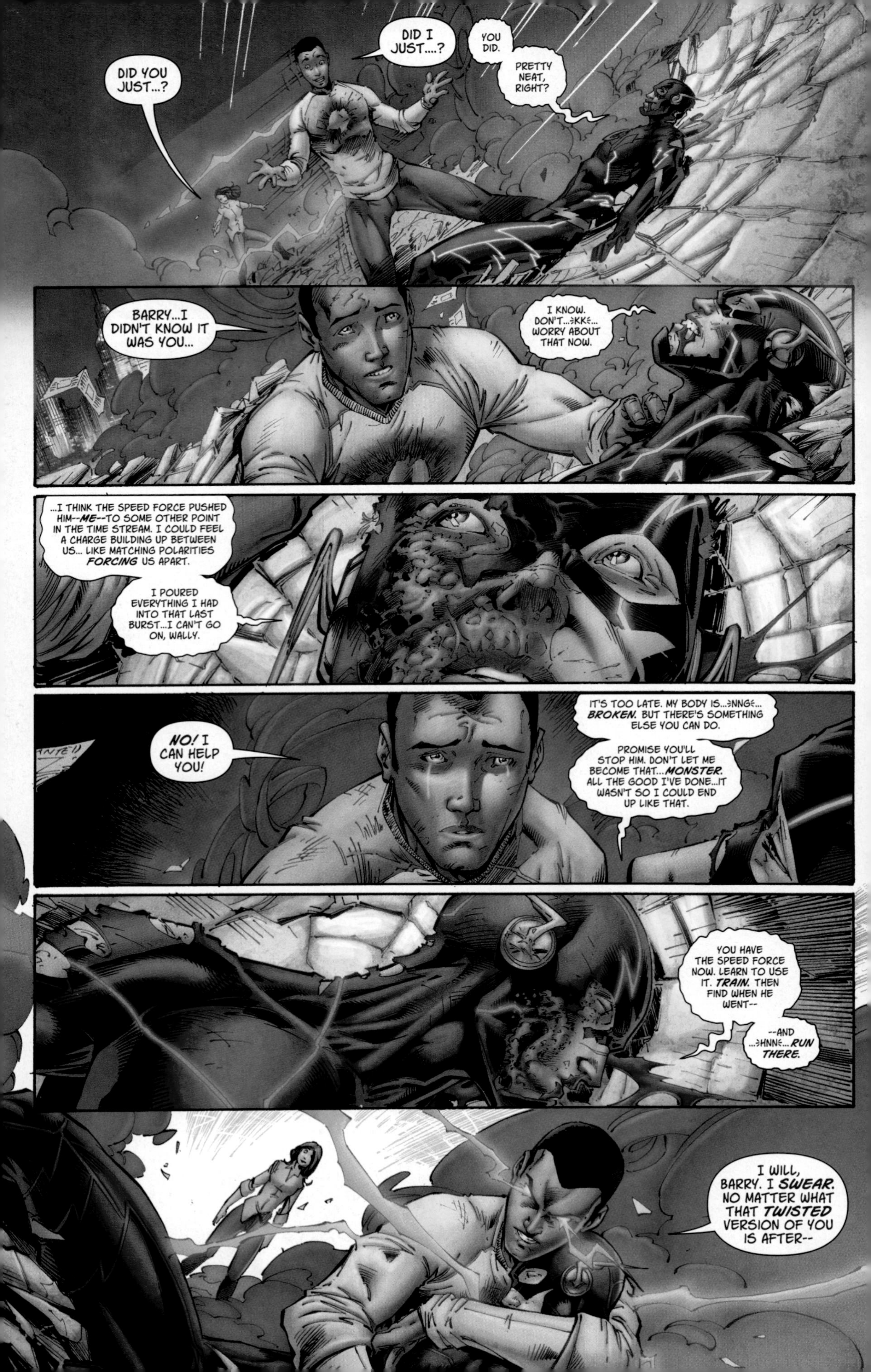
DID YOU JUST...?
DID I JUST....?
YOU DID.
PRETTY NEAT, RIGHT?
BARRY...I DIDN'T KNOW IT WAS YOU...
I KNOW. DON'T...ƎKK६... WORRY ABOUT THAT NOW.
...I THINK THE SPEED FORCE PUSHED HIM--ME--TO SOME OTHER POINT IN THE TIME STREAM. I COULD FEEL A CHARGE BUILDING UP BETWEEN US... LIKE MATCHING POLARITIES FORCING US APART.
I POURED EVERYTHING I HAD INTO THAT LAST BURST...I CAN'T GO ON, WALLY.
NO! I CAN HELP YOU!
IT'S TOO LATE. MY BODY IS...ƎNNG६... BROKEN. BUT THERE'S SOMETHING ELSE YOU CAN DO.
PROMISE YOU'LL STOP HIM. DON'T LET ME BECOME THAT...MONSTER. ALL THE GOOD I'VE DONE...IT WASN'T SO I COULD END UP LIKE THAT.
YOU HAVE THE SPEED FORCE NOW. LEARN TO USE IT. TRAIN. THEN FIND WHEN HE WENT--
--AND ...ƎHNN६...RUN THERE.
I WILL, BARRY. I SWEAR. NO MATTER WHAT THAT TWISTED VERSION OF YOU IS AFTER--

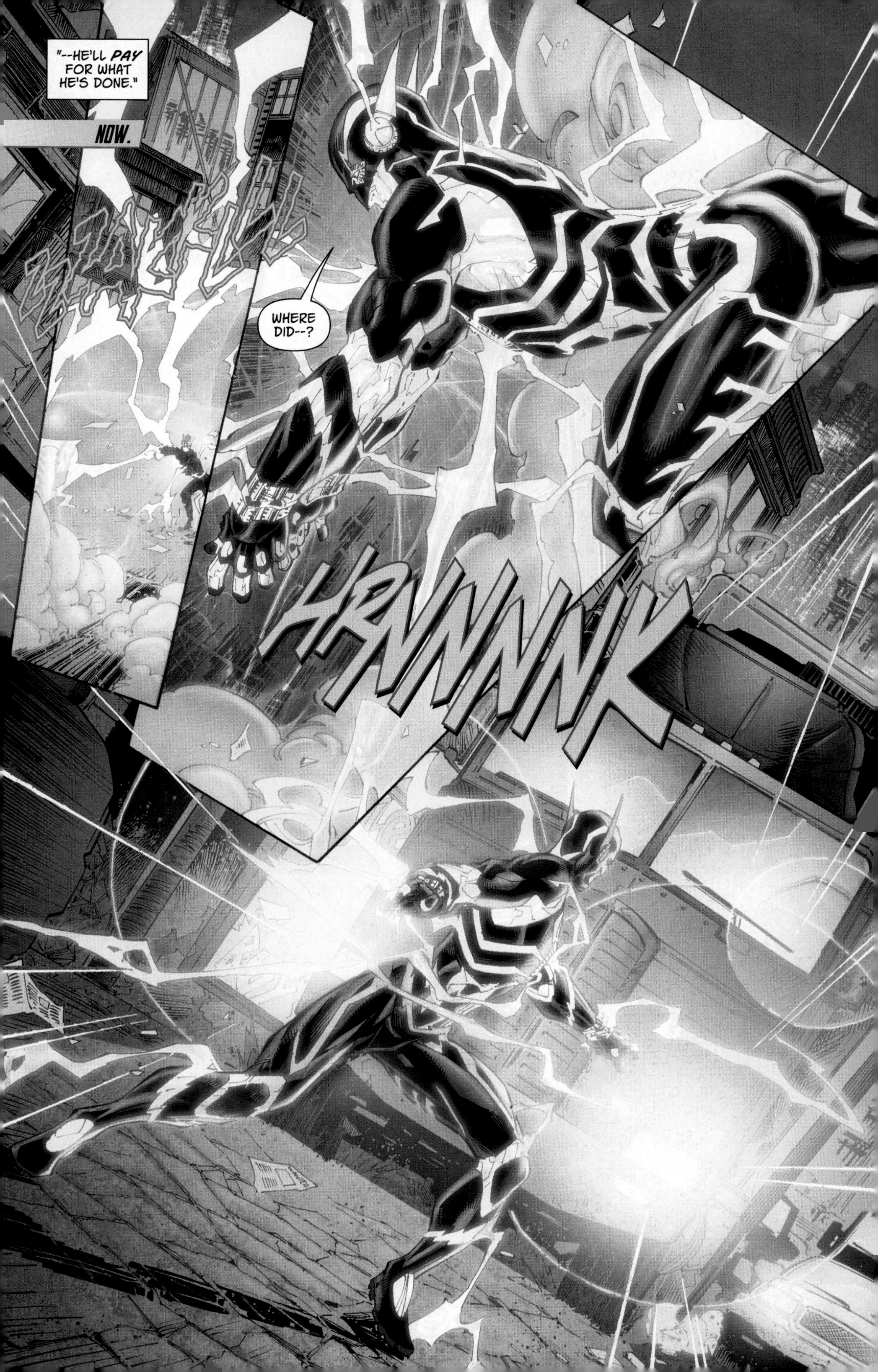
"--HE'LL PAY FOR WHAT HE'S DONE."
NOW.
ZZAAAKK
WHERE DID--?
HRNNNNK

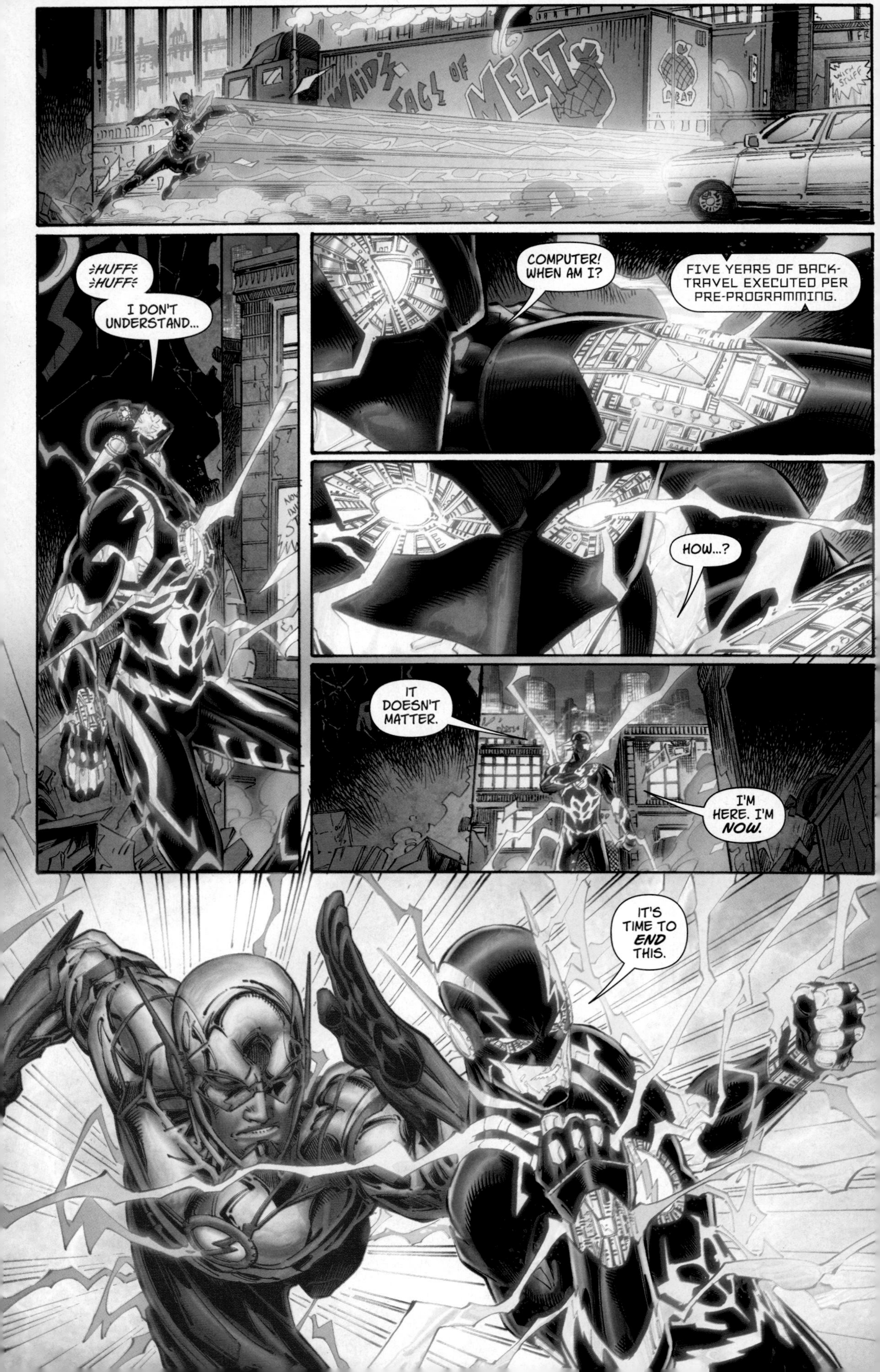
WAID'S CAGE OF MEAT
WITH STUFF
≶HUFF≶ ≶HUFF≶
I DON'T UNDERSTAND...
COMPUTER! WHEN AM I?
FIVE YEARS OF BACK-TRAVEL EXECUTED PER PRE-PROGRAMMING.
HOW...?
IT DOESN'T MATTER.
I'M HERE. I'M *NOW*.
IT'S TIME TO *END* THIS.

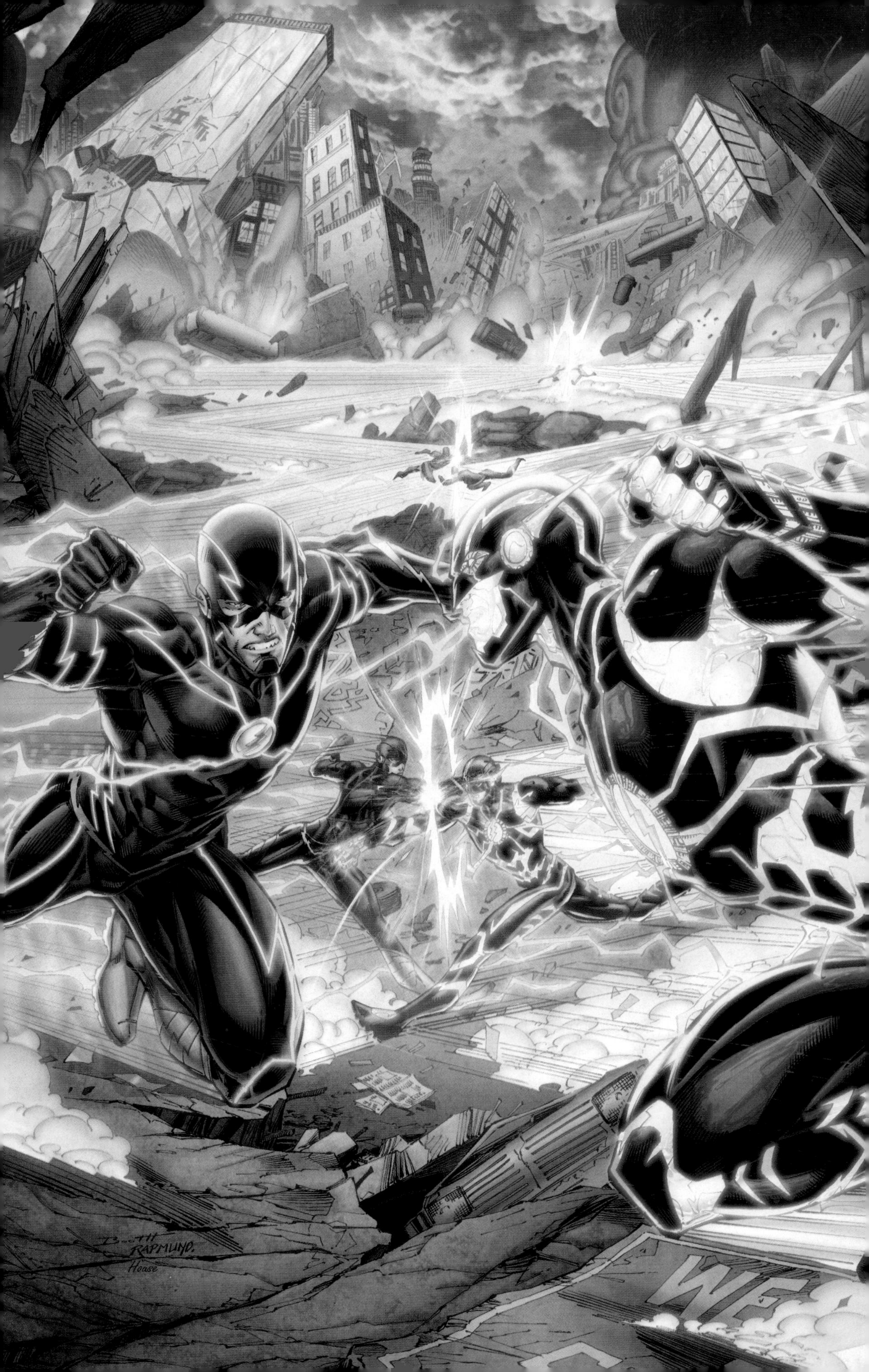

OUT OF TIME

ROBERT VENDITTI & VAN JENSEN writers BRETT BOOTH penciller NORM RAPMUND inker

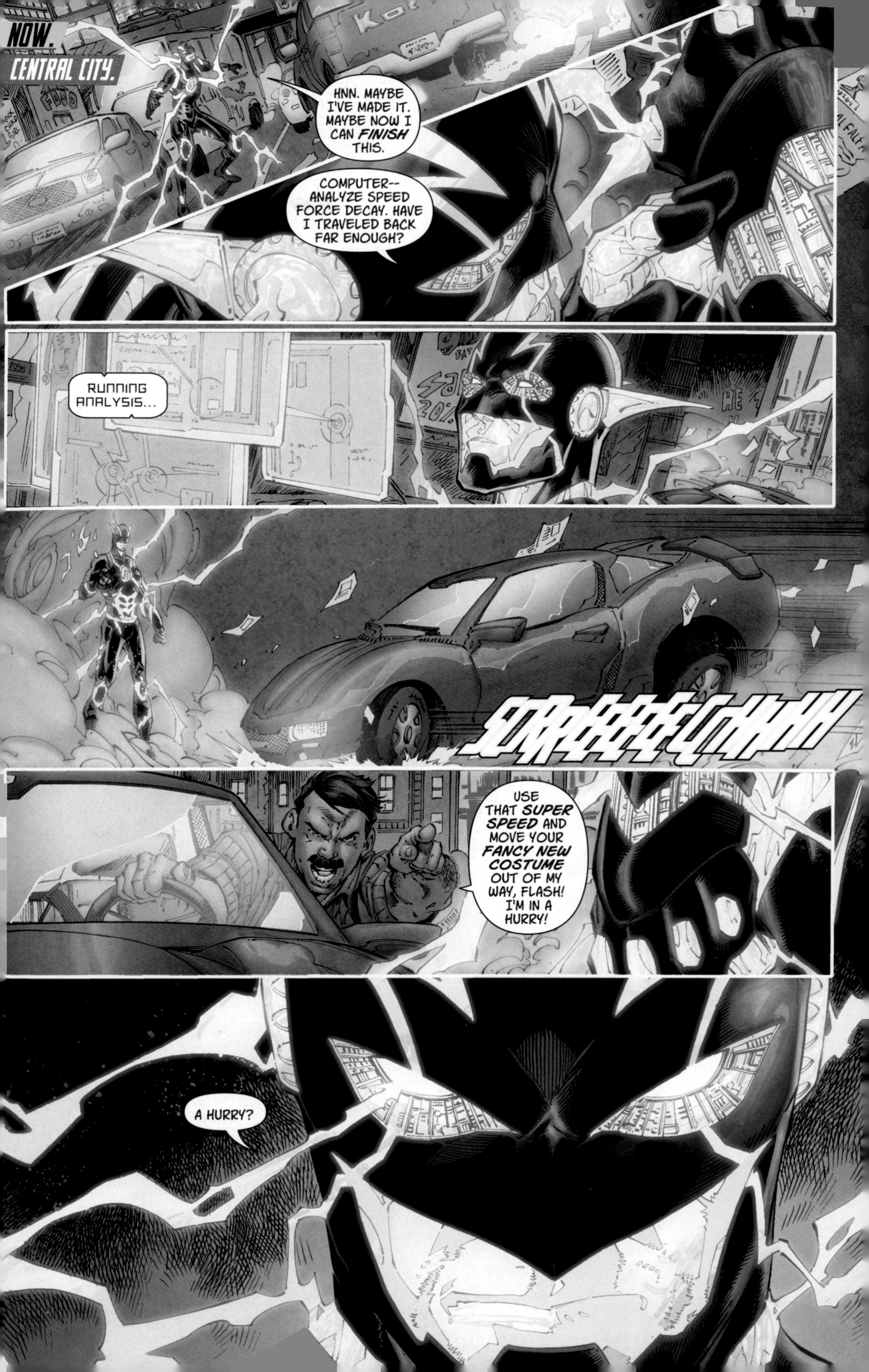
NOW.
CENTRAL CITY.
HNN. MAYBE I'VE MADE IT. MAYBE NOW I CAN FINISH THIS.
COMPUTER-- ANALYZE SPEED FORCE DECAY. HAVE I TRAVELED BACK FAR ENOUGH?
RUNNING ANALYSIS...
SCRRRRREECHHHHH
USE THAT SUPER SPEED AND MOVE YOUR FANCY NEW COSTUME OUT OF MY WAY, FLASH! I'M IN A HURRY!
A HURRY?

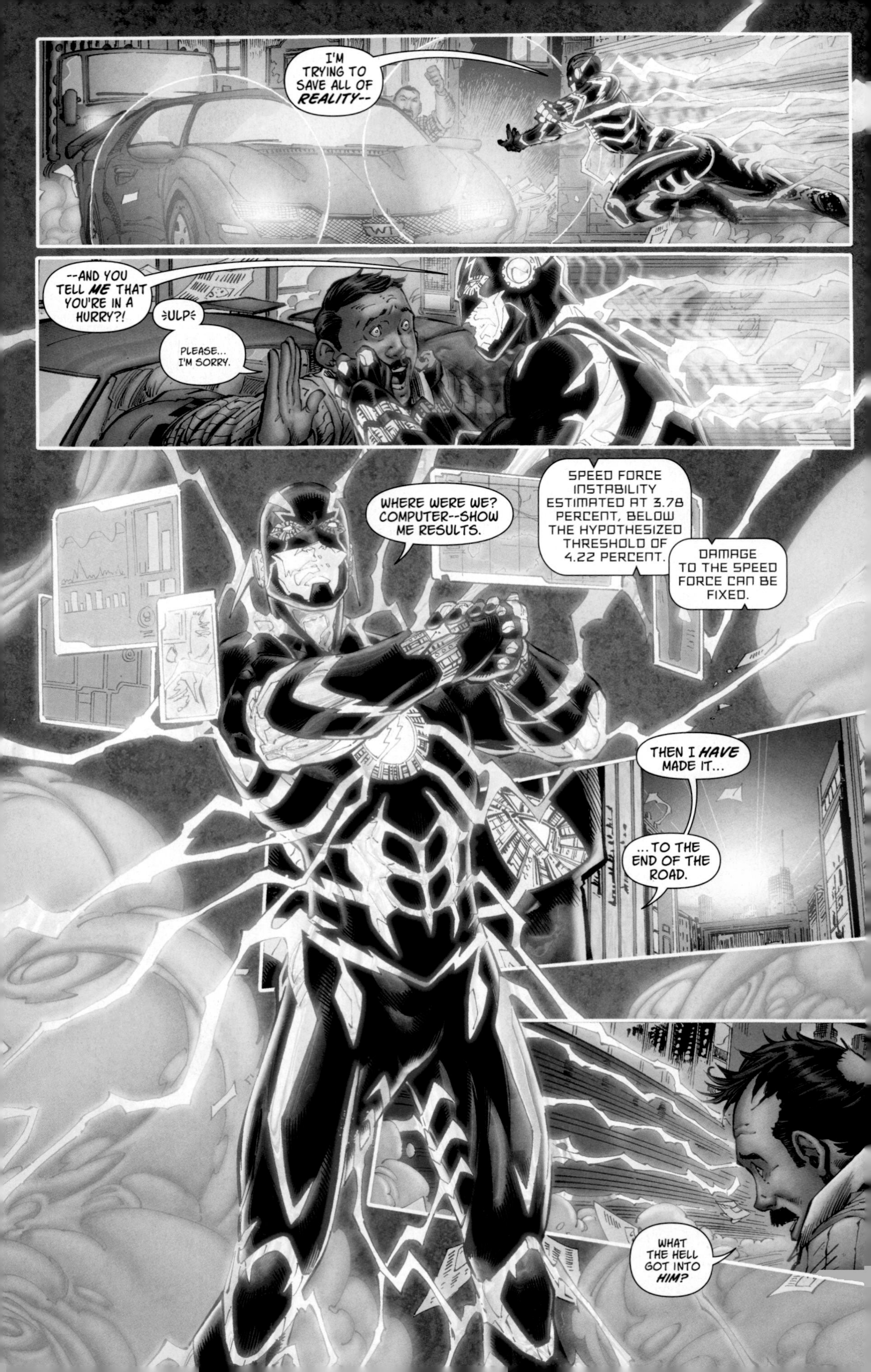
I'M TRYING TO SAVE ALL OF REALITY--
--AND YOU TELL ME THAT YOU'RE IN A HURRY?!
ULP
PLEASE... I'M SORRY.
WHERE WERE WE? COMPUTER--SHOW ME RESULTS.
SPEED FORCE INSTABILITY ESTIMATED AT 3.78 PERCENT, BELOW THE HYPOTHESIZED THRESHOLD OF 4.22 PERCENT.
DAMAGE TO THE SPEED FORCE CAN BE FIXED.
THEN I HAVE MADE IT...
...TO THE END OF THE ROAD.
WHAT THE HELL GOT INTO HIM?

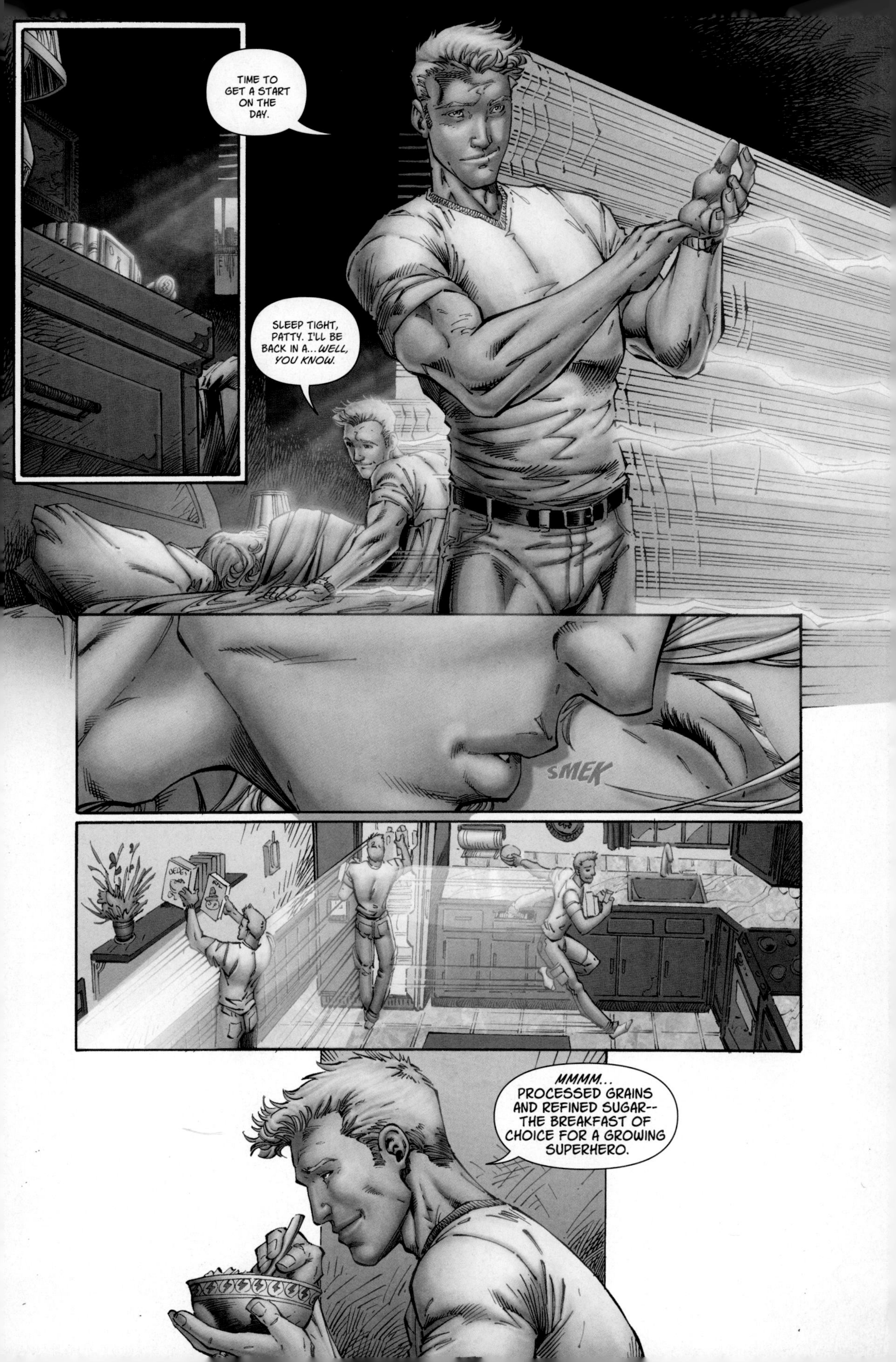
TIME TO GET A START ON THE DAY.
SLEEP TIGHT, PATTY. I'LL BE BACK IN A... *WELL, YOU KNOW.*
SMEK
MMMM... PROCESSED GRAINS AND REFINED SUGAR-- THE BREAKFAST OF CHOICE FOR A GROWING SUPERHERO.

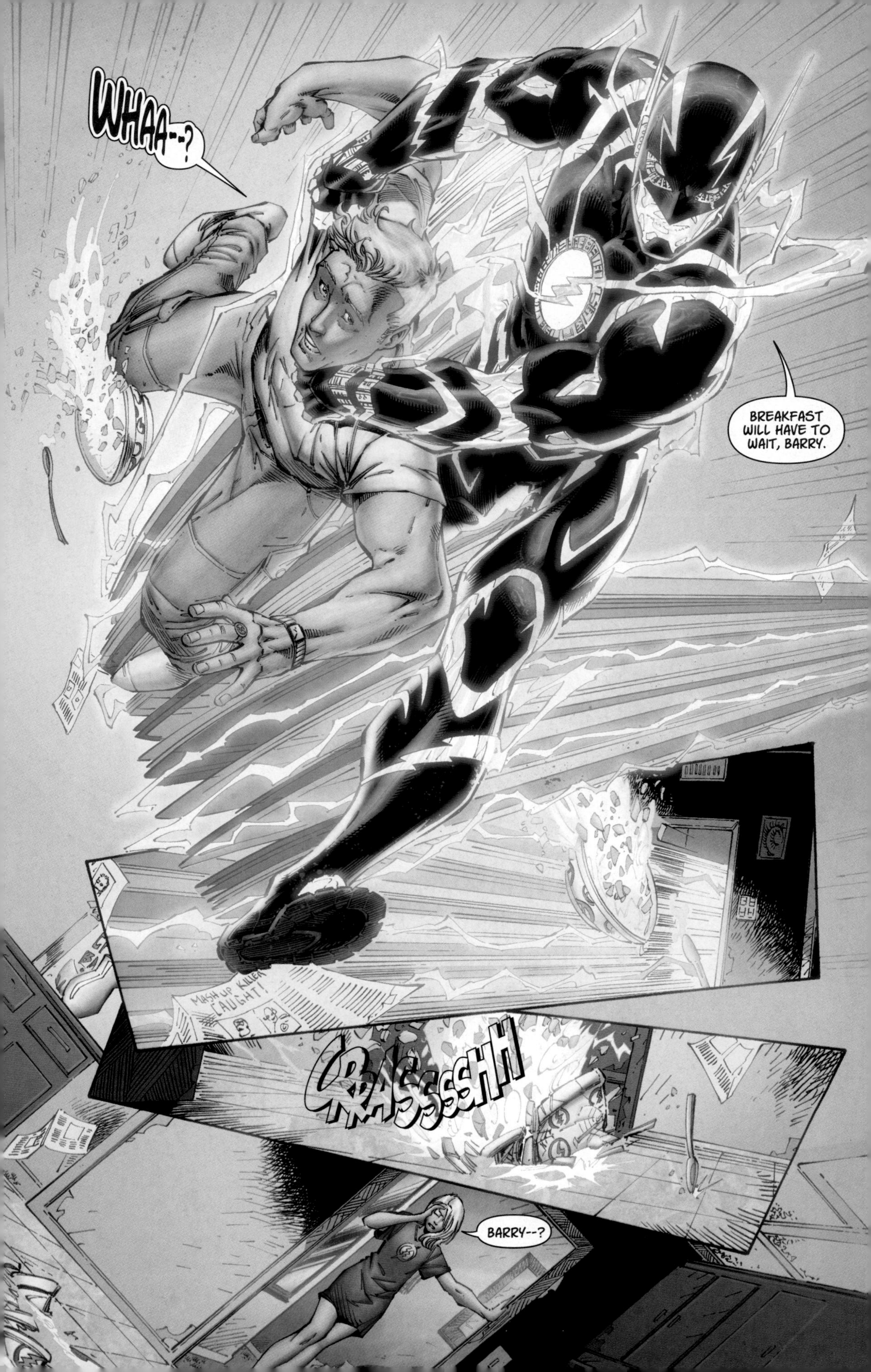
WHAA--?
BREAKFAST WILL HAVE TO WAIT, BARRY.
MASH UP KILLER CAUGHT!
CRASSSSSHH
BARRY--?

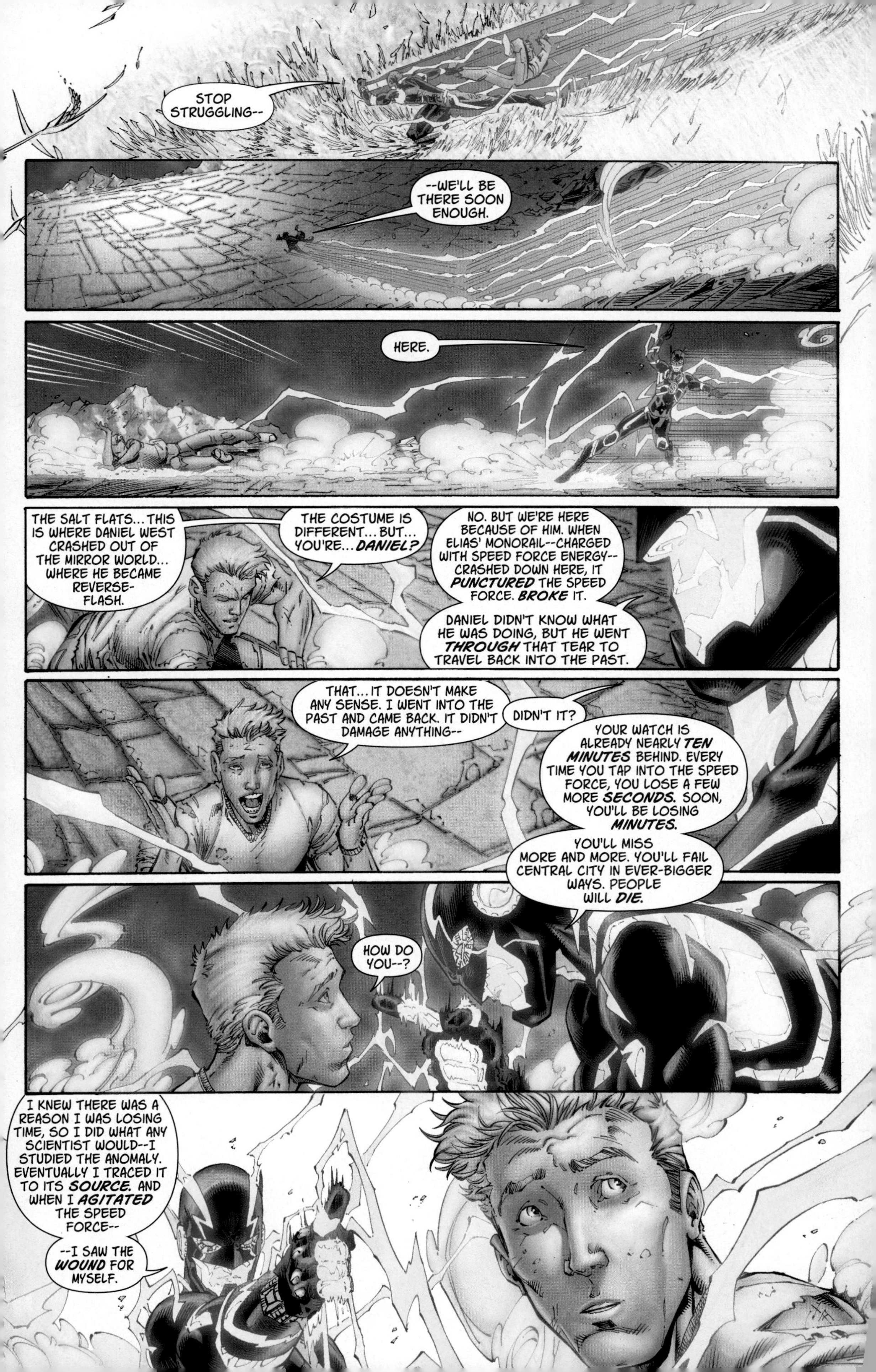
STOP STRUGGLING--
--WE'LL BE THERE SOON ENOUGH.
HERE.
THE SALT FLATS... THIS IS WHERE DANIEL WEST CRASHED OUT OF THE MIRROR WORLD... WHERE HE BECAME REVERSE-FLASH.
THE COSTUME IS DIFFERENT... BUT... YOU'RE... *DANIEL?*
NO. BUT WE'RE HERE BECAUSE OF HIM. WHEN ELIAS' MONORAIL--CHARGED WITH SPEED FORCE ENERGY--CRASHED DOWN HERE, IT *PUNCTURED* THE SPEED FORCE. *BROKE* IT.
DANIEL DIDN'T KNOW WHAT HE WAS DOING, BUT HE WENT *THROUGH* THAT TEAR TO TRAVEL BACK INTO THE PAST.
THAT... IT DOESN'T MAKE ANY SENSE. I WENT INTO THE PAST AND CAME BACK. IT DIDN'T DAMAGE ANYTHING--
DIDN'T IT?
YOUR WATCH IS ALREADY NEARLY *TEN MINUTES* BEHIND. EVERY TIME YOU TAP INTO THE SPEED FORCE, YOU LOSE A FEW MORE *SECONDS.* SOON, YOU'LL BE LOSING *MINUTES.*
YOU'LL MISS MORE AND MORE. YOU'LL FAIL CENTRAL CITY IN EVER-BIGGER WAYS. PEOPLE WILL *DIE.*
HOW DO YOU--?
I KNEW THERE WAS A REASON I WAS LOSING TIME, SO I DID WHAT ANY SCIENTIST WOULD--I STUDIED THE ANOMALY. EVENTUALLY I TRACED IT TO ITS *SOURCE.* AND WHEN I *AGITATED* THE SPEED FORCE--
--I SAW THE *WOUND* FOR MYSELF.

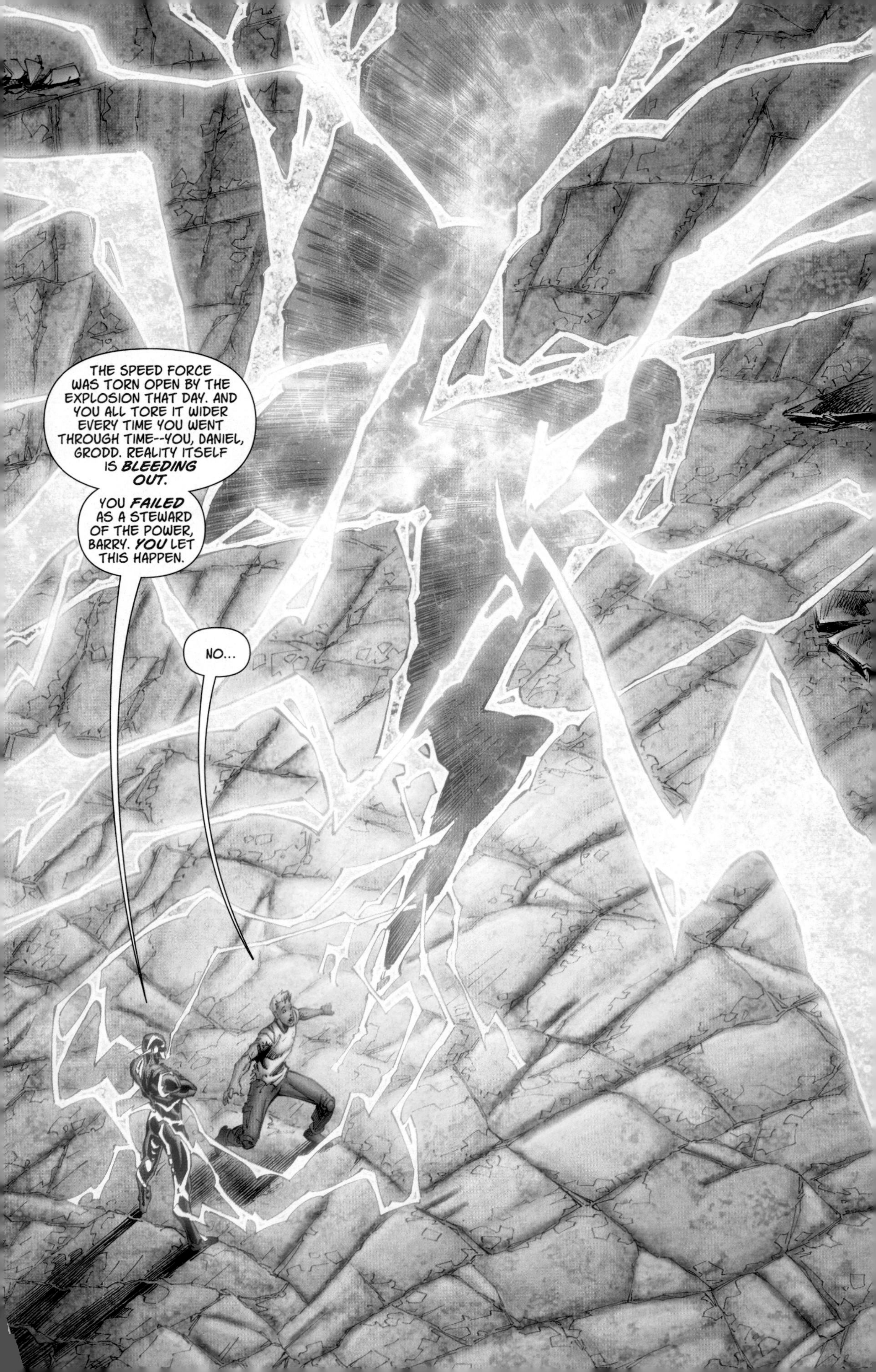
THE SPEED FORCE WAS TORN OPEN BY THE EXPLOSION THAT DAY. AND YOU ALL TORE IT WIDER EVERY TIME YOU WENT THROUGH TIME--YOU, DANIEL, GRODD. REALITY ITSELF IS **BLEEDING OUT**.
YOU **FAILED** AS A STEWARD OF THE POWER, BARRY. **YOU** LET THIS HAPPEN.
NO...

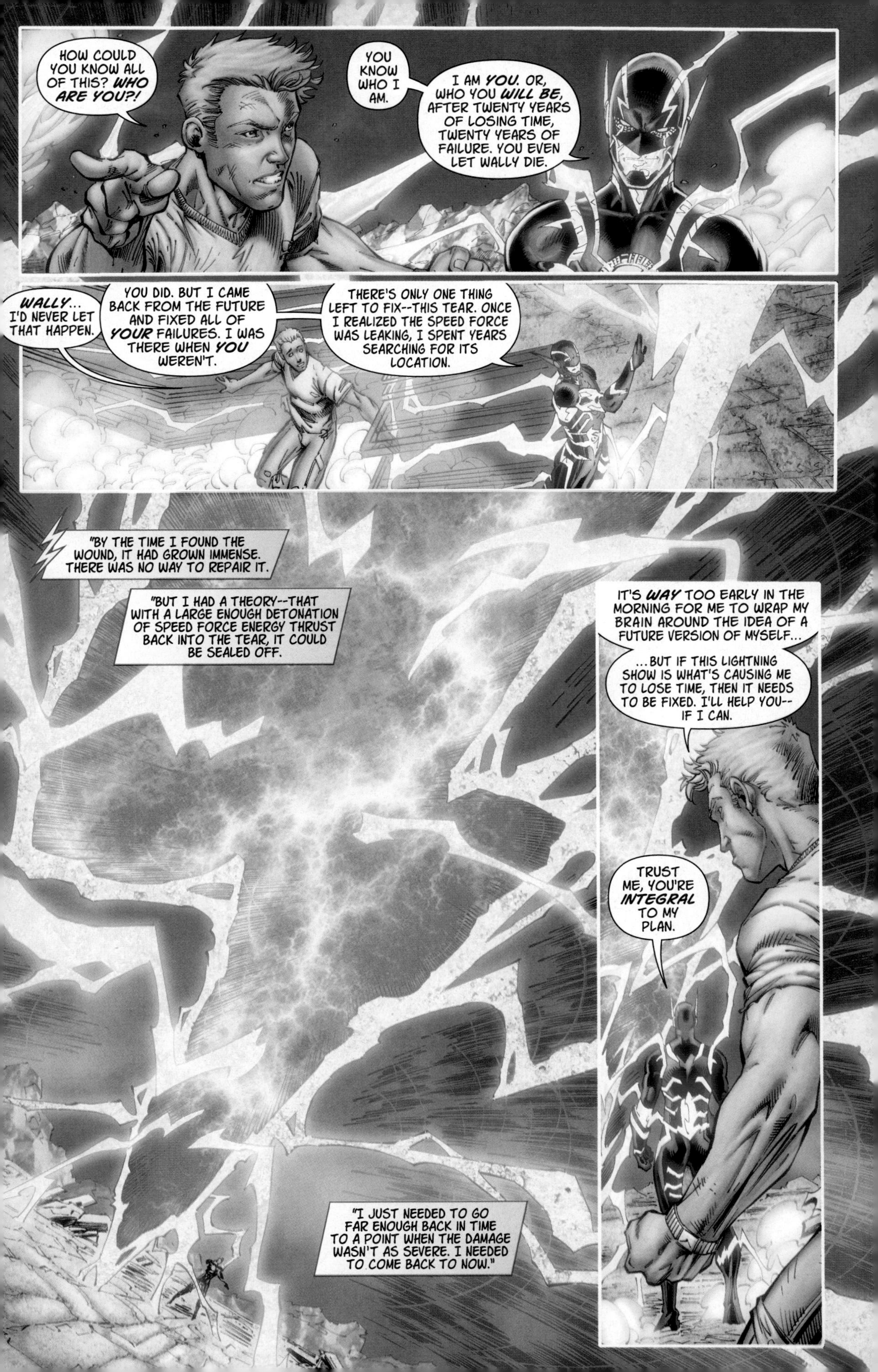

HOW COULD YOU KNOW ALL OF THIS? WHO ARE YOU?!
YOU KNOW WHO I AM.
I AM YOU. OR, WHO YOU WILL BE, AFTER TWENTY YEARS OF LOSING TIME, TWENTY YEARS OF FAILURE. YOU EVEN LET WALLY DIE.
WALLY... I'D NEVER LET THAT HAPPEN.
YOU DID. BUT I CAME BACK FROM THE FUTURE AND FIXED ALL OF YOUR FAILURES. I WAS THERE WHEN YOU WEREN'T.
THERE'S ONLY ONE THING LEFT TO FIX--THIS TEAR. ONCE I REALIZED THE SPEED FORCE WAS LEAKING, I SPENT YEARS SEARCHING FOR ITS LOCATION.
"BY THE TIME I FOUND THE WOUND, IT HAD GROWN IMMENSE. THERE WAS NO WAY TO REPAIR IT.
"BUT I HAD A THEORY--THAT WITH A LARGE ENOUGH DETONATION OF SPEED FORCE ENERGY THRUST BACK INTO THE TEAR, IT COULD BE SEALED OFF.
"I JUST NEEDED TO GO FAR ENOUGH BACK IN TIME TO A POINT WHEN THE DAMAGE WASN'T AS SEVERE. I NEEDED TO COME BACK TO NOW."
IT'S WAY TOO EARLY IN THE MORNING FOR ME TO WRAP MY BRAIN AROUND THE IDEA OF A FUTURE VERSION OF MYSELF...
...BUT IF THIS LIGHTNING SHOW IS WHAT'S CAUSING ME TO LOSE TIME, THEN IT NEEDS TO BE FIXED. I'LL HELP YOU-- IF I CAN.
TRUST ME, YOU'RE INTEGRAL TO MY PLAN.

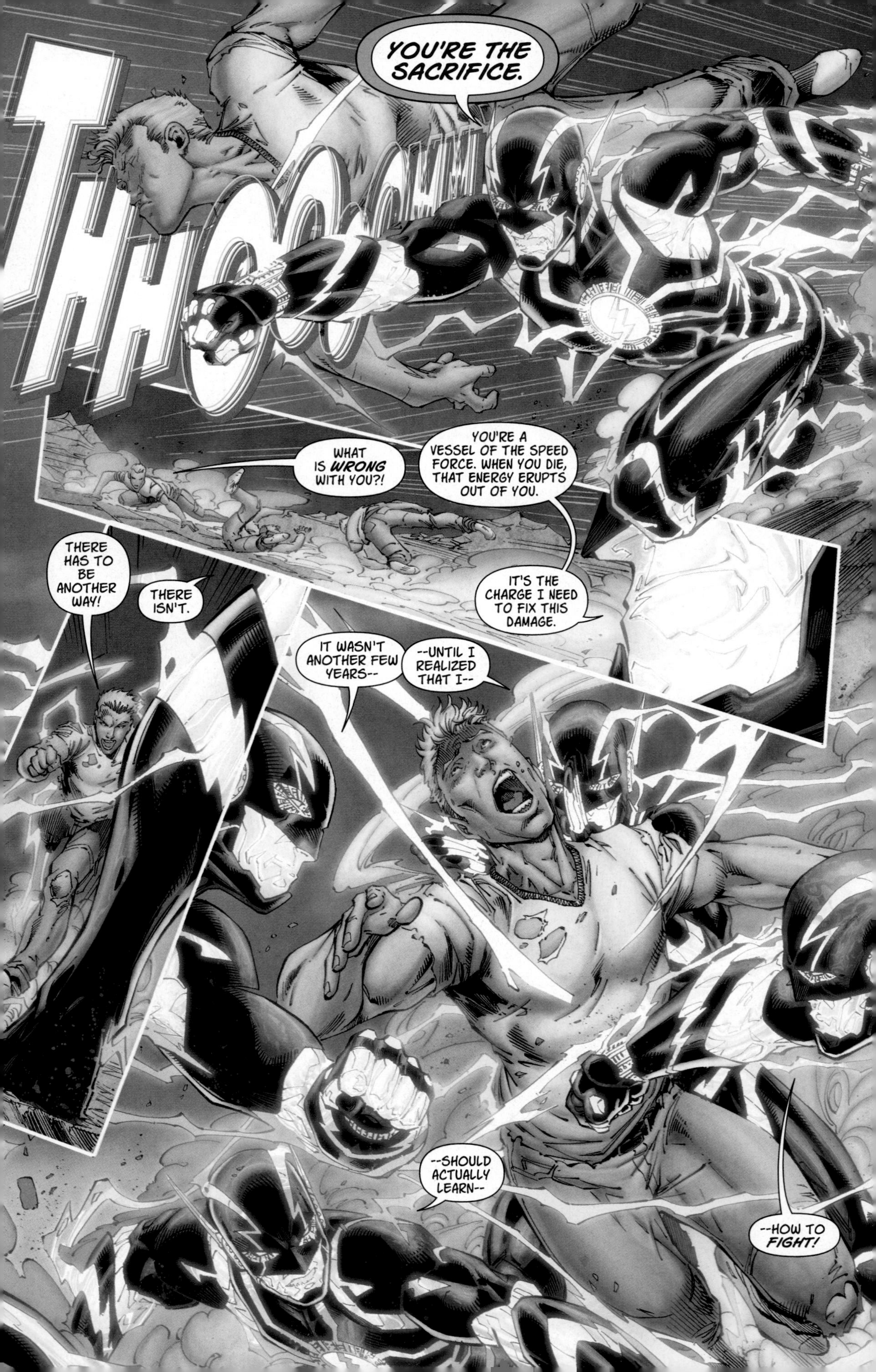

YOU'RE THE SACRIFICE.
THOOOOOM
WHAT IS *WRONG* WITH YOU?!
YOU'RE A VESSEL OF THE SPEED FORCE. WHEN YOU DIE, THAT ENERGY ERUPTS OUT OF YOU.
IT'S THE CHARGE I NEED TO FIX THIS DAMAGE.
THERE HAS TO BE ANOTHER WAY!
THERE ISN'T.
IT WASN'T ANOTHER FEW YEARS--
--UNTIL I REALIZED THAT I--
--SHOULD ACTUALLY LEARN--
--HOW TO *FIGHT!*

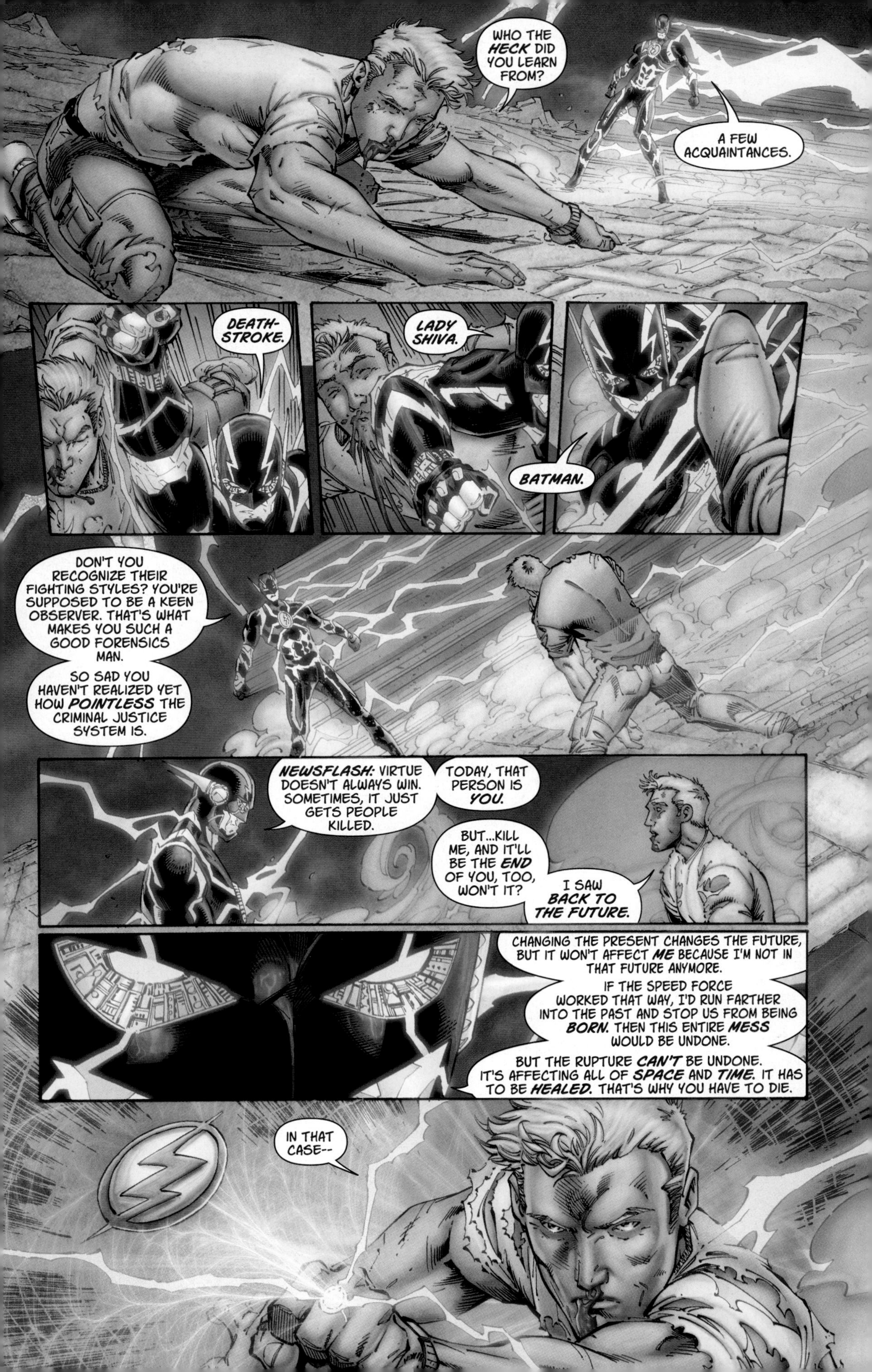

WHO THE HECK DID YOU LEARN FROM?
A FEW ACQUAINTANCES.
DEATH-STROKE.
LADY SHIVA.
BATMAN.
DON'T YOU RECOGNIZE THEIR FIGHTING STYLES? YOU'RE SUPPOSED TO BE A KEEN OBSERVER. THAT'S WHAT MAKES YOU SUCH A GOOD FORENSICS MAN.
SO SAD YOU HAVEN'T REALIZED YET HOW POINTLESS THE CRIMINAL JUSTICE SYSTEM IS.
NEWSFLASH: VIRTUE DOESN'T ALWAYS WIN. SOMETIMES, IT JUST GETS PEOPLE KILLED.
TODAY, THAT PERSON IS YOU.
BUT...KILL ME, AND IT'LL BE THE END OF YOU, TOO, WON'T IT?
I SAW BACK TO THE FUTURE.
CHANGING THE PRESENT CHANGES THE FUTURE, BUT IT WON'T AFFECT ME BECAUSE I'M NOT IN THAT FUTURE ANYMORE.
IF THE SPEED FORCE WORKED THAT WAY, I'D RUN FARTHER INTO THE PAST AND STOP US FROM BEING BORN. THEN THIS ENTIRE MESS WOULD BE UNDONE.
BUT THE RUPTURE CAN'T BE UNDONE. IT'S AFFECTING ALL OF SPACE AND TIME. IT HAS TO BE HEALED. THAT'S WHY YOU HAVE TO DIE.
IN THAT CASE--

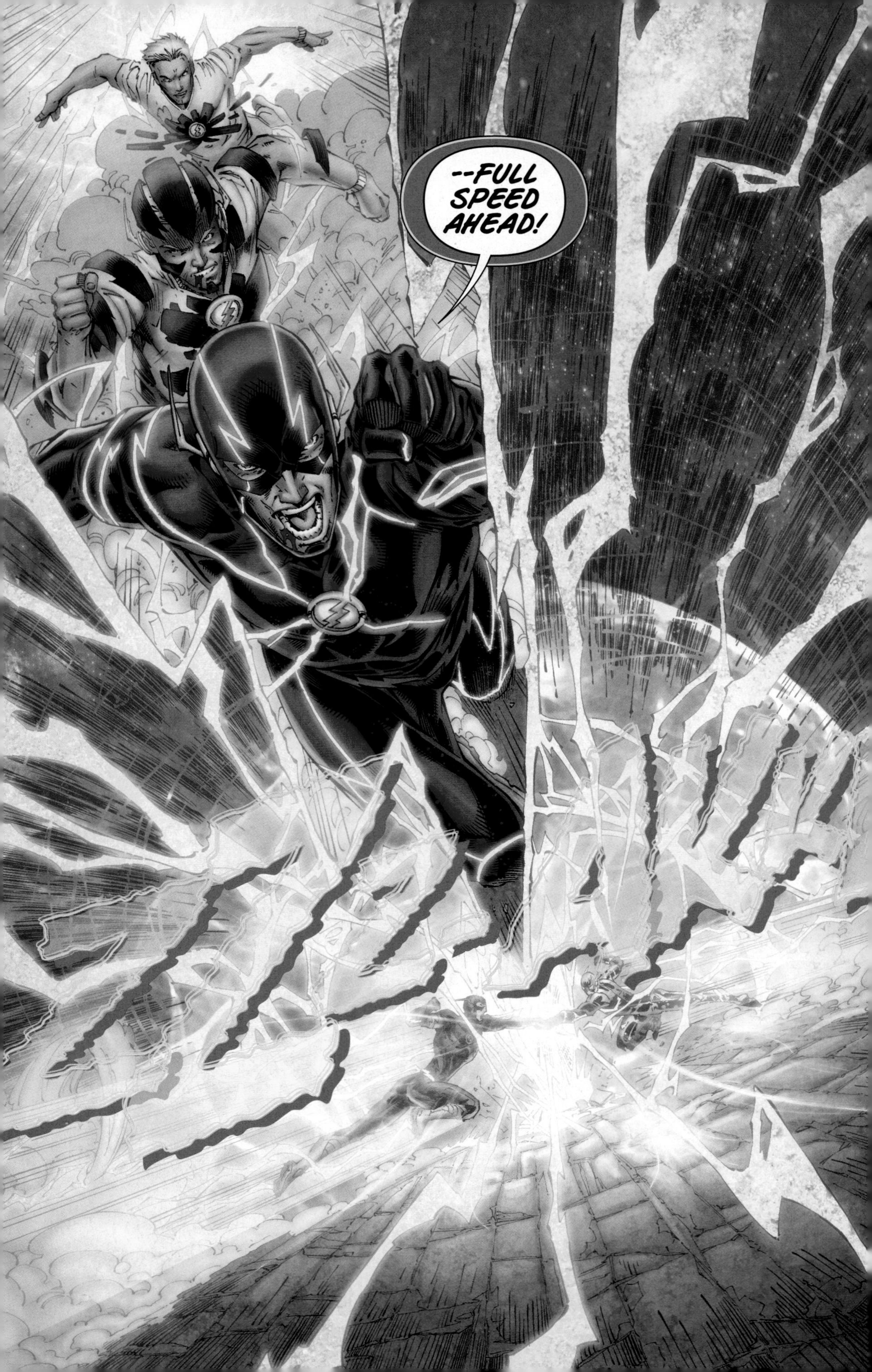
--FULL SPEED AHEAD!

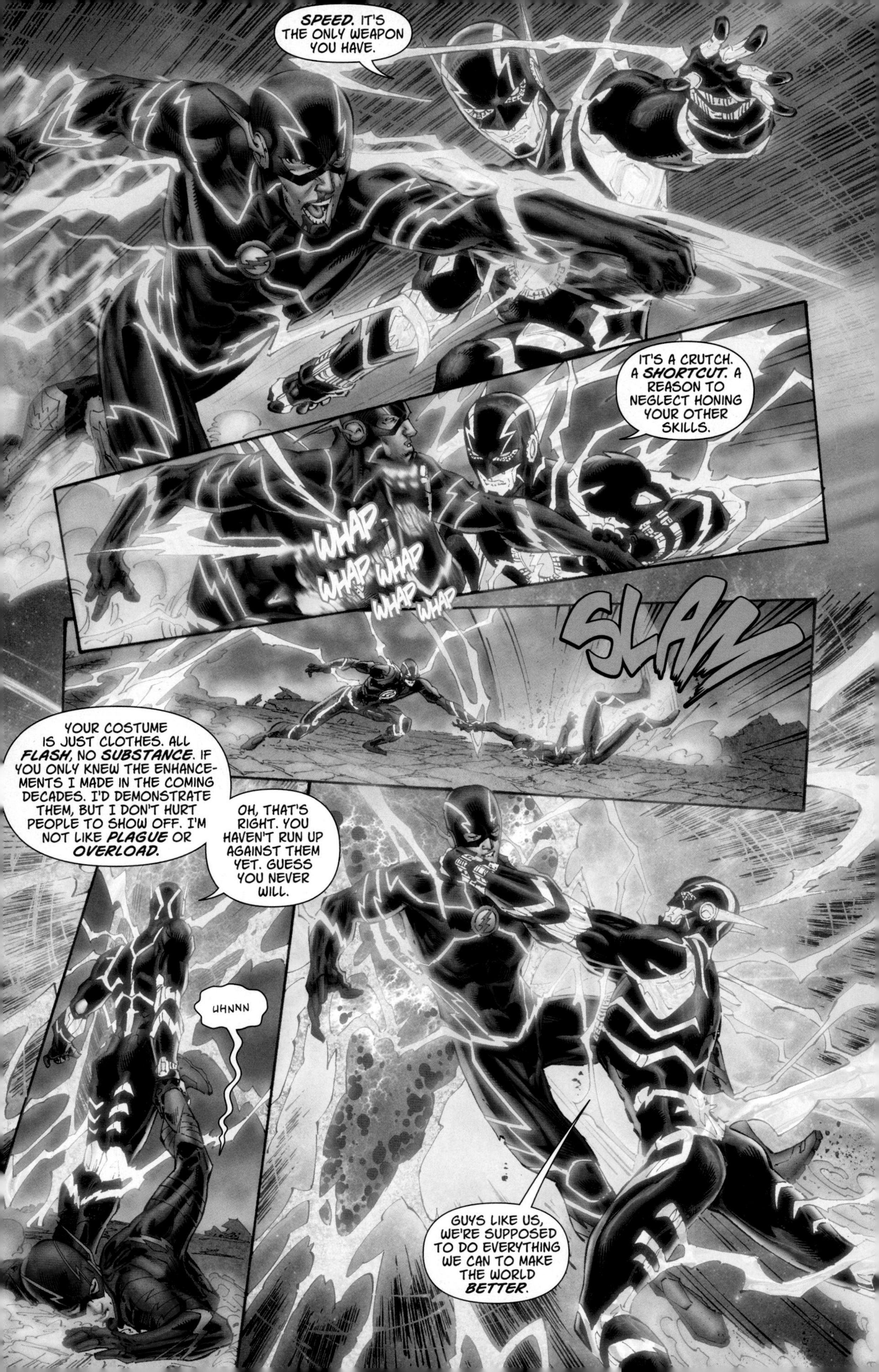
SPEED. IT'S THE ONLY WEAPON YOU HAVE.
IT'S A CRUTCH. A SHORTCUT. A REASON TO NEGLECT HONING YOUR OTHER SKILLS.
WHAP WHAP WHAP WHAP WHAP
SLAM
YOUR COSTUME IS JUST CLOTHES. ALL FLASH, NO SUBSTANCE. IF YOU ONLY KNEW THE ENHANCEMENTS I MADE IN THE COMING DECADES. I'D DEMONSTRATE THEM, BUT I DON'T HURT PEOPLE TO SHOW OFF. I'M NOT LIKE PLAGUE OR OVERLOAD.
OH, THAT'S RIGHT. YOU HAVEN'T RUN UP AGAINST THEM YET. GUESS YOU NEVER WILL.
UHNNN
GUYS LIKE US, WE'RE SUPPOSED TO DO EVERYTHING WE CAN TO MAKE THE WORLD BETTER.

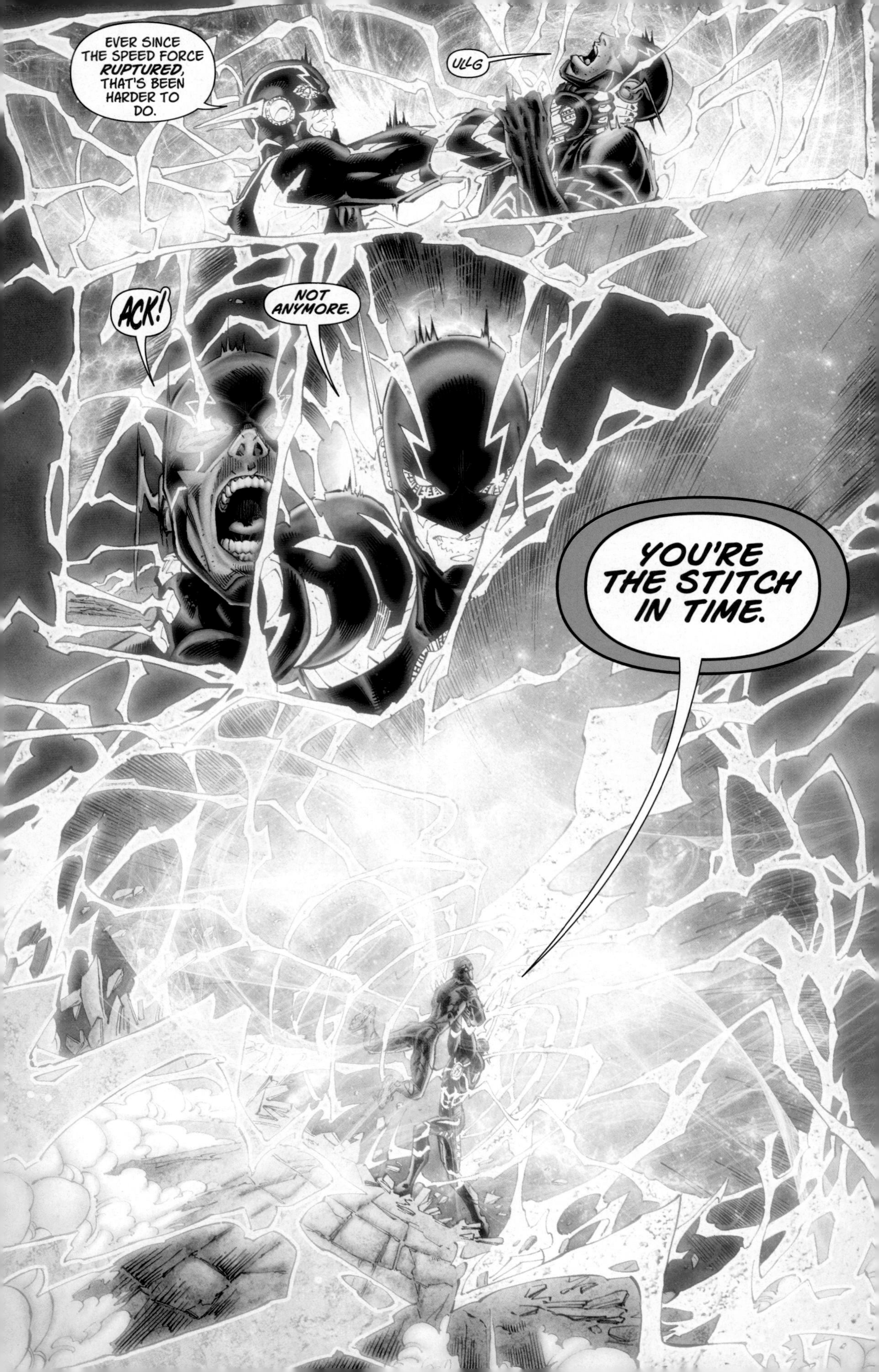
EVER SINCE THE SPEED FORCE RUPTURED, THAT'S BEEN HARDER TO DO.
ULLG
ACK!
NOT ANYMORE.
YOU'RE THE STITCH IN TIME.

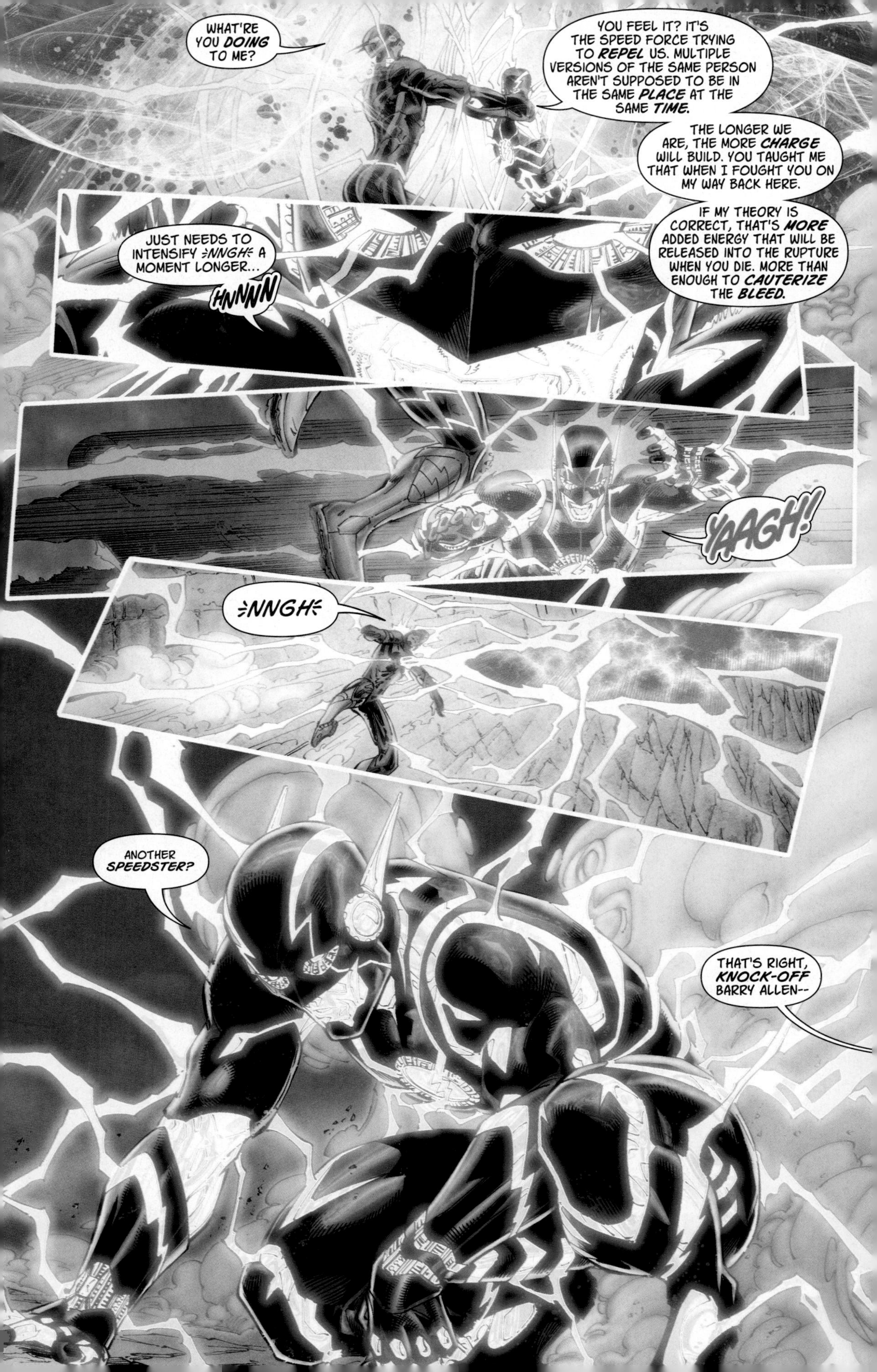
WHAT'RE YOU DOING TO ME?
YOU FEEL IT? IT'S THE SPEED FORCE TRYING TO REPEL US. MULTIPLE VERSIONS OF THE SAME PERSON AREN'T SUPPOSED TO BE IN THE SAME PLACE AT THE SAME TIME.
THE LONGER WE ARE, THE MORE CHARGE WILL BUILD. YOU TAUGHT ME THAT WHEN I FOUGHT YOU ON MY WAY BACK HERE.
JUST NEEDS TO INTENSIFY NNGH A MOMENT LONGER...
HNNNN
IF MY THEORY IS CORRECT, THAT'S MORE ADDED ENERGY THAT WILL BE RELEASED INTO THE RUPTURE WHEN YOU DIE. MORE THAN ENOUGH TO CAUTERIZE THE BLEED.
YAAGH!
NNGH
ANOTHER SPEEDSTER?
THAT'S RIGHT, KNOCK-OFF BARRY ALLEN--

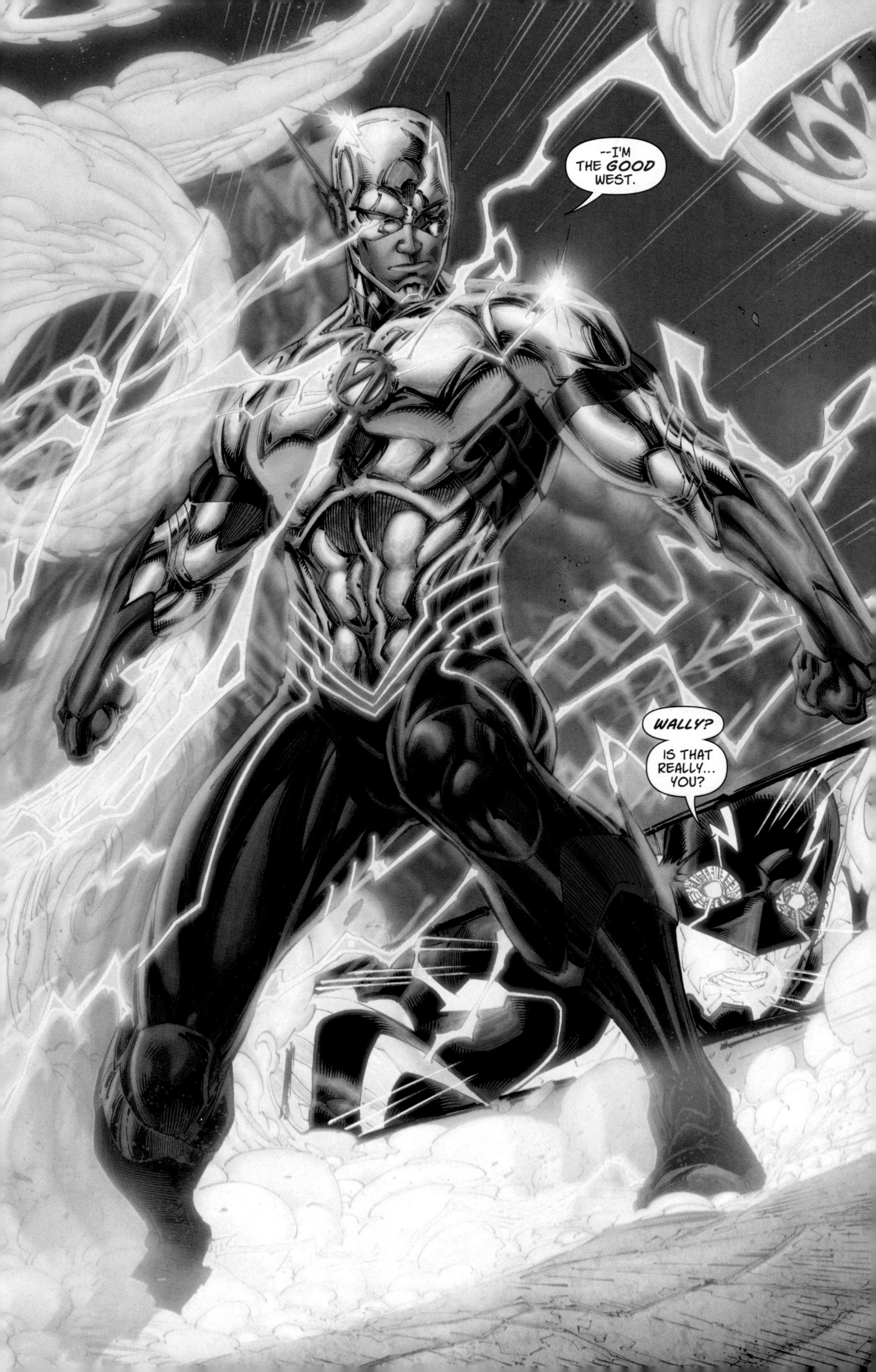
--I'M THE *GOOD* WEST.
WALLY?
IS THAT REALLY... YOU?

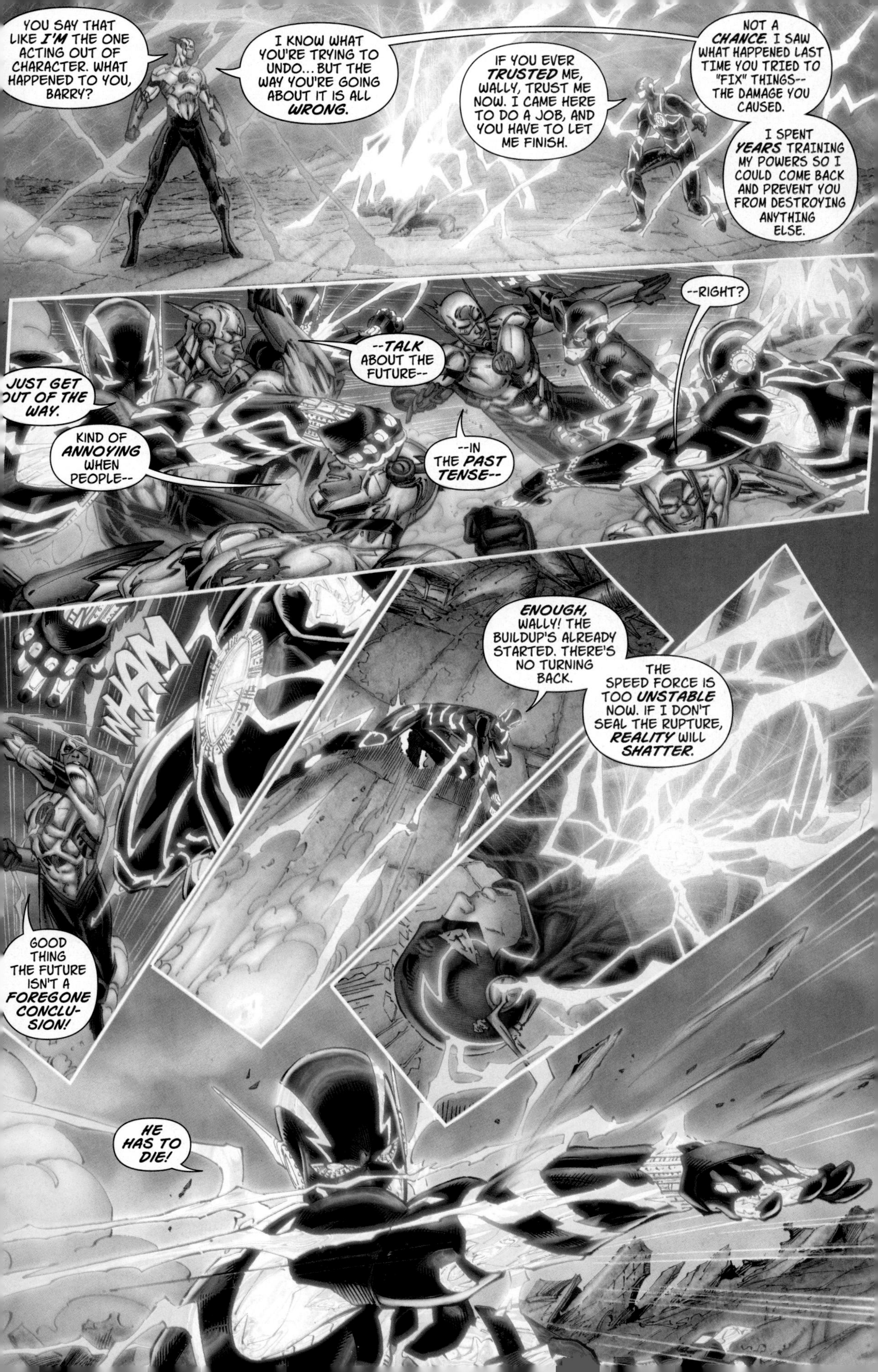

YOU SAY THAT LIKE *I'M* THE ONE ACTING OUT OF CHARACTER. WHAT HAPPENED TO YOU, BARRY?
I KNOW WHAT YOU'RE TRYING TO UNDO... BUT THE WAY YOU'RE GOING ABOUT IT IS ALL *WRONG.*
NOT A *CHANCE.* I SAW WHAT HAPPENED LAST TIME YOU TRIED TO "FIX" THINGS-- THE DAMAGE YOU CAUSED.
I SPENT *YEARS* TRAINING MY POWERS SO I COULD COME BACK AND PREVENT YOU FROM DESTROYING ANYTHING ELSE.
IF YOU EVER *TRUSTED* ME, WALLY, TRUST ME NOW. I CAME HERE TO DO A JOB, AND YOU HAVE TO LET ME FINISH.
JUST GET OUT OF THE WAY.
KIND OF *ANNOYING* WHEN PEOPLE--
--*TALK* ABOUT THE FUTURE--
--IN THE *PAST TENSE*--
--RIGHT?
WHAM
GOOD THING THE FUTURE ISN'T A *FOREGONE CONCLUSION!*
ENOUGH, WALLY! THE BUILDUP'S ALREADY STARTED. THERE'S NO TURNING BACK.
THE SPEED FORCE IS TOO *UNSTABLE* NOW. IF I DON'T SEAL THE RUPTURE, *REALITY* WILL *SHATTER.*
HE HAS TO DIE!

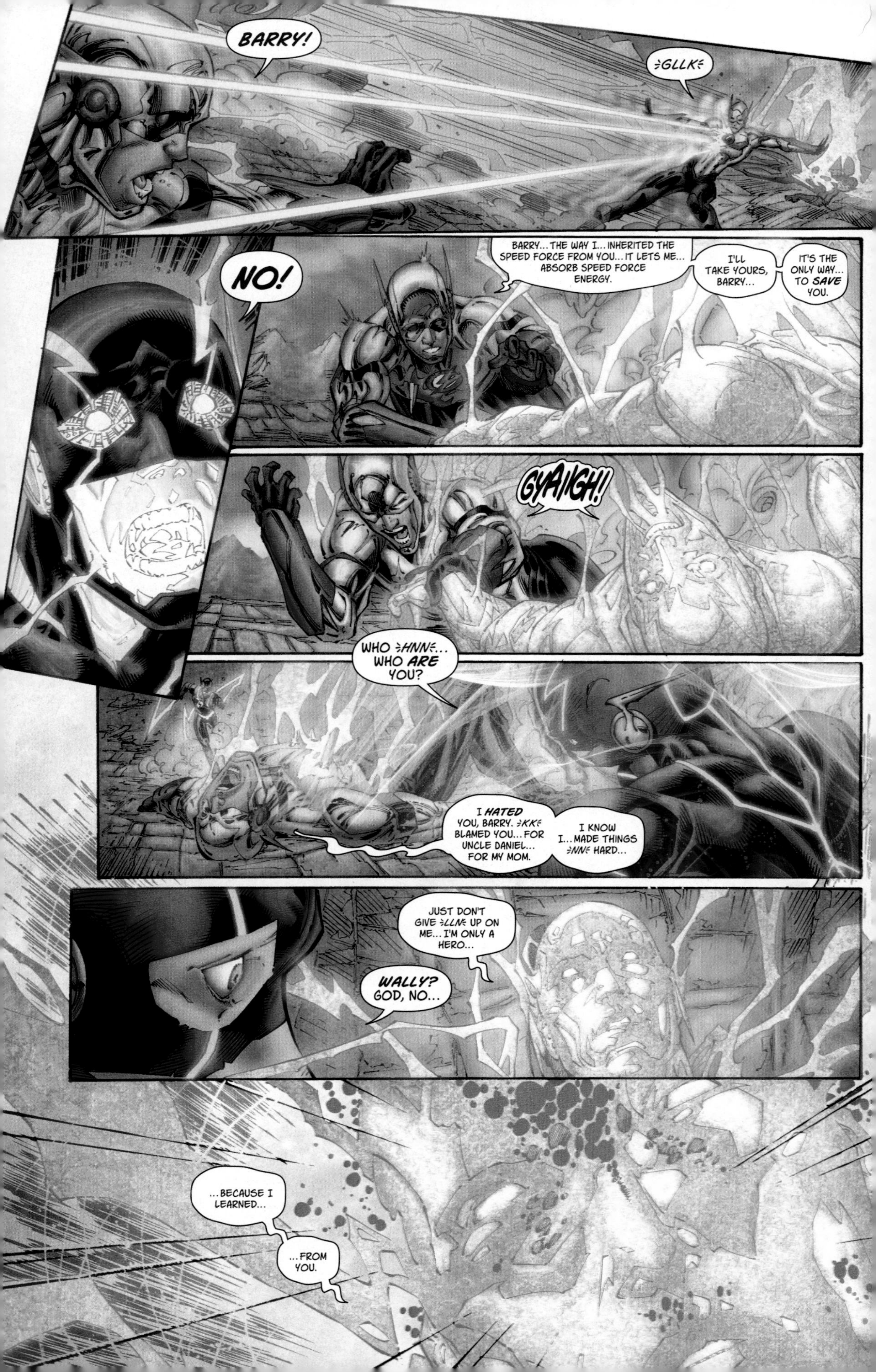

BARRY!
GLLK
NO!
BARRY... THE WAY I... INHERITED THE SPEED FORCE FROM YOU... IT LETS ME... ABSORB SPEED FORCE ENERGY.
I'LL TAKE YOURS, BARRY...
IT'S THE ONLY WAY... TO SAVE YOU.
GYAIIGH!
WHO HNN... WHO ARE YOU?
I HATED YOU, BARRY. KK BLAMED YOU... FOR UNCLE DANIEL... FOR MY MOM.
I KNOW I... MADE THINGS NN HARD...
JUST DON'T GIVE LLN UP ON ME... I'M ONLY A HERO...
WALLY? GOD, NO...
...BECAUSE I LEARNED...
...FROM YOU.

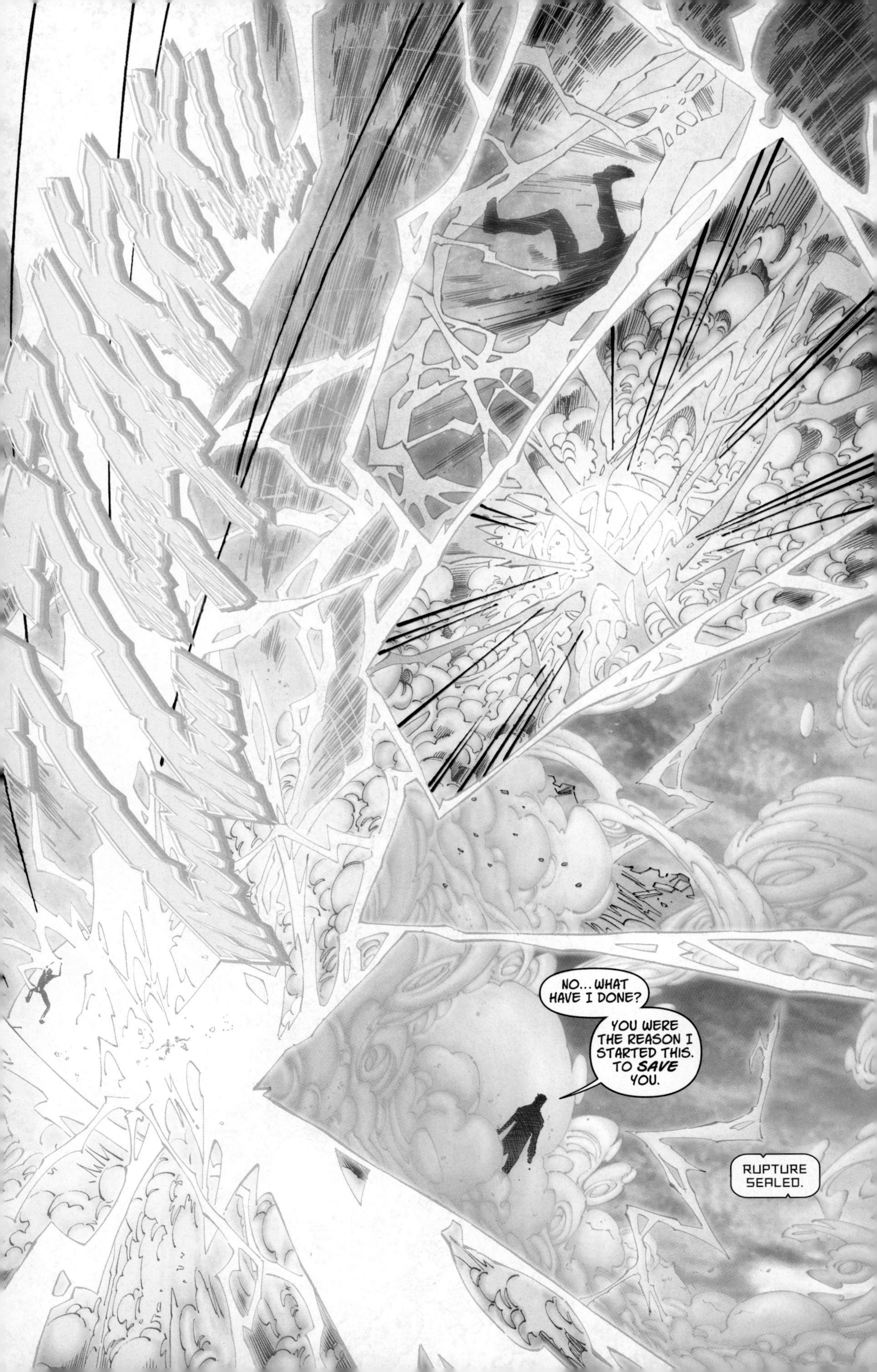
NO... WHAT HAVE I DONE?
YOU WERE THE REASON I STARTED THIS. TO SAVE YOU.
RUPTURE SEALED.

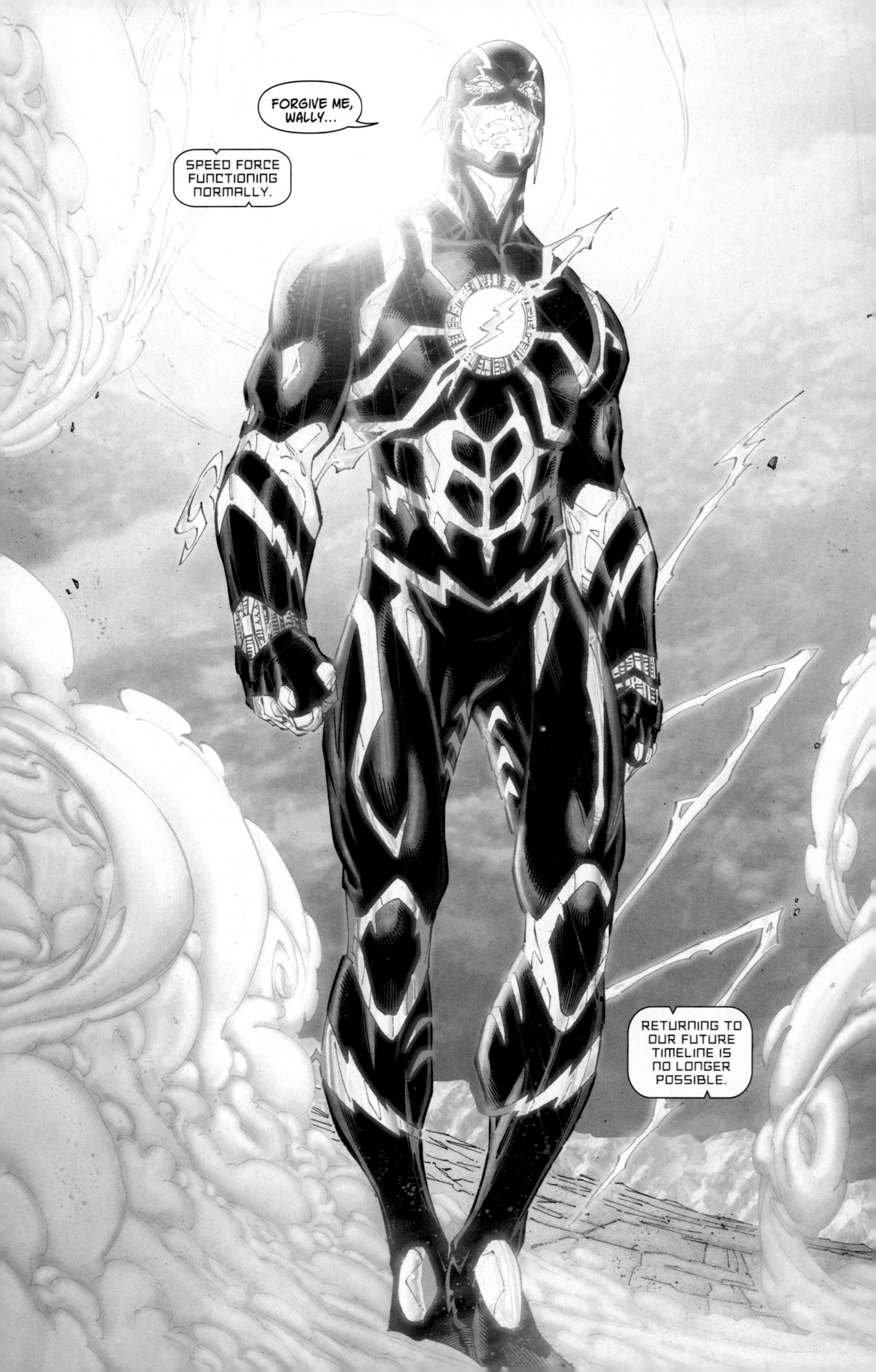
FORGIVE ME, WALLY...
SPEED FORCE FUNCTIONING NORMALLY.
RETURNING TO OUR FUTURE TIMELINE IS NO LONGER POSSIBLE.

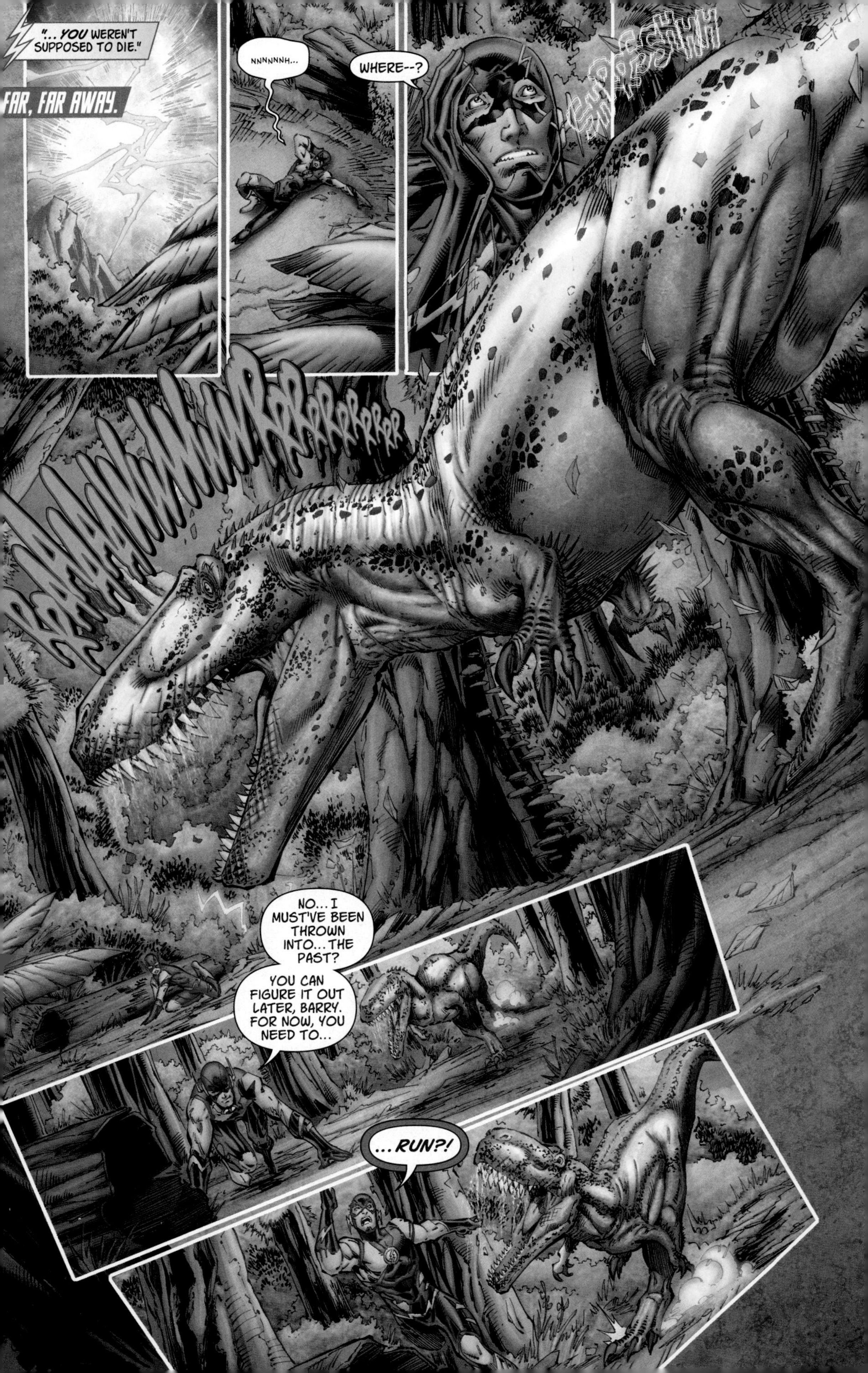
"...YOU WEREN'T SUPPOSED TO DIE."
FAR, FAR AWAY.
NNNNNNH...
WHERE--?
SHHHHH
RRAAAHHHWWRRRRRRRRRR
NO... I MUST'VE BEEN THROWN INTO... THE PAST?
YOU CAN FIGURE IT OUT LATER, BARRY. FOR NOW, YOU NEED TO...
...RUN?!

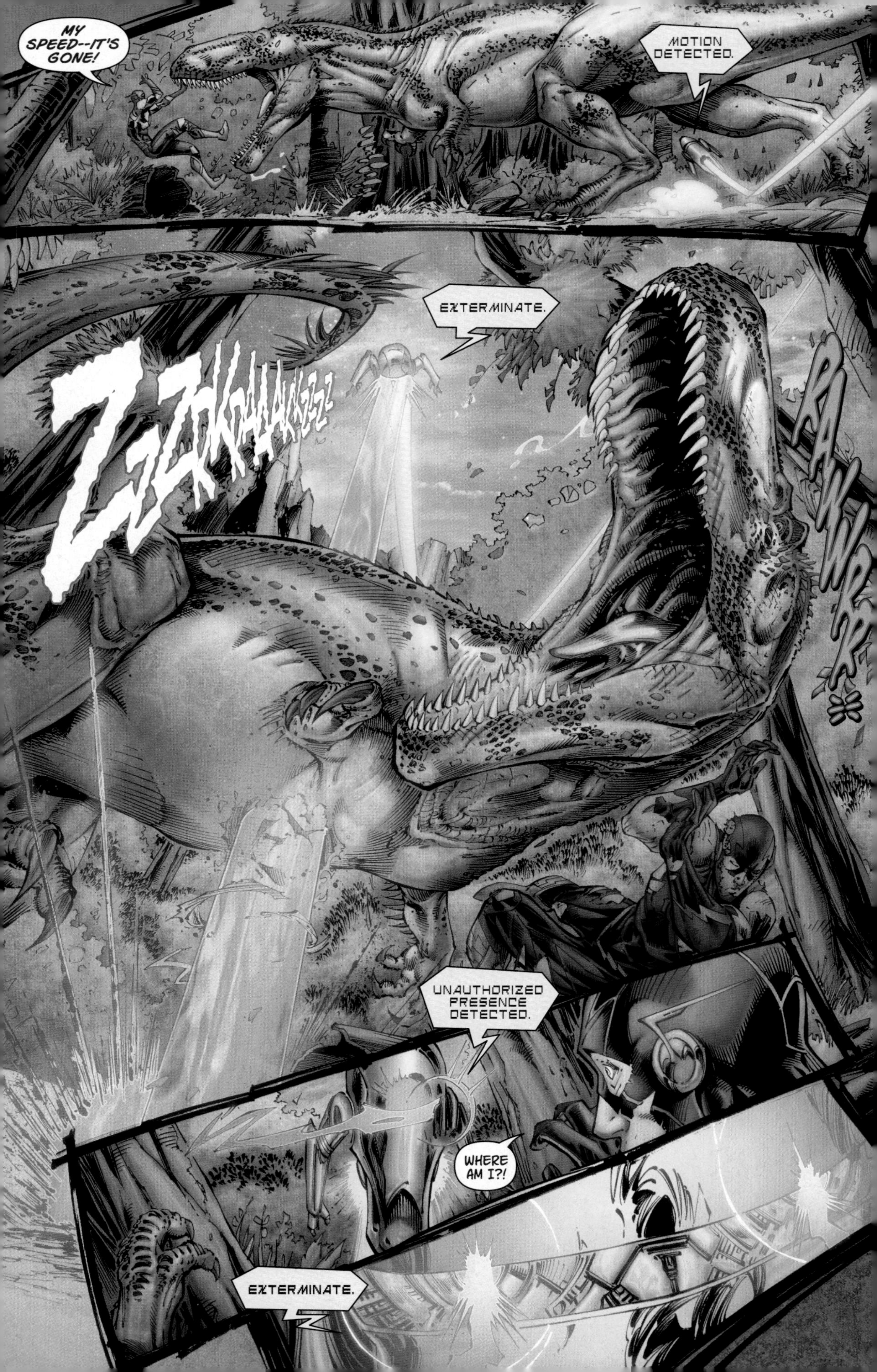
MY SPEED--IT'S GONE!
MOTION DETECTED.
EXTERMINATE.
ZZZKRAAAKKZZZZ
RAWWRRK
UNAUTHORIZED PRESENCE DETECTED.
WHERE AM I?!
EXTERMINATE.

VARIANT COVER GALLERY

FLASH #30
MAD variant cover by Anton Emoin

FLASH #31
Batman '66 Variant cover by Mike and Laura Allred

FLASH #32
Bombshell variant cover by Ant Lucia

FLASH #33
Batman 75th Anniversary variant cover by Kim Jung Gi

FLASH #34
Selfie variant cover by Eddy Barrows, Eber Ferreira and HI-FI

FLASH: FUTURES END #1
Brett Booth, Norm Rapmund and Andrew Dalhouse

FLASH #35
Monsters of the Month variant cover by Ryan Ottley and FCO Plascencia

FLASH #30
MAD variant cover by Anton Emoin

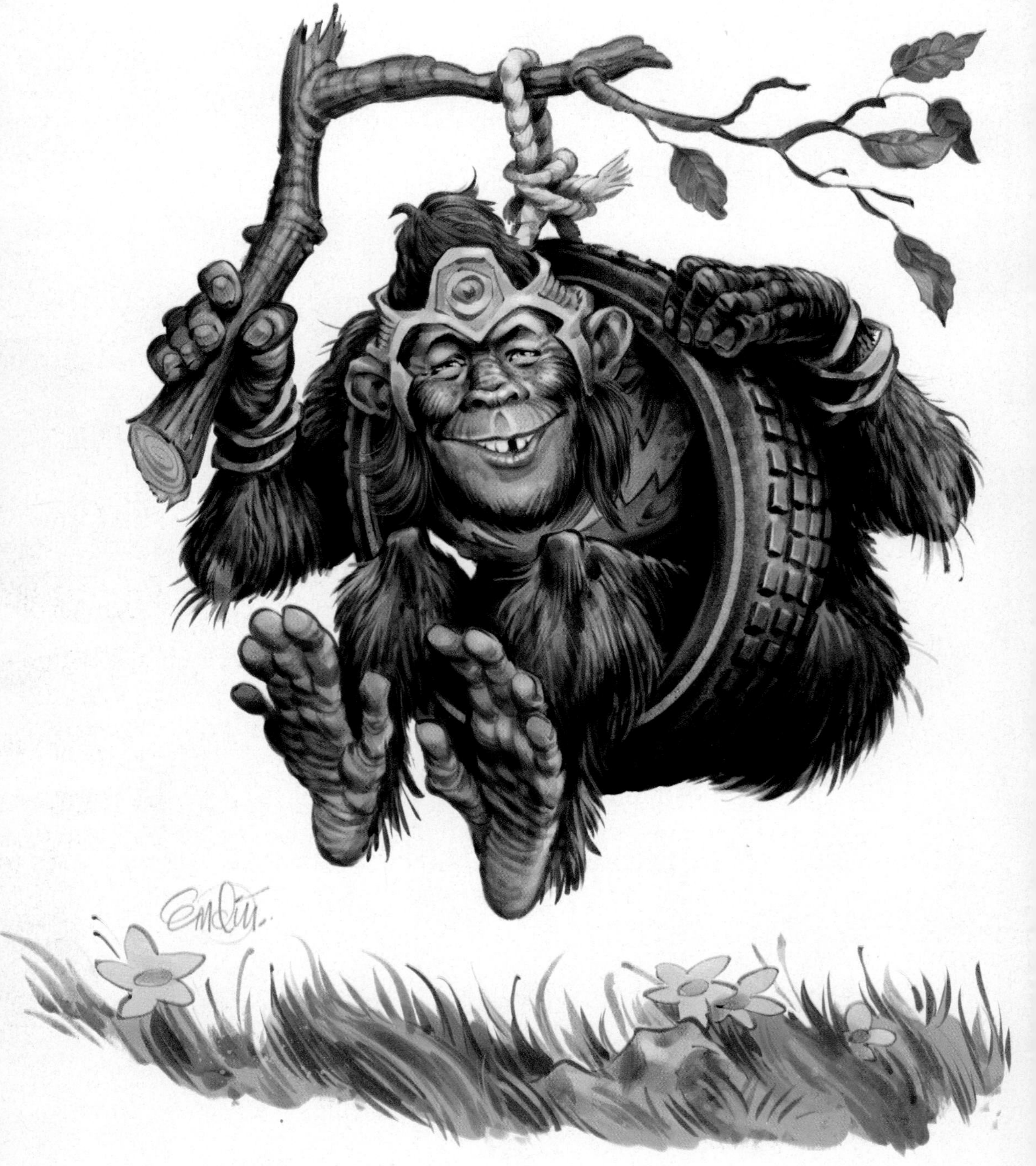

FLASH #31
Batman 66 Variant cover by Mike and Laura Allred

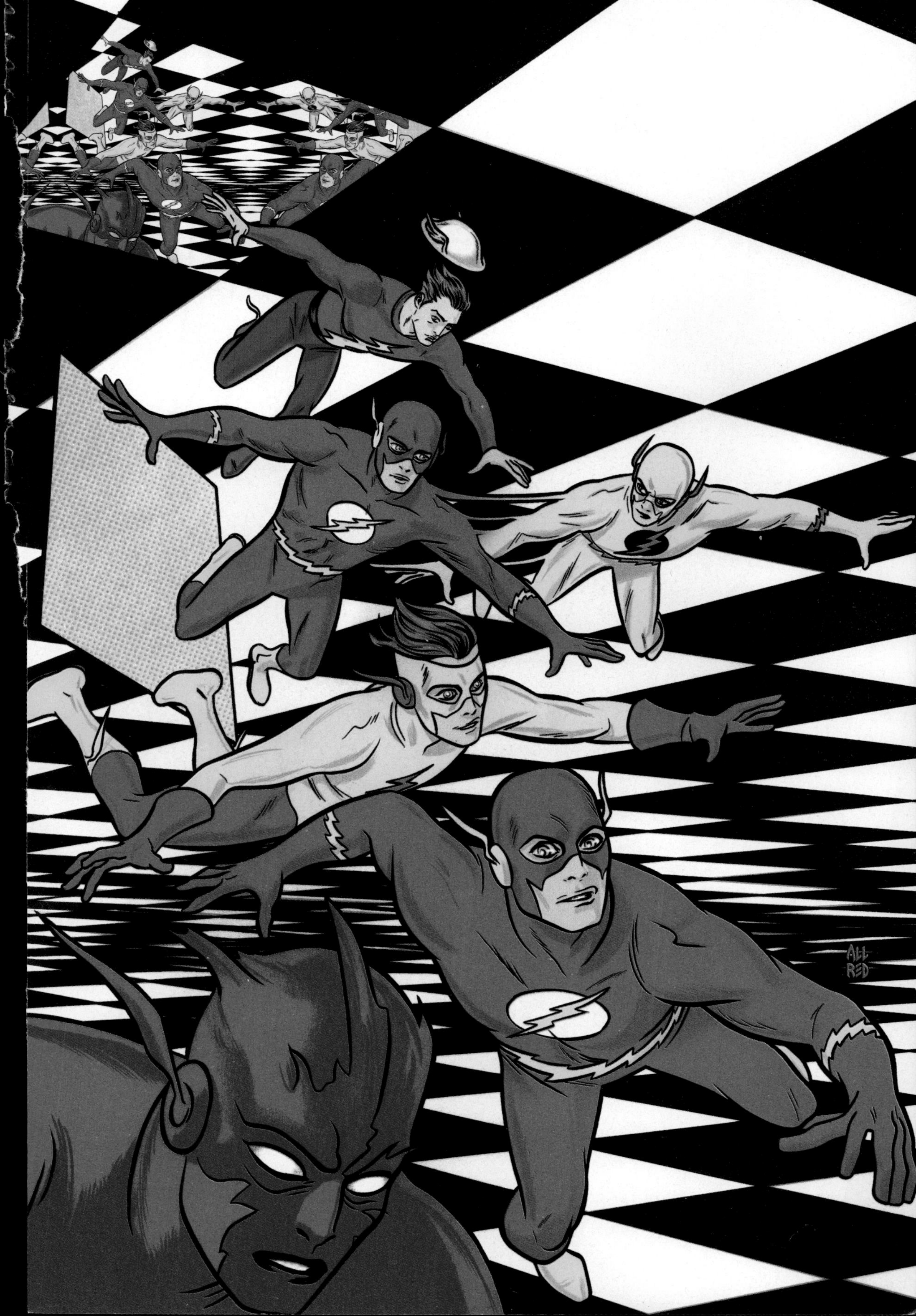

FLASH #32
Bombshell variant cover by Ant Lucia

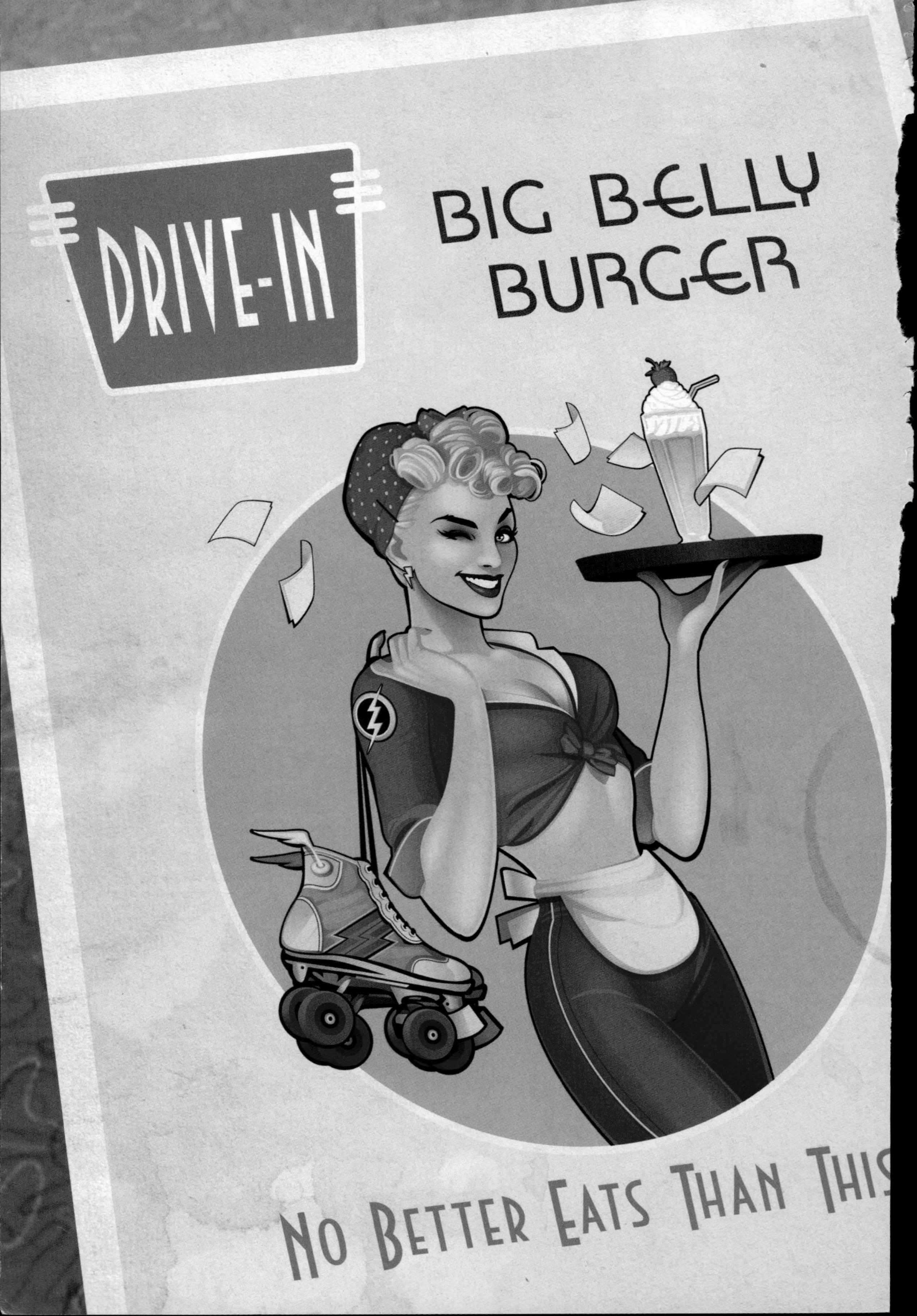
DRIVE-IN
BIG BELLY BURGER
NO BETTER EATS THAN THIS

FLASH #34

Selfie variant cover by Eddy Barrows, Eber Ferreira and HI-FI

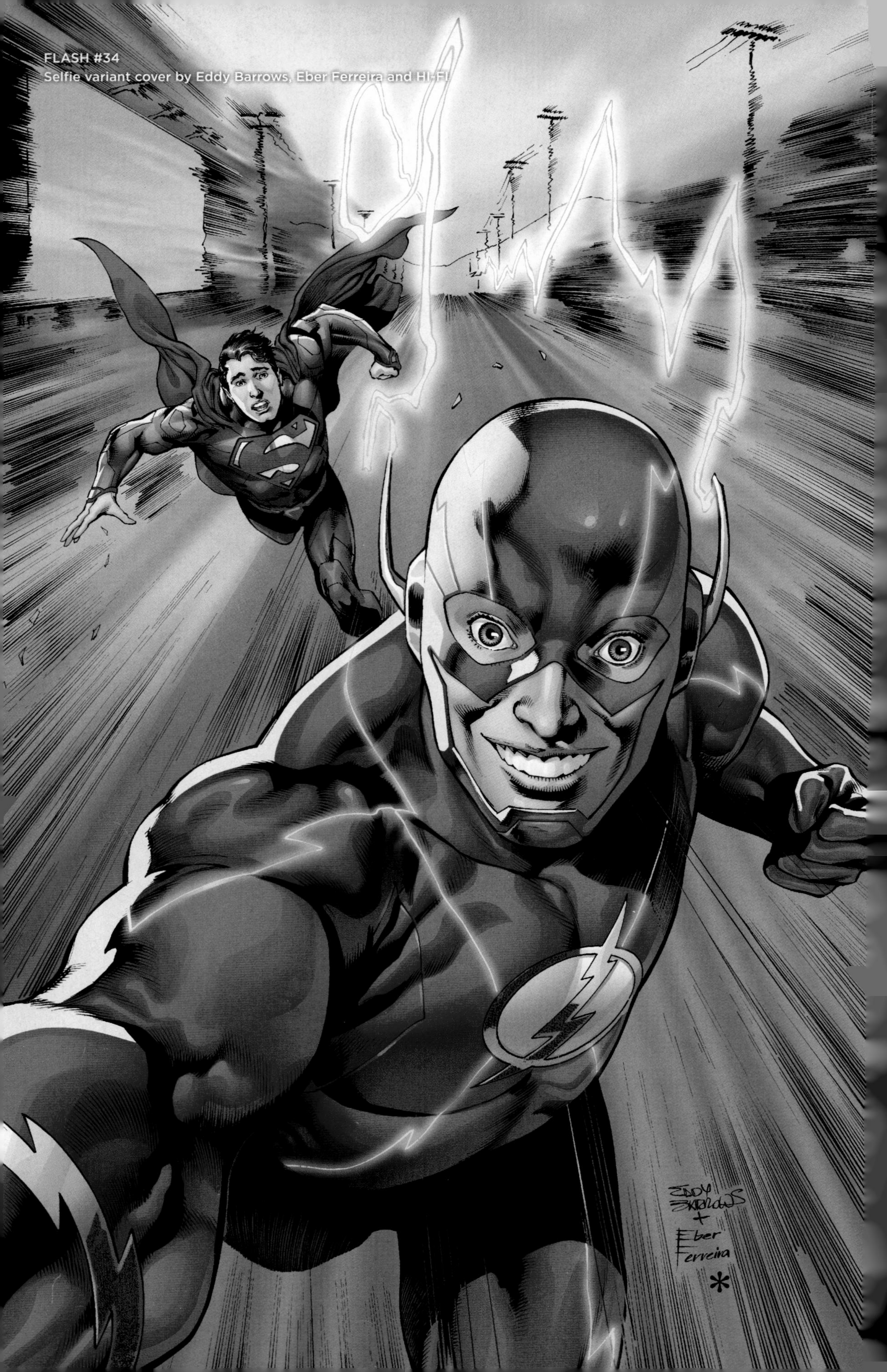
EDDY BARROWS
+
Eber
Ferreira

FLASH: FUTURES END #1
Brett Booth, Norm Rapmund and Andrew Dalhouse

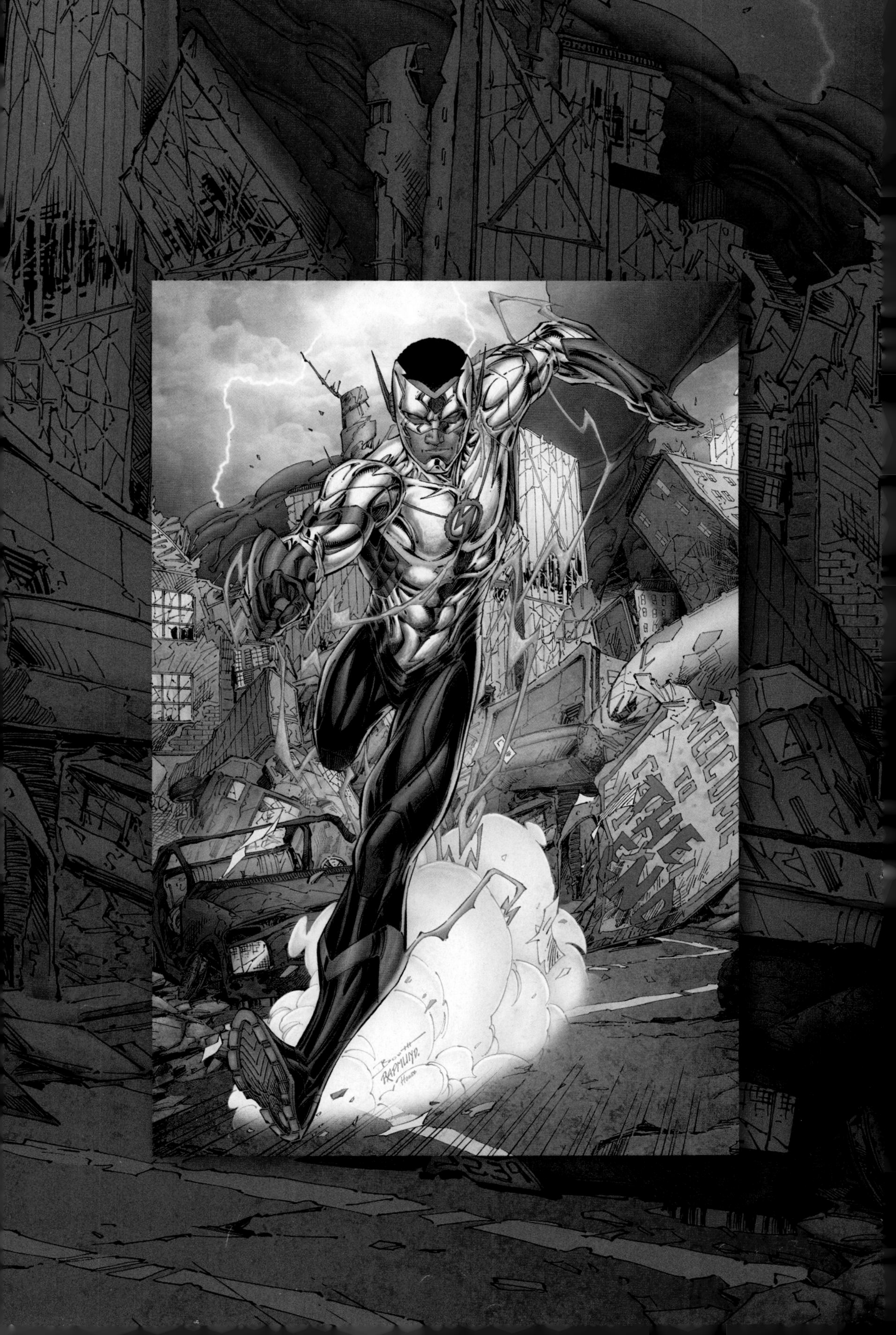

FLASH #35
Monsters of the Month variant cover by Ryan Ottley and FCO Plascencia

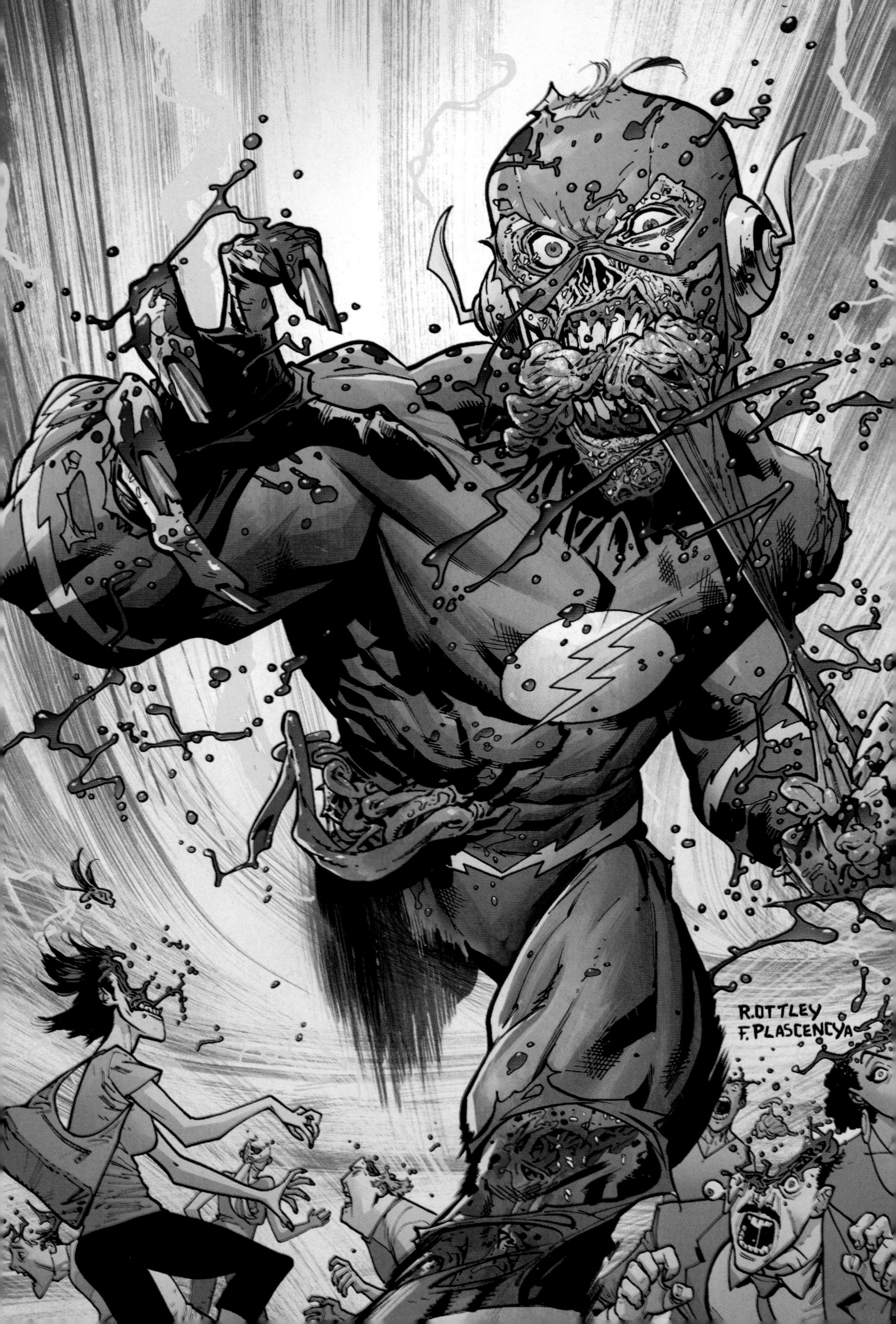
R.OTTLEY
F.PLASCENCYA

DC COMICS™

"Dynamite."
—IGN

"Intriguing."
—AIN'T IT COOL NEWS

"Comic-book art at its finest."
—ENTERTAINMENT WEEKLY SHELF LIFE

"Ambitious."
—USA TODAY

FLASHPOINT
GEOFF JOHNS with ANDY KUBERT

FLASHPOINT: THE WORLD OF FLASHPOINT FEATURING BATMAN

FLASHPOINT: THE WORLD OF FLASHPOINT FEATURING GREEN LANTERN

READ THE ENTIRE EPIC!

FLASHPOINT

FLASHPOINT: THE WORLD OF FLASHPOINT FEATURING BATMAN

FLASHPOINT: THE WORLD OF FLASHPOINT FEATURING THE FLASH

FLASHPOINT: THE WORLD OF FLASHPOINT FEATURING GREEN LANTERN

FLASHPOINT: THE WORLD OF FLASHPOINT FEATURING SUPERMAN

FLASHPOINT: THE WORLD OF FLASHPOINT FEATURING WONDER WOMAN

"Flash fans should breathe a sigh of relief that the character is 100% in the right hands." —MTV GEEK

START AT THE BEGINNING!

THE FLASH
VOLUME 1: MOVE FORWARD

THE FLASH VOL. 2:
ROGUES REVOLUTION

THE FLASH VOL. 3:
GORILLA WARFARE

JUSTICE LEAGUE
VOL. 1: ORIGIN

© 2012 DC Comics. All Rights Reserved.